TRUTH

AND

THE

HERETIC

TRUTH AND THE
HERETIC CRISES OF

KNOWLEDGE IN

MEDIEVAL

FRENCH

LITERATURE

KAREN SULLIVAN

THE UNIVERSITY OF CHICAGO PRESS

CHICAGO AND LONDON

Karen Sullivan is associate professor of literature at Bard College and the author of *The Interrogation of Joan of Arc* (1999).

The University of Chicago Press, Chicago 60637
The University of Chicago Press, Ltd., London
© 2005 by The University of Chicago
All rights reserved. Published 2005
Printed in the United States of America

14 13 12 11 10 09 08 07 06 05   1 2 3 4 5

ISBN: 0-226-78169-0 (cloth)

Library of Congress Cataloging-in-Publication Data

Sullivan, Karen, 1964–
    Truth and the heretic : crises of knowledge in medieval French literature / Karen Sullivan.
        p. cm.
    Includes bibliographical references and index.
    ISBN: 0-226-78169-0 (cloth : alk. paper))
    1. French literature—To 1500—History and criticism.   2. Heresy in literature.   I. Title.
PQ155.H38S85 2005
840.9'382628—dc22

2005002673

♾ The paper used in this publication meets the minimum requirements of the American National Standard for Information Sciences—Permanence of Paper for Printed Library Materials, ANSI Z39.48-1992.

For Katie Pitt

CONTENTS

ACKNOWLEDGMENTS

This book owes much to many people. I am grateful to Deirdre d'Albertis and Mark Lambert for having read the manuscript at various points and offered insightful suggestions. I am particularly beholden to Walter Stephens and the other readers at the University of Chicago Press for the constructive advice they provided at a crucial stage in the book's genesis. Marina van Zuylen, Cami Townsend, Michèle Dominy, Nathan Rutenbeck, and Geoff Sanborn discussed with me many of the issues addressed in the book and helped me think them through. Randolph Petilos stands out for his trust in this project and his patience with its development, as does Margaret Mahan in her careful and intelligent editing of the text. In Carcassonne, the staff of the Centre d'Etudes Cathares was invaluable in the assistance they offered with their holdings. In Annandale, Jane Hryshko, Parul Desai, and Betsy Cawley were no less essential in helping me track down often obscure sources. The Bard College Faculty Research Council provided funding for this project when it was most needed. As always, any faults in the finished work remain my own.

ABBREVIATIONS

Bouquet   Martin Bouquet et al., eds. *Recueil des historiens des Gaules et de la France.* 24 vols. Paris: Aux dépens des librairies, 1739–1904.

CC   *Corpus christianorum, Series Latina.* Turholti: Brepols, 1953–.

CCCM   *Corpus Christianorum, Continuatio Mediaevalis.* Turnolti: Brepols, 1971–.

Fearns   James Fearns, ed. *Ketzer und Ketzerbekämpfung in Hochmittelalter.* Göttingen: Vandenhoeck & Ruprecht, 1968.

MGH   *Monumenta Germaniae historica inde ab anno Christi quingentesimo usque ad annum millesimum et quingentesimum . . . Scriptores.* 32 vols. Stuttgart and Hanover: Hannsche Buchhandlung, 1823–96.

Mansi   Giovan Domenico Mansi, ed. *Sacrorum conciliorum nova et amplissima collectio . . . .* 53 vols. Florentiae: Expensis Antonii Zatta Veneti; Paris: H. Welter, 1759–1927.

Moore   Moore. R. I., ed. *The Birth of Popular Heresy.* New York: Edward Arnold, 1975. Rpt. Toronto: Medieval Academy of America, 1995.

Peters   Peters, Edward, ed. *Heresy and Authority in Medieval Europe: Documents in Translation.* Philadelphia: University of Pennsylvania Press, 1980.

PG   Jacques Paul Migne, ed. *Patrologiae cursus completus . . . ab aevo Photiano ad Concilii usque Florentini tempora . . . series graeca.* 161 vols. Paris: Garnier Frères, 1857–91.

PL   Jacques Paul Migne, ed. *Patrologiae cursus completus . . . ab aevo apostolico ad tempora Innocentii III, anno 1216 . . . series latina.* 221 vols. Paris: Garnier Frères, 1844–64.

Wakefield   Walter L. Wakefield and Austin P. Evans, eds. *Heresies of the*
and Evans   *High Middle Ages: Selected Sources, Translated and Annotated.*
            New York: Columbia University Press, 1969. Rpt. 1991.

INTRODUCTION

The heretic of the Middle Ages, it would seem, never existed as a heretic.[1] A Jew admitted that he was a Jew, and a Muslim that he was a Muslim, but a heretic, however much he knew himself to lie outside the Church's fold, invariably denied that he was a heretic, insisting, instead, that he was a good Christian.[2] If the heretic were perchance to have

1. Scholars have addressed the medieval stereotype of the heretic in scattered paragraphs and articles. See Herbert Grundmann, "Der Typus des Ketzers in Mittelalterlicher Anschauung," in *Kultur- und Universalgeschichte: Walter Goetz, zu seinem 60. Geburtstage* (Leipzig: B. G. Teubner, 1927), pp. 91–107; and "*Oportet et haereses esse*: Das Problem der Ketzerei im Spiegel des mittelalterlichen Bibelexegese," *Archiv für Kulturgeschichte* 45, no. 2 (1963): 129–64; R. I. Moore, "Heresy as Disease," in *The Concept of Heresy in the Middle Ages (11th–13th c.)* (Proceedings of the International Conference, Louvain, May 13–16, 1973), ed. W. Lourdaux and D. Verhelst (The Hague: Martinus Nijhoff, 1976; rpt. Leuven: University Press, 1983), pp. 1–11; and *The Origins of European Dissent* (London: Alan Lane, 1977; rpt. Toronto: University of Toronto Press, 1985), pp. 246–50; Edward Peters, *Inquisition* (New York: Free Press, 1988; rpt. Berkeley: University of California Press, 1989), pp. 22 and 42; Alexander Patschovsky, "Der Ketzer als Teufelsdiener," *Papsttum, Kirche, und Recht im Mittelalter*, ed. Horst Fuhrmann and Hubert Mordek (Tübingen: Max Niemeyer, 1991), pp. 317–34; Malcolm Lambert, *Medieval Heresy: Popular Movements from the Gregorian Reform to the Reformation*, 3rd ed. (Oxford: Blackwell, 2002), pp. 3–5; Beverly Mayne Kienzle, *Cistercians, Heresy, and the Crusade in Occitania, 1145–1229: Preaching in the Lord's Vineyard* (Woodbridge: York Medieval Press, 2001), passim. Though these scholars have acknowledged the importance of the stereotype of the medieval heretic, none of them has provided a full-length study of this figure, let alone connected him with contemporaneous literary characters.

2. Medieval clerics envisaged "the heretic" as male, to the point where they speak of "the heretics and their women," as we shall see. There were *haereticae* as well as *haeretici*, of course, and these female sectaries often stand out from their male counterparts in the pages of chronicles: their weakness makes them vulnerable to the seductions of heresiarchs, who lead them astray both spiritually and physically; their beauty makes them appealing to the sympathies of

acknowledged that he was a heretic, his very recognition of his error would have made him cease to be in error and, hence, cease to fall in this category. All religious and social minorities of the Middle Ages enjoyed a somewhat phantasmatic status in the minds of the majority population, but the heretic alone functioned as an exclusively imaginary concept, which everyone perceived as existing but no one saw himself as being.[3] Unstable in his own meaning, the heretic made the meanings of the texts he read seem unstable. No matter what the level of his education, a heretic always had access to the words of Scripture and the Church Fathers, whether through authorized Latin versions, vernacular translations, or oral recitations, and he insisted upon interpreting these texts otherwise than Catholic clerics saw fit.[4] As part of an alternative "textual community," he demonstrated the fact that texts give rise to multiple readings and that these readings cannot always be reconciled to the satisfaction of all.[5] In doing so, he represented the possibility, not only that these works might contain meanings different from those their Catholic exegetes had derived from them, but, even more dangerously, that they might contain no fixed meanings in the end. Having rejected the single, generally accepted interpretation of a work in favor of what would become multiple and conflicting readings, the heretic became, in the medieval imagination, the figure of textual and even

---

Catholic observers, who long to save them from the pyre; and their obstinacy makes them resistant to all such attempts at conversion. Because the stereotype of "the heretic" is masculine, I will be referring to this figure with masculine pronouns throughout this study, though I hope to remain sensitive to the gendered nature of this category.

3. It is perhaps because of their purely subjective identification that heretics, in contrast to Jews and Muslims, are unrecognizable in medieval art. Debra Higgs Strickland writes in *Saracens, Demons, and Jews: Making Monsters in Medieval Art* (Princeton: Princeton University Press, 2003), "It is normally impossible to identify an image of a heretic without an inscription or accompanying text; there does not seem to be a distinct pictorial code for heretics" (p. 9).

4. From at least the third century, Christian authors used the word "Catholic" (*katholikos* or *catholicus*) to describe the universal Church in contrast to heretical sects. Around 252, for example, Cyprian writes his treatise "On the Unity of the Catholic Church," where he clearly distinguishes the "Catholic" Church from its heretical offshoots. Augustine later points out that even heretics commonly refer to the Catholic Church as "Catholic" in contrast to their own groups. The use of the term "Catholic" remains consistent through the Middle Ages, with representatives of the dominant, Roman Church referring to themselves as "Catholics" and members of the more marginal, scattered sects terming themselves "Christians" but not "Catholics."

5. On "textual communities," see Brian Stock, *The Implications of Literacy: Written Language and Models of Interpretation in the Eleventh and Twelfth Centuries* (Princeton: Princeton University Press, 1983), pp. 88–240.

epistemological indeterminacy. Whether this figure was to be condemned or celebrated depended, as we shall see, upon whether or not it was a literary text that was representing him.

But, one might object, the Church Fathers and the medieval clerics who followed them established that a heretic was not an epistemological construct but, rather, a theological reality. Recalling the etymology of the word "heresy," Jerome writes, "'Heresy' comes from the Greek 'choice,' that is, when each person chooses for himself a doctrine he thinks to be the better one."[6] Thomas Aquinas adds to Jerome's explanation that a heretic is "anyone who, from among the many things taught by the Church, picks some and not others as he chooses, not . . . hold[ing] fast to the Church teaching as an infallible rule, but to his own will."[7] While Catholics passively receive the doctrines that have been transmitted to them in their entirety, acknowledging the divine otherness present in Scripture and the Church tradition which has interpreted that Scripture, heretics actively resist those doctrines and that tradition, interposing their human selves within the divine otherness and, in doing so, failing to recognize the essential difference between these categories. According to Vincent of Lérins, while Catholics, as members of the universal, eternal Church, accept "what has been believed everywhere, always, and by all," heretics "are possessed by a permanent desire to change religion, to add something and to take something away—as though the dogma were not divine . . . [but] a merely human institution which cannot be perfected except by constant emendation, rather, by constant correction."[8] Whereas Catholics recognize that truth lies in the other rather than in the self, in tradition rather than in innovation, and in antiquity rather than in modernity, heretics are perceived as blinded to the truth because of their love of themselves and their own powers of invention. Given the vanity that lies at the heart of heresy, it was not so much their errors as their stubbornness in defending their errors that was seen as setting them apart. For

6. "Haeresis graece ab electione dicitur, quod scilicet eam sibi unusquisque eligat disciplinam quam putat esse meliorem," Jerome, *In Galat.* III, on Gal 5: 19, in PL 26, col. 445. All translations are my own unless otherwise indicated.

7. "Alioquin, si de his quae Ecclesia docet quae vult tenet et quae non vult non tenet, non jam inhaeret Ecclesiae doctrinae sicut infallibili regulae, sed propriae voluntati," Saint Thomas Aquinas, *Summa Theologiae*, Blackfriars (London: Eyre & Spottiswoode, 1964–81), vol. 31, *Faith (2a2ae. 1–7)*, ed. and trans. T. C. O'Brien, Qu. 5, Art. 3, Reply, p. 158.

8. Vincent of Lérins, *The Commonitories*, trans. Rudolph E. Morris (New York: Fathers of the Church, 1949), ch. 21, p. 306. "sed terrena institutio, quae aliter perfici nisi adsidua emendatione, immo potius reprehensione, non posset," Vincent of Lérins, *Commonitorium*, CC 69, p. 175.

Peter Abelard "it is not ignorance but pride that makes a heretic," and the tendency among dialecticians to so glory in their intelligence that they resist all efforts at correction makes them particularly liable to this sin.[9] As medieval clerics saw it, just as Catholics are people whose love of God makes them submit themselves to Scripture and the Church, heretics are people whose love of self makes them mistake their error for God's truth and refuse to abandon their error when it is exposed to them.

Despite the confidence of medieval theologians in the objective reality of heretics, however, it was not always easy to distinguish between those who believe what divine and ecclesiastical authorities dictate and those who believe what they choose. A heretic, we are told, relies upon himself rather than upon Scripture or Church tradition in determining what is true, but those condemned for heresy over the years invariably cited biblical passages and institutional practices that seemed, at least to them, to justify their stances. A heretic counts upon his own human, immanent reason in arriving at his beliefs, while a Catholic depends upon the other's divine, transcendent grace in achieving that end, but the tendency of even the best-intentioned to mistake the self for the other, the interpretation for the text, and, hence, heresy for orthodoxy was often admitted. Even as Hilary of Poitiers writes that "the best reader is he who looks for the meaning of his words in the words themselves rather than reads his meaning into them," he fears that he himself could resemble heretics, who, he alleges, read their own meaning into these words.[10] In interpreting the authors of Scripture, Hilary finds it necessary to pray to God "that we may understand their words in no other sense than that in which they spoke them, and that we may explain the proper meaning of the words in accordance with the realities they signify."[11] Even as Abelard chastises professors who are so persuaded of their intelligence as to refuse to accept criticism of their heterodoxy, this philosopher lashes out at the participants at the councils of Soissons and Sens who are so obtuse as to find errors in his own writings. It was one thing

9. "Non enim ignorantia haereticum facit sed superbia," Peter Abelard, *Opera Theologica*, vol. 2, *Theologia Christiana*, ed. M. Buytaert, CCCM 12, pp. 69–372, at p. 202.

10. Hilary of Poitiers, *The Trinity*, trans. Stephen McKenna, Fathers of the Church (Washington, DC: Catholic University of America Press, 1954), bk. 1, ch. 18, p. 18. "Optimus enim lector est, qui dictorum intellegentiam expectet ex dictis potius quam inponat," Hilary of Poitiers, *De Trinitate*, CC 62, bk. 1, ch. 18, p. 18.

11. Hilary of Poitiers, *The Trinity*, bk. 1, ch. 38, p. 34. "ut dicta eorum non alio quam ipsi locuti sunt sensu adpraehendamus, verborumque proprietates hisdem rerum significationibus exsequamur," Hilary of Poitiers, *De Trinitate*, bk. 1, ch. 38, p. 36.

to know abstractly that one should seek the divine other instead of the human self in the text, but it was another thing to trust one's contemporaries' judgments instead of one's own reasoning as to whether one has succeeded in this endeavor. Many of the most influential Christian theologians of both late antique and medieval times, including Tertullian, Origen, John Scotus Erigena, Gilbert of Poitiers, and Siger of Brabant, were seen as occasionally mistaking their own human errors for divine truths and as defending their views when confronted. Even Thomas Aquinas, the theologian who, by the end of the Middle Ages, would be widely recognized as the most important expositor of Catholic thought since Augustine, espoused doctrines that were condemned as heretical by the bishop of Paris and the archbishop of Canterbury shortly after his death. Someone considered a Catholic one day could be regarded as a heretic the next, it was admitted, and even the most venerated doctors of the Church could be believed, at times, to have erred in the faith.

However difficult it may be to establish the reality of heretics from a theological point of view, one might argue, it is nevertheless possible to establish that reality from a historical perspective. According to the reports of medieval chroniclers, heretics resurfaced in Western Europe around the year 1000 and proliferated throughout France, Italy, Germany, and the Low Countries, only to disappear almost entirely again from these lands by the mid-fourteenth century.[12] At first, the desire for spiritual leaders uncorrupted by their affiliations with secular lords, which had been nurtured by the Gregorian Reform, found expression in the development of cults surrounding either individual preachers, both orthodox and heterodox, or small groups devoted to ascetic practices, both inside and outside the Church. Prominent among these groups were so-called Manichaeans, who were perceived as arising in scattered locales and reviving the dualist doctrines of their late antique predecessors.[13] As the twelfth century progressed, these "Manichaeans" gave way to the similarly dualist

12. I do not mean to diminish the importance of late medieval heresies, yet the dissident movements of these years either occurred in lands outside those where high medieval heresies had flourished (as did the Lollards of England or the Hussites of Bohemia) or wavered on the border of heterodoxy and orthodoxy (as did the Béguines and Beghards). See, for example, Richard Kieckhefer, *Repression of Heresy in Medieval Germany* (Philadelphia: University of Pennsylvania Press, 1979); Robert E. Lerner, *The Heresy of the Free Spirit in the Later Middle Ages* (Berkeley: University of California Press, 1972; rpt. Notre Dame: University of Notre Dame Press, 1991).

13. Because "Manichaean" is used in this book exclusively of the eleventh-century heretics so called, I omit quotation marks around this term in the text.

Cathars or Albigensians, who established themselves as such a presence in Occitania (or the area now known as southern France),[14] in particular, that they provoked the pope to declare the Albigensian Crusade of 1209–29 against them. These sectaries held that there were two gods or two forces, one good, who had created the spiritual world, including our souls, and the other evil, who had created the material world, including the bodies that imprison those souls. During the same years, the Waldensians also formed as a distinct group, spreading out from Lyon throughout the surrounding lands. They rejected the special status of the priest, insisting, instead, that any good man (or woman) could preach, absolve people of sin, and administer the sacraments. Other, more minor sects also proliferated during this time, but they tended to follow either the Cathar model in its radical dualism or the Waldensian model in its reformist criticism of the Church. There is no reason to think that these heretical groups were the invention of clerical imaginations, as is often alleged of the witch covens of the early modern era. Though most of the information we possess about the accused heretics derives from Catholic sources, a few Cathar and Waldensian theological texts have survived, exhibiting doctrines at odds with those of their Catholic opponents. Abbots, bishops, and, later, inquisitors describe their encounters with heretics with details so precise and idiosyncratic that their portraits of their opponents in the faith do not seem to spring from a cleric's fantasy alone. However theologians define a heretic, there clearly existed people who perceived themselves and were perceived by others as adhering to a version of Christianity at odds with that espoused by the Catholic Church.

14. Though I here use "France" to refer to the lands we now perceive as encompassed by this term, in the Middle Ages, this word designated only the territories directly held by the French king, which radiated out from Paris and the Ile-de-France but did not include regions such as Brittany, Normandy, Aquitaine, Lorraine, or Burgundy. Most importantly for my purposes, "France" did not encompass the territories south of the Loire Valley, whose inhabitants spoke a different language, obeyed different laws, and followed different customs than did their northern neighbors. During the twelfth and early thirteenth centuries, this southern district constituted a patchwork of largely independent fiefdoms, including those of Toulouse, Foix, and Comminges, so that no one appellation was regularly used to refer to the lands as a whole. The word "Provence" (*Proensa*) was occasionally put into service in the Middle Ages, but it threatens to confuse readers nowadays, given its current limitation to the territories east of the Rhône. As inhabitants of this region referred to themselves as speaking the *lingua occitana*, there is some precedent in calling these lands "Languedoc," but, again, this word can cause perplexity, given its current restriction to the lands west of this river. Regional patriots of the twentieth century have brought "Occitania" into favor, and I follow scholarly precedent in adopting this term as well, though it, too, suggests a greater unity among these lands than existed in the Middle Ages.

Still, despite the abundance of chronicles and other written proofs of heretics' existence, recent studies have argued that what changed in Western Europe during the High Middle Ages was not so much that heretics arose and were recognized as such by Catholic clerics as that Catholic clerics arose and began to label people as heretics. In *The Formation of a Persecuting Society*, R. I. Moore linked the rise in prosecutions of heresy to the rise in prosecutions of Jews, sodomites, prostitutes, and lepers, who came to constitute the foil against which a changing society defined itself.[15] At the origin of many heretical movements, Moore and other scholars have shown, one finds not so much a doctrinal innovation as a political and social tension articulated in doctrinal terms. In the wake of the Gregorian Reform, the difference between a preacher who decried the corruption of local ecclesiastics in the hope of strengthening the Church and one who made the same complaints with the aim of creating a schism may have been in the eyes of the beholder. At a time when the Cistercians and other new monastic orders were reviving the ascetical spirit of the early Church, the difference between Catholic mortifications of the flesh and Cathar poverty, abstinence, and celibacy could likewise be hard to discern. With the sacramental nature of marriage and the annual necessity of penance only recently established, Waldensian objections to the Church's intervention in everyday spirituality could be seen either as defending tradition or as opposing the defenders of tradition. During an era when the Church itself was in flux, both those who were overzealous in support of the changes and those who were resistant to them could be viewed as antagonistic to the Church and, hence, as heretical in their beliefs. Once Catholic clerics had identified various sorts of dissidence as heresy, their formalization of the heretics' religious views, their exclusion from the Church of those who held these views, and their condemnation to the stake of those who refused to abjure these views could be instrumental in teaching otherwise vague dissenters that they were members of a special group, with their own defined doctrines, rites, and martyrs.[16] People

15. See R. I. Moore, *The Formation of a Persecuting Society* (Oxford: Blackwell, 1987; rpt. 1996). Much recent work on heretics has adopted Moore's Foucauldian line, including the recent collection of essays edited by Monique Zerner, *Inventer l'hérésie? Discours polémiques et pouvoirs avant l'Inquisition* (Nice: Z'éditions, 1998).

16. In *I Benandanti: Richerche sulla stregoneria e sui culti agrari tra Cinquecento e Seicento* (Torino: G. Einaudi, 1966), trans. John and Anne Tedeschi as *Night Battles: Witchcraft and Agrarian Cults in the Sixteenth and Seventeenth Centuries* (Baltimore: Johns Hopkins University Press, 1983), Carlo Ginzburg describes how inhabitants of the Friuli region of Italy had believed that people who were born with a caul were capable of fighting witches during

accused of heresy may have developed their own beliefs, drafted their own writings, and defended them before Catholic clerics, but the Church may have helped them to perceive themselves as essentially different from its other members in the first place.

Given the elusiveness of the heretic when he is defined theologically or historically, it is not surprising that many didactic authors ended up depicting him characterologically. If one considers didactic writings of the Middle Ages, theological genres like the *summa hereticorum*, which address heresy more than the heretic, tend to represent this figure in terms of his doctrines, yet historical and pastoral genres like the chronicle, the sermon, and the *exemplum*, which speak of the heretic more than of his heresy, depict him either wholly or partly in terms of his stereotypical behavior.[17] Time and again, the heretic is portrayed in such works as someone who challenges not only *what* we know to be the truth, with his alternate religious creed, but *how* we know the truth, with his ambiguous persona. Time and again, the heretic is portrayed not just as someone who does not perceive himself to be a heretic but as someone who does not seem to others to be a heretic either. Indeed, in many of these texts, the clearest sign by which one can identify a heretic is that he does not appear to be a heretic at all. The ambiguity of the heretic's character, far from making the authors more sympathetic to him, makes them more harsh. If these writers repudiate heretics as consistently and unequivocally as they do, it is because they are appalled not only by the perversity of the heretics' beliefs but also by the multiplicity of interpretations these perverse beliefs reflect. Insofar as there exists any commonality among didactic texts of the Middle Ages, it lies in their tendency to prioritize one stable point of view, clearly identified with the

---

the Ember Days until they learned from visiting inquisitors that those who combat witches are to be considered witches themselves. Ginzburg illustrates well how an originally neutral or even pro-Catholic folkloric belief could come to seem heretical in the eyes of a community under ecclesiastical surveillance.

17. My point here, I would like to stress, is not to suggest any clear, consistent, or reliable distinction between medieval didactic and literary texts. However much didactic genres may claim to differ from their literary counterparts because of their recourse to "truth" rather than "fiction," literary texts undermine this claim by making it themselves. See, for example, Roger Dragonetti, *Le Mirage des sources: L'Art du faux dans le roman médiéval* (Paris: Editions du Seuil, 1981), and Jeanette M. A. Beer, *Narrative Conventions of Truth of the Middle Ages* (Genève: Droz, 1981). On a more general level, Peter Lamarque and Stein Haugom Olsen, *Truth, Fiction, and Literature: A Philosophical Perspective* (Oxford: Clarendon Press, 1994), Mario J. Valdés, *World-Making: The Literary Truth-Claim and the Interpretation of Texts* (Toronto: University of Toronto Press, 1992), and Michael Riffaterre, *Fictional Truth* (Baltimore: Johns Hopkins University Press, 1990) might also be considered.

author, to the exclusion of other perspectives. Such texts may draw upon non-Catholic traditions, including Greco-Latin, Jewish, or Muslim bodies of knowledge, but they strive to subsume these diverse, contradictory traditions into a unified, coherent whole. If the heretic is a dangerous figure for didactic authors, it is, at least to some degree, because he represents a point of view which is neither Christian nor non-Christian, neither familiar nor foreign, neither the same nor other, and which, by its very bifurcation of Christian identity into opposing camps, resists assimilation into an imagined unity. The didactic text asks for all readers to interpret it in the same way, in accordance with the author's stated intentions, and, in doing so, it necessarily opposes the heretic, who always interprets texts in a different way, in accordance with his own desire. Emphasizing the part at the expense of the whole, the letter at the expense of the spirit, and the detail at the expense of the primary theme, the heretic prevents not only Christians from agreeing on one interpretation of Scripture but readers in general from agreeing on one interpretation of a text, to the distress of any author who wants to be read in one set manner.

However the heretic is depicted in medieval didactic writings, one could still protest, in contrast to what has been implied so far, that he bears no relation to the literature of this time period, from which he remains strangely absent. French and Occitan literary texts of that era present Saracens, prostitutes, and criminals of every variety, but they feature no deviants from the faith. The chansons de geste include no heretics among their many characters, even when they sing of the crusade waged against them.[18] Troubadour and trouvère lyrics forefront no heretics, even in the Occitan *sirventes*, where they address topical issues. It is perhaps to be expected that romance, with its emphasis upon an ideal, often mythical past, fails to represent this population, but it is noteworthy that the fabliau, with its emphasis upon a real, occasionally gritty present, is likewise silent about them. Even a work as encyclopedic as Jean de Meun's contribution to the *Roman de la Rose*, despite its strong opinions about religious hypocrites, has no heretics emerge in its roster of characters. To turn to Italian literature, Dante Alighieri's *Commedia* devotes an entire circle of Hell to heretics, but it places no members of the major medieval sects in it: the sinners who are highlighted there are ancient Epicureans and their medieval successors in the Guelf and Ghibilline parties,

---

18. *Renaut de Montauban, édition critique du manuscrit Douce*, ed. Jacques Thomas (Genève: Droz, 1989), does feature an apostate but not a heretic.

known more for their political views than for their religious beliefs.[19] Dante is able to compare the lustful who burn in Purgatory to criminals who burn in city squares, as if he has witnessed such pyres himself, but he remains silent about the actual heretics he may have seen executed in this manner. Similarly, Giovanni Boccaccio's *Decameron* contains tales about religious and social minorities of every stripe (including one about an inquisitor), but it includes no stories about heretics. Even Ser Cepperello, the character who has reportedly committed every sin possible to mankind, appears to be orthodox. In England, Geoffrey Chaucer's *Canterbury Tales* provides portraits of any number of religious malefactors, but none of Lollards, the sole medieval English heretics, let alone of their continental counterparts.[20] Thematized in virtually no literary work during these years, heretics are mentioned only in a minus-

19. Virgil informs the Dante pilgrim as they approach the sixth circle, "Here are the heresiarchs with all their followers of every sect [*Qui son li eresïarche / con lor seguaci, d'ogne setta*]." Dante Alighieri, *The Divine Comedy*, ed. and trans. Charles S. Singleton (Princeton: Princeton University Press, 1970–75), vol. 1, *Inferno*, canto IX, vv. 127–29, but of these sects Virgil identifies only "Epicurus with all his followers / who make the soul die with the body [*con Epicuro tutti suoi seguaci / che l'anima col corpo morta fanno*]" (ibid., canto X, vv. 14–15). Of the five heretics Dante names, three are Ghibilline leaders (the emperor Frederick II, the cardinal Ottaviano degli Ubaldini, and the Florentine patriot Farinata degli Uberti) and one a Guelf leader (Cavalcante de' Cavalcanti, the poet Guido's father). The fifth heretic is the fifth-century pope Athanasius, who was alleged to have denied the divine origin of Christ. For a rich but ultimately inconclusive discussion of Dante's resistance to placing the heretics of his time in this circle, see Alfonso De Savio, *Dante and Heresy* (Baltimore: Waverly Press, 1936).

20. Chaucer refers to Lollards only once in *The Canterbury Tales*, in the epilogue to the Man of Law's Tale, after the Parson reproaches the Host for swearing. Recalling the Lollards' distaste for profane oaths, the Host retorts, "I smelle a Lollere in the wynd," and he predicts, "This Lollere heer wil prechen us somwhat," *The Riverside Chaucer*, ed. Larry D. Benson, 3rd ed. (Boston: Houghton Mifflin Co., 1987), vv. 1173–77. See also Paul Strohm, "Chaucer's Lollard Joke: History and the Textual Unconscious," *Studies in the Age of Chaucer* 17 (1995): 23–42, and Alcuin Blamires, "The Wife of Bath and Lollardy," *Medium Aevum* 58, no. 2 (1989): 224–42. In *The Legend of Good Women*, Prologue, text F, the God of Love informs the narrator, ". . . Thou maist yt nat denye, / For in pleyn text, withouten nede of glose, / Thou hast translated the Romaunce of the Rose, / That is an heresye ayeins my lawe, / And makest wise folk fro me withdrawe," *The Riverside Chaucer*, ed. Benson, vv. 327–31. On the Lollard Sir John Oldcastle's revolt against Henry V and poetic responses to this event, see V. J. Scattergood, *Politics and Poetry in the Fifteenth Century* (London: Blanford Press, 1971; rpt. New York: Barnes & Noble, 1972), pp. 129–34, as well as *Thomas Hoccleve's Minor Poems*, ed. Frederick J. Furnivall, 3 vols. (London: Publications for the Early English Text Society by K. Paul, 1892–1925), poems 2, 5, and 8; Thomas Hoccleve, *The Regiment of Princes*, ed. Charles R. Blyth (Kalamazoo, MI: Medieval Institute Publications, 1999); and the anonymous "Defend Us from All Lollardy," in R. H. Robbins, ed., *Historical Poems of the XIVth and XVth Centuries* (New York: Columbia University Press, 1959), poem 64.

cule number and there only in passing.[21] One might assume that the authors of these texts avoid representing heretics for fear of being identified with their characters, but there is no evidence to suggest that any literary writer from this period was ever prosecuted for heresy on account of his writings. On the contrary, the regularity with which literary authors depict the sins of the Catholic clergy, to the point of anticlerical diatribe, testifies to the freedom from ecclesiastical censure under which they wrote. It was not until the end of the Middle Ages that a literary text, the *Roman de la Rose*, was attacked as heretical, but it was a woman writer marginal to the Parisian literary establishment who levied this charge, and the establishment itself—including representatives of the Church—that rose to the work's defense.[22] Though no external cause prevented medieval literary authors from representing heretics in their works, they nonetheless refrained from doing so.

When the heretic is imagined theologically or historically as a person who believes a deviant type of doctrine, he is indeed absent from medieval literature, yet when he is imagined characterologically, as a deviant type of person, I am proposing here, he can be found throughout literary texts of this period. While didactic authors (who were almost always Catholic clerics, writing as Catholic clerics) were describing heretics as people who caused epistemological instability in those around them, literary authors (who were also typically Catholic clerics, though not writing as such) were featuring in their works protagonists not labeled as heretics per se but virtually identical to these figures in the confusion they provoke. In the late twelfth and early thirteenth centuries, when the struggle between Catholic clerics and heretics was at its height, and in France and Occitania, where the conflict between these forces was best documented, literary authors highlighted in their texts figures who seem to be different from what they are and who mislead those around them through this discrepancy. Historians might account for the growing fascination with deceptive characters in literary writings at this time by explaining that as Europe

---

21. In addition to the literary texts addressed in this book, see "Le Débat d'Izarn et de Sicart de Figueiras," ed. Paul Meyer, *Annuaire bulletin de la Société de l'Histoire de la France* 16 (1879): 233–84, which depicts a debate between a Cathar heretic and an inquisitor; *Tenson provençal*, ed. David J. Jones (Paris: Droz, 1934), pp. 89–93, where the Waldensians are mentioned; and *The Romance of Flamenca*, ed. and trans. E. D. Blodgett (New York: Garland Publishing Co., 1995), v. 1260, where a character is compared to a Patarine. For discussion, see René Nelli, *L'Erotique des troubadours* (Toulouse: Editions Privat, 1963), pp. 221–46.

22. See my article "The Inquisitorial Origins of Literary Debate," *Romanic Review* 88, no. 1 (January 1997): 27–51, on Christine de Pizan's role in the *querelle de la Rose*.

shifted from a shame culture to a guilt culture, people's perception of themselves ceased to be based upon their external acts, as perceived by others, and began to be grounded in their internal intentions, as perceived by themselves alone; increasingly aware of the potential discrepancy between act and intention, people began to suspect that unscrupulous individuals could take advantage of this gap to trick others. Yet if literary authors were influenced by representations of heretics, particularly in their depictions of their protagonists, as I am arguing that they were, it is because the heretic constitutes not one type of dissimulator among others but, rather, the incarnation, in this culture at this time, of the dissimulation at the heart of literary writing. Insofar as there exists any commonality among what are usually considered literary texts, it can be said to lie in their tendency to include a multiplicity of voices, any one (or none) of which can be seen as privileged. While medieval literary authors, no less than their didactic peers, typically present themselves as teaching a lesson, they aim to disguise the bitter medicine of their teaching with the sweet honey of pleasure, calling upon classical, Celtic, and Germanic traditions, with their pagan origins, or upon courtly and chivalric customs, with their similarly non-Christian roots, to enrich and beautify their texts for this purpose. Cobbled together from different sources, their works are multiple, scattered, contradictory, with what they say often in conflict with what they show, to the point where they encourage their readers to interpret them in different ways. Even as didactic authors condemn the heretic because the profusion of possible interpretations he reflects threatens the single, definitive reading they demand of their works, literary authors celebrate his characterological counterpart because he invites the multiple and inconclusive readings of their texts they seek. Whereas in the context of a didactic work the heretic is condemned for undermining the distinction between truth and falsity upon which such straightforward texts rely, in the context of a literary work his twin is celebrated for supporting the truthfulness of that falsity upon which these more ambiguous texts depend.

A few disclaimers about this project may be in order at this point. First, in most of the book I will be discussing not the historical reality of so-called heretics in the Middle Ages but, rather, the textual representation of this population in didactic writings and their counterparts in literary works. I am interested in heretics not insofar as they actually existed but insofar as they were imagined as existing by their Catholic opponents and as their imagined personae influenced the literature of their time. For medieval Catholics, heretics were people one encountered not through one's own experiences but through a textual tradition of antiheretical writings or, perhaps, through one's own experiences as mediated and informed by that textual tradition. It is upon this textual tradition that I will be concentrating. Second, I do not mean to imply that the heretic was the only figure in medieval culture suspected of seeming to be different from what he was. Vassals were regularly thought to betray their lords with false oaths of loyalty, friars to deceive laymen with hypocritical pretensions to sanctity, and merchants to cheat customers with fraudulent professions of honesty. Yet even if the heretic shares features with these other characters, he remains the only figure who functions in didactic texts, not just as a theme, threatening the coherence of society, but as a trope, threatening the coherence of the text. The heretic was the only figure whose capacity to disconcert those around him was rooted in his alternate reading of a text and, hence, in the possibility he represented that all texts could be subjected to alternate readings. Finally, I am not suggesting that the authors of literary works were consciously or intentionally attempting to represent the character of the heretic as it was being portrayed in didactic writings of this time. Rather, I propose that these authors were responding to the epistemological crisis identified with the heretic during these years and that the works they were composing, by virtue of their very literariness, forced them to take the side of this figure against his opponents. With so little known about most medieval literary authors, there is no reason to suspect large numbers of them of heretical sympathies or to identify the particularities of their works with such deviant inclinations. If their writings champion characters of a "heretical" type, as I argue they do, it is because the logic of these writings ensures that figures who provoke epistemological uncertainty will cause pleasure rather than anxiety in their audiences. If literary works do not and probably cannot represent heretics as such, it may well be because any character defined by his demonstration of multiple possible interpretations of a text would necessarily emerge as their hero.

While this book as a whole is concerned with representations of heretics in texts, as opposed to the actual existence of so-called heretics in the world, it is appropriate that it begin by noting that Catholics' stereotypes about heretics do not appear to have differed significantly from accused heretics' own perceptions of themselves. The Cathar and Waldensian writings that have survived to this day focus upon theological issues at the expense of lived experience, but inquisitorial records, with their transcriptions of the often detailed confessions of accused heretics, partially supplement this lack. In chapter 1, the registers from the last prosecution of Cathars show that the "perfected" members of the sect, who had undergone the rite of *consolamentum*, who ate only bread, fish, and vegetables, who practiced sexual continence, and who ministered to other members of the cult, concealed themselves from view out of fear of pursuit, even as they revealed themselves to potential converts.[23] The non-"perfected" adherents to this heresy, who pursued ordinary secular lives, also concealed themselves, not physically but verbally, employing double entendres to convey their meaning to supporters of the cult and to keep it from potential opponents. In these inquisitorial registers, as in the literary works that surround them, the covertness of the heretics in hiding themselves from Catholic clerics and informers overlaps with the covertness of lovers in hiding themselves from their families, and the resultant intimacy of the heterodox sect, united against an orthodox world, intersects with the intimacy of lovers, united against more normative social structures. The epistemological instability heretics are typically depicted as causing can be seen here to be at least in part based on a historical reality, though this reality is experienced differently by the heretics who seek to preserve themselves from arrest and by the Catholic clerics who hunt them down.

Turning from heretics' views of themselves to Catholics' views of heretics, we see that the heretic is envisioned in orthodox texts first as secretive.[24] For Catholic clerics, as we will see in chapter 2, the Manichaeans and the Cathars who followed them conceal their beliefs, their rituals, and the meaning of their words in order to elude the just supervision of the authorities under whose jurisdiction they lie. One hides something because one has something to hide, the clerics surmise, and only that which is not of God has to be hidden. For the troubadours, however, as will become apparent in chapter 3, lovers must con-

---

23. Jean Duvernoy, "L'Acceptation: *Haereticus* (*Iretge*) ='parfait cathare' en Languedoc au XIIIe siècle," in *The Concept of Heresy in the Middle Ages,* ed. Lourdeaux and Verhelst, pp. 189–210.

24. A few scholars have begun to consider the secretiveness associated with the heretic in medieval society. See "Histoire et clandestinité (du Moyen-Age à la Première Guerre mondiale)," (Colloque de Privas, 20–22 mai 1977), especially Dominique Barthélemy and Jacques Chiffoleau, "Les Sources et la notion de clandestinité au Moyen-Age"; Annie Cazenave, "Cathares clandestins: De la puissance à l'exil"; and Monique Zerner, "Les Cathares au temps de la croisade albigeoise d'après les sources littéraires: Informations, déformations, ignorances" (typescript B 1844, Centre d'Etudes Cathares / René Nelli, Carcassonne). Others, such as Karma Lochrie, in *Covert Operations: The Medieval Uses of Secrecy* (Philadelphia: University of Pennsylvania Press, 1999), have begun to explore the related issue of secrecy in medieval society. Still others, such as Sissela Bok, in *Secrets: On the Ethics of Concealment and Revelation* (New York: Vintage Books, 1983), and Jacques Derrida, in "La Littérature au secret: Une filiation impossible," in Chantal Zabus, ed., *Le Secret: Motif et moteur de la littérature: Etudes réunies et présentées* (Louvain-la-Neuve: Collège Erasme, Bureau de Recueil, 1999), have approached this topic in a more general manner.

ceal the names of their ladies in order to preserve their liaisons from husbands and guardians, poets must conceal the significance of their poems in order to protect their value from unworthy audiences, and burghers must conceal their criticisms of inquisitors in order to avoid charges of heresy. These parties are secretive not because they implicitly recognize the iniquity of what they hide and try to prevent others from recognizing it themselves, as the clerics would have it, but because they perceive its value and aim to preserve their access to it from meddlers or trespassers. Though secretiveness troubles clerical authors because it excludes them from what they believe they deserve to know, it delights the troubadours because it includes them in a small coterie of people with special knowledge.

Secretive, the heretic is also viewed by Catholic authors as singular. As the clerics see it (chapter 4 will show), the noblemen and noblewomen among the Cathars seem to themselves and to many of their contemporaries so individual that they cannot be assimilated to any group, let alone one as degraded as that of heretics. Because nobles resemble heretics in their traditional resistance to the extension of Church power, they can seem to be heretics insofar as they stand up against ecclesiastical ambitions, but they can also seem to be Catholics insofar as what would be condemned in other populations as heretical behavior can be dismissed in them as the habits of their class. As Béroul, the author of the *Roman de Tristran*, sees it (chapter 5 will argue), the aristocratic Tristan and Iseut seem to themselves and to their supporters to be so distinctive that they cannot be held accountable to ordinary moral standards. Like heretics, the lovers deny the freedom of their will and their consequent responsibility for their actions, but like aristocrats, they limit their theological deviance to their own particular case. Singularity disturbs clerical authors because it allows nobility to trump orthodoxy of faith, yet it pleases romance authors because it suggests that individual excellence, upon which the nobility prides itself, should place people outside the categories in which the masses are judged.

When not annulling his identity through his secretiveness or rendering it unique and, hence, unreadable through his singularity, the heretic is doubling it through his duplicity. According to the clerics, as we will see in chapter 6, the Waldensians are Protean characters, transforming themselves (or, rather, pretending to transform themselves) into merchants, harvesters, pilgrims, or members of other groups, with all the accoutrements of these ways of life, in order to mislead people as to their true, heretical identity. Worst of all, they adopt the personae of clerics, studying Scripture and the Church Fathers, though they have obtained no formal learning, and preaching about what they have learned to mixed crowds, though they have received no authorization to do so. Cloaking who they are under these assumed identities, they subvert a legitimate social hierarchy, which sets learned and approved clerics over illiterate and inconsequential laymen. According to the authors of a series of interlinked comic narratives, as will become evident in chapter 7, the prostitute Richeut and her son Samson, the simpleton Trubert, and the fox Renart are also inclined to take on the guise of different social and even religious roles in order to deceive others as to their true, malicious intentions. Though these authors agree that the assumption of alternate identities provides a way of attaining a power in one's society one would not otherwise possess, they justify this tactic as necessary to those who are disadvantaged in a corrupt world where others are unfairly set above them.

Literary texts end up affirming the heretic so condemned in didactic writings through their recognition of a complexity of experience irreducible to any one creed, yet they can never prevent the heretic from being condemned. In this context, literature functions not unlike play, as Johan Huizinga defined this activity many years ago. "Play is . . . a stepping out of 'real' life into a temporary sphere of activity, with a disposition all of its own," Huizinga writes. "Inside the circle of the game, the laws and customs of ordinary life no longer count."[25] The experience of play is, for Huizinga, the experience of freedom, but this freedom is contingent upon the restriction of play to specified times and places, sharply demarcated from "real" life, or, in the case of literature, to specified linguistic conventions, clearly distinguished from "real" speech. The fool is allowed to speak the truth with impunity only because he is understood to speak follies, which are not to be taken seriously. The literary author who questions, not whether Catholicism is to be preferred to Catharism or Waldensianism, but, more radically, whether any orthodoxy can ever do justice to the heteroclite nature of experience is allowed to voice his concerns without suffering reprisals only because he is composing fictions, which are also not to be taken seriously. Literature permitted medieval society to express truths about heretics and the anxieties they aroused which could not be uttered otherwise, but the very distance from reality which prevented its authors from being prosecuted for heresy also prevented its insights from tempering such prosecutions.

---

25. Johan Huizinga, *Homo Ludens: A Study of the Play-Element in Culture* (Boston: Beacon Press, 1955), pp. 8 and 12.

1

THE HALF-OPENED DOOR, THE LOWERED HOOD, THE SMILE

Béatris de Planissoles and the Heretics of Montaillou

Between 1300 and 1318, three-quarters of a century after the defeat of Occitania in the Albigensian Crusade and half a century after the fall of the Cathar citadel of Montségur, the dualist heresy witnessed a resurgence in the Sarbathès, the mountainous region of the county of Foix that includes the villages of Montaillou and Prades.[1] According to one witness's version of the events, Peire Autier, a notary in nearby Ax-les-Thermes, was reading a book one day when he discovered a passage in it which struck him so much that he showed it to his brother Guilhem, another clerk.[2] "Now

---

1. For an account of this resurgence, see Jean Duvernoy, "Pierre Autier," *Cahiers d'études cathares* 21, no. 47 (automne 1970): 9–49, and *Le Catharisme*, vol. 2, *L'Histoire des Cathares* (Toulouse: Privat, 1979), pp. 315–33. MS Lat. Vat. 4030, which documents the rebirth of heresy in this region during these years, has already been subjected to numerous studies. See Célestin Douais, ed., *Documents pour servir à l'histoire de l'Inquisition dans le Languedoc*, vol. 1 (Paris: Renouard, 1890), pp. ciii–cxiii, and J. M. Vidal's numerous articles on topics addressed in this manuscript, including the campaigns against Jews and lepers and the last Albigeois ministers. The most famous study is Emmanuel Le Roy Ladurie's *Montaillou: Village occitan de 1294 à 1324* (Paris: Editions Gallimard, 1975), trans. and abr. Barbara Bray as *Montaillou: The Promised Land of Error* (New York: George Brazillier, 1978; rpt., New York: Vintage Books, 1979), which approaches the manuscript from an anthropological perspective. See also Matthias Benad, *Domus und Religion in Montaillou: Katholische Kirche und Katharismus im Überlebenskampf der Familie des Pfarrers Petrus Clerici am Anfang des 14. Jahrhunderts* (Tübingen: Mohr, 1990). On the Inquisition in this area, see James B. Given, *Inquisition and Medieval Society: Power, Discipline, and Resistance in Languedoc* (Ithaca: Cornell University Press, 1997), and John H. Arnold, *Inquisition and Power: Catharism and the Confessing Subject in Medieval Languedoc* (Philadelphia: University of Pennsylvania Press, 2001).

2. I will be referring to individuals by the medieval, vernacular versions of their first names, whether in Occitan, French, Italian, German, or English, depending upon their native tongue,

17

what, my brother?" Peire asked.[3] "It seems to me that we have lost our souls,"
Guilhem replied.[4] "Let us leave, then, brother, and go seek the salvation of our
souls," Peire concluded.[5] Though the two men each had a wife, children, and
a prosperous household, they abandoned all that they had and traveled to
Lombardy, where a Cathar hierarchy was still in existence, and there they
became "perfected" heretics under these surviving ministers' hands.[6] Whatever
the reasons for the Autier brothers' departure from the Occitan region and
consecration in the heretical faith—and tongues wagged that they were fleeing
debts as much as they were pursuing sanctity—the two men returned to their
homeland before long and began to preach to their compatriots with remarkable effectiveness. The Benet, Belot, and Rives families welcomed the brothers
to the village and into their houses, which soon became the chief meeting-
places for the heretics and their believers, while the Clergue household added
the authority of the priest Peire and the *bayle* (or bailiff) Bernart to the
renascent faith. In addition to these four important clans, the Guilhaberts, the
Martys, the Maurs, and the Maurys also joined the sect.[7] So thoroughly did the

---

and by the modern, vernacular versions of their places of origin. For the more obscure Occitan
names cited in Latin texts, I have been aided by Anne Brenon, *Le Petit Livre aventureux des
prénoms occitans au temps du catharisme* (Toulouse: Editions Loubatières, 1992). Only in the
cases of well-known figures, whose names are already familiar to readers in their English (or
occasionally French) equivalents, have I deviated from this rule. The disjunction between
Occitan first names and French last names may be linguistically offensive to some, but given
the backdrop of the Albigensian Crusade behind the events being discussed here, it seemed
best to acknowledge, as much as possible, the Occitan identity of these figures.

3. "Et quid est, frater?" *Le Registre d'Inquisition de Jacques Fournier, Evêque de Pamiers
(1318–1325),* ed. Jean Duvernoy (Toulouse: Privat, 1965), vol. 2, p. 404. This edition has not
escaped criticism, though Duvernoy published a list of corrections in 1972. See Antoine
Dondaine, "Le Registre d'Inquisition de Jacques Fournier: A propos d'une édition récente:
Examen critique de l'édition donnée par M. Jean Duvernoy," *Revue de l'histoire des religions*
178 (octobre 1970): 49–56.

4. "Videtur michi quod animas nostras perdidimus," *Registre,* vol. 2, p. 404.

5. "Eamus ergo, frater, et queramus salvationem animarum nostrarum," ibid.

6. On the Occitan refugee community in Lombardy, see Eugène Dupré-Theseider, "Le
Catharisme languedocien et l'Italie," *Cahiers de Fanjeaux,* vol. 3, *Cathares en Languedoc*
(Toulouse: Privat, 1963): 299–316. The Inquisition, so strong in Occitania, was paralyzed in
the urban centers that dominated the Italian political landscape, which, playing off the Church
and the Empire, tended to remain independent of both. The region south of Turin, especially
the city of Coni, where the Autier brothers stayed, proved to be especially welcoming to the
foreign heretics.

7. On the phenomenon of the *genus hereticorum,* see Michel Roquebert, "Le Catharisme
comme tradition dans la 'Familia' languedocienne," *Cahiers de Fanjeaux,* vol. 20, *Effacement
du catharisme? (XIIIe–XIVe s.)* (Toulouse: Privat, 1985), pp. 221–42.

inhabitants of Montaillou shift to the heretical camp that when Geoffroy d'Ablis, the inquisitor of Carcassonne, arrived in this village in 1308, he found it necessary to arrest its entire adult population, and even after the Autier brothers were executed in the following months, the belief they had kindled persisted.[8] Between 1319 and 1324, when Jacques Fournier, the bishop of Pamiers, took over the responsibility of pursuing heretics in his see, twenty-eight of the cases he examined, or over a fourth of the total number, were from these two villages.[9] As a result of the work of the inquisitor and, even more, that of the bishop, three heretics, namely, Prades Tavernier, Pons Sicre, and Felip d'Alaryac, and a few resolute believers, including Sebèlia Baille and Guilhem Fort, followed the Autiers to the flames, while scores of repentant believers spent years in prison only to find, when they emerged, their houses razed, their property confiscated, and their livelihoods destroyed. Refugees from this troubled region trekked across the Pyrenees and founded a community in Spain, but after Arnaut Sicre, son of Sebèlia Baille, had lured Guilhem Bélibaste, the last-known heretic, back onto the lands of the county of Foix in 1321 so that he might redeem his forfeited heritage with perfected blood, there appear to have been no more heretics and eventually no more believers either. The Cathar faith, as far as we know, had finally been extinguished in the southern lands.

The inquisitorial records of Jacques Fournier have long been recognized as some of the richest documents concerning medieval heretics, unique in the information they provide about the day-to-day lives of some of the last Cathars. Among the principal families of Montaillou and Prades, several of the most active figures in the revival of heresy during this period had already died by the time these registers were compiled, yet twenty-seven others, including seventeen women and ten men, gave lengthy and detailed confessions. The records of these avowals cannot, obviously, be taken at face value.[10] The villagers spoke only because they had been summoned to respond in matters of faith or even, on occasion, because they had been arrested and forcibly brought to court. If

8. See *L'Inquisiteur Geoffroy d'Ablis et les cathares du comté de Foix (1308–1309)*, ed. and trans. Annette Palès-Gobilliard (Paris: CNRS, 1984).

9. On Fournier, see Jacques Paul, "Jacques Fournier, inquisiteur," in *Cahiers de Fanjeaux*, vol. 26, *La Papauté d'Avignon et le Languedoc, 1316–1342* (Toulouse: Privat, 1991), pp. 39–67.

10. On the dangers of doing so, see Leonard Boyle, "Montaillou Revisited: *Mentalité* and Methodology," in *Pathways to Medieval Peasants*, ed. J. A. Raftis (Toronto: Pontifical Institute of Mediaeval Studies, 1981), pp. 119–40, and Renato Rosaldo, "From the Door of His Tent: The Fieldworker and the Inquisitor," in James Clifford and George E. Marcus, eds., *Writing Culture: The Poetics and Politics of Ethnography* (Berkeley: University of California Press, 1986), pp. 77–97.

the bishop was persuaded that they had confessed all that they and their acquaintances had done in matters of heresy, he forgave them and subjected them to the normal series of penances for their sins, including pilgrimages, incarcerations, and the wearing of double crosses; yet if he had reason to suspect that they had not acknowledged all that they or others had done, he kept them in prison until they were more forthcoming. Even if we can assume that the bishop persuaded the villagers to speak fully about their participation in the heterodox cult, the notaries transformed their words, transcribing their oral utterances into written confessions, translating the original Occitan of these dialogues into Latin, and condensing answers to multiple questions into one single response.[11] Given the multiple levels of mediation which separate us from the villagers' original words, let alone their original thoughts, we might reasonably expect that the statements attributed to them reflect more clerical preconceptions about heresy than popular experience. Nonetheless, the villagers' confessions contain such vivid, almost novelistic accounts of their lives, replete with information helpful, harmful, or indifferent to their cases, that they clearly reflect far more than the projections of a Catholic prelate's prejudices against Cathars.[12] For the many scholars who have exploited these registers, it is in this text, more than in any other medieval source, that we can gain some sense of the lived experience of heretics during those years.

Considering the exceptional value of the villagers' confessions in Fournier's records, the elusiveness of the heretic in these pages is all the more striking. Is a heretic someone, referred to as a "heretic" in these registers, who has become a perfected member of the sect and thus devotes himself to preaching its creed and administering its sacraments, despite the threat of punishment that forces him to live underground? Is a heretic someone, referred to not as a heretic but as a "believer" in these volumes but no less charged with heresy, who gives credence to the doctrines she has learned from the perfected members of the cult but does not adopt their radical lifestyle? Is a heretic someone, occasionally defined as "suspected" of heresy, who listens to the sermons of the perfected members of the sect, who retains their lessons in his or her mem-

---

11. On the production of this manuscript, see J. M. Vidal, *Le Tribunal d'Inquisition de Pamiers* (Toulouse: Privat, 1906). Vidal identifies Guilhem Peire-Barthe as the notary who prepared the original paper version of the registers and the first 133 folios of the final parchment version, and he names Joan Jabbaud and Rainaut Jabbaud (who are possibly the same individual) as the officials who completed the text after Peire-Barthe's death.

12. On this point, see Natalie Zemon Davis, "Les Conteurs de Montaillou," *Annales E. S. G.* 34, no. 1 (janvier–février 1979): 61–73.

ory, and who repeats them to other people, without, perhaps, giving credence to these beliefs? Is a heretic someone, at times described as a "receiver" or a "favorer" of heretics, who supports perfected members of the sect by offering them shelter, by providing them escort in their travels, or by sending them gifts, but is not otherwise committed to this cult? Perhaps because of the coercive circumstances in which these confessions were recorded, the heretic surfaces in this text either as an earlier, heterodox member of the community, now dead or disappeared, or as an earlier, heterodox version of the speaker, now replaced by the current, orthodox self. The heretic dominates these pages, but as the empty center around which both the accused and the accusing parties situate themselves.

THE HERETICS

If we are to believe her confession, Fournier's most celebrated defendant, Béatris de Planissoles, never met the Autier brothers, once they had become perfected, or any other heretics of their rank, despite repeated inducements to do so. In 1294, well before the Autiers began to preach in the Sarbathès, Béatris was *châtelaine* of Montaillou, living near the castle with her husband, when she found herself importuned by Raimon Roussel of Prades, the manager and steward of her house, to depart with him for the "Good Men" of Lombardy.[13] A fellow noblewoman from the area, Estevena de Châteauverdun, had already fled across the Alps with Prades Tavernier to join the Italian heretics, who were said to be able to practice their faith in greater security, and Raimon encouraged Béatris to follow her example. He praised the heretics' sermons enthusiastically, informing Béatris that "after a man heard them speak a single time, he could not do without them, and if she heard them a single time, she would adhere to them forever."[14] If the heretics could not be found in the Sarbathès, Raimon explained, it was because "they dared not live here, because the wolves and dogs persecuted them"; these "wolves and dogs," he explained, were "the bishops and Friars Preachers who persecuted the Good Christians and hunted them

---

13. On Béatris's social context, see Jean Duvernoy, "La Noblesse du comté de Foix au début du XIVe siècle," in *Pays de l'Ariège: Archéologie, histoire, géographie* (Actes du XVIe Congrès d'Etudes de la Fédération des sociétés académiques et savantes de Languedoc, Pyrénées, Gascogne, Foix, 28–30 mai 1960) (Montpellier: Fédération des sociétés académiques et savantes de Languedoc-Pyrénées-Gascogne, 1961), pp. 123–40.

14. "postquam semel homo audiverat eos loquentes, non poterat carere ipsis, et si ipsa semel audivisset eos, perpetuo eis adhereret," *Registre*, vol. 1, p. 219.

from these parts."[15] Though seemingly tempted by Raimon's proposal, Béatris decided to stay in Montaillou when she discovered the steward's intentions toward her to be less spiritual than carnal in nature, and Raimon soon abandoned his position and returned to his hometown. A few years later, after her husband had died, Béatris became the mistress of the priest Peire Clergue, from whom she heard praises of the heterodox sect and lessons about their doctrine. At this time the heretics had begun to visit the Benet, Belot, and Rives families, and Béatris received invitations to meet them at the Rives' house. She tells how Azalaïs Rives one day tried to entice her to come to where she lived, at first claiming that she needed to borrow some vinegar, then alleging that her daughter Guillelma Clergue needed to see her, and finally admitting that "her brother Prades Tavernier was in her house and wanted to speak with her" because he had a message from the fugitive Estevena.[16] Another companion, Raimonda de Luzenac, urged her to accept such invitations to meet the heretics, insisting that "if she had seen and heard them a single time, she would never want to hear anything else."[17] Even after 1301, when Béatris descended from these mountainous regions to Dalou to marry her second husband, opportunities to encounter the heretics did not end. Bernart Belot arrived at her house and told her that, although the heretics generally did not like to visit these lands because of the dangers that awaited them there, "the Good Christians, if they dared, would ask her to see them, because, as it was said, no one could be firm in their faith without having seen them and heard them speak."[18] Once again, however, she alleges that she refused Bernart's offer. Béatris does not explain why she declined to meet the heretics time and again, but if she is speaking the truth in claiming to have kept her distance from these sectaries, her wariness of such encounters most likely lies in a hope of avoiding prosecution for heresy. Whatever the reasons for her failure to meet Prades or his confrères, the heretics as she depicts them functioned as an abstraction in her spiritual life, idealized missionaries who, once heard, would confirm her in their faith but who remained an image rather than a memory in her mind.

---

15. "non audebant hic morari, quia lupi et canes persequebantur eos," ibid.; "episcopi et Fratres Predicatores qui persequebantur bonos christianos et fugebant eos de partibus istis," ibid.

16. "frater eius scilicet Pradas Tavernir erat in domo sua, et volebat loqui cum ipsa," *Registre*, vol. 1, p. 223.

17. "si semel eos vidisset et audivisset nunquam alius audire vellet," *Registre*, vol. 1, p. 238.

18. "boni christiani, si auderent, rogarent quod ipsa videret eos, quia, ut dicebatur, nullus poterat esse firmus in eorum fide, nisi eos vidisset, et eciam loquentes audivisset," *Registre*, vol. 1, pp. 233.

While Béatris's neighbors in the Sarbathès admit to having met the heretics, they too emphasize the mysteriousness of their covert ways, recalling how the heretics hid themselves inside the houses and outbuildings of their believers. It happened that the heretics concealed themselves so effectively that they were not actually seen but only ascertained through circumstantial evidence to have been present. The servant Raimonda Testanière noticed an ornate bed with a silk-worked cushion in the *solier* (or upstairs) of the Belot household. The registers relate, "Seeing this bed, she was amazed because she had not seen a bed or such a cushion anywhere else in the *solier*, and she thought suddenly, on account of the words she had heard from Arnaut Vidal, that heretics had slept in this bed the night before."[19] Later, Raimonda observed wine and honey being slipped into this bedroom, as another servant espied wine, bread, and other items being brought there. More often the heretics were seen, but they were seen as people intended to go unseen. Seven of the women villagers describe stopping by a neighbor's house, most often that of the Benets, the Belots, or the Rives, to borrow an item, only to discover a heretic, or a man they suspected of being a heretic, on the property.[20] Hidden within these buildings, the heretics were, on occasion, hidden behind special barriers, most often locked doors through which their low voices could be heard, but also blankets, as in the Benets' *solier*, or wine casks, as in Guillelma Maury's cellar. When apprehended in these internal or doubly internal spaces, the heretics often attempted to flee their interlopers' sight, thus underscoring their covert status. At the Benets' house, Azalaïs Azéma entered the *foganha* (or kitchen) one night to find Guilhem Autier sitting on a bench near the fire with a few other men, all of whom rose abruptly when they saw her. Gauzia Clergue ventured into this same abode to find an old man in a long coat, known as a *balandrun*, in a room near the *foganha*, leaning against a chest with his feet propped up on a bed and quoting Saint Paul to the family's father and son. "Seeing her, he sank into the bed in such a way, she said, that she could not see his face fully, but she saw only that he had white hair above his forehead."[21] At the Belots',

19. "lectum videns ipsa mirata fuit, quia non viderat alias in dicto solario lectum nec talem minhotum, et statim opinata fuit propter verba que audiverat a dicto Arnaldo Vidalis quod heretici in dicto lecto iacuisset nocte precedenti," *Registre*, vol. 1, p. 459.

20. These villagers were Guillelma Arzelier, Azalaïs Azéma, Raimonda Belot, Gauzia Clergue, Guillelma Clergue, Bruna Pourcel, and Faurèsa Rives.

21. "videns ipsam loquentem declinavit se super dictum lectum, sic quod ipsa loquens, ut dixit, non potuit videre ad plenum faciem eius, sed solum vidit quod supra frontem habebat pilos canos," *Registre*, vol. 3, p. 358.

Guillelma Clergue, née Rives, detected two men dressed in green in the *solier* and returned to investigate who they might be; she reports, "Seeing her come back, the two men, receding, hid inside the bedroom."[22] At the Rives', Guillelma penetrated the family's *foganha* despite her brother Pons's effort to bar her way and discovered Prades Tavernier seated on a bench by the fire. "Seeing her, Prades rose and entered the bedroom."[23] At another time, in this compound's straw loft she found the same heretic reading a small book in the sunlight. "Seeing her, Prades rose, troubled, as if he wanted to hide."[24] Heretics are described as men not seen but only suspected of being there or as seen only briefly as they hastily withdrew.

The heretics were perceived as hiding no less outdoors than indoors. They were said to emerge at dusk. Raimonda Arsen observed Guilhem Autier conversing with Guilhem Belot outside the Belots' farm at twilight, and Guillelma Clergue noticed Prades Tavernier talking with her brother Pons outside the Rives' house at this hour. So nocturnal in their habits that they impressed observers with their pallor, the heretics were said to travel from one house to another almost exclusively after sunset. Guillelma Benet and Sebèlia Peyre recall their arriving after the hour when most people had gone to bed and not leaving until the following evening. Peire Maury is said to have guided Felip d'Alayrac to Cubières, "although the night was dark to the point where one could hardly see."[25] Raimon Azéma once led Guilhem Autier to nearby Luzenac, where a man "whom he did not recognize on account of the darkness of the night" met them and took the heretic away with him.[26] Cathar believers were expected to become heretics on their deathbed so as to ensure their salvation, and those who are asked to testify about hereticacions of invalids often recall the darkness of the hour at which the ministers arrived to perform this ceremony. Faurèsa Rives, who had been nursing the young Azalaïs Benet, was sent away from the house during the night; as she was departing, she witnessed two men, "whom she did not recognize because the hour was dark,"[27]

22. "dicti duo homines videntes ipsam retrocedentem absconderunt se in dicta camera," *Registre*, vol. 1, p. 347.

23. "videntes eam dictus Pradas surrexit et intravit cameram," *Registre*, vol. 1, p. 337.

24. "dictus Pradas videns ipsam stupefactus surrexit ac si se abscondere vellet," *Registre*, vol. 1, p. 341.

25. "licet obscura esset dicta nox in tantum quod vix poterat videre," *Registre*, vol. 3, p. 141.

26. "quem ipse . . . non cognovit propter obscuritatem noctis," *Registre*, vol. 1, p. 313.

27. "quos ipsa non cognovit, quia tempus erat obscuram," *Registre*, vol. 1, 323.

emerging from the cellar. When Guilhem Guilhabert's two brothers-in-law were waiting outdoors for a heretic to arrive to console their sick relative, they at first failed to recognize him because of the obscurity. Shielded by the darkness as they traveled, the heretics were also shielded by felt hats, hoods, and *balandruns*. One of Guilhem Guilhabert's brothers-in-law mentions that it was only when the heretic uncovered his head at the foot of the invalid's bed that he recognized him as Prades Tavernier. Raimonda Belot recalls heretics' wearing hoods that covered almost all of their faces; another villager remembers their lowering these hoods over their eyes to ensure that they would not be identified. When the heretics were obliged to undertake a journey by day, they not only concealed but disguised themselves. Azalaïs Faure explains that Prades Tavernier was able to travel in the sunlight to hereticate a certain invalid because he carried a skin and staff over his shoulder and a skein of spun wool in his hands, so that he might seem to be a merchant to those he passed. On the day that the inquisitor's men came to search for heretics in Montaillou, Joan Pelessier saw Arnaut Vidal pass by the field, leading into the woods two men wearing brown *balandruns* and carrying axes. Joan's companion, not fooled by their costume, joked, "Are they from Lavanalet, these two woodcutters? They look like it!"[28] When not hiding in a believer's compound, heretics are said to appear only at night and under cover.

Recalled as hiding, whether indoors or outdoors, the heretics were often remembered as wavering, physically, between exposed and concealed places. Faurèsa Rives, visiting the Clergues' house to borrow a pitcher, was bidden to fetch the container and leave quickly. "When she passed before the door of the rector's bedroom, which was half open, she looked into the bedroom and saw the 'clothed' heretic Guilhem Autier standing by the window which overlooks the canal."[29] Of Azalaïs Azéma, who stopped by the Belots' house to borrow a cauldron, we learn, "When she was in the house, she saw Guilhem Autier the heretic standing in the doorway of the bedroom that communicates with the *foganha*, and he had his body inside and his head outside."[30] Bruna Pourcel

28. "Et sunt de Avellaneto illi duo boscaterii? Parent!" *Registre*, vol. 3, p. 85.

29. "cum transerit ante hostium camere dicti rectoris, quod erat semi apertum, respexit intus cameram et vidit ibi stantem iuxta fenestram que respicit versus la Canal Guillelmum Auterii hereticum indutum," *Registre*, vol. 1, p. 327. "Clothed" here refers to the special clothing worn by perfected heretics.

30. "cum fuit in dicta domo, vidit Guillelmum Auterii hereticum in hostio camere, que se tenebat cum foganha, stantem, et erat corpus intra et capud tenebat extra," *Registre*, vol. 1, p. 317.

notes that once when she entered the Rives' house, she saw Prades Tavernier
"standing in the doorway of the bedroom" and that after she had sat down by
the hearth with her aunt Azalaïs, "the heretic stood in the doorway of the bedroom, without coming toward them."[31] On other occasions, Bruna recalls
Prades' opening the door of the house "a little" and standing "at the door of
the bedroom" with some other men.[32] Guilhem Maurs states that when one
day he and some others were finishing a meal at Guillelma Maury's house, "he
saw Guillelma Maury with one of the men who had eaten there approach the
door of a bedroom in the house and, with the door of the bedroom half-open,
speak, apparently to someone who was in the bedroom" who, he indicates,
turned out to be Guilhelm Bélibaste.[33] Lingering at windows or in doorways,
the heretics were also said to hover in passageways specially constructed for
them. Sebèlia Peyre was dining with others in the *foganha* of a house in Limoux
when, she reports, she saw Peire Autier poke his head through a hole in the wall
that was normally covered by a board. Between the Benet, Belot, and Rives
houses partitions appear to have been built, through which the heretics were
able to travel. According to Guillelma Clergue, "Prades entered the great house
of her father through the partition that was in the straw loft, from which a board
had been removed, and he put his head through the hole where this board had
been removed."[34] Even when the villagers do not depict the heretics as occupying some in-between zone, half outside and half inside, half exposed and half
concealed, they portray them as emerging from and returning to their lairs with
such discretion that the public world seems to be, for them, just such a zone.
The same Prades Tavernier who had at first withdrawn from Guillelma Clergue
and Bruna Pourcel when they discovered him by chance in the Rives' household, fearful, it seems, of their potential denunciation of him, ended up asking
the one young woman, "'Won't you sit here with us?'" and helping the other
to carry her bread from the oven, while he preached to her "not to say or do
evil to anyone, and not to take the possessions of another, . . . and to believe in

31. "stantem in hostio cuiusdam camere," *Registre*, vol. 1, p. 382; "dictus hereticus stetit
in hostio camere supradicte, non veniendo ad ipsas," ibid.

32. "aliquantulum," *Registre*, vol. 1, p. 385; "ad hostium dicte camere," *Registre*, vol. 1, p.
384.

33. "Vidit . . . dicta Guillelma Maurina cum uno homo de illis qui ibi comederant acces-
sit ad hostium cuiusdam camere dicte domus et semiaperto dicto hostio dicte camere loque-
bantur, ut videbatur, cum aliquo qui erat in dicta camera," *Registre*, vol. 2, p. 184.

34. "dictus Pradas intravit per posticium quod erat in palherio de quo una postis erat
amota domum maiorem patris ipsius, et tenebat caput extractum per foramen unde dicta
postis fuerat amota," *Registre*, vol. 1, p. 341.

him."[35] Wavering in liminal places, such as windows, doorways, passageways, or even, as we have seen, the edge of a forest, the heretics were wary of being discovered and betrayed by the villagers but also eager to meet and convert them to their faith.

In general, the villagers interpreted the secretive habits of the heretics sympathetically, as the necessary result of their persecution by the Church. At times, it is true, they may have compared the heretics to brigands, like those from Belcaire de Sault, who were pursued on account of their criminality, but more often they compared them to Jesus Christ, the Apostles, and the martyrs, who were pursued because of their sanctity.[36] Peire Autier informed Peire Maury, "It is not surprising that the world hates us, because it also bore hatred toward our Lord, whom it persecuted, along with his Apostles. We are hated and persecuted on account of his law, which we keep firmly."[37] Guilhem Maury and Guilhem Belot instructed Peire, similarly, that the heretics hide "because of the lust for dominion of the Church, which persecutes them because these men observe truth and justice, just as the Apostles suffered persecution because they defended truth and justice."[38] When Guillelma Benet brought Raymonda Belot to her house to meet Guilhem Autier, she explained to her guest "that he followed the way of the Apostles Peter and Paul and sustained persecution for God."[39] If Raimonda perceived the heretic as secretive, Guillelma stated, the reason for this was that "he did not dare circulate openly in public because he suffered persecution."[40] For these villagers, the world is not a good place for those who are good, whether they be Jesus Christ, the Apostles, or the

35. "non sedebitis hic nobiscum?" *Registre*, vol. 1, p. 336; "ne diceret malum alicui vel faceret, et quod non acciperet aliquid de alieno, . . . et quod crederet ei," *Registre*, vol. 1, p. 386.

36. See Guilhem Buscail's testimony, *Registre*, vol. 1, p. 488. Raimonda Arsen, Guillelma Arzelier, Mengarda Buscail, Guillelma Clergue, Peire Maury, and Bruna Pourcel all claim to have asked interlocutors, with more or less similar words, "If these were good men and they had a good faith, why did they hide themselves? [*quare, ex quo dicti homines erant boni homines et bonam fidem tenebant, se abscondebant?*]" *Registre*, vol. 3, p. 92 et passim.

37. "non est mirum si odit nos mundus, quia etiam odio habuit Dominum nostrum, quem persequtus fuit et apostolos suos. Et nos sumus odio habiti et persequti propter Legem eius, quam firme tenemus," *Registre*, vol. 3, p. 123.

38. "propter sobransariam Ecclesie, que eos persequitur pro eo quia predicti homines tenent veritatem et iusticiam, sicut Apostoli passi fuerunt persecutionem, quia veritatem et iusticiam manutenebant," *Registre*, vol. 3, p. 120. Duvernoy glosses "subransana" as "volonté de domination," *Registre*, trans. Duvernoy, vol. 3, p. 1024.

39. "tenebat viam Apostolorum Petri et Pauli, et sustinebat persecutionem propter Deum," *Registre*, vol. 3, p. 69.

40. "non audebat ire palam et publice, quia persecutionem paciebatur," *Registre*, vol. 3, p. 68.

so-called heretics, because it is dominated by the wicked, who inevitably persecute the good, hating their observance of truth, justice, and the law. The
heretics' perception of the world as evil is rooted in their theology. Joan Maury
cites a Cathar prayer which extols the "legitimate God," who created "good
spirits" such as Jesus Christ, the Apostles, and their heretical successors, and
contrasts him with the "stranger god," who created the material beings who
persecute these holy men.[41] Of these "good spirits," the prayer proclaims, "We
are not of the world and the world is not of us."[42] By refusing themselves sexual procreation, animal consumption, and material accumulation, the heretics
sought to exist outside the life cycles in which other, more material people were
captured. If individuals such as the bishop and the inquisitor or institutions
such as the Church and the kingdom of France enter into conflict with the
heretics, it is as part of a larger, cosmic combat between "the world of
the stranger god" and the Good Men.[43] For themselves and their followers, the
heretics represent the ideal of "good spirits," of people whose spiritual existence provokes the wrath of material powers and who must conceal themselves
in order to avoid extermination.

Occupying the doorway between the here and the there, the now and the
then, the transitory world and the eternal heavens, the heretics were seen, even
during the time they roamed these highlands, as people who would soon be
gone or who, even when present, seemed already absent. Azalaïs Azéma relates
that in 1302, seven years before the Autiers and their companions began to be
arrested, Raimon Benet invited her into his house, telling her that "she should
enter because she would see in his house something that would never be seen
again."[44] Entering the *foganha*, Azalaïs beheld, again "near the doorway of the
bedroom," the heretics Guilhem Autier and Pons Sicre.[45] Asked why Raimon
had told her that she would not see figures of this sort again, Azalaïs explains
that it was because "it was already said that people would come to seek out and
arrest these heretics."[46] Even as external persecution threatened the heretics'
physical existence, internal temptation endangered their spiritual integrity, and,

---

41. "Dieu dreyturier," *Registre*, vol. 2, p. 461; "bons speritz," ibid.; "dieu estranh," ibid.

42. "nos no em del mon nil mon no es de nos," ibid.

43. "al mon de dieu estranh," ibid.

44. "intraret, quia videret in domo eius aliqua que postea nunquam visura esset," *Registre*,
vol. 1, p. 311.

45. "iuxta hostium cuiusdam camere," ibid.

46. "iam dicebatur quod aliqui venire debebant ad explorandum et capiendum dictos
hereticos," ibid.

in doing so, made them seem no less ephemeral. For their believers, the heretics embodied a certain ideal. Newcomers to the faith first learned not so much about the doctrines of Catharism as about the special status of the "Good Christians," whose harsh diet, poverty, and itinerancy made their lives more ascetic than those of even their most austere Catholic counterparts. Believers sought not to imitate the rigorous routines of the heretics but to acknowledge the unbridgeable gap between these holy men and themselves. In the *meliora-mentum*, believers knelt down before the heretics, placed their hands on the floor, and cast their head three times onto their hands, asking, each time, "*Benedicte, senher*" and thus recognizing the heretics' spiritual power over them. Believers fulfilled their responsibilities toward their religion, not by praying or lighting candles, as Catholics did, but by escorting heretics from one village to another and by providing them with food, lodging, or other sustenance. Even when dying believers underwent the *consolamentum* and became heretics themselves, their refusal to eat or drink anything but water after the ceremony reflected a conviction that if they survived, they could not sustain the arduous lifestyle the heretics had chosen. At the same time as the heretics represented an ideal to their believers, they tended to fall short of that ideal. While heretics were supposed to accept money only for their present needs, Sebèlia Peyre testifies that Guilhem and Peire Autier amassed funds far beyond this purpose. While heretics were supposed to remain celibate, Peire Maury makes clear that Guilhem Bélibaste enjoyed a concubine and that when she became pregnant, he persuaded Peire to marry her. The heretics were supposed to represent an ideal, namely, the capacity for a human being to transcend the material, corruptible, transitory world and to attain a purely spiritual, immutable, and eternal realm of existence, yet as representatives of that ideal they seemed to function better at a distance than nearby. Vulnerable to destruction either by an outer world that would inevitably defeat them or by an inner weakness that would almost as inevitably prove them inadequate to their intention, the heretics were remembered nostalgically, even during the height of their revival, as a concept that was, in its very being, more powerful than the reality behind it.

THE BELIEVERS

Though Béatris represents herself to Fournier as having kept her distance from the heretics, she admits, nonetheless, to having frequented their believers, who opened up the heretical world to her once she gained their confidence. One day, after the death of her first husband, Béatris relates, she was warming herself by Azalaïs Maury's fire when Gauzia Clergue arrived to ask Azalaïs if

Guillelma Faure had died. When Azalaïs replied affirmatively, Béatris recalls during her confession, "Gauzia said then, 'And you have done well [*bene*]?' Azalaïs responded, 'Yes, by my faith, well.' Gauzia said then, 'And you have done well, well [*bene, bene*]? Nothing was missing on your part?' Azalaïs responded that they had done 'well' and that they had had no hindrance to doing so."[47] After this dialogue, Gauzia exclaimed, "Thanks be to God,"[48] and sat down at the fire with them. At the time, Béatris did not understand what the words between the two women meant, and a few days later she asked Azalaïs about them. At first, Azalaïs claimed that these words meant nothing, but then, when pressed, she admitted that she dared not reveal their meaning to Béatris. It was only after Béatris promised to keep secret whatever Azalaïs told her that she learned the hidden meaning of Gauzia's words: in asking if Azalaïs had done "well," Gauzia had been inquiring if Guillelma had been hereticated before her death, and, in asking if nothing had been missing, she had been attempting to learn whether Guillelma had refused to eat after the ceremony and had thus ensured her death in this holy state. In speaking of doing "well," Gauzia had been employing a traditional Cathar term, as we shall see, but her vagueness was not unintentional. The fact that Gauzia repeated her question three times shows that she was unsure whether she was getting her meaning across, and the fact that she refused to speak more explicitly despite this uncertainty shows that she did not want to get her meaning across to all persons present. By refusing, at first, to explain Gauzia's words to Béatris, Azalaïs confirmed the impression that she was being guarded. Yet even as the heretical code functions as a barrier, preventing Béatris from understanding her companions' conversation, it also functions as a portal, allowing her entrance into the society of believers. Once she has induced Azalaïs to disclose to her what was done "well" at Guillelma's deathbed, Béatris states that "Azalaïs began to frequent her, and she spoke to her of the Good Christians."[49] If the heretics conceal themselves physically, with their hidden lairs, nocturnal travels, and disguises, the believers, like Azalaïs, conceal the heretics and themselves verbally, with their ambiguity of speech. Residing openly in the world yet

---

47. "dicta Gauzia dixit: 'Et fecistis bene?,' et dicta Alazaicis respondit: 'Ita, per fidem meam, bene,' et tunc dicta Gauzia dixit: 'Et fecistis bene, bene, et defuit vobis aliquid?' et dicta Alazaicis respondit quod bene fecerant, et nullum impedimentum habuerant in faciendo," *Registre*, vol. i, p. 235.

48. "Deo gratias," ibid.

49. "dicta Alazaicis incepit ipsam que loquitur frequentare, et loquebatur ei de illis bonis christianis," *Registre*, vol. i, p. 236.

adhering secretly to the heretical sect, the believers function as mediators between the heretics and the uninitiated, shielding them from those who might do them harm, introducing them to those who might help them, and in both cases using veiled words as the medium of this filtration. Like the doorways that hide and reveal heretics to others, ambiguous speech functions as a membrane that helps to regulate admission into a new, secret society.

The heretics portrayed in these registers strove to ensure that their words would be truthful on the most literal level, even when speaking about the most quotidian of matters, though this veiled truthfulness could lead to confusion. Arnaut Sicre recalls Peire Maury's telling him about a heretic who had borrowed some money from a woman and had promised to return it to her within two weeks. When the woman requested that the heretic be more precise as to when he would repay her, he refused to oblige, claiming that he would risk lying if he did so. The heretic presumably feared that if he named a date on which he would give the woman her coins and failed to fulfill this task on that day, he would have misrepresented himself, even if the woman understood him to be speaking approximately rather than exactly. Similarly, when Bernart Clergue first found Guilhem Autier in the Belots' *solier*, sewing sleeves or hose, he asked, "We have here a tailor?" To which the heretic replied, "We are one, as we believe."[50] Looking through a window or a chink in the wall, the heretic noticed that pigs had wandered into the yard below, and he warned his new companion, "But we believe that these pigs are doing damage in the gardens," so that Bernart rushed down to shoo them away.[51] Later, when Bernart found Guilhem Autier at the Belots again, along with Prades Tavernier, and asked who was there, the heretics answered, "We, as we believe."[52] The heretics qualified even these seemingly innocuous affirmations of their occupation as tailor, the invasion of some pigs, or their own presence in the house, with the phrase "we believe," wary, once again, of asserting an absolute truth that might turn out to be invalid. During his interrogation, Peire Maury is asked, "Why do the heretics speak with words of double meaning and with qualifications?" to which he responds, "They do it because they say that they must not lie, and for that reason they speak with words of double meaning, saying with qualification, 'A

50. "Et habemus hic sartorem?" *Registre*, vol. 2, p. 273; "Ita sumus, ut credimus," ibid.
51. "Aquo pur nos credimus quod illi porci inferant dampnum in illis ortis," *Registre*, vol. 2, p. 274.
52. "Nos, ut credimus," *Registre*, vol. 2, p. 275. Duvernoy comments, "On notera l'automatisme de la précaution verbale dans une réponse où les risques de mensonge étaient évidemment bien limités," ibid.

man could say this or that,' 'This or that could be good, if God wished,' or saying, 'My father thus named,' or 'my mother thus named,' and thus with other
such qualifications."[53] While Peire's interrogator interprets the heretics' habit-
ual speech patterns negatively, suggesting that these men are duplicitous and
deceptive, Peire understands them more positively, as the result of an almost
Jesuitical desire for precision.

Concerned with words in and of themselves rather than as vehicles of com-
munication, the heretics felt free to take advantage of their words to lead astray
those who were not of their faith. They disdained the cross as the instrument
of Christ's torture, finding Catholics' worship of this object to be as perverse
as would be a son's worship of the tree from which his father was hanged. Upon
entering a church, however, they crossed themselves no less than Catholic con-
gregants would do because they attached a different meaning to this act.
According to Bernart Clergue and Sebèlia Peyre, when making this gesture the
heretics said to themselves, "Here is the forehead, and here is the beard, and
here is one ear, and here is another."[54] According to Arnaut Sicre, Guilhelm
Bélibaste claimed to cross himself because doing so was a good way of chasing
flies from one's face. The heretics were forbidden to kill, even in self-defense,
but some villagers recall Guilhem Autier's telling them that "they could all the
same threaten those who persecuted them with death, even drawing out a
sword or blade if they carried one, or brandishing a lance, saying, 'If you
approach you will die,' meaning, 'You will die,' not in the sense that they will
be killed, but that they will die one day."[55] With these lines, the heretics did
not act in any way that they would see as false in and of itself: they did not venerate the symbol of Christ's execution, nor did they announce their intention

53. "quare dicti heretici loquntur verbis duplicibus et cum retinencia," *Registre*, vol. 3, p.
250; "hoc ideo faciebant quia dicebant quod non debebant mentiri, et propter hoc vel loque-
bantur verbis duplicibus, retinemento dicendo: 'Posset homo dicere quod hoc vel illud est,'
'posset esse bonum hoc vel illud si Deus vellet,' vel dicendo, 'Pater meus dictus' vel 'mater
mea dicta,' et sic de aliis retinementis," ibid.

54. "Asi es le front, et aysi es la barba, et aysi la una aurelha et aysi l'autre," *Registre*, vol.
2, p. 284. Bertomieu Auriliac reports Bernart Clergue as quoting these words. Sebèlia Peyre
recalls the heretics' saying, similarly, "hic est frons, et hic est barba, et hic est una auris et hic
alia," *Registre*, vol. 2, p. 422.

55. "licet possent cominari de interfectione illos qui persequebantur eos, et extrahere
eciam spadam vel gladium, si portabant ipsum, vel lanceam opponere, dicendo, 'Si appropin-
quas hic, morieris,' interpretando 'morieris' non quod ipsi occiderent, sed quod aliquando
moreretur," *Registre*, vol. 1, p. 294. See *Registre*, vol. 2, pp. 106–7 for another version of this
tactic.

to kill their would-be assassins. By playing with the inherent gap between signifier and signified, however, they misled others, and they did so, from what
the records suggest, with delight in their cleverness. The bond of trust between
speaker and listener or, at least, between heretical speaker and orthodox listener
is here seen as something that can be abused profitably in order to afford the
heretic secrecy and protection from potential harm.

The believers, like the heretics, speak ambiguously about their faith, at
times, it seems, with no more intention to deceive than their ministers have
when adding restrictions to their statements. Throughout these records,
believers refer to *Be*, or "the Good," a word left in Occitan in the Latin tran-
scripts apparently out of the notaries' own recognition of its slipperiness. At
times, this *Be* seems to refer to the heretics themselves. Guillelma Maury asks
Arnaut Sicre, whom she encounters in Spain, "Would you not give thanks to
God if the *Be* were to be shown to you?"[56] as if this *Be* were people, like the
heretics, who could be physically apprehended. Of Arnaut, it is stated,
"Understanding that she was speaking of the heretics, he answered her that he
did not want to see this *Be*."[57] Peire Maury, another member of this exile community, complained to Arnaut of "the *Be* that there is,"[58] contrasting Guilhelm
Bélibaste, who, he says, does not know how to preach, with the late Peire and
Jacme Autier. He commented, "When one sees now the *Be* that there is, and
one saw the one that there used to be, one should burst."[59] Peire recalls that
when he stayed away from Guilhelm Bélibaste, Mersenda Marty told him he
was wrong to distance himself from "the *Be*, that is, from the heretic."[60] At
times, the *Be* seems to signify the cluster of believers who surround the heretic
as well as the heretic himself. When Arnaut is traveling to see another believer,
Peire advises him to inform her "that he had found the *Be*, that is, Peire [sic]
Bélibaste, Peire Maury, Guillelma Maury, her sons Arnaut and Joan, and Peire
Maury, the brother of this Guillelma," as if this *Be* spreads out from the first-
named figure to his followers.[61] Guilhelm Bélibaste himself recommended,

56. "Et vos non regraciaremini Deo si ostendaretur vobis le be?" *Registre*, vol. 2, p. 22.

57. "ipse attendens quod de hereticis loquebatur, respondit ei quod nolebat videre illud
be," ibid.

58. "le be quod est," *Registre*, vol. 2, p. 28.

59. "Qui modo videt le be quod est, et vidit illud quod fuit, crepare deberet," ibid.

60. "dicti be (id est de heretico)," *Registre*, vol. 3, p. 183.

61. "quod ipse invenerat le be, id est dictum Petrum Belibasta, Petrum Maurini,
Guillelmam Maurinam, Arnaldum et Iohannam filios eius, et Petrum Maurini fratrem dicte
Guillelme," *Registre*, vol. 2, p. 44. Heretics often assumed new names upon their heretica-
tion, so that Guilhem Bélibaste became Peire Bélibaste.

"We should all stay together, as then one can warm the other in the *Be*."[62] At times, this *Be* seems to mean the Holy Spirit that descends into the heretic, the group he is among, or the ceremony he is administering. At Guilhem Guilhabert's heretication, when Prades Tavernier attempted to send one of Guilhem's brothers-in-law away, the latter protested, "'But, lord, I also need my part of the *Be*,' believing that what the heretic wanted to do was good and wanting to have his own part in this good,"[63] as if *Be* were something which would surface during the heretical ceremony and in which its observers would partake. For these villagers, *Be* appears ultimately to be the divine presence which descends into the heretics at the moment of their heretication and radiates out from them, in a series of concentric circles, to encompass the believers who live in their midst and the witnesses who participate in their ceremonies. If *Be* has multiple meanings here, it is only because members of the faith understand this term in several ways.

Even if the believers used multivalent words among themselves, as part of the jargon of their religion, it is also true that they used such terms among those of whom they were less sure, as a screening device. In their confessions, the villagers cite themselves and others as having used expressions, often based upon the root of "good" (*bonus*) or "well" (*bene*), in such an obscure manner that they are asked to specify how they understood what was being said. Azalaïs Azéma remembers Raimonda de Luzenac's meeting her, embracing her, and telling her that she loved her because her son Raimon went among the "Good People" (*bonis gentibus*). Raimonda then advised her "to be good [*bona*] and faithful, and to hold her tongue lest any misfortune occur because of her words, and not to do evil to any thing."[64] Apparently prompted by her interrogator, Azalaïs clarifies "that she understood that she was warning me to be good [*bona*] and faithful toward the heretics, and to say nothing against them, and not to reveal them."[65] Guillelma Clergue remembers Azalaïs Maury's praising her family because they did good to "all good things" (*omni rei bone*).[66] Again,

---

62. "omnes nos simul stare debemus, qui sic unus alium calefaceret en le be," *Registre*, vol. 2, p. 42.

63. "'Cor, senher, tabe m'auria obs ma part del be,' credens quod bonum esset illud quod dictus hereticus facere volebat, et de dicto bono volens partem habere," *Registre*, vol. 1, p. 437.

64. "quod esset bona et fidelis et quod custodiret os suum ne propter verba eius alicui malum eveniret, et quod non faceret malum alicui rei," *Registre*, vol. 1, p. 313.

65. "et ipsa . . . intellexit quod moneret eam quod esset bona et fidelis hereticis, et quod non loqueretur aliquid contra eos vel eciam eos revelaret," ibid.

66. "omni rei bone," *Registre*, vol. 1, p. 345.

seemingly under the interrogator's influence, "She said she believed that Azalaïs meant by 'good things [*bonas res*]' the heretics to whom the people of her father's house were good."[67] This code of "Good Men," "being" or "doing good," and "good things" which Raimonda and Azalaïs employed here would sound vague and meaningless to those not familiar with these terms but precise and meaningful to those familiar with them, and the believers appear to have exploited this gap in understanding. When Guillelma Maury first met Arnaut Sicre, for example, she inquired if he had "understanding of the Good [*entendement de Be*]?" and then, as we have seen, if he would like to be shown such *Be*.[68] When Arnaut asked what she means by this *entendement de Be*, she referred to his grandfather and his mother, who had possessed *Be*, and to his father, who had not. It was only in the course of all of these coded words that Arnaut understood Guillelma as referring to the heresy for which his mother had been burned at the stake and against which his father had led the forces of the Inquisition. Alarmed by this realization, Arnaut answered that he did not want to see this *Be* because of the misfortunes his family had suffered as a result of it. He recounts, "Hearing this, Guillelma changed her words and said that she was not speaking to him with the aim that she would show him the heretics."[69] She had spoken of the *Be* and had suggested that it might "be shown [*ostendaretur*]" to Arnaut; faced with his hostile tone, she denied that she would be the one who "would show [*ostenderet*]" it to him. As Peire Maury told Arnaut, in sending him to see another adherent of the heretical faith, "Our believers do not manifest themselves easily to our other believers, especially when they are young," so that it would be best for him to mention the *Be* he has found as "a sign from other believers" in order to bring her to trust him.[70] Just as the secretive heretic constituted the center around which the believers' spiritual lives were organized, so the secretive speech of these believers served as the means through which their spiritual community was constructed.

67. "et ipsa loquens tunc credidit, ut dixit, quod dicta Alazaicis vocasset bonas res quibus benefaciebant illi de domo patris sui hereticos," ibid.

68. *Registre*, vol. 1, p. 22. Jean Duvernoy comments upon this phrase in *Inquisition à Pamiers, cathares, juifs, lépreux . . . devant leurs juges* (Toulouse: Edouard Privat, 1966), "Le sens de cette formule, qui sert de mot de passe, est bien proche du mot 'gnose,' que seul l'anachronisme empêche de retenir" (p. 158, n. 7).

69. "Quod audiens dicta Guillelma mutavit verba et dixit quod non loquebatur sibi ad illum finem ut ostenderet ei hereticos," *Registre*, vol. 2, p. 22.

70. "Credentes nostri non faciliter se manifestant credentibus nobis, et maxime quando sunt iuvenes," *Registre*, vol. 2, p. 44. "aliqua signa de aliis credentibus," ibid.

THE LOVERS

If in Béatris's youth, when the heretics were frequenting Montaillou and Prades, secrecy had constituted the empty center around which her relationships with her heretical lovers and companions were organized, in her old age, when these heretics had long since disappeared, it continued to structure her last known liaison, with the Catholic priest Bertomieu d'Auriliac. Earlier, as if vacillating between the heterodox and the orthodox creeds, Béatris had employed ambiguities of speech in order to shroud her beliefs from enemies and partisans of this faith. Now, as if reminiscent of these vacillations, she employed such ambiguities again in order to conceal her beliefs from her Catholic lover. At times, the dynamic between Bertomieu and Béatris resembles that between an inquisitor and an accused heretic, who, opposed to each other in their religious views, hold themselves back from each other through duplicitous words. At other times, it resembles that between two lovers, who, allied with each other against a hostile world, communicate through a shared code. Heresy and love overlap, in Bertomieu's as well as Béatris's confession, to the point where, despite his Catholicism, the priest too is condemned to the prison in Carcassonne for his protection of his onetime heretical lover.

In general, Béatris appears to have been in the habit of concealing her thoughts by quoting others and leaving uncertain the degree to which she shared the views she had cited. Her trial opened when a witness testified to having heard her say that if the Eucharist were truly the body of Christ, it would have long since been consumed by the clergy alone, even if it were as large as Mount Marguail. While the witness assumed that Béatris was revealing her own skepticism about transubstantiation in making this remark, Béatris insists, first, that she was merely quoting a mason she had heard in Celles when she was a child and, later, that she was merely quoting Raimon Roussel, who was in turn citing someone else. Concerning the mason, we are informed, "She sometimes cited the words that she heard this man say, without putting faith in them."[71] At another point, Béatris reports that after she had seen an invalid receive the Eucharist with great devotion, she repeated the mason's comment to a companion in order to favorably contrast the invalid's veneration of the host with another person's disdain for the sacrament. When the companion reproached her, warning her that her words could be held against her, she replied that "she

---

71. "ista verba que audivit a dicto homine, aliquociens recitando, non alias, ut dixit, fidem habendo," *Registre*, vol. 1, p. 218.

did not say them in a wicked way, but was citing the words of the wicked man who had said this."[72] Attributing her heterodox statements to others, she attributes her orthodox statements to such people no less. When she was preparing to descend to the low country for her second marriage, Peire Clergue told her that he would send a Good Christian to her if she would like to be received into the sect. With the words of her Catholic sister Gentils, from Limoux, she answered that "she did not want to be received into such a sect, but she wanted to be saved in the faith in which she found herself, alleging the saying of her sister Gentils, who had said this first."[73] As these various examples show, when Béatris cites another person, it can be with approval, with disapproval, or with indifference for what she has heard, but it is always with an ambiguous judgment, so that her listener can, as Béatris claims, misinterpret this purpose or so that she herself can, it appears, attribute different intentions to the same speech at different times. With citations, Béatris at once reveals and conceals her meaning or, rather, reveals a meaning whose identity is never entirely stable and can, as a result, be revised in retrospect.

In her interactions with Bertomieu, in particular, Béatris appears to have quoted others, again leaving open how the words she has cited were to be evaluated. According to Bertomieu, a certain Peire Clergue was a "great friend of hers . . . and a crony."[74] One day in Montaillou, Béatris told him, she had received a message from Estevena bidding that she "do good to the Good Christians" and had gone to the said Peire for advice about this request.[75] He had advised that she do good to them, as Estevena had recommended, and he had praised the Good Christians as people who acted justly, who spoke truthfully, and who suffered persecution for God. Upon hearing of Peire's counsel, Bertomieu protested, "The priest who told you that was a heretic,"[76] yet Béatris denied that this was the case, insisting, instead, that Peire was "a good and worthy man, and that he was held to be a worthy man in this place."[77] She told Bertomieu shortly thereafter that, as he later puts it, "Chaplains more

72. "ipsa non dicebat pro malo, sed recitabat illa verba illius mali hominis qui hoc dixerat," *Registre*, vol. 1, p. 240.

73. "nolebat ad talem sectam recipi, sed in fide in qua erat volebat salvari, allegando ad hoc dictum Gentilis sororis sue, que hoc primo dixerat," *Registre*, vol. 1, p. 231.

74. "magnus amicus eius . . . et compater," *Registre*, vol. 1, p. 253.

75. "bene faceret bonis christianis," ibid.

76. "Ille sacerdos qui predicta vobis dixit hereticus erat," ibid.

77. "erat bonus homo et probus, et pro probo homine faciebat se teneri in dicto loco," ibid.

confirmed than he was were of the sect of the Good Christians."[78] In this exchange, Béatris did not show herself to think highly of the heretics, nor did she encourage Bertomieu to think highly of them, but she did offer him a model of a Catholic priest even "more confirmed" than himself, who experienced no contradiction between his orthodox role and his heterodox beliefs. Whereas Bertomieu considered someone who holds views contrary to those of the Church to be a heretic, Béatris suggested that whatever a man's views may be, he cannot be held to be a heretic if he is respected by his community. Juxtaposing the heterodox priest, with the high esteem in which he was held, with the orthodox priest, with his lesser social status, Béatris indicated implicitly, but not explicitly, that her current clerical lover might do well to take after his predecessor. Quoting Estevena and Peire on the advisability of doing good to the heretics, without distinguishing her views from those of these respected persons, Béatris also quoted the people of Montaillou in general, again without making such a distinction. She reported to Bertomieu, "It was commonly said in this place that people should do good to all pilgrims and to all 'poor in the faith,' and they understood by those 'poor in the faith' the heretics whom they called Good Christians."[79] Once again, Béatris offered no comment on this opinion, yet her very citation of it implies that it was attractive to her. In all of these passages, Béatris continued to take advantage of the gap between the content of a citation and the purpose with which she uttered that citation, at once conveying support for the heretics and distancing herself from that support, as she had conveyed a positive portrait of a heretical priest and had left Bertomieu to make of that portrait what he would.

In addition to quotations, Béatris seems to have used indirect speech to shield her views from those around her. To her interrogators, she acknowledged openly that she had believed the heretics were good men who suffered martyrdom for God and that she had shared their errors "fully and perfectly,"[80] to the point where she would have undergone anything in defense of them. Yet with her fellow villagers she was not so frank. When Azalaïs Maury extolled to her the Good Christians and those who gave them alms, Béatris did not second her approval of them but, rather, asked her, "Do these Christians accept

78. "certiores capellani quam ipse esset erant de secta dictorum bonorum christianorum," ibid.

79. "communiter dicebatur in dicto loco quod homines debent bene facere omnibus peregrinis et pauperibus fidei, et intelligebant per dictos pauperes fidei hereticos quos ipsi vocabant bonos christianos," *Registre*, vol. I, p. 255.

80. "plene et perfecte," *Registre*, vol. I, p. 232.

flour?"[81] and then offered her a quart of flour for the men. Later, when Bernart Belot visited her in the low country and told her that the heretics would like to see her, she stated at first that she did not want to see them, but then, when encouraged to send a "sign of recognition," she asked, "And what could I send to the Good Christians?"[82] She ultimately donated five sous *parisis*. Responding to these villagers with practical questions rather than with doctrinal avowals, she refrained from giving voice to the moment when she must, logically, have come to acknowledge the goodness of the Good Christians, concerning herself only with how she might best act upon that acknowledgment. Similarly, when Azalaïs Azéma commended to her the Good Christians, to whom her son Raimon carried food, Béatris "did not answer except to say that misfortune would befall her son if he were arrested carrying his scrip to the Good Christians."[83] When Raimonda de Luzenac inquired if Béatris had seen the heretics, as the two women walked to church in Caussou, Béatris replied that she had not done so and had no desire to do so. Her companion went on to praise the heretics' sermons, and, we are told, "There were no more words between them on this matter, but they entered into the church and heard Mass."[84] With her worries about the dangers Azalaïs's son risks in assisting the heretics and her own resistance to meeting the Good Christians, Béatris appears to fear the consequences of coming into contact with these men, and this fear seems to contribute to her tacit rather than avowed support of them.

With Bertomieu in particular, Béatris seems to have employed indirection to make her meaning ambiguous. When the priest accused her of being a heretic, she protested that this was not the case. When he asked her if she had believed what Peire had told her about heretics, she denied that she had ever accepted his words. When he inquired if she had ever seen heretics or given or sent them anything, she insisted that she had not done so, though her own confession to the bishop indicates otherwise. At the same time, it is possible that she was not using the word "heretic" in the same way that Bertomieu was using it. If a heretic is defined narrowly, as someone who has been hereticated, then she is certainly innocent of this charge. If a heretic is construed more broadly,

81. "Et illi boni christiani accipiunt farinam?" *Registre*, vol. 1, p. 236.

82. "signum recognicionis," *Registre*, vol. 1, p. 233; "Et quid ego mittere possem dictis bonis christianis?" ibid.

83. "nichil ad hec respondit, nisi solum quod dixit quod male accideret filio suo predicto si caperetur portans predictum cabacium ad dictos bonos christianos," *Registre*, vol. 1, p. 237.

84. "plura verba inter eos non fuerunt, ut dixit, de ista materia, sed intraverunt ecclesiam et audiverunt missam," *Registre*, vol. 1, p. 238.

as someone who sees the heretics, adores them, listens to their sermons, or participates in their ceremonies, then she is also clearly innocent of this accusation, as she has taken care to be. Asked by Bertomieu why the bishop was summoning her on charges of heresy, Béatris replied "that she did not know and was not afraid, for she did not feel herself to be guilty [*non sentiebat se culpabilem*]."[85] In her own confession, she explained that she told Bertomieu that "she did not feel herself to be guilty [*non sentiret se . . . culpabilem*] because she had never seen the heretics Peire and Guilhem Autier after they had become heretics."[86] In each these utterances, Béatris maintained her innocence of heresy, yet she did so by defining guilt of this crime not in terms of belief in the deviant creed or support of its ministers, of which she was indeed culpable, but in terms of encounters with such ministers. She declared not that she "was not guilty" but that she "did not feel herself to be guilty," as if aware of the possible disjunction between the impersonal conception of heresy, under which the bishop was operating, and her own personal conception of this crime. Confronted directly with a question, she denied her guilt, but she undermined the force of that denial with her subsequent statements.

Faced with these mixed signals, Bertomieu discounts Béatris's claims to orthodoxy. He appears suspicious that Béatris is, in fact, a believer of the heretics, or at least was one in the past, and convinced that she, like all such believers, should submit herself to the tribunal the Church has set up for those erring in the faith. When he heard how she had considered assisting the Good Christians, how she had consulted a priest who had encouraged her to do so, and how she now defended this priest against his condemnation, he reports having told her that "if he were in the bishopric of Pamiers, in a place where there was an inquisitor, he would have her arrested, and she knew much more about heresy than she said," at which point, he adds, "she smiled."[87] Later, after Bertomieu heard more of Béatris's tales from Montaillou, he remarked to her that "if people were so addressed and solicited about heresy by the people of Montaillou and other places in the Sarbathès, it was surprising that she was not a heretic," to which she replied that "God had given her a great grace" in

85. "quod nesciebat, et quod eciam non timebat, quia non sentiebat se culpabilem," *Registre*, vol. 1, p. 256.

86. "non sentiret se . . . culpabilem . . . quia non viderat Petrum et Guillelmum Auterii hereticos postquam fuerunt heretici," *Registre*, vol. 1, p. 247.

87. "si ipse esset in episcopatu Appamiarum vel in loco in quo esset inquisitor, ipse faceret eam capi, et multa plura sciebat de heresi quam diceret," *Registre*, vol. 1, p. 253; "ipsa subrisit," *Registre*, ibid.

bringing her down from this region when he did, for she would have been drawn to the heretics if she had stayed there another year.[88] Bertomieu acknowledges that once during a quarrel with Béatris he called her a "wicked old woman and a heretic" and reproached her for having come from a "heretical land."[89] Given his evident suspicions of Béatris and his pro-Catholic sentiments, it is unsurprising that when the bishop summoned Béatris to appear before him in matters of heresy, Bertomieu urged her to obey this order, "for the lord bishop would not do her injustice."[90]

Even as Bertomieu questions Béatris's Catholicism, however, he allows his judgment of her to be tempered by his compassion. When Béatris responded to the bishop's summons, she was alarmed by the prelate's hostility toward her and escaped the region rather than return before him a second time. In her own confession, Béatris accounts for her flight by stressing her implication in matters of heresy and her father's earlier implication in this crime, yet in his version of her departure, Bertomieu plays down the legitimate evidence against Béatris and emphasizes the bishop's illegitimate harshness toward her. With far more heightened rhetoric than his paramour, he cites this bishop as having told Béatris that she was a "wicked heretic," that her father had worn crosses, and that "from a wicked tree is born wicked fruit."[91] He claims that the bishop had refused to listen to two ecclesiastics who had defended Béatris and that he had declared, instead, that he would listen to nothing in her favor until she had spoken the truth. In general, he affirms, "It seemed to Béatris that [the bishop] was a wicked and cruel man" and that "the bishop had received her severely."[92] Insisting upon the bishop's cruelty toward Béatris, Bertomieu also insists upon Béatris's fear of this figure. When she saw the bishop, he states, "she was overwhelmed," and, when she saw how many people had arrived to arrest her, "she was terrified."[93] He describes her as coming to him "crying" and begging him to take her to Gentils' house in Limoux, where the bishop would not seek her, "saying that she had no counsel or help except from him in whom she was

---

88. "ex quo tot ei dicebantur et sollicitabantur de heresi per homines de Alione et aliis locis Savartesii, mirum fuit quod ipsa non fuit heretica," *Registre*, vol. 1, p. 253; "Deus fecerat ei magnam gratiam," ibid.

89. "vetulam malam et hereticam," *Registre*, vol. 1, p. 253; "terra hereticali," ibid.

90. "quia dictus dominus episcopus non faceret ei iniusticiam," *Registre*, vol. 1, p. 256.

91. "mala heretica," *Registre*, vol. 1, p. 257; "de mala arbore malus fructus nascitur," ibid.

92. "videbatur ipsi Beatrici quod esset malus homo et crudelis," *Registre*, vol. 1, p. 257; "episcopus receperat eam graviter," *Registre*, vol. 1, p. 256.

93. "ipsa valde fuit stupefacta," *Registre*, vol. 1, p. 257; "territa fuerat," ibid.

confiding."[94] Though Bertomieu reproached Béatris for fleeing the bishop, he also told her, as Béatris recalls, "If this is the way it is and if I cannot keep you back, take this money."[95] Though he tried to separate himself from her en route to Limoux, he states, she again appealed to him "weeping,"[96] and he again softened before her plea. He admits that "having compassion for her, . . . he went with her."[97] As a Catholic, Bertomieu clearly had no sympathy either for the heretics or for those who shared their beliefs. As a lover, however, Bertomieu's emotion overcame his reason, his pity overcame his justice, and his mercy overcame his condemnation, which he believed should have happened in the heart of the bishop, though it did not.

If Bertomieu depicts himself as having become increasingly implicated in Béatris's heresy, it is because in his narrative, as in hers, heresy and love are intricately intertwined. We have seen how the heretics and their believers met in secret, yet it is no less true that lovers gathered with each other in the darkness or in hidden locations. At Montaillou, Peire Clergue would come to Béatris's house near the castle at night two or three times a week, and she came to his house at night twice. At Prades, Peire sent a schoolboy to lead her, through "a very dark night,"[98] to a church where he then slept with her, escorting her back to her residence before dawn. Still later, at Dalou, Peire descended into the cellar with Béatris while a servant stood in the middle of the open doorway, "so that if someone came by, he would not believe that something wicked was going on between the priest and her."[99] As for Bertomieu, her new clerical lover, he relates that Béatris invited him to come to see her "one evening,"[100] which he did, and that she then told him of her love for him and her desire to have carnal relations with him, to which he consented. Afterwards, they did not sleep together at night, but, we are told, "they kept a lookout, he and she, for the moment during the day when her daughters and servant would not be in the house, and then they committed

94. "plorando," *Registre*, vol. 1, p. 258; "dicendo quod quia non habebat aliud consilium nec adiutorium nisi ipsum in quo confideret," ibid.

95. "Ex quo ita est, quod ego non possum vos nunc tenere, [accipiatis] istam peccuniam," *Registre*, vol. 1, p. 247.

96. "flendo," *Registre*, vol. 1, p. 258.

97. "compatiens ei, . . . ivit cum ea," ibid.

98. "nox valde obscura," *Registre*, vol. 1, p. 243.

99. "si superveniret, quod extimaret quod nichil mali committeretur inter ipsam et dictum sacerdotem," *Registre*, vol. 1, p. 239.

100. "in sero," *Registre*, vol. 1, p. 254.

this carnal sin."[101] Béatris's fear that the bishop would punish her for the reports he had heard about her heresy caused her to flee to Limoux, yet her fears that her brothers would punish her for the rumors about her liaison with Bertomieu had already prompted her to escape to Catalonia, where she had lived for a year with the priest in his native region. At times, the secretiveness with which believers conversed with each other about their heresy appears indistinguishable from the secretiveness with which lovers entered into their trysts. When Peire talked to Béatris about heresy, "at her house, sometimes near a window that overlooked the road, while she deloused the head of the priest, sometimes near the fire, and sometimes when he was in bed with her," she recollects, "they kept themselves from being heard by others as much as possible."[102] She warned Bernart Belot, who brought up the same topic during a visit to her in the low country, not to come to her again, "for if you frequent the house my husband will think something wrongful on my account, either shamelessness or some other wicked thing."[103] If men and women seek each other out in private, it appears to be for heretical or for carnal intercourse—or for both.

Lovers resembled partisans of the heretical faith insofar as they met in secret, yet they could also become such partisans in order to justify their liaisons. Peire taught Béatris not only that it was no worse to sleep with a priest than with one's own husband but that a man and a woman could commit any sort of sin during their lives and be saved at the end, so long as they were received into the heretical faith on their deathbeds. "And, with these words and many others," she confesses, "this rector influenced her to the point that, in the octave of the feasts of the Apostles Peter and Paul, she consented that this priest would know her carnally."[104] Bertomieu, though not himself a Cathar, possessed certain opinions about clerical celibacy that predated the

101. "explorabant ipsa et ipse quando filie et ancilla dicte Beatricis non essent in domo de die, et tunc committebant peccatum suum carnale," *Registre*, vol. 1, p. 252.

102. "in domo sua predicta aliquando iuxta quamdam fenestram, que respiciebat versus viam, quando expediculabat ipsa capud dicti sacerdotis, aliquando iuxta ignem, et aliquando etiam quando cum ipsa erat in lecto," *Registre*, vol. 1, p. 227; "custodiebant se quantum poterant ne ab aliis audirentur," ibid.

103. "si frequentaretis domum meam, statim maritus meus extimaret aliquid sinistrum de me vel de inhoneste, vel de aliquo alio malo," *Registre*, vol. 1, p. 234.

104. "Et propter verba predicta et multa alia dictus rector sic induxit ipsam que loquitur quod in octabis festi apostolorum Petri et Pauli ipsa consenciit quod dictus sacerdos eam cognosceret carnaliter," *Registre*, vol. 1, p. 226.

Gregorian Reform and would by this point be considered heterodox. In the region from which he came, he told her, priests were allowed to take concubines, and these women and their children enjoyed all of the legal rights of laymen's wives and progeny. According to Bertomieu, Béatris told him (with a somewhat Catharist conviction in a deity's responsibility for human weaknesses) that God should have given priests and other ecclesiastics the ability to reject sin, but instead he made them desire women even more than other men do. Without distinguishing his lover's heterodox views from his own, Bertomieu states that "it is thus that she tried to excuse the sin of the flesh that she committed with him."[105] For men like Peire or Bertomieu, to consort with a woman like Béatris, to whom they are not and cannot be married, is a grave sin, and for them to defend their actions and thus deny the gravity of this sin is to run counter to Catholic orthodoxy, whatever form their defense takes. Love, according to the literary conventions of the Middle Ages, is necessarily secretive because it is necessarily forbidden, and here, at least, it is necessarily heretical or at least aligned with heresy when its practitioners attempt to justify it.

As we have seen, when Bertomieu suggested to Béatris that she knew much more about heresy than she was letting on and that he would have her arrested, were the bishop or the inquisitor nearby, "she smiled." The meaning of this smile is rich, if ambiguous. Did Béatris smile because she did know more than she avowed? Guilhem Maurs recounts that when he heard Peire Maury speak of having sold a pair of shoes to the son of the heretical Sebèlia Baille, he accused him of knowing every wicked devil in the world, at which point Peire "smiled and did not respond."[106] When Guilhem reproached Guillelma Maury with similar words, he remembers, likewise, that "she began to smile."[107] If Peire's and Guilhelma's smiles acknowledge their heresy, as they appear to do in these contexts, Béatris's smile may bespeak a similar guilt. It is possible that Béatris retained the heretical beliefs for which, she states, she was once willing to die and that she was purposefully misrepresenting herself, first to Bertomieu and then to the bishop, in order to pass as a Catholic in a Catholic world. When Béatris spoke to Bertomieu of the "Good Christians" whom Estevena bid her assist, of the "poor in the faith" whom the people of Montaillou commended, and of the priest who was a "good and worthy" man, however much he might

---

105. "isto modo nitebatur excusare peccatum carnis quod committebant cum ipso qui loquitur," *Registre*, vol. 1, p. 255.

106. "subrisit et nichil respondit ei," *Registre*, vol. 2, p. 185.

107. "Et tunc ipsa incepit subridere," *Registre*, vol. 2, p. 189.

support the heretics, she did not distinguish her current opinions from the ones held by her former neighbors. At the same time, it is also possible that Béatris long ago repudiated those beliefs, as she says she did. When Béatris descended into the low country to marry her second husband, she tells the bishop, she heard the Dominicans and Franciscans preach and decided that it was better to listen to their sermons than to the tales of the heretics and their believers. From what she told Peire, when he visited with her in these valleys, it was in the Catholic faith that she wanted to be saved, to the point that, when she was ill, she regretted deeply their heretical conversations. She insists to the bishop that she regrets all that she did or said in matters of heresy, persuading him of the sincerity of her repentance. Yet it is also possible, and perhaps even probable, that Béatris experienced her beliefs not as a unified and coherent system, whether Catholic or Cathar, but as a scattered and jumbled collection of ideas, some, at some times, deriving from one creed, others, at other times, deriving from another. Her use of questions, examples, citations, and circumlocutions may reflect not just the desire to keep her views uncertain to her interlocutor but also the reality that her views were, in fact, uncertain, even to herself. An example or a quotation from Montaillou may have made an impression upon her without her being entirely sure of what that impression was. Yet, it may also be asked, did Béatris smile, not because she was keeping secrets from Bertomieu, but because she was confident that whatever secrets she might have, he would not turn her in even when he could have done so? Did she smile because she knew that just as her beliefs were neither entirely orthodox nor entirely heterodox, the priest's response to these beliefs was neither entirely rigorous nor entirely lax? The silent knowledge implicit in her smile seems to reflect the gray, inarticulable zone that both of them inhabit, between their two religions.

It was with her smile that Béatris acknowledged having a secret and hence revealed herself to be on the side of the heretics. In Montaillou and Prades, the registers make clear, heretics were believed to be secretive people, and secretive people were believed to be heretics. It was because Faurèsa Rives saw two visitors emerge from Raimon Belot's cellar after she left the house that she concluded that they were heretics. It was because Guillelma Clergue espied two men at the Belots' residence conceal themselves when she went back to look at them that she decided that they were heretics. Secretive conversations, no less than secretive habitations, betray people as members of the deviant sect. We are told, for example, that Azalaïs Azéma paid visits to Estevena de Châteauverdun and that "when Azalaïs arrived, Estevena rose for her and went to speak with her secretly, to the side."[108] During one such exchange, Arnaut de Château-verdun, Estevena's son, approached his mother and asked, "And so, madam, will these wicked counsels last forever?"[109] Estevena replied, "Be quiet, for we are not saying anything wicked," yet Arnaut retorted that "she had never said anything good and would not do any better in the future."[110] To reveal that one is concealing, as Béatris does with her smile, is to occupy the same episte-mological space that adherents to heresy occupy. For the villagers, the secre-tiveness of the heretics and believers leads to curiosity, the curiosity about the sectaries leads to learning, and the learning about the cult leads to conversion. For lovers, like Bertomieu, the secretiveness of the beloved, whose present character seems clear but whose past involvements remain forever masked, sim-ilarly increases her mystery and fascination.

108. "quando dicta Alazaicis venit, dicta Estevena assurrexit ei et ivit loqutum cum ipsa secrete ad partem," *Registre*, vol. 1, p. 281.

109. "Et domina, et semper durabunt ista consilia mala?" ibid.

110. "Tace, quia nichil mali dicimus," ibid.; "nunquam dixerat aliquid boni, nec in posterum faceret," ibid. Mengarda Clergue and Na Roqua, Raimon Lizier and Guillelma Belot, Azalaïs Azéma and Raimonda de Luzenac are all described by various villagers as speak-ing secretly with each other and are all imputed to be heretics as a result.

2 A GARDEN OF HOLY COMPANIONSHIP

The Secrecy of the "Manichaeans" and Cathars

Ecclesiastical chroniclers depicted heretics as concealing themselves from those they distrust, just as the heretics depicted themselves as doing. Between the early eleventh and mid-twelfth centuries, clerics began to observe the existence of heretical groups, often identified—anachronistically, it is now thought—as Manichaean in their beliefs, and to deplore the furtiveness of their ways.[1] In 1018, the chronicler Adémar de Chabannes wrote, "Manichaeans appeared throughout Aquitaine, seducing the people."[2] In 1022 he observed again of these heretics, "Messengers of Antichrist arose, took care to conceal themselves in hiding-places and subverted whatever men and women they could."[3] In the same year, a cluster of

1. On the eleventh-century heresies, see, for example, Pierre Bonnassaie and Richard Landes, "Une nouvelle hérésie est née dans le monde," in *Les Sociétés méridionales autour de l'An Mil: Répertoire des sources et documents commentés*, ed. Michael Zimmermann (Paris: CNRS, 1992), pp. 435–59; Richard Landes, "La Vie apostolique en Aquitaine en l'An Mil: Paix de Dieu, culte des reliques, et communauté hérétiques," *Annales E. S. G.* 3 (mai–juin 1991): 573–93; Guy Lobrichon, "The Chiaroscuro of Heresy: Early Eleventh-Century Aquitaine as Seen from Auxerre," in *The Peace of God: Social Violence and Religious Response in France around the Year 1000*, ed. Thomas Head and Richard Landes (Ithaca, NY: Cornell University Press, 1992), pp. 80–103; and Malcolm Lambert, *Medieval Heresy: Popular Movements from the Gregorian Reform to the Reformation*, 3rd ed. (Oxford: Blackwell, 2002), pp. 14–21.

2. "'Manichaeans' in Aquitaine," in Wakefield and Evans, pp. 73–74, at p. 74; "exorti sunt per Aquitaniam Manichei, seducentes plebem," Adémar de Chabannes, *Historiarum Libri III*, MGH *Scriptores* 4, bk. 3, ch. 49, p. 138.

3. "Heresy at Orléans: A Report by Adémar of Chabannes," in Wakefield and Evans, pp. 75–76, at p. 75, translation modified; "nuntii antichristi exorti, per latibula sese occultare curabant, et quoscumque poterant viros et mulieres subvertebant," Adémar de Chabannes, *Historiarum Libri III*, bk. 3, ch. 59, p. 143.

ten to twenty heretics, whom Adémar once again terms Manichaean, was uncovered in Orléans, centered around Lisois, a canon of the Cathedral of the Holy
Cross, and Etienne, a canon of the collegiate Church of Saint Peter.[4] The secretiveness of this sect was also noted and seen to contribute to its dangerousness.
Raoul Glaber writes of its heresy, "Having long sprouted in secrecy, it burst forth
with evil abundance into a damnable harvest" and "a secret malady was afflicting
the flock." Glaber imagines the Manichaean creed, as other authors would do, as
a weed furtively germinating underground or a poison or cancer furtively cours-
ing through a human body.[5] By 1026, Manichaeans were considered such a threat
that Guilhem V, duke of Aquitaine, called a council at Charroux where bishops,
abbots, and noblemen debated how best to eliminate them. Despite the duke's
and other leaders' efforts, in the 1040s, in Châlons-sur-Marne, and in 1114, near
Soissons, Manichaeans were still being observed and still being characterized as
secretive. In the second half of the twelfth century, the scattered groups identified as Manichaean gave way to the unified sect of the Cathars, or Albigensians,
which would rise to prominence during the following decades. The relation
between the eleventh- and early twelfth-century Manichaeans and the late
twelfth-, thirteenth-, and early fourteenth-century Cathars, who were termed
Manichaeans as well, has been hotly contested by generations of historians, but
the stereotype of the secretive heretic, so closely identified with the early sectaries,
is clearly inherited by their dualist successors.[6] In the places they assemble, the
deeds they perform, and the words they speak, both Manichaeans and Cathars
are regularly portrayed as secretive and their secretiveness as troubling.

If the clerics who write of the Manichaeans and Cathars are disturbed by
their covert ways, it is because, by concealing themselves, the heretics present

---

4. "Heresy at Orléans: A Report by Adémar of Chabannes," p. 75. "Manichei," Adémar
de Chabannes, *Historiarum Libri III*, bk. 3, ch. 59, p. 143.

5. "diutius occulte germinata in perditionis segetem male," Rodolfus Glaber, *The Five
Books of the Histories / Historiarum Libri Quinque*, ed. and trans. John France (Oxford:
Clarendon Press, 1989), bk. 3, ch. 8, p. 139; "faciens clamdestinam . . . ovium pestem," ibid.,
bk. 3, ch. 8, p. 138.

6. See Christine Thouzellier, "Cathares et Manichéens," in *"Sapientiae Doctrina":
Mélanges de théologie et de littérature médiévales offerts à Dom Hildebrand Bascour, O. S. B.*,
ed. Roland Hissette, Guibert Michiels, and Dirk van den Auweele (Leuven: Abbaye du mont
César, 1980), pp. 312–26. The bibliography on Catharism is voluminous. For some of the more
recent studies, see Malcolm Lambert, *The Cathars* (Oxford: Blackwell, 1998), and *Medieval
Heresy*, pp. 115–57; Malcolm Barber, *The Cathars: Dualist Heretics in Languedoc in the High
Middle Ages* (Harlow, UK: Longman's, 2000); and *Cahiers de Fanjeaux*, vol. 3, *Cathares en
Languedoc* (Toulouse: Privat, 1968), and vol. 20, *Effacement du catharisme? (XIIIe–XIVe s.)*
(Toulouse: Privat, 1985).

epistemological challenges to the ecclesiastical authorities who pursue them. Time and again, these authors represent abbots, bishops, and inquisitors as vaguely aware of the existence of heretics among them but unable to distinguish these sectaries from their Catholic neighbors. Even when authorities are convinced they have apprehended heretics, these authors depict them as unable to demonstrate the accused parties' guilt to skeptical neighbors. Despite the difficulties they experience, the authorities are invariably portrayed, in the end, as succeeding in unmasking the guilty and in winning their onetime defenders to their side or at least silencing their objections. Insofar as the representatives of Catholicism triumph over their opponents, it is because the secretiveness of the accused heretics becomes, in the absence of other evidence against them, proof of their heresy.[7]

GUIBERT DE NOGENT

The case of the heretics of Soissons is one of the more obscure in the history of heterodoxy, as it is recounted only in the memoir of Guibert, the abbot of the Benedictine monastery of Nogent, yet it illustrates well the challenges confronted by ecclesiastics in dealing with such deviants.[8] From what Guibert tells us, a cluster of Manichaeans was detected in the village of Bucy-le-Long, three miles from Soissons and not far from his abbey. Two peasant brothers by the names of Clement and Evrard were arrested and, as Guibert puts it, "were charged by the bishop [Lisiard of Soissons] with holding meetings outside the

---

7. See R. I. Moore, "New Sects and Secret Meetings," *Studies in Church History* 23, *Voluntary Religion* (1986): 47–68.

8. MS B.III.7 at Durham Cathedral, which contains a version of Guibert's account, identifies the heretics as people "who are called *Telier* or *Deimai* in the French language [*qui Gallica lingua dicuntur Telier vel Deimai*]" (fol. 364). On Guibert de Nogent, see Bernard Monod, *Le Moine Guibert et son temps (1053–1124)* (Paris: Librairie Hachette, 1905); Edmond-René Labande, "L'Art de Guibert de Nogent," in *Economies et sociétés au Moyen Age: Mélanges offerts à Edouard Perroy* (Paris: Publications de la Sorbonne, 1973), pp. 608–25; John F. Benton's introduction to *Self and Society in Medieval France: The Memoirs of Abbot Guibert of Nogent (1064–c. 1125)*, trans. C. C. Swinton Bland, rev. John F. Benton (New York: Harper & Row, 1970; rpt. Toronto: University of Toronto Press, 1984), pp. 7–33; Paul J. Archambault's introduction to his translation of *A Monk's Confession: The Memoirs of Guibert of Nogent* (University Park, PA: Pennsylvania State University Press, 1996), pp. xiii–xl; and Labande's introduction to his edition and translation of the monk's *Autobiographie* (Paris: Les Belles Lettres, 1981), pp. ix–xxiii. On this sect, see also Jeffrey Burton Russell, *Dissent and Reform in the Early Middle Ages* (Berkeley: University of California Press, 1965), pp. 78–81, and R. I. Moore, *The Origins of European Dissent* (London: Allen Lane, 1977; rpt. Toronto: University of Toronto Press, 1985), pp. 67–69.

Church and were said to be heretics by their neighbors."[9] When they were confronted with attending such conventicles, Guibert reports, "They . . . did not deny their meetings."[10] When accused of holding heterodox beliefs, however, the brothers did not avow their guilt so quickly. Clement seems to have admitted and justified their identification as heretics, perhaps because of some misunderstanding about the term's meaning, yet when he and his brother were interrogated about the faith, Guibert observes, "they gave most Christian answers."[11] In response to an inquiry about infant baptism, for example, the brothers replied, with echoes of the Gospel of Mark, "He that believeth and is baptized shall be saved"; in answer to a query about those baptized in other faiths, they begged not to be questioned so deeply.[12] "We believe everything you say," they told their examiners, with the appropriate deference of ignorant peasants to learned clerics.[13] If Clement and Evrard were not forthcoming about their heretical beliefs, neither were the neighbors who were said to have defamed them. Jean, the notorious count of Soissons, was reported to have regarded Clement as the wisest of men; an unnamed lady was alleged to have been deceived by Clement for a year; and an unnamed deacon was said to have been exposed to his sermons—yet none of these potential witnesses appears to have been present for the brothers' trial or to have contributed formal testimony against them. Guibert acknowledges the lack of this evidence when he reports informing the bishop that "the witnesses who heard them professing such beliefs are not present."[14] In the absence of the confessions or depositions that would normally cause such a case to be pursued, Guibert appears persuaded of the brothers' guilt, as we shall see, not so much because of what

9. Guibert of Nogent, *Self and Society*, p. 213; "ab episcopo ingereretur, quod conventus praeter ecclesiam facerent et haeretici ab affinibus dicerentur," Guibert de Nogent, *Autobiographie*, p. 432.

10. Guibert of Nogent, *Self and Society*, p. 213; "conventicula tamen non negarunt," Guibert de Nogent, *Autobiographie*, p. 430.

11. Guibert of Nogent, *Self and Society*, p. 213; "christianissime responderunt," Guibert de Nogent, *Autobiographie*, p. 432.

12. Guibert of Nogent, *Self and Society*, p. 213. "Qui crediderit, et baptisatus fuerit, salvus erit," Guibert de Nogent, *Autobiographie*, p. 432. Cf. Mk 16:16. All biblical citations are from *The Holy Bible, Douay Version, Translated from the Latin Vulgate* (New York: P. J. Kenedy & Sons, 1914), and *Biblia Sacra iuxta vulgatam versionem*, ed. Robert Weber et al. (Stuttgart: Deutsche Bibelgesellschaft, 1969; rpt. 1994).

13. Guibert of Nogent, *Self and Society*, p. 213; "Nos omnia quae dicitis credimus," Guibert de Nogent, *Autobiographie*, p. 432.

14. Guibert of Nogent, *Self and Society*, p. 214; "testes absunt qui eos talia dogmatizantes audierunt," Guibert de Nogent, *Autobiographie*, p. 432.

he was able to apprehend in their beliefs and behavior as because of what he was not able to apprehend. Having familiarized himself with patristic and medieval accounts of heretics, Guibert has learned that heretics are secretive, and he concludes that because these brothers are secretive, they must therefore be heretics.

From his readings of the Church Fathers, Guibert appears to have discovered that heretics hold secret doctrines. In the early years of the Church, even Catholic catechists withheld knowledge about the deepest mysteries of the faith, such as the Trinity and the Eucharist, from "hearers" (*auditores*), who professed an interest in the faith, and "catechumens" (*catechumeni*), who were receiving instruction in its teachings, reserving the full understanding of Christian doctrine for baptized members of their cult.[15] Augustine suggests that this knowledge was withheld, at least in part, in order to whet initiates' appetite for these teachings and thus to increase their desire to enter the faith. He writes, for example, that "the sacraments of the believers are not revealed . . . in order that they may be the more ardently desired, the more that they are hidden from them, out of a greater respect."[16] Yet this tendency to conceal teachings among Catholics differs sharply, the Fathers insist, from a similar tendency toward esotericism observable among heretics. In Proverbs, a "foolish woman," whom Augustine identifies as at once a harlot and a heretic, is said to sit at the door of her house and to urge passersby to enter it, luring them with the words, "Stolen waters are sweeter, and hidden bread is more pleasant," and thus inviting them to participate in carnal sin and spiritual error.[17] If the harlot

15. The catechumenate, which developed over the course of the second and third centuries, reached its apogee during the fourth century and declined after the fifth century, when the bulk of converts had shifted from adults from pagan families to infants from Christian families. See Jean Daniélou, *La Catéchèse aux premiers siècles*, ed. Régine du Charlat (Paris: Fayard, 1968); Michel Dujarier, *The History of the Catechumenate*, trans. Edward J. Haasl (New York: Saldier, 1979); Everett Ferguson, ed., *Conversion, Catechumenate, and Baptism in the Early Church* (New York: Garland Publishing Co., 1993), especially Lawrence D. Folkdemer, "A Study of the Catechumenate [1946], pp. 244–65, A. Turck, "Aux Origines du catéchumenat" [1964], pp. 266–77, and Jean Daniélou, "La Catéchèse dans la tradition patristique," [1960], pp. 279–92; and William Harmless, *Augustine and the Catechumenate* (Collegeville, MN: Liturgical Press, 1995).

16. Augustine, *Tractates on the Gospel of John*, trans. John W. Rettig, vol. 5, The Fathers of the Church (Washington, DC: Catholic University of America Press, 1995), *Tractates 55–111*, Tractate 96, p. 197, translation modified; "non eis fidelium sacramenta produntur . . . ut ab eis tanto ardentius concupiscantur, quanto eis honorabilis occultantur," Augustine, *In Iohannis Evangelium Tractatus CXXIV*, CC 36, Tractate 96, p. 571.

17. "stulta," Prv 9:13; "aquae furtivae dulciores sunt et panis absconditus suavior," Prv 9:17.

compares her offerings, in their illicitness and secretiveness, to "stolen waters" and "hidden bread," Augustine explains, it is only in order to arouse men's curiosity and desire. He explains, "That mention of the secret and the stolen, by which it is said, 'Take with pleasure hidden breads and the sweetness of holy water,' causes an itching for those hearing, in their ears committing spiritual fornication, just as the integrity of chastity is likewise corrupted in the flesh by a certain itching of lust."[18] A harlot entices a man by appealing to a lust which, since the Fall, has ceased to be fully subject to reason, and a heretic entices an initiate by appealing to a curiosity which, since that same fatal moment, also seems to have vied against his better instincts. A heretic, like this woman, seduces the initiate by offering him what others are not permitted and by convincing him that because what is great is often hidden and restricted in its access, what is hidden and restricted in access must therefore be great. This paradoxical allurement succeeds, Augustine explains, because "those things may be heard and done which are forbidden to be said and believed openly in the Church. For indeed, by their very hiddenness, wicked readers, so to speak, season their poisons for the curious, so that they may suppose that they are learning something great, for the very reason that it deserved to contain a secret."[19] Hippolytus of Rome, like Augustine, maintains that heretics hide their doctrines from all but an elite in their sects in order to make their initiates yearn to possess this knowledge and thus "advance to the rank of those admitted to the higher mysteries."[20] By promising their disciples a hidden gnosis, the heretics, Hippolytus writes, "acquire a complete ascendancy over [them] and perceive [them] eagerly panting after the promised disclosure."[21] Though Catholics concealed their deepest mysteries from newcomers in order to inspire them to

18. Augustine, *Tractates on the Gospel of John*, Tractate 97, p. 204; "Illa enim secreti furtique commemoratio qua dicitur, 'Panes occultos libenter adtingite, et aquae furtivae dulcedinem,' pruritum facit audientibus in auribus spiritualiter fornicantibus, sicut pruritu quodam libidinis etiam in carne corrumpitur integritas castitatis," *In Iohannis Evangelium Tractatus CXXIV*, Tractate 97, p. 575.

19. Augustine, *Tractates on the Gospel of John*, Tractate 97, pp. 202–3; "quae palam in ecclesia dici credique prohibentur. Ipsa quippe occultatione condiunt quodammodo nefarii doctores sua venena curiosis; ut ideo se existiment aliquid discere magnum, quia meruit habere secretum," Augustine, *In Iohannis Evangelium Tractatus CXXIV*, Tractate 97, p. 574.

20. Hippolytus, *The Refutation of All Heresies, with Fragments from His Commentaries on Various Books of Scripture*, trans. S. D. F. Salmond, Ante-Nicene Christian Library (Edinburgh: T. & T. Clark, 1868), bk. 6, ch. 36, p. 246. Hippolytus, *Refutatio omnium haeresium*, ed. Miroslav Marcovich (Berlin: W. de Gruyter, 1986), bk. 6, ch. 36, pp. 250–51.

21. Hippolytus, *The Refutation of All Heresies*, Proemium, p. 27. Hippolytus, *Refutatio omnium haeresium*, Proemium, p. 54.

a virtuous longing to enter the faith, heretics are seen as hiding their core beliefs from initiates in order to inflame them with a sinful curiosity to know what others do not know and a sinful pride in finally joining those who do possess such knowledge.

Adhering to secret doctrines, heretics also practice secret rituals, Guibert would have learned from his study of the Fathers. In the diatribes of Roman pagans, early Christians in general are accused of gathering for "secret and nocturnal rites" in rooms illuminated by lamps and then indulging in gluttonous feasts.[22] When they finish their meal, it is alleged, the Christians toss meat to dogs that have been tied to the lamps, and the dogs, rushing at the meat, overturn and extinguish the lights. Released by the cover of darkness, the revelers grab whoever is next to them, even if she be their mother or sister, and engage in incestuous intercourse with her. If a child is conceived in the course of this orgy, the celebrants meet again, killing the infant by passing it through a flame or submitting it to some other sort of violence and then eating its remains. Though these allegations of "Oedipal" and "Thyestian" crimes appear to have derived from misunderstandings about the brotherly affection expressed during Christians' "love feasts" (*agapae*) and about the flesh and blood consumed during their Masses, Justin Martyr proposes that such claims may, in fact, be valid—if only about the secret rites of the heretics. After describing certain heretical sects, he adds, insinuatingly, "We do not know whether they are guilty of those disgraceful and fabulous deeds, the upsetting of the lamp, promiscuous intercourse, and anthropophagy."[23] When heretics welcome newcomers to their sect, Augustine alleges, they promise them access not only to secret teachings but to secret rituals, again reserved for those few deemed worthy of them. Jesus bade his followers, "If any man have ears to hear, let him hear,"[24] and the heretics inform their initiates that if they have such ears, they will not recoil in horror from those rites but, rather, will embrace them. Augustine warns, "There are some evils that no human sense of decency can bear, and there are

22. *Tertullian, Apogetical Words and Minucius Felix, Octavius,* trans. Rudolph Arbesmann, Emily Joseph Daly, and Edwin A. Quain, Fathers of the Church (Washington, DC: Catholic University of America Press, 1950), pp. 313–402, at ch. 3, p. 336; "occultis ac nocturnis sacris," Minucius Félix, *Octavius,* ed. Jean Beaujeu, 2nd ed. (Paris: Les Belles Letttres, 1974), p. 13.

23. Justin Martyr, *The First Apology; The Second Apology; Dialogue with Trypho; Exhortation to the Greeks; The Monarchy, or The Rule of God,* trans. Thomas B. Falls (Washington, DC: Catholic University of America Press, 1948), "The First Apology," pp. 33–114, at ch. 26, p. 63. Justin Martyr, "Apologia prima," PG 1, cols. 327–440, at col. 369.

24. "si quis habet aures audiendi audiat," Mk 4:23.

some goods that our small human understanding cannot bear,"[25] but the
heretics confuse these categories, affirming that mysteries so low that the common people would rightly condemn them are, in fact, so high that these people cannot grasp them. Once the initiate has been inducted into these occult
rites, the secrecy that blinded him to that which he was entering is replaced by
a new secrecy, which he now uses to blind others in turn. Having sworn, earlier, not to divulge the rituals to which he would be exposed, Hippolytus
explains, the heretical initiate now has no need for such an oath. "He . . . will
feel himself sufficiently under an obligation not to divulge them; for if he once
disclose wickedness of this description, he would neither be reckoned among
men, nor be deemed worthy to behold the light, since not even irrational animals would attempt such an enormity."[26] The darkness of ignorance has now
been supplanted by the darkness of shame, and the secrecy which once prevented the initiate from gaining access to the cult and its ceremonies now prevents him from separating himself from them. Just as the heretics had used
secrecy to make their profane doctrines seem sacred and, hence, attractive to
potential imitates, when they would not seem so if apprehended in full face, so
do they use secrecy to make their wicked rituals seem holy and appealing to
newcomers, who would be appalled if they knew from the start their true
nature.

Secretive in their teachings and their rites, heretics are also secretive in their
speech, Guibert would have discovered from the Fathers. In the early years of
the Church, Catholics spoke cryptically to believers who were not yet full members of the Church. Jesus Christ, one recalls, first reveals himself as the Son of
God to a small band of followers, and speaks in parables, which obscure his
meaning, when he addresses an audience beyond his own companions. Christ
explains the rationale behind this difference in approach when he advises his listeners, "Give not that which is holy to dogs, neither cast ye your pearls before
swine."[27] In his epistles, Paul pursues Christ's distinction of the common people, who are unworthy or even incapable of the truth, and an elite deserving

---

25. Augustine, *Tractates on the Gospel of John*, Tractate 96, p. 199; "Alia sunt mala quae
portare non potest qualiscumque pudor humanus, et alia sunt bona quae portare non potest
parvus sensus humanus," Augustine, *In Iohannis Evangelium Tractatus CXXIV*, Tractate 96,
p. 572.

26. Hippolytus, *Refutation of All Heresies*, Proemium, pp. 27–28; Hippolytus, *Refutatio
omnium haeresium*, Proemium, p. 55.

27. "Nolite dare sanctum canibus neque mittatis margaritas vestras ante porcos," Mt 7:6.

and prepared to receive it when he contrasts the "carnal," who apprehend only the death-dealing letter of the text, and the "spiritual," who transcend the letter and attain the life-giving meaning as well, though he represents the difference between these two groups as reflecting more their stage of development than their essential nature. The Apostle informs the Corinthians, "And I, brethren, could not speak to you as unto spiritual, but as unto carnal. As unto little ones in Christ, I gave you milk to drink, not meat, for you were not able as yet."[28] Among Catholics, Augustine states, the milk to which Paul refers takes the form of faith, upon which the simple must rely for their beliefs, and the meat the form of understanding, upon which the learned may also depend, but there exists no essential contradiction between these two levels of meaning. "Far be it," Augustine exclaims, "that incompatible with this milk is the food of spiritual things, which must be grasped with firm understanding."[29] Among heretics, however, he adds, there exists a contradiction between the often orthodox lessons initiates are first given, when they are entering the sect, and the heterodox teachings they are later provided, when they have advanced in its ranks, so that the earlier lessons mislead newcomers as to the ultimate doctrines of the faith. Augustine cautions the unwary about the heretic who, to excuse the novelty of his teachings, explains that "these things were not said to you sooner when you were being nourished with milk because you did not yet have your heart suited for grasping truths." He then declares, "This man is not preparing food for you, but poison."[30] Far from offering an esoteric understanding which will deepen and reinforce the exoteric revelation, as Catholics do, the heretic offers a new, heretical falsehood, which counters the old, orthodox truth. While Catholics may have spoken in a veiled manner to newcomers to the faith when welcoming them to their assemblies, they are remembered as openly declaring their adherence to this religion when dragged before Roman tribunal, whereas heretics are remembered as denying their membership in their sects in similar circumstances. In a phrase that would later be attributed

---

28. "ego fratres non potui vobis loqui quasi spiritualibus sed quasi carnalibus tamquam parvulis in Christo lac vobis potum dedi non escam nondum enim poteratis," 1 Cor 3:1–2.

29. Augustine, *Tractates on the Gospel of John*, Tractate 98, p. 213; "Sed huic lacti absit ut sit contrarius cibus rerum spiritualium firma intelligentia capiendus," Augustine, *In Iohannis Evangelium tractatus CXXIV*, Tractate 98, p. 579.

30. Augustine, *Tractates on the Gospel of John*, Tractate 98, p. 215; haec enim vobis pius ideo non dicebantur, quando lacte nutriebamini, quoniam ad vera capienda cor nondum habebatis idoneum; non vobis iste cibum praeparet, sed venenum," Augustine, *In Iohannis Evangelium Tractatus CXXIV*, Tractate 98, p. 580.

to any number of heterodox groups, Augustine cites the heretical Priscillianists as advising their coreligionists, "Swear truly or falsely, but betray not the secret."[31] While Catholics are supposed to speak truthfully to strangers to the faith as well as to neighbors, in the conviction that the one will only be induced to become the other by being treated by such, Augustine writes, the heretics regard it as "lawful and dutiful to tell a lie to those who are not our neighbors."[32] While Catholics preach "on the rooftops"[33] because the truth of their words testifies to the truth of their beliefs, heretics speak cryptically or even mendaciously because their falsehoods must, inevitably, reflect the falsity of their creed.

If Guibert had run across the account of the Manichaeans at Orléans by Paul de Saint-Père de Chartres, a fellow Norman monk who contributed to the records of his abbey around 1072, he would have learned that medieval heretics held secret doctrines no less than their late antique predecessors.[34] According to Paul, a Norman knight by the name of Aréfast learned of the existence of the

31. Augustine, *Letters*, trans. Wilfred Parsons, vol. 5 *(204–270)* (New York: Fathers of the Church, 1956), letter 237, pp. 182–89, at p. 184; "Iura, periura, secretum prodere noli," Augustine, *Epistola* 237, PL 33, col. 1033. See also *The "De Haerisibus" of Saint Augustine*, trans. Liguori G. Müller (Washington, DC: Catholic University of America Press, 1956), pp. 110–11 and Augustine, *De Haeresibus*, CC 46, pp. 236–345, at p. 333.

32. Augustine, "Against Lying," in *Treatises on Various Subjects*, trans. Harold B. Jaffee (New York: Fathers of the Church, 1952), pp. 125–79, at p. 127; "ore autem ad alienos proferre falsum, nullum esse peccatum," Augustine, "Contra mendacium ad Consentium," PL 6, cols. 517–48, at col. 519.

33. "in tectis," Lk 12: 3.

34. In addition to Adémar de Chabannes and Raoul Glaber, the authors who provide accounts of this heretical sect are André de Fleury, *Vie de Gauzlin, abbé de Fleury/ Vita Gauzlini, abbatis Floriacensis monasterii*, ed. and trans. Robert-Henri Bautier and Gilette Labory (Paris: CNRS, 1969), p. 235; André de Fleury et al., *Les Miracles de Saint Benoît, écrits par Adrevald, Aimon, André, Raoul Tortaire et Hughes de Sainte Marie, moines de Fleury*, ed. Eugène de Certain (Paris: Renouard, 1858); Paul de Saint-Père de Chartres, *Cartulaire de l'abbaye de Saint-Père de Chartres*, ed. Benjamin Edamé-Charles Guérard, 2 vols. (Paris: Crapelet, 1840), vol. 1, pp. 109–15, and "Heresy at Orléans: The Narrative of Paul, a Monk of Chartres," in Wakefield and Evans, pp. 76–81; and the various brief notices in Bouquet 10, such as Jean de Ripoll, *Vie de Gauzelin*, pp. 180–83, the *Historia Francicae*, pp. 211–12, the *Chronicon Sancti Petri Vivi Senonensis*, p. 224, the *Chronicon Turonense*, p. 284, Jean de Ripoll's letter to Abbot Oliba, p. 498, and the diploma of Robert the Pious, p. 607. The most influential study on this sect is Robert-Henri Bautier's "L'Hérésie d'Orléans et le mouvement intellectuel au début du XIe siècle. Documents et hypothèses," in *Enseignement et vie intellectuelle (IXe–XVIe siècle)* (Actes du 95e Congrès national des sociétés savantes, Section de philologie et histoire jusqu'à 1610, Reims, 1970), vol. 1 (the only volume to have been published) (Paris: Bibliothèque nationale, 1975), pp. 63–88. Bautier situates this group in the context of other eleventh-century heretical movements, finding it to be distinguished by the elite, intellectual

heretical sect in this city, and he traveled there "in the guise of an ignorant disciple" to expose them in their errors.[35] It was only after time passed and the heretics came to trust Aréfast, Paul relates, that he "was admitted within a house [*domum*]" of the sect and not just an ordinary, literal house of brick or stone but a figurative "house of errors [*domum herroneorum*]," to which a select few appear to have been allowed entry.[36] It was only after more time passed and the heretics perceived Aréfast attending to their words "with submissive ear, like a perfect disciple" that they began to disclose to him their hidden mysteries.[37] Again employing the image of a closed, walled space, restricted to the chosen few, the heretics informed their pupil, "You are to be treated by us like a tree of the forest, . . . transplanted into a garden," by which they meant, "You . . . [will be] transferred from the evil world into our holy companionship."[38] And, as such a tree might be watered, pruned of thorns, grafted onto

---

cast of its members. He also sketches a background of political intrigue both between King Robert the Pious and Count Eudes II de Blois and between Robert and Queen Constance. Thierry, the bishop of Orléans, who was supported by the royal party and belonged to the same circles as the accused canons, was deposed from his office in 1022 and replaced by Odalric, who was sponsored by Eudes and may well have been opposed to this coterie. In *The Origins of European Dissent* (pp. 25–30 and pp. 285–89), R. I. Moore addresses this background to the heresy, and in *The Formation of a Persecuting Society: Power and Deviance in Western Europe* (Oxford: Blackwell, 1987), he asserts, "The Orléans affair . . . must be understood as a successful attack on an influential court circle united by ties of spiritual tendency and patronage, planned and carried out by a similarly coherent and similarly motivated rival faction (p. 16). From another perspective, Brian Stock, in *The Implications of Literacy: Written Language and Models of Interpretation in the Eleventh and Twelfth Centuries* (Princeton: Princeton University Press, 1983), pp. 106–20, reads Paul de Saint-Père de Chartres' account as "an exemplum of lay piety" (pp. 108–9), where the knight Aréfast sets out on a chivalrous quest, overcomes the temptations offered by the heretics, and succeeds in establishing his own hermeneutical competence by seeing through the holy appearance of these clerics. As Stock reads the account, Aréfast's lay piety and the canons' heresy are intertwined, both reflections of new communities of reading which developed after the millennium. See also Ilarino da Milano, "Le eresie populari nel secolo XI nell'Europa occidentale," in G. B. Borino, ed., *Studie Gregoriani per la storia di Gregorio VII e della riforma Gregoriana* (Roma: Abbazia di san Paolo, 1947), pp. 43–89, especially pp. 52–60; Russell, *Dissent and Reform*, pp. 103–6; and Lambert, *Medieval Heresies*, pp. 9–16.

35. "Heresy at Orléans: The Narrative of Paul, a Monk of Chartres," p. 77; "ad instar rudis discipuli," Paul de Saint-Père de Chartres, *Cartulaire de l'abbaye*, p. 110.

36. "Heresy at Orléans: The Narrative of Paul, a Monk of Chartres," p. 77; Paul de Saint-Père de Chartres, *Cartulaire de l'abbaye*, p. 110.

37. "Heresy at Orléans: The Narrative of Paul, a Monk of Chartres," p. 77; "more perfecti discipuli, subdita aure intentum," Paul de Saint-Père de Chartres, *Cartulaire de l'abbaye*, p. 110.

38. "Heresy at Orléans: The Narrative of Paul, a Monk of Chartres," p. 77; "Tractandus es . . . a nobis ut arbor silvestris qui translatus in viridiario, " Paul de Saint-Père de Chartres,

a superior growth, and brought to fruition, Aréfast, they suggested, would be "well supplied with the water of wisdom"; he would be "shorn of the thorns of evil," including "absurd teachings"; and he would then "receive with purity of mind [their] own teaching, bestowed by the Holy Spirit."[39] If Aréfast has thus far resembled a tree raised in the open, wild, and savage surroundings of a forest, now that he was being inducted into their sect, he will resemble a tree transplanted into the closed, cultivated, and holy environs of a garden. The horticultural metaphor the heretics used in describing Aréfast's entry into their sect recalls the metaphor early Catholic catechists employed in depicting catechumens' initiation into the Church. Cyril of Jerusalem, for example, echoes the biblical image of a branch cut off from a wild olive tree and grafted onto a domesticated olive tree so as to partake of its fatness when he informs candidates for baptism of the change they are about to undergo.[40] After relating that these candidates are about to enter a "garden" (*paradeison*), Cyril declares, "From now on, you are grafted upon the stock of the spiritual olive, like a slip transplanted from the wild olive into the good olive tree, from sin to righteousness, from corruption to purity," and he adds that they will then be watered and brought to bear good fruit.[41] Once again, we see heretics hiding their doctrines from an initiate and making that hiddenness seem attractive to him. Through their use of the traditional catechistic image of the tree and the

---

Cartulaire de l'abbaye, pp. 110–11; "Heresy at Orléans: The Narrative of Paul, a Monk of Chartres,"p. 77; "Itaque tu, simili modo translatus de iniquo seculo in nostro sancto collegio," Paul de Saint-Père de Chartres, *Cartulaire de l'abbaye*, p. 111.

39. "Heresy at Orléans: The Narrative of Paul, a Monk of Chartres," p. 77.; "aquis perfunderis sapientiae," Paul de Saint-Père de Chartres, *Cartulaire de l'abbaye*, p. 111; "Heresy at Orléans: The Narrative of Paul, a Monk of Chartres," p. 77; "viciorum spinis carere," Paul de Saint-Père de Chartres, *Cartulaire de l'abbaye*, p. 111; "Heresy at Orléans: The Narrative of Paul, a Monk of Chartres," p. 77; "insula doctrina," Paul de Saint-Père de Chartres, *Cartulaire de l'abbaye*, p. 111; "Heresy at Orléans: The Narrative of Paul, a Monk of Chartres," p. 77; "nostram doctrinam a Sancto Spiritu traditam mentis puritate possis excipere," Paul de Saint-Père de Chartres, *Cartulaire de l'abbaye*, p. 111.

40. Cf. Rom 11:17–24. For other treatments of this metaphor, see Irenaeus, *Against the Heresies*, bk. 5, ch. 10; Clement of Alexandria, *Stromata*, bk. 6, Pt. 1, ch. 1; Augustine, *Reply to Faustus the Manichaean*, bk. 9, ch. 2; Augustine, *Sermons on Selected Lessons of the New Testament*, sermon 27, chs. 12–15, and *The Oration and Panegyric Addressed to Origen*, arg. 7.

41. Cyril of Jerusalem, "Lenten Lectures (Catecheses)," in *The Works of Saint Cyril of Jerusalem*, trans. Leo P. McCauley and Antony A. Stephenson, Fathers of the Church (Washington, DC: Catholic University of America Press, 1969), vol. 1, pp. 67–85, at Catechesis 1, ch. 4, p. 93; Cyril of Jerusalem, "Catecheses," PG 33, cols. 331–1060, at col. 373.

garden, the heretics introduced Aréfast to the idea of moving from a forest to a garden, without identifying the forest he is living as the Church or the garden he was entering as a sect; to being pruned of thorns and grafted onto a better shoot, without identifying these thorns as truths and the shoot as errors; and to being brought to bear fruit, without identifying these products as infamous crimes. Like his late antique predecessors, Paul represents heretics as persuading initiates to enter their cults by introducing them to the structure of such a transition, even as they conceal its horrifying content.

If Guibert had perused Paul's text, he would have known that medieval heretics, like their late antique counterparts, perform secret deeds within their secret enclosures. On certain nights, Paul relates, the heretics assembled "in a designated house" to chant the names of devil until they saw a demon appear in the form of a small animal in their midst.[42] At that point, he continues, they extinguished the lights, grabbed the woman closest to them, even if she was their mother, their sister, or a nun, and fornicated with her. If a child was born as a result of this orgy, the heretics gathered together again, tossed the infant through flames, and made of its ashes a viaticum of such power that whoever ate of it could not depart this sect. It is difficult to reconcile Paul's account of this heretical gluttony, incest, sacrilege, infanticide, and cannibalism—so resonant with late antique accusations against orthodox and heterodox Christians—with his principal narrative. He acknowledges that his account constitutes a "digression," which is based upon unnamed, presumably textual sources derived from the Church Fathers, from the rest of the narrative, which appears to be grounded, instead, upon Aréfast's oral report to the monks of Chartres when he entered their monastery.[43] He admits, too, that the infamous behavior attributed to the heretics contradicts the comportment one might expect from canons who were, he states, "in popular repute distinguished above all others in words, eminent in holiness and piety, bountiful in charity," to the point where Etienne had become confessor to the queen and Lisois a man beloved of the king.[44] Other chroniclers similarly stress the discrepancy

---

42. "Heresy at Orléans: The Narrative of Paul, a Monk of Chartres," p. 78; "in domo denominata," Paul de Saint-Père de Chartres, *Cartulaire de l'abbaye*, p. 112.

43. "Heresy at Orléans: The Narrative of Paul, a Monk of Chartres," p. 79; "digressionem," translation modified; Paul de Saint-Père de Chartres, *Cartulaire de l'abbaye*, p. 112.

44. "Heresy at Orléans: The Narrative of Paul, a Monk of Chartres," p. 76; "aput omnes sapientia clari, sanctitate ac religione magnifici, elemosinis largi, opinione habebantur vulgi," Paul de Saint-Père de Chartres, *Cartulaire de l'abbaye*, p. 109.

between what the canons were thought to be and what they were. Adémar, for example, writes of the heretics, "In obedience to [the devil's] works, in private, they completely rejected Christ and secretly practiced abominations and crimes of which it is shameful to speak, while publicly they pretended to be true Christians."[45] Of another member of the sect, Adémar adds, "A certain cantor of the canons of Orléans, named Theodatus, had given every appearance of piety, but, as trustworthy persons declared, had died in their heresy three years before."[46] While the celebrants at the nocturnal rites were both male and female, both clerical and lay, and familially grouped, the canons were exclusively male, clerical, and professionally organized. Yet if heretics are understood to be people who conceal the notorious deeds they perform among themselves underneath the laudatory behavior they exemplify before others, the very contradiction between the wickedness suspected of the canons in private, and the goodness apparent in them in public, becomes, by a perverse logic, evidence of their guilt.

If Guibert had read Paul's test, he would have known that medieval heretics continued to use secret words, which hid their beliefs under veils, when introducing newcomers to the faith, and lies, which denied their beliefs altogether, when dealing with outsiders to the sect. The heretics of Orléans are seen as having expressed their views on Catholics when they responded to the bishop who attempted to persuade them of orthodox views on creation. They sneered, "You may spin stories in that way to those who have earthly bodies and believe the fictions of carnal men, scribbled on animal skins. To us, however, who have the law written upon the heart by the Holy Spirit (and we recognize nothing but what we have learned from God, Creator of all), in vain you spin out superfluities and things inconsistent with the Divinity."[47] Those outside their sect,

45. "Heresy at Orléans: A Report by Adémar of Chabannes," p. 74; "Cuius verbis obedientes, penitus Christum latenter respuerant, et abhominationes et crimina, quae dici etiam flagitium est, in occulto exercebant, et in aperto christianos veros se fallebant," Adémar de Chabannes, *Historiarum Libri III*, bk. 3, ch. 59, p. 143.

46. "Heresy at Orléans: A Report by Adémar of Chabannes," p. 75; "Quidam etiam Aurelianis canonicus cantor, nomine Theodatus, qui mortuus erat ante triennum in illa haeresi, ut perhibebant probati viri, religiosus visus fuerat," Adémar de Chabannes, *Historiarum Libri III*, bk. 3, ch. 59, p. 143.

47. "Heresy at Orléans: The Narrative of Paul, a Monk of Chartres," p. 81; "Ista illis narrare potes, qui terrena sapiunt atque credunt ficta carnalium hominum, scripta in membranulis animalium; nobis autem qui legem scriptam habemus in interiori homine a Spiritu Sancto, et nichil aliud sapimus, nisi quod a Deo, omnium conditore, didicimus, incassum superflua et a Divinitate devia profers," Paul de Saint-Père de Chartres, *Cartulaire de l'abbaye*, p. 114.

the heretics suggested, are "carnal" men who rely upon external, physical texts, which they themselves have made, while those inside the sect are, in contrast, spiritual men, who depend, instead, upon internal, abstract illumination, which the Holy Ghost has imparted to them. As we have seen, the heretics began their instruction of their disciples with exoteric, Catholic lessons from Scripture and only gradually moved to disclosing their own esoteric, heretical teachings, which contradicted what they had earlier taught. As we have seen, they are said to have relied upon "similitudes," like that of the tree and the garden, and other obscure manners of speaking which at once revealed the truth of their beliefs and rites to those who knew how to interpret their words and concealed this truth from those who were not so discerning.[48] Disguising the truth about their heresy to Aréfast through their doubled speech, the heretics concealed it altogether, at first, from the secular and sacred authorities who examined them. When initially questioned by the king and the bishop, Paul recounts, "the enemies of all truth . . . had no intention of entering upon the filthiness of their heresy by any avenue."[49] Aréfast reproached his teachers for their denials of what they had taught him, stating, "I thought to have in you masters of truth, not error" and thus suggesting that by lying about that apparent truth, they have revealed it to be a lie.[50] Through their falsehoods, Paul asserts, the heretics have exposed themselves as "enemies of all truth," both in this particular situation and in their essential being. Whether in their veiled or their mendacious speech, the heretics' very manner of expressing themselves becomes, in its perceived secretiveness, testimony against them.

On the basis of his reading of these antique and medieval texts about heretics, Guibert comes to perceive the secretiveness of Clement and Evrard as proof of their heresy. Like Paul, who interrupts his specific, empirically based narrative about Aréfast's encounter with the heretics with a general, textually grounded description of nefarious rituals, Guibert interweaves his account of Clement and Evrard's trial, which is bound in time and space and which he himself has observed, with descriptions of their sect's beliefs and rituals which are not

48. "Heresy at Orléans: The Narrative of Paul, a Monk of Chartres," p. 77, translation modified; "similitudinibus," Paul de Saint-Père de Chartres, *Cartulaire de l'abbaye*, p. 110.

49. "Heresy at Orléans: The Narrative of Paul, a Monk of Chartres," p. 80; "totius veritatis inimici, alia pro aliis dicentes, intra suae heresis foeditatem nullo aditu introire volebant," Paul de Saint-Père de Chartres, *Cartulaire de l'abbaye*, p. 113.

50. "Heresy at Orléans: The Narrative of Paul, a Monk of Chartres," p. 80; "Veritatis magistros, non herroris, vos habere putavi," Paul de Saint-Père de Chartres, *Cartulaire de l'abbaye*, p. 113.

limited by such parameters and not obtained by such experience. At first discouraged by Clement and Evrard's orthodox replies to his questions, Guibert relates, "I then remembered that line to which the Priscillianists formerly agreed, that is, 'Swear truly or falsely, but betray not the secret,'" and he adds, "I perceived that with them a good saying covers much wickedness."[51] If Guibert knows, in particular, that Clement and Evrard are lying when they profess to hold only orthodox views, it is because he knows, in general, that "such people deny charges and always draw away the hearts of the dull-witted in secret."[52] The brothers' repudiation of heretical views exposed them as heretics, who are also said to repudiate heretical views, Guibert deduces, though his logic makes it hard to imagine how a genuinely orthodox individual could persuade such judges of his or her orthodoxy. As Clement and Evrard's presumed secretiveness about their heretical doctrines revealed them to be heretics, their secretiveness about their heretical rituals similarly implicated them. Accused of "holding meetings outside the Church," as we have seen, "they did not deny the meetings." Though Guibert apparently never learned what the brothers and their supposed companions did during these gatherings, he asserts that heretics in general "have their meetings in underground vaults or unfrequented cellars" and that they commit infamous deeds at these times.[53] Gathering together at night, Guibert relates, the heretics extinguish the candles, cry out, "Chaos!" and then couple with whatever woman is next to them.[54] If a child is born as a result of this orgy, he continues, they meet again and toss it through the flames, bake its ashes into a loaf of bread, and distribute this substance as their host; anyone who eats of it can leave the sect only with great difficulty. As Paul was unconcerned by discrepancies between Aréfast's observations about the heretics of Orléans and his own account of their nefarious rites, so Guibert is untroubled by contradictions between the composition he perceives of their cult and the

---

51. Guibert of Nogent, *Self and Society*, p. 214; "Tunc recordans versus illius in quem priscillianistae olim consenserant, scilicet 'jura, perjura, secretum prodere noli,'" Guibert de Nogent, *Autobiographie*, p. 432; Guibert of Nogent, *Self and Society*, p. 213; "in bona sententia magnam quantum ad ipsos intelligerem latere nequitiam," Guibert de Nogent, *Autobiographie*, p. 432.

52. Guibert of Nogent, *Self and Society*, p. 213; "Ad quia talium est negare et semper hebetum clam corda seducere," Guibert de Nogent, *Autobiographie*, p. 432.

53. Guibert of Nogent, *Self and Society*, p. 212. "Conventicula faciunt in ypogeis aut penetralibus abditis," Guibert de Nogent, *Autobiographie*, p. 430.

54. Guibert of Nogent, *Self and Society*, p. 213; "Chaos!" Guibert de Nogent, *Autobiographie*, p. 430.

practice he attributes to these brothers. Though no more than five men and one woman are judged to have belonged to their sect, they are said to have conducted orgies among themselves. Though the heretics are said to have repudiated heterosexual intercourse, they are also believed to have engaged in this act as part of their central rite. When describing the brothers' doctrines and rituals, Guibert usually leaves unclear how he has obtained his information, but at one point he makes his source known. "If you review the heresies described by Augustine," he writes, "you will find this like none of them so much as that of the Manichaeans."[55] It appears that secretiveness and heresy became so linked in the clerical imagination through readings of patristic and medieval sources that those who were judged to be secretive, like these brothers, could be judged to be heretics on that basis.

BERNARD OF CLAIRVAUX

In the 1140s, Bernard, abbot of the Cistercian monastery of Clairvaux, turned to the problem of the "new heretics" whom his contemporaries appear to have been struggling to expose around this time.[56] In his *Sermons on the Song of Songs*, Bernard cites bishops and noblemen who have hesitated to prosecute heretics and who, when reproached for their inactivity, have argued, "But how . . . are we to condemn men who neither have been convicted of error nor admit it?"[57] For these ecclesiastical and secular lords, the challenge of heresy lies in the fact that although one may suspect certain individuals of error, it remains difficult to transform that suspicion into certainty and, hence, difficult to justify

55. Guibert of Nogent, *Self and Society*, p. 213; "Si relegas haereses ab Augustino disgestas, nulli magis quam manicheorum reperies convenire," Guibert de Nogent, *Autobiographie*, p. 430.

56. Bernard of Clairvaux, *Sermons on the Song of Songs*, trans. Kilian Walsh and Irene M. Edmonds (Kalamazoo, MI: Cistercian Publications, 1979), vol. 3, 65: 1; "novi haeretici," Bernard of Clairvaux, *Opera*, ed. Jean Leclercq, C. H. Talbot, and Henri Rochais (Roma: Editiones Cistercienses, 1957–77), vol. 2, *Sermones super Cantica canticorum, 38–86* (1958), 65:1. References to Bernard's *Sermons on the Song of Songs* will cite the sermon number and the section number within the sermon; they will apply both to the English translation and to the Latin original. On Bernard's *Sermons on the Song of Songs*, see Jean Leclercq, *Recueil d'études sur Saint Bernard et ses écrits* (Roma: Edizioni di storia et letteratura, 1962), vol. 1; Raoul Manselli, "Everino di Steinfeld e san Bernardo di Clairvaux," in *Studie sulle eresie del secolo XII*, 2nd ed. (Rome: Istituto Palazzo Borremini, 1975), pp. 145–56; and Arno Borst, *Die Katharer* (Stuttgart: Hiersemann, 1953), pp. 4–7 et passim.

57. "Et quomodo . . . damnabimus nec convictos nec confessos?" Bernard of Clairvaux, *Sermones* 66:14, translation modified.

their exclusion from Christian society. In responding to these authorities, Bernard acknowledges the difficulty of proving people to be heretics, especially those who seem to be more Christian than their neighbors, like the heretics he encountered during his preaching campaign in Occitania in 1145 or those his correspondent Everwin, the prior of the Premonastratensian abbey at Steinfeld, met near Cologne around that time. "It is not for man to know what is in man," he concedes, admitting, through his recollection of the Gospel of John,[58] that only God possesses this power. At the same time, Bernard qualifies his admission of the inscrutability of men's souls to other men by adding that man cannot know what is in man, "unless he is enlightened for this very purpose by the Spirit of God or guided by angelic activity."[59] Elsewhere, he states of the sins with which heresy is identified that "they cannot be avoided except by the perfect and the experienced, and by such as have the eyes of their souls enlightened for the discernment of good and evil, and particularly for the discernment of spirits."[60] Even though Bernard establishes the limitations of man's insight, he also suggests that man can transcend these limitations through divine or angelic illumination or, more specifically, through the understanding that can result from such illumination. If the external crisis Christendom is now facing, where heretics go about unchecked and uncorrected, is rooted in an internal crisis experienced by bishops and noblemen, who find themselves paralyzed by their uncertainty as to the state of their subjects' souls, Bernard insists, with his customary emphasis upon divine grace rather than human reason, that God can help some of them in this quandary, enabling them to see the heresy they would not otherwise apprehend. Throughout his sermons on heretics, Bernard acknowledges and even amplifies the epistemological problems heretics are seen as posing by seeming not to be heretics, but he also shows himself able, through a mysterious interpretive power, to use these apparent obstacles to prosecution as evidence against them.

Like the eleventh- and early twelfth-century ecclesiastics who came before him, who found heretics to be so difficult to apprehend, Bernard depicts these

58. "Non est autem hominis scire quid sit in homine"; cf. John 2:25.

59. "nisi quis forte ad hoc ipsum fuerit vel illuminatus Spiritu Dei, vel angelica informatus industria," Bernard of Clairvaux, *Sermones* 64:6.

60. "nisi dumtaxat a perfectis et exercitatis, et qui habeant illuminatos oculos cordis ad discretionem boni et mali, maximeque ad discretionem spirituum," Bernard of Clairvaux, *Sermones* 65:4. The "discernment of spirits" (*discretio spirituum*) is one of the gifts of the Holy Spirit, alongside faith-healing and the performance of miracles, that Paul mentions in 1 Cor 12: 8–10.

deviants as physically secretive. By sermon 63, he had reached chapter 2, verse 15, of the Song of Songs, where the reader is urged, "Catch us the little foxes that destroy the vines."[61] Bernard interprets these "little foxes" as all the various subtle temptations one encounters in the spiritual life but especially as heretics, who incarnate one such subtle temptation. Since late antiquity, foxes had been held to resemble heretics because of their trickiness, their deceptiveness, and their furtiveness.[62] In accordance with this tradition, Bernard informs the heretics that although they claim to resemble the Apostles in their lifestyle, they differ from them because "they [are] in public, you in corners; they fly like a cloud, you lurk in darkness and in underground houses."[63] Heretics, he states, constantly seek "hiding-places for themselves."[64] Instead of attacking

61. "Capite nobis vulpes parvulas, quae demoliuntur vineas."

62. In addition to this passage from the Song of Songs, foxes are mentioned in Judges 15:4, where Samson catches three hundred such animals, places them in pairs, tail to tail, and attaches torches to each set of tails, so that, when freed, they burn the grain fields and vineyards of the Philistines. Foxes are also mentioned in the gospels of Matthew 8:20 and Luke 9: 58, where Jesus complains "The foxes have holes and the birds of the air nests, but the Son of man hath not where to lay his head [*vulpes foveas habent et volucres caeli tabernacula. Filius autem hominis non habet ubi caput reclinet*]." Origen is considered to be the first Christian author to identify the scriptural foxes with heretics. See *Commentarium in Cant. Can.*, PG 13, col. 196. Jerome also makes this connection in *Epistola* 15, PL 22, cols. 374–75. Ambrose of Milan remarks, "It is to heretics that [Christ] compares foxes. . . . For the fox is an animal full of ruses, digging his den and wanting always to be buried in his lair [*Haereticis autem vulpes conparat . . . ; vulpes enim plenum fraudis est animal fouveam parans et in fovea semper latere desiderans*]," *Traité sur l'Evangile de s. Luc*, ed. Gabriel Tissot, Sources chrétiennes (Paris: Editions du Cerf, 1959), vol. 2, bk. 7, chs. 30–31, p. 19. See also *Comment, In Ps. CXVII*, sermon 11, PL 15, col. 1360. Augustine agrees with his mentor, writing that "foxes symbolize insidious men and above all heretics: tricksters and knaves who hide themselves and deceive with hollowed-out windings [*Vulpes insidiosos, maximeque haereticos significant: dolosos, fraudulentos, cavernosis anfractibus latentes et decipientes*]," (*En. in Ps.* 80, 14, PL 37, col. 1040). For discussion of this metaphor, see See G. M. Dubarle, "Les Renards de Samson," *Revue du Moyen Age latin* 7 (1951): 174–76; Yves Marie-Joseph Congar, "Henri de Marcy, abbé de Clairvaux, cardinal-évêque d'Albano et légat pontifical," *Analecta Monastica*, ser. 5, *Studia Anselmiana* 43 (1958): 1–19 at 13, n. 37; Maddelena Scopello, "Le Renard symbole de l'hérésie dans les polémiques patristiques contre les gnostiques," *Revue d'Histoire et de philosophie religieuses* 71 (1991): 73–88; and Jacques Voisenet, "Le Renart dans les bestiares des clercs médiévaux," *Reinardus* 9 (1996): 179–88. Many of the qualities Scopello sees as most often attributed to foxes, such as "trickery" (*dolus*), "cunning" (*calliditas*), "ruses" (*versutiae*), "fallacies" (*fallaciae*), and "sophistries" (*sophismata*), are also attributed to heretics in general. Voisenet notes, interestingly, that, while most other animals condemned by Christian texts, including wolves and snakes, are occasionally depicted positively, foxes are never portrayed in this manner.

63. "illi in publico, vos in angulo; illi ut nubes volant, vos in tenebris ac subterraneis domibus delitescitis," Bernard of Clairvaux, *Sermones* 65:4, translation modified.

64. "latebras sibi," ibid., 65:2.

boldly and openly, they reside in their dens, emerge slyly and covertly to spoil the vines, and then retreat back to their lairs, managing "by I know not what art"[65] to conceal their footprints so that no one can perceive their means of access to the vineyard. Whether influenced by the abbot's thought or by the exegetical tradition before him, many subsequent authors also described the Cathars, in particular, as covert in their physical habits. In the 1160s, not long after these heretics resurfaced in Cologne, Eckbert, a Benedictine monk from Schönau, wrote of them, "They are the hidden men, perverted and perverting, who have lain hidden through the ages. They have secretly corrupted the Christian faith of many foolish and simple men, so that they have multiplied in every land."[66] These heretics hold their meetings, he reports, "in corners," "in cellars, in weavers' huts, and such underground houses."[67] Time and again, these later clerics characterize the Cathars as "little foxes," hiding away in their holes when the vigilance of prelates forces them underground and emerging to wreak havoc upon the vineyard when the increasing laxity of the ecclesiastics or their own increasing boldness encourages them to appear, but always acting stealthily. In addition, the Cathars are imagined as "moles," again because "they buried themselves in hiding-places in the ground and hollowed-out cellars, so that they could gnaw and destroy the roots of the holy plants"; as "grubs," because "they crawl through [the Catholic faith] cunningly, undermining it"; as "crabs," because they "scuttle about secretly"; and, in general, as "wild beasts, whose timidity and confusion has driven them, like loathsome reptiles, into holes underground."[68] So absolute does this association of heretics and hidden spaces become that Pope Lucius III, in his 1184 bull *Ad Abolendum*, ordered

---

65. "nescio qua arte," ibid., 65:5, translation modified.

66. Eckbert of Schönau, "Sermon Against the Cathars," in Moore, *The Origins of European Dissent*, pp. 88–94, at p. 90, translation modified; "Ecce enim quidam latibulosi homines perversi et perversores, qui per multa tempora latuerunt, et occulte fidem Christianam in multis stultae simplicitatis hominibus corruperunt ita per omnes terras multiplicati sunt," Eckbert von Schönau, *Sermones contra Catharos*, in PL 195, cols. 11–102 at cols. 13–14.

67. My translation; "in angulis," Eckbert von Schönau, *Sermones contra Catharos*, col. 19; Eckbert of Schönau, "Sermon against the Cathars," p. 90; "in cellariis et in textrinis, et in hujusmodi subterraneis domibus," Eckbert von Schönau, *Sermones contra Catharos*, col. 14.

68. On moles, see Henry of Clairvaux, "Legation in the Languedoc," in Moore, *The origins of European Heresy*, p. 116–22, at p. 117; "talpas . . . jam terrarum latebris, jam sese cellulis immergerent cavernosis et plantaria sacra . . . corroderent et necarent," Henri de Clairvaux, *Epistolae*, PL 204, cols. 215–52, *Epistola* 29, cols. 235–40, at cols. 236–37. On grubs, see Eckbert of Schönau, "Sermon against the Cathars," p. 89; "Catholicae fidei, quam velut tineae demoliuntur et corrumpunt, ambulantes in astutia multa," Eckbert von Schönau, *Sermones contra*

bishops or their delegates to visit parishes suspected of heresy once a year and there to investigate "heretics . . . or any persons holding secret conventicles," and the Fourth Lateran Council of 1215 reiterated this mandate.[69] The Council of Toulouse of 1229 went so far as to command these authorities to "search all houses and subterranean chambers which lie under any suspicion" and to "look . . . for appendages or outbuildings in the roofs themselves, or any other kind of hiding place, all which we direct to be destroyed."[70] If Bernard and his successors depict heretics as concealing themselves, like foxes, in "hiding-places," "cellars," and "underground houses," they are speaking both figuratively, to evoke the general covertness of the heretics' character, and also literally, to suggest the specific covertness of their habitations.

Secretive physically, the heretics, as Bernard represents them, are secretive verbally as well. Though the heretics purport to imitate the Apostles, Bernard recalls, those original Christians were hardly silent about their creed. As he tells the heretics, "They shout their teaching," spreading their doctrine throughout the world and converting the multitudes.[71] In contrast to their alleged models, Bernard cites the heretics as maintaining, "We must not reveal our mystery," and he reports, "They consider that their mystery, whatever it is, should be kept from anyone, without exception, who does not belong to their sect."[72] If the heretics are so taciturn about their faith, Bernard speculates, it may be because they genuinely believe themselves to follow the scriptural precept not "to give what is holy to dogs, or . . . to cast pearls before swine."[73] The heretics

---

Catharos, cols. 13–14. On crabs, see Eckbert of Schönau, "Sermons against the Cathars," p. 90; "sermo eorum serpit ut cancer," Eckbert von Schönau, *Sermones contra Catharos*, col. 13. On wild beasts, see Henry of Claivaux, "Legation in the Languedoc," p. 118; "cum feris bestiis . . . quos timor et confusio tanquam ignobile reptile in ima terrae detruserant," Henri de Clairvaux, *Epistola* 29, col. 237.

69. "Pope Lucius III: The Decretal *Ad Abolendum*, 1184," Peters, pp. 170–73, at p. 173; "haereticus . . . vel aliquos occulte conventicula celebrantes," "Das Edikt 'Ad abolendam' von Lucius III. (1184)," in Fearns, pp. 61–63, at p. 63.

70. "The Council of Toulouse, 1229," in Peters, pp. 195–95; "domos singulas et cameras subterraneas aliqua suspicione notabiles perscrutando, seu adjuncta in ipsis tectis aedificia, seu quaecumque alia latibula, quae omnia destrui praecipimus, perquirendo," "Beschlüsse des Konzils von Toulouse zur Verfolgung der Ketzer (1229)," in Fearns, pp. 69–72, at p. 69.

71. "Hi clamant," Bernard of Clairvaux, *Sermones* 65:4, translation modified.

72. "ne mysterium publicemus," ibid., 65:2, translation modified; "Sine exceptione enim omnibus qui de sua secta non sunt, suum illud, quidquid est, subtrahendum existimant," ibid., 65:3, translation modified.

73. "sanctum dare canibus et margaritas porcis," ibid., 65:3.

regard themselves as "the only followers of the true Gospel" and scorn all who
do not already adhere to their faith.[74] If the heretics are so guarded, Bernard
wonders, it may also be because they adhere to the Priscillianists' rule, "Swear
truly or falsely, but betray not the secret."[75] In the manner of the heretics of
old, they strive to keep their esoteric creed from the exoteric masses, even if
they must perjure themselves to do so. Depicting the heretics as "whispering"
their beliefs to their cohorts,[76] Bernard attributes to them an unchristian,
uncharitable elitism, which would preserve an allegedly salutary truth for a
handpicked few, at the expense of all others. Eckbert von Schönau expands
upon Bernard's thoughts. Like the Cistercian abbot, he contrasts the heretics'
silence about their creed to the loquaciousness of the Apostles they claim to
follow. The Apostles obeyed Christ's command to place their lamps not under
a bushel basket but on a lampstand, in order to allow their light to shine before
all. "You, however, have hidden yourselves and concealed your doctrine," he
informs the heretics, "and you have placed your lantern under a bushel basket,
nor do you ever manifest it to anyone about whom you are afraid, lest he make
you manifest."[77] The heretics may think themselves to be keeping what is holy
from dogs and pearls from swine, Eckbert recognizes, but in doing so they
overlook the intent of these words, which was to restrict the Gospel only from
those who, like the Jews, had repeatedly mocked and rejected its truths. Again
like Bernard, Eckbert hypothesizes that the heretics follow the Priscillianists'
dictum not to betray the secret. With their reluctance to disclose their creed,
he charges, they contradict the spirit of an evangelical religion. Even if they fear
being prosecuted for heresy, Eckbert urges, they should follow the words of the
Prophet: "Get thee up upon a high mountain, . . . lift up your voice with
strength, . . . lift it up; fear not."[78] If the heretics genuinely believed their faith
necessary for salvation, they would act as if this were the case by proselytizing
it to one and all, whatever they might risk in doing so. Even when the heretics
are drawn out from their hiding-places, Bernard and his followers contend,

---

74. "se Evangelii . . . aemulatores, et solos," ibid., 65:3.

75. "Iura, perjura; secretum prodere noli," ibid., 65:2.

76. "vos susurratis," ibid., 65:4, translation modified.

77. My translation; "vos autem semper absconditi fuistis, et doctrinam vestra occultastis,
et ita lucernam vestram sub modio timoris positam habetis, nec unquam eam alicui manifes-
tastis, de quo timetis, quod vos faciat manifestos," Eckbert von Schönau, *Sermones contra
Catharos*, col. 19.

78. "Super montem excelsum ascende tu . . . , exalta vocem tuam, . . . exalta, noli timere,"
ibid., col. 20. Cf. Is 40:9.

they are still inclined to hide, now in a silence which shows the falsity of their apostolic claims.

Secretive physically and verbally, the heretics are, at last, according to Bernard, secretive morally. Everwin had already complained to Bernard that when the heretics from near Cologne were examined by the bishop and other prelates, they pointed out that their lives of labor, fasting, and prayer were holier than those of Catholic monks and canons. Bernard now concedes of the archetypal heretic, "As far as his life and his conduct are concerned, he harms no one, distresses no one, does not set himself above anyone. His face is pale from fasting, he does not eat the bread of idleness, he supports himself with the labor of his hands."[79] In his duties toward the Church as well as toward his fellow man, Bernard recognizes the heretic to be without fault. "What you see is a man frequenting the church, honoring the clergy, offering his gifts, making his confession, receiving the sacraments," he writes. "What can be more orthodox?"[80] When the man is apprehended and examined on account of his heresy, he continues to appear exemplary. "If you question him about his faith, nothing could be more Christian," Bernard reports. "If [you question him] as to his way of life, nothing could be more irreproachable."[81] Even when he is condemned to death, the heretic still seems to personify Christian ideals. Everwin had informed Bernard that when the heretics at Cologne were cast into the flames, they endured their torments "not merely courageously but joyfully."[82] Reflecting upon the heretics' comportment in the pyre, Everwin writes, "I wish I were with you, holy father, to hear you explain how such great fortitude comes to these tools of the devil in their heresy as is seldom found among the truly religious in the faith of Christ."[83] It is perhaps of this group of heretics that Bernard now admits, "They declared [their guilt] openly, alleging that it

79. "Iam quod ad vitam moresque spectat, neminem concutit, neminem circumvenit, neminem supergreditur. Pallent insuper ora ieiuniis, panem non comedit otiosus, operatur manibus unde vitam sustentat," Bernard of Clairvaux, *Sermones* 65:4.

80. "Videas hominem in testimonium suae fidei frequentare ecclesiam, honorare presbyteros, offerre munus suum, confessionem facere, sacramentis communicare. Quid fidelius?" ibid., 65:4.

81. "Denique si fidem interroges, nihil christianius; si conversationem, nihil irreprehensibilius," ibid., 65:5, translation modified.

82. "Eversin of Steinfeld,"p. 75; "non solum cum patientia, sed cum laetitia," Everwin von Steinfeld, *Epistola*, col. 677.

83. "Eversin of Steinfeld," p. 75; "Hic, sancte pater, vellem, si praesens essem, habere responsionem tuam, unde istis diaboli membris tanta fortitudo in sua haeresi, quanta vix etiam invenitur in valde religiosis in fide Christi," Everwin von Steinfeld, *Epistola*, col. 677.

was true piety, and for it they have been ready to suffer death," and when faced with this fate, "they were led to death not only with patience, but also, it seems, joyfully."[84] Later clerics shared Bernard's perception of these heretics' virtuous lifestyles. The Dominican Peter Ferrand cites heretics as contrasting their humility, industry, and poverty with the pride and ostentatiousness of the Catholic clerics, without denying the justice of their self-description.[85] The Franciscan Giacomo Capelli grants, "For we know that they suppose their behavior to be virtuous, and they do many things that are in the nature of good works; in frequent prayer, in vigils, in sparseness of food and clothing, and— let me acknowledge the truth—in austerity of abstinence they surpass all other religions."[86] Bernard's depiction of the heretics as willingly sacrificing their lives for their beliefs becomes a commonplace in clerical writings. The Cistercian Pierre des Vaux-de-Cernay, for example, represents the heretics seized at Minerve during the Albigensian Crusade as announcing, "Neither death nor life can separate us from the beliefs we hold," and remaining stead-fast even as they were cast into the flames.[87] If the heretics are secretive in their actions, as Bernard contends that they are, it is not because they use an apparent goodness to conceal their actual wickedness (as, for example, the heretics at Orléans were alleged to have done), but, rather, because a heretic's virtue constitutes just another form of vice. "This heresy knows so well how to lie,

84. "professi sunt, palam pietatem astruentes et pro ea mortem subire parati," Bernard of Clairvaux, *Sermones* 66: 12; "non modo patienter, sed et laeti, ut videbatur, ducerentur ad mortem," ibid., *Sermones* 66:13, translation modified.

85. See, for example, Peter Ferrand, who states that "they assumed, as usual, a remarkable air of humility in the clothing they wore and pleasantness of speech, together with an unusual austerity in regard to food [*Pretendebant enim, ut assolent, miram humilitatem in habitu, simplicitatem in gestu, dulcedinem in affatu, nimiam austeritatem in victu*]," *Legenda S. Dominici*, ed. Marie-Hyacinthe Laurent, Monumenta Ordinis Fratrum Praedicatorum Historica (Rome: Institutum Historicum FF. Praedicatorum ad S. Sabinae, 1935), pp. 197–260, at p. 225.

86. "James Capelli on the Cathars," in Wakefield and Evans, pp. 301–6, at pp. 303–4; "Scimus enim quoniam se bona opera credunt et multa quae sunt de genere bonorum faciunt in ieiuniis, in crebis orationibus, in vigiliis, in parcitate victus et vestitus, et ut vera fatear, fere omnes alios religiosos per austeritatem abstinentiae excedunt," Giacomo Capelli, *Summa contra haereticos*, in Dino Bazzocchi, *L'Eresia Catara* (Bologna: Licinio Cappelli, 1920), pp. i–ccx, at p. cxxxix.

87. Pierre des Les Vaux-de-Cernay, *The History of the Albigensian Crusade*, trans. W. A. Silby and M. D. Silby (Woodbridge, Suffolk: Boydell Press, 1998; rpt. 2000), § 155, p. 85. "A secta quam tenemus neque mors neque vita nos poterit revocare," Pierre des Vaux-de-Cernay, *Hystoria Albigensis*, ed. Pascal Guébin and Ernest Lyon (Paris: Honoré Champion, 1926),vol. 1, § 155, p. 160.

not only with its tongue, but with its life,"[88] writes Bernard. Not only does the heretic deceive by making a falsehood seem to be a truth, Bernard maintains, but when he acts like a virtuous and holy person, he deceives by making a heretic seem to be a good man. If the devil recruits people of such admirable habits to serve him, it is because he knows that, as Bernard puts it, "malice always has less power to harm when it is obvious. No good man is ever deceived except by a simulation of goodness."[89] Of such heretics, he states, "It is to cause the downfall of the good that they strive to appear good."[90] For Bernard, heretics conceal themselves not by appearing to be good but by being good, which in a heretic is by definition only an appearance.

Acknowledging that the heretics are difficult to apprehend, Bernard instructs his audience that it can nonetheless recognize heretics by looking not at their actions, which are admirable in themselves, but at the causes of those actions, which are not so admirable. The heretics may seem more chaste than their Catholic counterparts because they renounce all carnal intercourse, including that performed between married partners, but, Bernard warns, "a man who condemns marriage opens the door to every kind of impurity," including concubinage, masturbation, and incest.[91] Bernard suggests that the heretics reject lawful wedlock not out of a desire to restrain all sexual acts, as they claim, but out of a desire to unleash illegitimate sexual acts by banning the only legitimate ones. If the heretics repudiate connubial relations, Bernard maintains, "they say this as hypocrites, with the cunning of foxes, pretending that their words are inspired by a love of chastity, whereas their motive is rather to foment and increase immorality."[92] In addition, the heretics may appear more abstinent than their Catholic counterparts because they renounce all animal-based foods and undergo frequent fasts even from the meager fare they do allow themselves, yet they do so, Bernard cautions, not out of a love of the spirit, but out of hatred of the flesh. He compares the motive which drives him, at times, to restrict his diet, namely, "a reparation due to sin," with the motive which drives the heretics to practice the same behavior, namely, "a superstition

88. "haeresis haec, docta mentiri non lingua tantum, sed vita," Bernard of Clairvaux, *Sermones* 65:4, translation modified.
89. "Etenim minus semper malitia palam nocuit, nec umquam bonus nisi boni simulatione deceptus est," ibid., 66:1, translation modified.
90. "Ita ergo in malum bonorum boni apparere student," ibid., 66:1.
91. "omni immunditatiae laxat habenas qui nuptias damnat," ibid., 66:3.
92. "In hypocrisi plane hoc et vulpina dolositate loquuntur, fingentes se amore id dicere castitatis, quod magis causa turpitudinis fovendae et multiplicandae adinvenerunt," ibid.

due to impiety."[93] As the heretics pursue celibacy out of a wicked rejection of the marital union, which God has sanctified, they pursue fasting out of a similarly wicked rejection of the material world, which God has created. Finally, heretics may seem more heroic than their Catholic peers because they are willing to go to the stake for their beliefs, yet they renounce earthly existence, not out of a hope for the next world, but out of despair at this one. Bernard compares the violence that heretics allow others to inflict upon them, through their refusal to convert, to the violence that suicides inflict upon themselves, through their self-slaughter. He writes of the heretics, "They are utterly subverted. This is proved by the fact that they would rather choose death than conversion. For them the end is destruction, for them fire is waiting at the last."[94] The heretics seek the flames of the temporal pyre because of the same self-destructiveness which makes them seek the flames of eternal damnation, and they reject the efforts of the clerics to dissuade them from this fate because of the same insensibility that makes them reject God. As a result, he concludes, "the obstinacy of these men has nothing in common with the constancy of the martyrs, for they were endowed by [their] piety with a contempt for death, whereas these others are prompted by their hardness of heart."[95] If one looks not at their external actions but at the internal motives which produce these actions, Bernard maintains, one sees that it is not a transcendence of the self but an aggression against the self which produces their indifference to death. If one considers not the action one sees but the intention one does not see, one can perceive, according to Bernard, the true iniquity of these sectaries.

Bernard instructs his audience that it can recognize the heretics by looking not only at the wicked causes that produce these persons' virtuous actions but also at the wicked effects that result from the virtuous actions, for, as Scripture tells us, it is by their fruits that one shall know them.[96] In pursuing this inquiry, Bernard concentrates upon the heretics' custom of traveling with women companions. At first, Bernard attempts to ascertain whether these women are, as the heretics claim, merely their companions or whether they are, as he suspects, their concubines, yet he encounters the same uncertainty which plagues bishops and

---

93. "satisfactio . . . pro peccatis," ibid., 66:6, translation modified; "superstitio pro impietate," ibid., translation modified.

94. "subversi sunt. Probatum est: mori magis eligunt, quam converti. Horum finis interitus, horum novissima incendium manet," ibid., 66:12, translation modified.

95. "Nihil ergo simile habent constantia martyrum et pertinacia horum, quia mortis contemptum in illis pietas, in istis cordis duritia operatur," ibid., 66:13.

96. Mt 7:16.

noblemen in their dealing with the heretics and prevents them from guarding their flocks as they should. He considers how the heretic's side touches the girl's side at table, how his bed touches her bed in their chamber, how his eyes meet her eyes in conversation, and how his hands meet her hands at work, and he speculates whether, given such contact between the heretic and the girl, the former could possibly be chaste, yet Bernard's thoughts remain speculations, without the conviction necessary to act against these people. Then, however, Bernard turns away from these conjectures toward a new, more productive line of thought. The heretic claims to be chaste, despite his women companions, and Bernard acknowledges, "It may be that you are," but he adds, "I have my suspicions. To me you are an object of scandal."[97] Bernard recalls that the Gospel condemns the man who scandalizes someone within the Church—who provides, through his own behavior, a stumbling block that causes others to fall, even if he himself has not sinned—and he concludes of the heretic, "If he does not remove the scandal when he can remove it, he is clearly disobedient to the Gospel."[98] Instead of focusing upon the uncertain action itself of the heretic, that is, his chastity or his lechery, Bernard focuses upon the certain fruits of this action, that is, the suspicion the heretic arouses in those around him. Even if the heretic is entirely chaste, the bad example he sets by his ambiguous relation with these women may well encourage others to be lecherous, and he will be held responsible for their ensuing sin. As evidence that the heretics have caused others to fall, Bernard recounts, "Women have left their husbands, and husbands their wives, to join these people. Clerics and priests, both young and old, have left the people and their churches and are to be found there among men and women weavers."[99] He asks, "Is this not great havoc? Is this not the work of foxes?"[100] Even if the heretics' deeds are unknowable or unassailable, the fruits which result from these deeds reveal their iniquity.

97. "Esto ut sis; sed ego suspicione non careo. Scandalo mihi es," Bernard of Clairvaux, *Sermones* 65:4.

98. "si non amovet scandalum cum amovere possit, transgressor tenetur Evangelii," ibid., 65:7. See Mt 18:6–9. According to Jerome, the Latin *scandalus* derives from the Greek *skandalon* and means "offensionem vel ruinam et impactionem pedis." The saint continues, "When we read, 'whoever scandalizes,' we understood by this, 'who gives an occasion of ruin in word or deed [*Quando legimus, Quicumque scandalizaverit, hoc intelligimus, Qui dicto vel facto occasionem ruinae dederit*],'" *S. Eusebii Hieronymi Commentariorum in evangelium Matthaei ad Eusebium*, in PL 26, col. 15–228, at col. 107.

99. "Mulieres, relictis viris, et item viri, dimissis uxoribus, ad istos se conferunt. Clerici et sacerdotes, populis ecclesiisque relictis, intonsi et barbati apud eos inter textores et textrices plerumque inventi sunt," Bernard of Clarivaux, *Sermones* 65: 5.

100. "Annon gravis demolitio ista? Annon opera vulpium haec?" ibid.

If the heretics' guilt can be ascertained from the causes and the effects of their behavior, it can also be determined from the very secretiveness with which they conceal that behavior. Bernard asks the heretic, "Tell me, O man wise beyond propriety and foolish beyond description, that mystery which you keep hidden—is it of God or not? If it is, why do you not expose it to his glory? For 'it is the glory of God to reveal teaching.' If it is not, why do you put faith in something not of God, unless you are a heretic?"[101] With this question, Bernard suggests that just as something that is "of God" is to be revealed, something that is not revealed must not be "of God." If the heretics conceal themselves physically, in their dens, he speculates, it is because they know that the profane nature of their teachings would be exposed if they emerged into the open. In the past, Bernard states, "a heretic would dispute in the open, for the desire for an open victory is the strongest motive of a heretic."[102] Now, he complains, "these foxes, the most malicious of all, . . . would rather inflict injury than win a victory in open fight."[103] In the past, heretics aspired to defeat the Church, yet now they know that their best hope is to damage it without being defeated themselves. As small, subtle, furtive creatures, Bernard contends, "they avoid any open conflict and defense. They are indeed a base and uncouth race, unlettered and wholly lacking in courage."[104] They are so weak that they know that they will be vanquished in any open combat with the Church, so cowardly that they dare not enter into any such combat, and so vicious that they resolve, all the same, to attack undercover. The heretics hide themselves verbally, Bernard maintains, because they think themselves superior to the Catholics around them, even though, in doing so, they create a division within the Church. He asks, "When they dismiss everyone within the Church as dogs and swine, is this not an open admission that they themselves are not within the Church?"[105] If the heretics conceal themselves morally, in their seemingly virtuous actions, Bernard hy-

---

101. "o homo qui plus quam oportet sapis, et plus quam dici potest desipis: Dei est, an non, myserium quod occultas? Si est, cur non ad eius gloriam pandis? Nam 'gloria dei revelare sermonem.' Si non, cur fidem habes in eo quod non est Dei, nisi quia haereticus es?" ibid., 65:3. Cf. Prv 25:2, as cited in Gregory the Great's *Homilies on Ezekiel* 1:6.

102. "Confligebat haereticus palam—nam inde haereticus maxime, quod palam vincere cupiebat," Bernard of Clairvaux, *Sermones* 65:1.

103. "his malignissimis vulpibus, . . . nocere quam vincere malunt," ibid., 65:2.

104. "Nam conflictus omnino ab his et defensio periit. Vile nempe hoc genus et rusticanum, ac sine litteris, et prorsus imbelle," ibid., 65:8.

105. "At istud aperte fateri est, se non esse de Ecclesia, qui omnes, qui de Ecclesia sunt, canes censet et porcos," ibid., 65:3.

pothesizes, it is because they know that the nefarious nature of their "myster-ies" would be revealed if they behaved otherwise. He does not attribute to the heretics the traditional narrative of nocturnal banquets, extinguished lamps, indiscriminate couplings, and ritualized infanticide, yet he cannot resist over-stepping his customary prudence to suggest, "I think it . . . likely that they would blush to expose their mystery, knowing it to be shameful. For it is said that they practice unspeakable obscenities in secret; just so, the hinder parts of foxes stink."[106] Throughout his discussion of the heretics, Bernard acknowledges that one cannot perceive these people's iniquity in their deeds and words, which seem, to the naked human eye, entirely good, but he insists that one can grasp their evil in the circumstances surrounding these deeds and words and, even more, in the concealment of other, more dubious, acts and utterances. When the center of the heretic's behavior remains obscured by its seeming innocence or even attractiveness, Bernard recommends, one must rely upon the silhouette of that behavior for indications as to its true nature.

GUILHEM PELHISSON

In the thirteenth century, the Dominican friars, like the Benedictine and Cistercian monks who pursued unbelievers before them, struggled to expose the heretics they perceived around them. According to Friar Guilhem Pelhisson, who composed a chronicle of his order's experience in Toulouse and Albi during the 1230s and early 1240s, the heretics and their supporters resisted the inquisitors' efforts to rout the land of the heterodox, but they did so sur-reptitiously.[107] At one point, when the friars accused a popular citizen of heresy, "the town was . . . very stirred up against the friars; there were even more threats

---

106. "mysterium . . . magis credo quod pandere erubescant, scientes inglorium. Nam nefanta et obscena dicuntur agere in secreto: siquidem et vulpium posteriora foestunt," ibid., 65:2, translation modified.

107. "The Chronicle of William Pelhisson," in Walter L. Wakefield, *Heresy, Crusade and Inquisition in Southern France, 1100–1250*, appendix 3, pp. 207–35; Guillaume Pelhisson, *Chronique (1229–1244), suivie du récit des troubles d'Albi (1234)*, ed. and trans. Jean Duvernoy (Paris: CNRS, 1994). For background on Toulouse in the Middle Ages, see John Hine Mundy, *Liberty and Political Power at Toulouse, 1050–1250* (New York: Columbia University Press, 1954), whose "Conclusion and Epilogue," pp. 159–67 sheds light on the time period under study here, and *Men and Women at Toulouse in the Age of the Cathars* (Toronto: Pontifical Institute of Mediaeval Studies, 1990), which addresses this era from a sociological point of view. On the Inquisition in Toulouse during these years, see especially Yves Dossat, *Les Crises de l'Inquisition toulousaine au XIIIe siècle (1233–1273)* (Bordeaux: Imprimerie Bière, 1959).

and speeches against them than usual, and many heretical persons incited the people to stone the friars and destroy their houses."[108] When the vicar tried to lead this citizen to the stake, Pelhisson continues, "those who defended the man raised an outcry against his doing any such thing, and everyone was muttering against the friar and the vicar."[109] When another reputable burgher was burned, "many of the people were stirred up against the friars and the vicar."[110] What is striking about the Toulousans' resistance to the inquisitors is that, however much it is expressed on the level of threats or rallying cries of destruction, it is not expressed on the level of rational arguments. Though the crowds are portrayed as either heretics or partisans of the heretics, none of them defend either the Cathars or the beliefs of this sect in order to justify their antagonism toward their persecutors. If the burghers speak out at all, it is only in the form of "threats and speeches" whose content Pelhisson does not convey and "mutterings" that suggest fear of expressing thoughts audibly to all. Because these citizens do not justify their opposition to the inquisitors with arguments, they appear unjustified, irrational, and therefore inexplicable in their opposition. Compelled by no sensible motivation in their hostility toward the friars, they appear motivated, instead, by the absolute malice which Augustine identifies with evil and which, in its very purity, can only be inspired by the devil. Because the Toulousans do not admit to being heretics and do not defend their antipathy toward the inquisitors on religious (or any other) grounds, their silence seems, in Pelhisson's account, to be proof of their diabolic affiliation. While heretics are not accused here of gathering in secret locales or performing secret rituals, they are charged, even more than before, of speaking a secret language, whose coded meanings only their fellow sectaries are thought to discern.

On those rare occasions in Pelhisson's chronicle when the Toulousans do speak, they do so, first, to deny that they are heretics. The first time that a Dominican friar decried the presence of heretics in Toulouse, Pelhisson relates,

---

108. "The Chronicle of William Pelhisson," p. 213. "commota est villa valde contra Fratres, et mine et verba multa fuerunt contra eos supra modum, et multi hereticales incitabant populum ut lapidarent Fratres, et domus eorum omnino diruerentur," Guillaume Pelhisson, *Chronique*, p. 52.

109. "The Chronicle of William Pelhisson," p. 213; "clamaverunt contra eum illi qui eum defendebant ne aliquo modo faceret, et murmurabant fere omnes contra Fratres et vicarium," Guillaume Pelhisson, *Chronique*, p. 52.

110. "The Chronicle of William Pelhisson," p. 215; "commoti sunt multi de populo contra Fratres et vicarium," Guillaume Pelhisson, *Chronique*, p. 60.

"the people of the town became very disturbed and agitated at hearing this."[111] The consuls who governed the city summoned the prior and advised him that the brethren should not preach that there were heretics in the city, "since no one among them, they insisted, was any such thing."[112] Bernart del Soler, accused of heresy in a personal quarrel, so rejected the validity of the charge that he complained of his accuser before the consuls and succeeded in having him condemned and punished for this alleged libel. Joan Tesseire, similarly charged, protested to the inquisitors, "Gentlemen, listen to me! I am not a heretic."[113] Of the suspect Arnaut Sans, Pelhisson writes that "the man denied everything, saying nothing in his own defense except that the charges were not true."[114] Despite their Catharist inclinations, the accused heretics all defended themselves not as Cathars but as Catholics. They argued, not that it is unjust for the inquisitors to prosecute Cathars, but that it is unjust for them to prosecute particular individuals as members of this sect. They thus acknowledged, implicitly, that, whatever their own religious beliefs, Cathars are not rhetorically defensible as Cathars, nor are inquisitors rhetorically assailable as inquisitors, but, on the contrary, that only false denials of Catharism can be used to support the one and to attack the other.

As the accused parties denied that they were heretics, their fellow citizens supported their repudiations of guilt. When del Soler argued his case before the bishop, he brought with him what Pelhisson describes as "a number of burghers and important people, all of whom took his part and raised violent and clamorous outcry against the other man."[115] When Tesseire was brought before the inquisitors, it is noted, similarly, that "he had many of the important heretical sympathizers of the town to defend him" and that these sympathizers defended his orthodoxy.[116] As the accused heretics did not deny their heresy

---

111. "The Chronicle of William Pelhisson," p. 214; "Quod audientes nomines de villa multum fuerunt inde perturbati et commoti," Guillaume Pelhisson, *Chronique*, pp. 40–42.

112. "The Chronicle of William Pelhisson," p. 210; "cum nullus, ut ipsi asserebant, inter eos esset talis," Guillaume Pelhisson, *Chronique*, p. 42.

113. "The Chronicle of William Pelhisson," p. 213; "Domini, audite me. Ego non sum hereticus," Guillaume Pelhisson, *Chronique*, p. 52.

114. "The Chronicle of William Pelhisson," p. 215; "Ipse vero negavit omnia, nihil aliud dicens ad sui defensionem, nisi quod non erat verum," Guillaume Pelhisson, *Chronique*, p. 58.

115. "The Chronicle of William Pelhisson," p. 212; "quamplurimos burgenses et maiores de villa et advocatos, qui omnes stabant pro illo, et contra alium potenter et clamose iangulabant," Guillaume Pelhisson, *Chronique*, p. 50.

116. "The Chronicle of William Pelhisson," p. 213; "multos de maioribus ville hereticalibus habuit defensores," Guillaume Pelhisson, *Chronique*, p. 52.

because they considered themselves to be orthodox, Pelhisson makes clear, neither did their supporters second their statements because they believed them to be Catholic. The partisans of the heretics are themselves described as "believers of heretics" (*credentes hereticorum*) and as "heretical sympathizers" or "heretical persons" (*hereticales*), as if in confirmation of the Church's contention that those who defend heretics are heretics in their own right. They are depicted as people who, though they might present themselves as championing the suspects altruistically because they believe them to be innocent of heresy, actually champion them selfishly because they know the accused—and themselves—to be guilty of this crime. When these suspects' guilt was revealed to all, their supporters were troubled, not because they knew themselves to have been duped by their pretense of Catholicism, but because they knew themselves no longer able to dupe others as to their own orthodoxy. After del Soler fled to Lombardy, Pelhisson notes, "his partisans stayed behind in confusion."[117] After Sans was burned at the stake, Pelhisson comments, "many of the people were both terrified and apprehensive; knowing themselves to be guilty, they were grievously afraid for themselves."[118] After Tesseire confessed to heresy, "all who had previously defended him were now covered with confusion, and they damned and cursed him, at least as far as words go."[119] Tesseire's former partisans, Pelhisson suggests, condemned him only publicly, with their words, out of a desire to establish their own orthodoxy to others, and not privately, with their hearts, out of a genuine repugnance to heresy. Like the accused parties, their supporters know of no way to defend someone accused of heresy except by rejecting the charge.

When the heretics and their supporters were not denying the crime of which they and their fellow citizens were accused, they were attempting to divert attention from this crime by accusing the inquisitors themselves of various misdeeds, whether judicial or political. After Guilhem Arnaut had aroused the wrath of the Toulousans through his prosecutions of heretics, Pelhisson tells us that Raimon VII, the count of Toulouse and Saint-Gilles, "came to the

---

117. "The Chronicle of William Pelhisson," p. 212; "adiutores eius remanserunt confusi," Guillaume Pelhisson, *Chronique*, p. 50.

118. "The Chronicle of William Pelhisson," p. 215; "Semel expavefacti et tremebundi plures de populo scientes se reos timebant valde sibi," Guillaume Pelhisson, *Chronique*, p. 60. This passage occurs in MSS A and C.

119. "The Chronicle of William Pelhisson," p. 214; "Tunc omnes qui eum ante defendebant confusi confusi et condempnaverunt eum publice ad minus verbotenus et maledixerunt," Guillaume Pelhisson, *Chronique*, p. 56. This passage occurs in MSS A and C.

inquisitors to ask them, out of consideration for him, to call a halt for a time, adducing his trifling reasons."[120] Pelhisson does not say what Raimon's reasons were, apparently judging them too frivolous to bear mentioning, but Gregory IX's bull of November 18, 1234, summarizes the objections the count made to the inquisitors. According to the pope, Raimon protested many of the judicial innovations identified with the Inquisition, such as concealing the charges made against the suspect, hiding the names of the witnesses who had made these charges, and restricting the suspect's rights to legal counsel and appeal. Raimon complains that some of the inquisitors prosecute his subjects "in accordance with their will, not in accordance with the judgment of reason," and that in doing so "they seem to labor more to bring the faithful to error than to lead the heretics back to the conception of truth."[121] Whatever merit an outside reader might find in Raimon's objections to the inquisitors, Pelhisson finds these complaints to be nothing more than ruses intended to prevent the inquisitors from routing heretics. When Toulousans were not citing legal quibbles to hinder the friars, Pelhisson alleges, they were inflaming political passions to achieve the same ends. As Tesseire was appealing to the people for support, for example, he informed them not only that he was innocent, despite the inquisitors' allegations, but that "They can accuse you as well as me. Look out for yourselves, for these wicked men want to ruin the town and honest men and take the town away from its lord."[122] As Sans was addressing the people, he too objected, "Look, all of you, at the injustice they do to me and the town, because I am a good Christian and believe in the Roman faith!"[123] For these suspects, the inquisitors are not accidentally prosecuting innocent persons in order to realize the universal, pastoral goals of the Church, but intentionally prosecuting "honest men" in order to achieve the local,

---

120. "The Chronicle of William Pelhisson," p. 217; "Qui veniens rogavit inquisitores quod cessarent ad tempus amore ipsius, ponens suas frivolas rationes," Guillaume Pelhisson, *Chronique*, p. 68.

121. "proprium sequentes arbitrium, non judicium rationis," *Registres de Grégoire IX: Recueil de bulles de ce pape, publiées ou analysées d'après les manuscrits originaux du Vatican*, ed. Lucien Auvray (Paris: Albert Fontemoing, 1896), vol. 1, no. 2218; "ut laborare potius videantur fideles trahere ad errorem, quam hereticos ad notitiam reducere veritatis," ibid.

122. "The Chronicle of William Pelhisson," p. 213; "Et ita poterunt vobis obicere sicut mihi. Cavete vobis, quia isti mali homines villam et probos homines volunt destruere et auferre villam domino," Guillaume Pelhisson, *Chronique*, p. 52.

123. "The Chronicle of William Pelhisson," p. 215; "Videte omnes quam iniuriam faciunt mihi et ville, quia ego bonus christianus sum, et credo fidem romanum," Guillaume Pelhisson, *Chronique*, p. 60.

political goals of the northern French lords. Pelhisson himself recounts how
the French authorities residing in the region of Carcassonne refused to burn
a condemned heretic because they feared that war would come of it, thus giving indirect voice to the southerners' association of the inquisitors' role in
repressing heretics, and the Frenchmen's role in repressing Occitania. While
the alliance between the Church and the French crown was real, however, this
reference to the Frenchmen at Carcassonne constitutes the only acknowledgment of the political circumstances surrounding the inquisitors' activities in
the chronicle. As Pelhisson sees it, the friars were pure in their motives in
attempting to eradicate heresy, and whoever complained of their extraordinary
judicial privileges or political support was merely seeking to distract attention
from their legitimate religious concerns.

Finally, when the Toulousans and their neighbors did not defend themselves
and their companions against accusations of heresy by denials or diversionary
counteraccusations, they did so by ambiguous words which, though literally
truthful, gave a false impression of innocence. Tesseire, for example, declared,
"Lords, listen to me! I am not a heretic, for I have a wife and I sleep with her.
I have sons, I eat meat, and I lie and swear, and I am a faithful Christian."[124]
On one level, Tesseire seemed to establish his innocence of heresy by asserting
that he engages in a series of behaviors contrary to the heretical faith. On
another level, however, Tesseire only appeared to proclaim this innocence.
Though a "heretic" was, broadly speaking, any adherent of a heterodox faith,
such a person was also, we recall, more narrowly defined, a perfected member
of the Cathar sect. When Tesseire claimed not to be a heretic, he may have been
doing no more than claiming not to be a such a consecrated individual, while
leaving open the possibility that he was one of their believers. When he recalled
that he slept with his wife, ate meat, lied, and swore, he may merely have been
recalling that he did not pursue the ascetic lifestyle required of the perfected
heretics, though, again, leaving open the option that he was fulfilling the more
lax requirements for one of their followers. When he declared that he was a
"faithful Christian," he did not specify what he understood by this phrase, so
that he may merely have affirmed that he was a faithful Cathar. It was of
such duplicities of words among the Cathars that Bernard Gui, the fourteenth-

---

124. "The Chronicle of William Pelhisson," p. 213; "Domini, audite me. Ego non sum
hereticus, quia uxorem habeo, et cum ipsa iaceo, et filios habeo, et carnes comedo, et men-
tior et iuro, et fidelis sum Christianus," Guillaume Pelhisson, *Chronique,* p. 52.

century inquisitor of Toulouse and contributor of an addendum to Pelhisson's chronicle, would warn other friars in his handbook for inquisitors. "Because of misleading expressions and terms, to inexperienced persons and to laymen they seem at first sight to profess the true faith," Gui cautions his readers.[125] "Yet, when the truth is more attentively tasted, sought for, and searched out, it appears that they utter all the foregoing in duplicity and falsehood . . . in order thus to deceive simple people and even highly educated men if they happen to be inexperienced."[126] If, on one level, Tesseire appeared to profess the "true faith" of Catholicism and, on a second level, only used "misleading expressions and terms" to give such an impression, on a third level he may have been mocking that "true faith" to which he purports to adhere. Identifying Catholics as people who enjoyed sexual intercourse, meat, lies, and oaths and heretics as people who refrained from these indulgences, Tesseire may have been making a jab at the inferiority of worldly Catholics to saintly Cathars, though he jocularly identified himself with worldliness as well. Pelhisson prefaces Tesseire's words by characterizing them as those of "wicked Joan," and in their ambiguity they may have been perceived as yet another means to avoid admitting to heresy.[127]

On rare occasions in Pelhisson's chronicle, heretics are depicted as eschewing denials, diversions, and duplicities of speech in favor of an open and honest confession of their heretical identity, yet Pelhisson responds to these individuals not with bafflement at their courage, as Everwin did before him, but with jubilation at their exposure as heretics. After Tesseire was imprisoned, he encountered some perfected heretics brought in from another city and became hereticated at their hands. As these heretics were being taken out to be examined, Pelhisson relates, "Joan said that he wished to go with them and to follow their way in all things," and he was condemned along with them.[128]

125. "Bernard Gui's Description of Heresies," In Wakefield and Evans, pp. 373–445, at 380; "palliatis verbis et vocabulis, prima facie videntur inexpertis hominibus et laycis confiteri veram fidem," Bernard Gui, Manuel de l'Inquisiteur, ed. and trans. Guillaume Mollat, (Paris: Champion, 1926–27), vol. 1, p. 14.

126. "Bernard Gui's Description of Heresies," pp. 380–81; "cum tamen, veritate diligentius examinata, inquisita et comperta, omnia predicta dicant in dupplicitate et falsitate secundum intellectum suum superius expressatum et declaratum, ut ita fallant simplices et etiam magnos litteratos inexpertos," Bernard Gui, Manuel de l'Inquisiteur, vol. 1, p. 16.

127. "The Chronicle of William Pelhisson," p. 213; "maledictus Iohannes," Guillaume Pelhisson, Chronique, p. 52.

128. "The Chronicle of William Pelhisson," p. 214; "dixit Iohannes quod ipse volebat exire cum eis et viam eorum sequi in omnibus," Guillaume Pelhisson, Chronique, p. 54.

With Tesseire finally revealed as the heretic he always was and burned at the stake without public protest, Pelhisson concludes, "In all things, blessed be God, who delivered the friars who were in grave danger and magnified his faith in the face of his enemies. Hence, Catholics rejoiced greatly, and heretical sympathizers were confused and refuted."[129] In another case, an old woman on her deathbed, thinking herself to be addressing a Cathar bishop instead of a Catholic prelate, promised her interlocutor, "My lord, what I say I believe, and I shall not change my commitment out of concern for the miserable remnant of my life."[130] Impenitent in her heresy, even when the bishop's Catholic identity was revealed to her, she allowed herself to be carried off to her death in her bed. Again, Pelhisson writes, "God performed these works on the first feast day of the Blessed Dominic, to the glory and praise of his name and of his servant, the Blessed Dominic, to the exaltation of the faith and to the discomfiture of the heretics and their believers."[131] Far from being troubled by these persons' apparent heroism, the friar rejoices in their confessions and the ensuing executions because he interprets the confessions as the means by which God makes manifest these individuals' heresy to all and thus justifies the inquisitors' actions in the eyes of the public. He delights in the confessions because "heretical persons" can no longer claim that there are no heretics among them and oppose the inquisitors with this excuse. Depicting the heretics as dissimulators of heresy, Pelhisson portrays the friars as unmaskers of these dissimulations, so that the heretics' avowals reflect not so much the bravery of those who will go to the stake for their faith as the acuity of those who know how to consign them to such a fate.

If, as we have seen, the secretiveness imputed to heretics becomes evidence of heresy, the authorities appointed in matters of faith can be said to be triumphing over these sectaries by transforming their means of concealing themselves into a means of exposure, but even as the original epistemological

129. "The Chronicle of William Pelhisson," p. 214; "Per omnia benedictus Deus qui liberavit Fratres qui erant in magno periculo, et magnificavit fidem suam coram inimicis suis. Unde gavisi sunt valde catholici, et hereticales confusi et confutati," Guillaume Pelhisson, *Chronique*, p. 56. This passage appears only in MS A of the text.

130. "The Chronicle of William Pelhisson," p. 216; "Ita credo, domine, sicut dico, nec propter modicam vitam miseram meam mutabo propositum," Guillaume Pelhisson, *Chronique*, p. 62.

131. "The Chronicle of William Pelhisson," p. 216; "Hec operatus est Dominus in prima sollempnitate beati Dominici, ad gloriam et laudem nominis sui et servi sui, beati Dominici, et exaltationem fidei et depressionem hereticorum et credencie eorumdem," Guillaume Pelhisson, *Chronique*, p. 64.

problem is solved, further difficulties arise. As one becomes persuaded of a heretic's guilt, not by what one knows about him but by what one does not know, the proof of his guilt lies, not in evidence acquired through one's own experience, but in knowledge attained through one's reading of another's text. An individual is accused of heresy, perhaps because he actually is a heretic, perhaps because he is falsely believed to be a heretic, or perhaps merely because someone is seeking his death. Once he has been accused, every effort the man makes to defend himself of this charge can be construed as evidence against him. He denies his heresy, but heretics are well known for such denials; he makes counteraccusations to explain why he has been accused, but heretics have been shown to attempt such diversions; he professes his Catholic faith, but every superficially orthodox word or phrase he uses can be interpreted as containing a hidden, heterodox meaning. As it is impossible to prove that one does not have a secret to someone who believes that one does, it becomes impossible for the accused heretic to prove that he is not a heretic to authorities who believe that he is legitimately charged.

3

A GARDEN, LOCKED AND FORTIFIED

Heresy, Secrecy, and Troubadour Lyric

Though their views are largely forgotten by scholars nowadays, for many years belletrists like Eugène Aroux, Joséphin Péladan, Otto Rahn, and Denis de Rougemont argued for an essential connection between the Cathar heretics who flourished in Occitania during the High Middle Ages and the troubadour poets who also prospered in this region for much of this time.[1] These authors point to circumstantial evidence which shows heretics and troubadours to have crossed paths in the twelfth

---

1. See Eugène Aroux, *Dante hérétique, socialiste et révolutionnaire: Révélations d'un catholique sur le Moyen Age* (Paris: Renouard, 1854), and *L'Hérésie de Dante, demontrée par Francesca de Rimini, devenue un moyen de propagande vaudoise; et coup-d'oeil sur les romans du St.-Graal* (Paris: Renouard, 1857); Joséphin Péladan, *Le Secret des troubadours: De Parsifal à Don Quichotte* (Caen: Ker-Ys, 1906); and Otto Rahn, *Kreuzzug gegen den Gral: Die Tragödie des Katharismus* (Freiburg-im-Breisgau: Urban Verlag, 1933); and Denis de Rougemont, *L'Amour et l'Occident* (Paris: Librairie Plon, 1939), trans. Montgomery Belgion as *Love in the Western World* (New York: Harcourt Brace and Co., 1940; rpt. New York: Schocken Books, 1983). See also, more derivatively, Gérard de Sède, *Le Trésor cathare* (Paris: Julliard, 1966), and Jean Blum, *Mystère et message des Cathares* (Monaco: Editions du Rocher, 1989). The earliest advocates of the Cathar thesis followed C. C. Fauriel, *Histoire de la Poésie provençale* (Paris: B. Duprat, 1846), who claims, with reference to Folquet de Marseille, that only one troubadour sided with the crusaders against the Albigensians (vol. 2, p. 214). Otto Rahn was a colonel in the SS, and his influential volume intersected with the Nazis' gnostic or mythological interests, as well as with their political ambitions in Occitania. For a discussion of Rahn's thesis, see Pierre Breillat, "Le Graal et les Albigeois," *Revue du Tarn*, n.s. 10 (1944): 458–70, and 11 (1945): 99–109 and Christian Bernardac, *Montségur et le Graal: Le Mystère Otto Rhan [sic]* (Paris: Editions France-Empire, 1994). See also René Nelli, "Du Catharisme à l'amour provençal (d'après M. Briffault)," *Revue de synthèse* 64 (1948): 31–38; "Les Troubadours et le catharisme," *Cahiers d'Etudes Cathares* 1 (1949): 18–22; *L'Erotique de troubadours* (Toulouse:

century, when many of the poets' patrons were known to be of heretical sympathies, and in the thirteenth century, when many of these supporters opposed the Albigensian crusaders and, thus, aligned themselves, to some extent, with the heterodox.[2] To those who protest that troubadour poems exhibit few, if any, overt references to heresy which might prove their authors' affiliation with the deviant creed, these writers respond that the troubadours, wary of persecution for their heretical beliefs, planted in their verses numerous covert references for audiences who knew how to decipher them. If the troubadours idealize their beloved lady and claim that it is only through her that they will acquire joy, refinement, and salvation, it is, according to these writers, because the lady represents their heretical church and because it is only through this church that they count on obtaining these benefits. If the troubadours refuse to name their lady and recourse to pseudonymous *senhals* in order to obscure

---

Privat, 1963), esp. pp. 221–46; "Le Catharisme vu à travers les troubadours," *Cahiers de Fanjeaux,* vol. 3, *Cathares en Languedoc* (Toulouse: Privat, 1968), pp. 177–97; and "Introduction" in *Ecrivains anti-conformistes du Moyen Age occitan,* vol. 2, *Hérétiques et Politiques,* (Paris: Phébus, 1977), pp. 9–31; Lucia Varga, "Peire Cardinal était-il hérétique?" *Revue de l'Histoire des Religions* 117 (juin 1938): 205–31; and Charles Camproux, "La Mentalité 'spirituelle' chez Peire Cardenal," *Cahiers de Fanjeaux,* vol. 10, *Franciscains d'Oc, Les Spirituels, ca. 1280–1324* (Toulouse: Privat, 1975), pp. 287–313. For a discussion of Catharism and the troubadours in the light of Nelli's work, see Maurice de Gandillac et al., "Débat autour du catharisme et de l'amour courtois," in *Entretiens sur la Renaissance du 12e siècle,* ed. Maurice de Gandillac and Edouard Jeauneau (Cerisy-la-Salle, 21–30 juillet 1965) (La Haye: Mouton, 1968), pp. 437–48. See also Joseph Garreau, "Hérésie et Politique chez Guilhem Figueria et Peire Cardinal," *Kentucky Romance Quarterly* 31, no. 3 (1984): 243–49, where Cardinal is characterized as less heretical than "engaged."

2. Peire Vidal sang the praises of Fanjeaux, Laurac, Gaillac, Saissac, and Montréal at a time when all of these fortresses were in the hands of Cathar lords and ladies. Peire d'Avernha spoke of composing a poem at Puivert during the years when the *châtelaine* of that castle is known to have been the Cathar Azalaïs de Carcassonne. Raimon Jordan had a wife who entered a convent of perfected ladies, and Guilhem de Durfort was one of the lords of Fanjeaux during the years when numerous Cathars were inhabiting the city. Azemar Jordan, Guilhem Figueria, Peire Cardinal, and Guilhem de Montanhagol were all attached to Occitan lords who defended their lands against the crusaders and, hence, were all aligned to some degree with the Cathars against whom the crusade was aimed. When Peire Rogier de Mirepoix was mortally wounded in battle, he had himself transported to Fanjeaux so that he could by hereticated, and his son defended the Cathar fortress of Montségur against royal armies. All together, approximately fifteen of the four hundred and sixty troubadours named by Alfred Jeanroy can be identified, on the basis of documentation, with the Cathar heresy, and some of the many others about whom no records survive can be assumed to have been implicated in the illicit faith as well. See Alfred Jeanroy, "Liste bio-bibliographique des troubadours des origines au milieu du XIVe siècle," in *La Poésie lyrique des troubadours* (Toulouse: Edouard Privat, 1934), vol. 1, pp. 236–436. For the best discussion of biographical connections between individual troubadours and Catharism, see Nelli, *L'Erotique des troubadours,* pp. 232–35.

her identity, it is again because the heretical church, represented by this lady, cannot be spoken of publicly. These poets often compose in what is known as *trobar clus*, the "closed" or "obscure" style, according to these authors, because they seek to cloak their true heretical meaning so that it is perceptible only to their fellow heretics. For Aroux, the troubadours and their jongleurs constitute missionaries of their religion, wandering about from castle to town, singing their songs, and revealing the true meaning of their lyrics to the extent to which their auditors appeared receptive to hearing it.[3] For Péladan "the *gay savoir* represented . . . the art of speaking, and, for an era when free speech led to the *in pace* or the stake, the art consisted of speaking without being understood by the profane. . . . He who does not have the right to show his face puts on a mask. That of the *joculator* or jongleur offered itself, excellent for propaganda."[4] For Rougemont "their work possessed an exact double meaning. . . . Symbols were sometimes vehicles of allegory . . . and took on a cryptographic guise."[5] For more conservative authors, like the Rougemont of later years or René Nelli and Lucia Varga, there may not always be a historical connection between the heretics and the troubadours, consciously and intentionally hidden within the ambiguous language of their poetry, but there still exists a spiritual link between these two groups, unconsciously and unintentionally interwoven between its lines. Even if a composer of troubadour *cansos* (or love songs) did not think of himself as a heretic, Rougemont maintains, his inclination to prize the soul over the body, death over life, and spiritual ascent over earthly reality is rooted in a theology more Cathar than Catholic in its foundation. Even if an author of troubadour *sirventes* (or satirical poems) did not profess heterodox beliefs, Nelli and Varga assert, the sharpness of his tone in criticizing the Church or praising a past cultural order, in the wake of the crusade, can be traced to a heterodox sensibility. Whether they find heresy in a poem's hidden content or in its ambiguous coloration, these belletrists believe the banned creed to have had its effect upon contemporaneous verse.

In more recent years, critics have tended to dismiss the possibility of a link between Catharism and troubadour verse, to the point where two new surveys of medieval Occitan poetry do not even bother to refute this notion.[6] Pierre Belperron and Henri Davenson argue that although the Cathars surfaced in the

3. Aroux, *Dante hérétique, révolutionnaire, et socialiste,* p. 14, or *L'Hérésie de Dante,* p. 21.

4. Péladan, *Le Secret des troubadours,* pp. 53–54.

5. Rougemont, *Love in the Western World,* p. 95.

6. F. R. P. Akehurst and Judith M. Davis, *A Handbook of the Troubadours* (Berkeley: University of California, 1995) says little about heresy. In Simon Gaunt and Sarah Kay, eds.,

1140s, the first troubadour with whose works we are familiar, Guilhem, the seventh count of Poitiers and the ninth duke of Aquitaine, preceded their appearance by seventy years and already demonstrated in his verses the characteristics that would later be considered most distinctive to troubadour lyric. Troubadours as important as Jaufre Rudel, Marcabru, and Bernart de Ventadorn likewise flourished well before the spread of heresy in this native land. In addition, these writers observe that whereas the Cathars would become most prominent in the regions of Toulouse, Carcassonne, and Foix, the first troubadours inhabited areas significantly to the north of those districts. Though both heretics and poets are present in medieval Occitania, their more precise temporal and geographical coordinates do not correspond. Even if their origins could be traced to the same time and place, no medieval sources attest to a connection between the Cathar heresy and troubadour lyric. Poets make virtually no mention of the heterodox creed in their songs, and heretics say little about the lyrics of their time, whether in their surviving writings or in their testimony before inquisitors. Catholic clerics, though they were quick to condemn aspects of Occitan culture they found contrary to their orthodox ethos, such as the importance of Jews in public life and the luxuriousness of feminine attire, did not cite the region's verse as one such aspect. Indeed, when the *Canso de la Crozada* depicts an individual's censuring troubadour poetry during a discussion of heresy, it is Raimon Rogier, the count of Foix, notoriously sympathetic toward the Cathars, who criticizes it, and Folquet de Marseille, the former troubadour and current bishop of Toulouse, notoriously antagonistic toward these heretics, who serves as the object of the count's reproach. Most of all, critics of the supposed Cathar source of troubadour lyric emphasize the danger of reading poems esoterically, to find hidden, heretical meanings, when there is no hint in any work from this era that these works were meant to be interpreted in this manner. Though Catholic clerics complain vociferously of

---

The Troubadours: An Introduction (Cambridge: Cambridge University Press, 1999), Michael Routledge devotes some attention to the Albigensian Crusade and its atermath in ch. 6, "The Later Troubadours: '. . . noels digz de nova maestra,'" pp. 99–112, but there is little direct discussion of the relation between heresy and troubadour poetry here or in the volume as a whole. For denials of Cathar influence upon troubadour poetry, see Pierre Belperron, *La Croisade contre les Albigeois et l'union du Languedoc à la France (1209–1249)* (Paris: Plon, 1942), p. 76, and La *"Joie d'Amour": Contribution à l'étude des troubadours et de l'amour courtois* (Paris: Plon, 1948), pp. 220–35; Henri Davenson (Henri-Irenée Marrou), "Denis de Rougemont: *L'Amour et l'Occident*," *Esprit* 7, no. 79 (1 avril 1939): 70–77, "Autour de *L'Amour et l'Occident*," *Esprit* 7, no. 84 (1 septembre 1939): 765–68, and *Les Troubadours* (Paris: Editions du Seuil, 1961), pp. 145–49.

the secretiveness of the heretics, as we have seen, they never identify it with troubadour poems, let alone depict this form of verse in general as a means of heterodox propaganda.

In bringing together heretics and troubadours once more, my purpose is not to argue that the poets had been persuaded or even influenced by the heterodox faith but, rather, to suggest that they came to share the fascination with secretiveness that permeated their culture. For the monks and friars we have considered so far, secretiveness is disturbing because they are outside the secret. As abbots promoting the word of God to an erring flock or as inquisitors summoning malefactors to their tribunals, they see themselves as possessing spiritual authority over these souls, but heretics, who do not acknowledge that authority, conceal themselves from them and hence thwart their efforts at supervision. Through such withdrawal, the heretics express distrust of the clerics' charitable intentions and fear of their salutary corrections, and this wariness only confirms the clerics' suspicions about them. Without any genuine knowledge of what heretics are doing or thinking, the clerics imagine their deeds and thoughts negatively. In their covert meeting places, during their covert rituals, and through their covert words, the heretics, the clerics assume, must be indulging in the darkest and most diabolical of sins. What is hidden (from them) must necessarily be evil, they deduce, because only what is evil would be concealed from their judgment. For the poets we turn to here, however, secretiveness is pleasurable because they are inside the secret. Like the heretics, the poets congregate in unknown locations and engage in unknown acts, but now, it is clear, the lasciviousness that is attributed to them can be assimilated to courtly love. Like the heretics, again, the poets address themselves to a small, chosen audience, which alone will understand and appreciate their works, but now this esotericism can be identified with *trobar clus*. Like heretics, finally, the poets speak with ambiguous words, capable of multiple interpretations.[7] Of Guilhem de Poitiers' oeuvre, in particular, Joseph J. Duggan has written that

---

7. Joan M. Ferrante has pointed out that the tendency of Occitan to abbreviate the Latin words from which its vocabulary derives obliged the same words to carry multiple meanings and that this abundance of homonyms made the language unusually obscure. See Joan M. Ferrante, "Ab joi mou lo vers e'l comens," in *The Interpretation of Medieval Lyric Poetry,* ed. W. T. J. Jackson (New York: Columbia University Press, 1980), pp. 113–41, at p. 113. William D. Paden has maintained that if it is not clear to modern readers whether the love described in these poems is consummated in sexual intercourse, it is because "The language of eroticism in troubadour lyric is distinguished by a pervasive ambiguity of reference which functions on linguistic levels from vocabulary to syntax, and in poetic conventions as well," William D. Paden, *"Utrum Copularentur:* Of *Cors,"* *L'Esprit Créateur* 19 (1979): 70–83, at p. 73.

"scarcely a poem of William's eleven extant pieces is lacking in purposely obscured intentionality or double meanings," and, of troubadour lyric in general, that "ambiguity was . . . not a problem to be surmounted, but a poetic value."[8] Laura Kendrick has gone so far as to cite plays on words and the ambiguity that follows from them as among the most characteristic motifs of these poets, while Aurelio Roncaglia has argued that the elusiveness of this verse, with its abstractions, its enigmas, and its baffling allusions, renders all *trobar clus*.[9] Even as clerics impugn the secretiveness of heretics, as a type of exclusiveness which prevents legitimate ecclesiastical oversight, troubadours affirm their own secretiveness, as a type of exclusiveness which transcends social, literary, and, as we shall see, even religious boundaries.

GUILHEM DE POITIERS

During the lifetime of Guilhem de Poitiers, from 1071 to 1129, the Cathars had not yet established themselves in Occitania, as they are usually believed to have done so in the second half of the twelfth century, but their Manichaean predecessors had already aroused concern among Catholic observers. It was in Aquitaine, the province over which Guilhem ruled, we recall, that Adémar de Chabannes had announced the spread of these dualists fifty-three years before the duke's birth, and it was there that Guilhem V, Guilhem's grandfather, was still attempting to quell the spread of Manichaeans eight years later. There is no mention of heresy's resurfacing in Guilhem's lands during his lifetime and no reason to imagine Guilhem in any way influenced by a heretical cult, yet the troubadour is intrigued by the secrecy which is identified with heretics no less than the clerics who write of them. While ecclesiastics express anxiety at concealment, suspecting the iniquity that lies beneath it, Guilhem expresses delight at the same tendency, interpreting that iniquity as eroticism. Inside the secret's circle, he experiences the exclusiveness of his position as an essential part of his pleasure.

Like heretics as the clerics depict them, Guilhem is drawn to secret spaces, here identified with the female sex or female sexuality.[10] In "Compaigno, non pus

---

8. Joseph J. Duggan, "Ambiguity in Twelfth-Century French and Provençal Literature: A Problem or a Value?" in *Jean Misrahi Memorial Volume,* ed. Hans R. Runte, Henri Niedziekski, and William L. Hendrickson (Columbia, SC: French Literature Publications Co., 1977), pp. 136–49, at p. 144 and p. 145.

9. Laura Kendrick, *The Game of Love: Troubadour Word Play* (Berkeley: University of California Press, 1988); Aurelio Roncaglia, "Trobar clus—discussion aperta," *Cultura neolatina* 29 (1969): 5–53, at p. 6.

10. R. Howard Bloch has already addressed the orientation of medieval lyric poetry, including that of Guilhem de Poitiers, around a lady identified with a hidden, unrepresentable,

mudar qu'eu non m'effrei," Guilhem informs his companions that a lady has
complained to him that her "guardians" "keep her locked up," confining her to
a closed room and even tying her down.[11] In "Companho, tant ai agutz d'avols
conres," the poet proclaims, "I do not like a guarded cunt," which he compares
to a "preserve," the section of a forest kept for the owner's private use.[12] In "Farai
un vers de dreit nien," he announces, in the *tornada* (or concluding stanza), that
he will send his song to one person who will, in turn, send it to another in the
direction of Anjou, "so that she might send me, for her coffer, / the counterkey."[13] Whether the secret space is identified with a chamber "locked up" by
its guardians, a hunting ground patrolled by its proprietors, or a chest secured by
its owners, it represents either the hidden locus within which the lady is confined
by her menfolk or the hidden locus within the lady herself, from which predators
are barred. Far from deterring Guilhem, the prohibition of these locales sparks
his longing, even more than the attractions of the lady herself. In "Farai un vers
de dreit nien," for example, Guilhem identifies as the object of his desire neither
the bodily interior of his lady nor the coffer which presumably represents that
bodily interior but, rather, the copy of the key to that coffer. He identifies as the
object of his desire not the end to which he presumably seeks access but, rather,
the counterfeit means by which he stands to gain access to that end.[14] Guilhem
writes similarly, in "Ab la dolchor del temps novel,"

---

unspeakable absolute; see *Medieval Misogyny and the Invention of Western Romantic Love*
(Chicago: University of Chicago Press, 1991). A. R. Press has also addressed this issue in "The
Theme of Concealed Love in Two French Poets of the Twelfth Century," in *Voices of
Conscience: Essays on Medieval and Modern French Literature in Memory of James D. Powell
and Rosemary Hodgins* (Philadelphia: Temple University Press, 1977), pp. 119–30, though I
would differ with this author's distinction of a negatively inflected "concealed love" and a positively viewed "secrecy-in-love."

11. "gardadors," in "Compaigno, non pus mudar qu'eu non m'effrei," *The Poetry of
William VII, Count of Poitiers, IX Duke of Aquitaine*, ed. and trans. Gerald A. Bond (New
York: Garland Publishing Co., 1982), pp. 6–9, v. 3; "la teno esserrada," ibid., v. 5.

12. "No m'zauta cons gardatz," in "Companho, tant ai agutz d'avols conres," ibid., pp.
10–13, v. 5; "un deveis," ibid., v. 14.

13. "Que·m tramezes del sieu estui / La contraclau," in "Farai un vers de dreit nien," ibid.,
pp. 14–17, vv. 47–48, translation modified.

14. This "counterkey" has been interpreted both literally, as the key to a chastity belt, and
metaphorically, as the key to the poem. See Nicolò Pasero, "'Devinalh,' 'non-senso,' e 'inte-
riorizzazione testuale': osservazioni sui rapporti fra strutture formali e contenuti ideologici
nella poesia provenzale," *Cultura neolatina* 28 (1968): 113–46; and Philippe Ménard, "Sens,
contresens, non-sens, réflexions sur la pièce 'Farai un vers de dreyt nien' de Guillaume IX,"
in *Mélanges de Langue et de littérature occitanes en hommage à Pierre Bec* (Poitiers: Université
de Poitiers, C. E. S. C. M., 1991), pp. 338–48.

> I still remember one morning
> When we put an end to war
> And when she gave me a gift so great:
> Her intimacy and her ring;
> God let me yet live long enough
> That I might have my hands underneath her cloak![15]

When Guilhem prays to God that he "might have [his] hands underneath her cloak," he begs not that he might touch a particular part of the lady's body but merely that he might venture underneath her cloak or outer garment. He envisions the cloak which serves as a barrier between the lady's body and the outside perception of that body; he envisions his hands slipping underneath that cloak and thus transgressing the barrier to reach that which others do not perceive; and it is this visual image, of his hands underneath the textile screen, that he finds exciting. What is erotic in these verses is not the noun of the lady's flesh, which is never mentioned, but, rather, the preposition "underneath" (*soz*), because this preposition symbolizes the poet's ability to attain that which is veiled from him. If one understands intimacy as access to that from which others are barred, this preposition stands out because it represents that intimacy. Whereas the clerics, appalled by the wickedness of those who congregate in secret spaces, condemn such people and attempt to draw them out of these sites, Guilhem, enticed by the eroticism he identifies with these areas, condemns those who would bar that entry and seeks to enter them himself.

Like the heretics, who are said to perform foul and unspeakable deeds in the secret locales in which they assemble, Guilhem depicts himself as engaging in illicit activities in such closed spaces, though he rejoices in their occurrence. In "Farai un vers, pos mi sonhel," he recounts how, dressed as a pilgrim, he is accosted by two ladies, identified at first as the wives of Lord Guari and Lord Bernart and later as Lady Aignés and Lady Hernessen. When Guilhem responds to the ladies' greeting with gibberish, Aignés informs Hernessen that they have found what they were looking for in this "mute"[16] and that they should give him lodging. She explains the reason for her satisfaction with him

---

15. "Enquer me menbra d'un mati / Que nos fezem de guera fi / E que·m donet un don tan gran: / Sa drudari'e son anel; / Enquer me lais Dieus viure tan / C'aia mas mans soz so mantel," in "Ab la dolchor del temps novel," *Poetry of William VII*, pp. 36–39, vv. 19–24, translation modified.

16. "Farai un vers, pos mi sonelh," ibid., pp. 18–23; "mutz," ibid., v. 34.

by stating, "Never through him will our secret / Be known."[17] Suspecting that
Guilhem may be "crafty"[18] and only pretending to be mute, however, the
ladies bring out a red cat with whose sharp claws they rake his naked body.
When the poet does not move his tongue, Aignés is persuaded that his silence
is not feigned and recommends that they prepare, literally, "for a bath / And
rest" and, figuratively, "for dalliance / And pleasure."[19] Once again, female
sexuality is identified with a secret space. The ladies are said to take Guilhem
from the open, public road where they found him and lead him to a tower,
where one of them "places [him] at the hearth in her chamber," that is, in a
closed, private room.[20] In this chamber, the ladies ply Guilhem with capons,
wine, and pepper, all foods believed to be conducive to sexual passion, and
they have him bathe—again a practice regularly undertaken in preparation for
a sexual encounter. The poet relates of the ladies, "One of them took me under
her cloak," as he dreams that the lady in "Ab la dolchor del temps novel" will
do, and thus allows him access to an intimacy similar to that of other verses.[21]
This secret space, like the secret spaces which the clerics describe as the locus
for "debauchery" and "abominations and crimes," is dramatized as the site of
forbidden, but highly pleasurable, carnal acts.

Finally, like the heretics, Guilhem seems to be saying one thing when he is
actually saying another. In "Companho, farai un vers tot convinen," he asserts
that he owns two horses, both of which are "good and brave in battle and worthy" but which do not tolerate each other.[22] He relates, of one of these horses,
that it is the swiftest of the mountain steeds but has recently become "so wild
and savage / that it refuses to carry [the equipment]," and of the other, that

17. ". . . ja per lui nostre conseilh / Non er sabutz," ibid., vv. 35–36.
18. "enginhos," ibid., v. 50.
19. "del bainh . . . / E del sojorn," ibid., vv. 75–76. Bond notes, "Although *bainh* and
sojorn literally mean 'bath' and 'rest,' there is ample evidence of the extended sense 'pleasure'
and 'fun' peculiar to OPr," ibid., p. 67, n. 75.
20. "E mes m'en la cambr'al fornel," ibid., v. 38.
21. "La una·m prese sotz son mantel," ibid., v. 37.
22. "Bon . . . ez ardit per armas e valen," in "Companho, farai un vers tot convinen,"
Poetry of William VII, pp. 2–5, v. 8. For detailed commentary of this poem, see Rita Lejeune,
"L'Extraordinaire insolence du troubadour Guillaume IX d'Aquitaine," in *Mélanges de
Langue et de littérature médiévales offerts à Pierre Le Gentil*, ed. Jean Dufournet and Daniel
Poirion (Paris: SEDES et CDU réunies, 1973), pp. 485–503. Allison Goddard Elliot provides
a useful reading of Guilhem's self-presentation as a poet in this poem in "The Manipulative
Poet: Guilhem IX and the 'Fabliau of the Red Cat,'" *Romance Philology* 38, no. 3 (February
1985): 293–99, as does David Rollo in "Sexual Escapades and Poetic Process: Three Poems by
William IX of Aquitaine," *Romanic Review* 81, no. 3 (May 1990): 293–311.

he gave to its master when it was still a grazing foal, "But I still retained something for myself through an agreement / that, if he kept it for a year, I would
keep it for a hundred."[23] Guilhem concludes of these two valiant but unruly
mounts, "If I could tame them to my liking / I would never want to take my
equipment elsewhere."[24] On the most literal level of the poem, Guilhem is
speaking of two steeds which he has difficulty controlling and bringing
together. On another, more figurative level, he indicates that he is speaking of
two women, identified by modern critics as Aignés de Gimel and Arsen de
Nieul, whom he is struggling to master and reconcile. In the eighth of the nine
stanzas, Guilhem declares, "I don't know with which I should remain, Lady
Aignés or Lady Arsen," and in the final stanza he boasts, "I own the castle of
Gimel and its command / And because of Niol I act proud toward everyone; /
For both are sworn and pledged to me by sacred oath."[25] If the horses are two
mistresses, the "battle" in which these steeds have proved themselves so worthy is lovemaking, and the "equipment" they bear his own body. Because the
castles with which these ladies are identified are located at opposite ends of
Guilhem's lands, Gimel in the southern Limousin and Niol (or Nieul) north-
west of Limoges, some critics believe that the poet is asserting a dominance
at once sexual, over the women of his vassals, and political, over the lands
within his realm.[26] On another, even more figurative level, some think
Guilhem is speaking not so much of two actual, historical women as of two
abstract, philosophical qualities, whether they be chivalry and courtliness,
masculinity and femininity, or Dionysian rhapsody and Apollonian restraint.[27]

23. ". . . tan fers et salvatge que de bailar si defen," "Companho, farai un vers tot convinen," v. 15; "Pero si·m retinc ieu tant de covenen / Que s'il lo teni'un an, qu'ieu lo tengues
mas de sen," ibid., v. 21.

24. "Si·ls pogues adomesgar a mon talen, / Ja no volgr' aillors mudar mon garnimen,"
ibid., vv. 10–11.

25. "E no sai ab cal me tenha, / de n'Ancnes ho de n'Arsen," ibid., v. 24. "De Gimel ai lo
castel e·l mandamen, / E per Niol fauc ergueill a tota gen; / C'ambedui me son jurat e plevit
per sagramen," ibid., vv. 25–27.

26. Judith M. Davis, for one, has denied that any deeper meaning exists in this poem
besides this comic affirmation of the *droit du seigneur*, see "A Fuller Reading of Guillaume
IX's 'Compahno, Faray un vers . . . convinen,'" *Romance Notes* 16, no. 2 (Winter 1975):
445–49.

27. See, respectively, Leo Pollmann, *Die Liebe in der hochmittelalterlichen Literatur
Frankreichs* (Frankfurt-am-Main: Vittorio Klostermann, 1966); Charles Camproux, "Faray un
vers *tot* covinen," in *Mélanges de Langue et de littérature du Moyen Age et de la Renaissance
offerts à Jean Frappier* (Genève: Droz, 1970), vol. 1, pp. 159–72; and Christopher Kertesz, "A
Full Reading of Guillaume IX's 'Companho, Farai un vers . . . covinen,'" *Romance Notes* 12,
no. 2 (Spring 1971): 461–65.

The poem's opening verses do seem to provide a clue as to how the work should be read:

> Comrades, I shall do a song that's very well made
> And in it there will be more folly than sense
> And it will be a total mixture of love, joy, and youthfulness.
> Hold him for a rustic who does not understand it
> Or who does not willingly take it to heart.[28]

These lines suggest an opposition between one group of people who are not "rustic" and who are, therefore, presumably "courtly," who understand and learn the poem by heart, and who can appreciate both the elegance of the song and the "folly," "love, joy, and youthfulness" it contains, and another group of people who are "rustics," who do not comprehend or memorize the poem, and who therefore cannot enjoy the qualities it contains. These verses suggest, in other words, a contrast between a cultivated elite capable of understanding and appreciation and vulgar masses possessing no such abilities. If the heretics' words resemble Guilhem's, it is in the secret meaning they reserve for an esoteric few, capable of discerning what others cannot detect, whether one conceives of this select audience as a heretical cult or a courtly coterie.

Ultimately, in Guilhem's poetry, the excessiveness of the erotic, which necessarily transgresses social boundaries, is related to the excessiveness of his signification. As the clerics see it, there should be a direct relation between the spoken word and the mental conception prompted by that word—that is, between signifier and signified. If they take exception to heretics' manner of speaking, it is because they suspect that such a direct relation does not exist in their utterances, so that they say one thing and their listeners understand another. The resultant confusion is, for the clerics, a source of unqualified distress. As Guilhem sees it, however, there is no need for so consistent a connection between what is said and what is grasped. When he declares of his poem, "Hold him for a rustic who does not understand it," he proposes a purposeful disjunction between the meaning intended for rough, vulgar audiences and the meaning aimed at more refined, courtly hearers. He is not troubled by the ensuing instability of his poem because he associates the excess of meaning

---

28. "Companho, farai un vers tot convinen / Ez aura·i mais de foudatz no·i a de sen / Ez er totz mesclatz d'amor e de joi e de joven, / E tenhatz lo per vilan qui no l'enten / O qu'ins en son cor volunteriers non l'apren," in "Companho, farai un vers tot covinen," *Poetry of William VII,* vv. 1–5.

which makes the clerics nervous with an excess of eros, energy, and high spirits, indeed, with the very qualities which would become the central values of troubadour poetry. The aspects of "Companho, farai un vers tot covinen" considered most ambiguous, including the identity of the female horses, the nature of the "battle" in which these steeds prove themselves worthy, and the nature of the "equipment" that they bear, are the elements which most lend themselves to an erotic interpretation, with all the exuberance with which eros is linked in this poem. It is not only the potentially erotic referents of these double entendres but the very gesture of the double entrendre itself, suggesting, but never confirming, the presence of an additional, overflowing meaning, which contributes to the excitement of the *canso*. The very "folly" which clerics so often condemn in heresy serves as the source of the jubilation which Guilhem promises in his poem.

If secret spaces are now identified with the female sex and female sexuality, from which unauthorized males are forbidden, and secret deeds with the carnal acts performed within these spaces despite this prohibition, the ladies within whom these spaces and deeds are located are depicted as at once desirous of opening up their bodies to lovers and fearful of the punishment they might suffer as a result. In "Farai un vers, pos me sonhel," as we have seen, the ladies are eager to consort with a lover, though they are married, but they choose what appears to be a mute for their companion and attempt to verify his silence before uniting with him. In "Farai un vers de dreit nien," the lady is ready to allow Guilhem access to her locked coffer, but she is expected not to break open her chest or even to steal the key to its interior but, rather, to send a copy of the key to Guilhem. In all of these poems, the lady, irrepressible, inexhaustible, insatiable in her desires, rebels against her menfolk, who patrol the secret space of her sex and sexuality to keep others from trespassing upon it, and she seeks to grant another, illegitimate man access to this space. At the same time, in the feudal context in which these ladies live, the ladies recognize that since men preside over the open, outside world of the road, they themselves must turn to the closed, inside world of the chamber in order to act as they wish. While men, who are not subject to the power of another sex, can afford to be open about what they do, women, who are subject to the power of men, must conceal their actions. While men are able to possess a single, coherent identity, where they appear as they are, women must possess a double, contradictory identity, where they seem different from what they are. Like the heretics who become secretive because they fear confronting the authority of the Church, the women in Guilhem's poems become secretive because they shrink from defying the

authority of their menfolk. While the clerics are anxious that heretics may succeed in escaping the supervision of the orthodox by keeping the secret of their
heresy, Guilhem is intrigued that these ladies may elude the guardianship of
their men by keeping the secret of their amorous adventures.

Even as the ladies in these poems know that their power resides in secrecy
and silence, they recognize that their male lovers' power lies in openness and
speech. At times, when the poem is narrative in its genre, comic in its sensibility, and carnal in the love it depicts, Guilhem resists the ladies' domination and
speaks openly of their activities. In "Farai un vers, pos mi sonelh," for example,
he announces of Aignés and Hernissen, "How often I screwed them you will
now hear: / One hundred and eighty-eight times!"[29] The shock of Guilhem's
assertion lies not merely in the boast of his prowess in bed but in the speech act
with which he overturns the ladies' domination of him with his own domination of them, repaying their violent testing of his muteness with his own violent destruction of their reputations. With these words, he submits the affair of
a private chamber to the judgment of a public view and, hence, the affair of a
feminine world of secrecy and silence to the judgment of a masculine world of
openness and speech. Similarly, in "Companho, farai un vers tot convinen,"
when Guilhem declares, after various hints as to these two equine ladies' identities, "I don't know with which I should remain, Lady Aignés or Lady Arsen,"
the interest of this statement lies in the speech act with which he reveals his mistresses' names to the "Comrades" and "Knights" addressed in the song[30] and,
hence, with which he subordinates the heterosexual encounters with the two
ladies to a homosocial encounter with these men. In both of these poems, the
climax lies not so much in the act of coitus with women as in the revelation of
this act to other men. Elsewhere, however, when the poem is lyrical in its genre,
courtly in its sensibility, and spiritual in its treatment of love, Guilhem submits
to the lady's dominance and refrains from speaking openly of their love. In
"Mout jauzens me prenc en amar," for example, he affirms,

> If milady wants to grant me her love,
> I am ready to take it and be grateful for it
> And to conceal it and to speak sweetly of it

---

29. "Tant las fotei com auziretz: / Cen e qatre vint et ueit vetz!" in "Farai un vers, pos mi
sonhel," vv. 79–80.

30. "Companho," in "Companho, farai un vers tot covinen," v. 1; "Cavalier," ibid., v. 22,
translation modified.

> And to say and do what pleases her
> And to hold dear her reputation
> And to promote her praise.[31]

In "Pos vezem de novel florir," he insists, likewise, upon the necessity that a refined man be "submissive" and "obeisant" in his love relationships and "that he guard himself from speaking in court / In a boorish way."[32] With these verses, Guilhem depicts the lady as *midons*, the masculine lord to whom he owes fealty and submission. Far from asserting his own dominance over the lady, as he does in the burlesque poems, he affirms that he wants to please her and, as part of that desire to please, to "conceal" her love, "hold dear" her reputation, and "promote" her praise. Instead of bragging of the liaison by naming the ladies with whom he has consorted, as he does in the burlesque poems, he alludes to her in "Pos vezem de novel florir" by the *senhal* (or pseudonym) "Esteve," and in "Ab la dolchor del temps novel" by the *senhal* "Good Neighbor."[33] Whether Guilhem accepts or resists the ladies' demand for silence, he associates the erotic not so much with carnal embraces as with the tension between masculine desire, in its possible legitimacy and overtness, and feminine desire, in its necessary illegitimacy and covertness.

In his poems, Guilhem depicts himself as secretive insofar as he joins ladies in hidden assignations, but ultimately he identifies no more with these ladies than with the menfolk from whom they attempt to hide. He enjoys the position of a feudal lord, in sex, class, and status no different from the ladies' husbands and guardians except in his higher nobility and greater power, but he undermines their authority through his adultery. He champions the ladies, encouraging their resistance to their lords, but he does so not because he sees the world from their angle but because he expects to benefit from their rebellion, as their amorous partner. While the clerics recognize only one code, that of Catholic orthodoxy, whose openness they see as linked to its inherent truthfulness and goodness, and while they refuse to recognize heresy, whose secrecy they see as related to its inherent falsity and wickedness, Guilhem recognizes

---

31. "Si·m vol midons s'amor donar, / Pres suy del penr' e del grazir / E del celar e del blandir / E de sos plazers dir e far / E de son pretz tenir en car / E de son laus enavantir," in "Mout jauzens me prenc en amar," *Poetry of William VII*, pp. 32–35, vv. 37–42.

32. "aclis," in "Pos vezem de novel florir," ibid., pp. 28–31, v. 36; "Obediëns," ibid., v. 30; "E que·s gart en cort de parlar / Vilanamens," ibid., vv. 35–36.

33. "Esteve," in "Pos vezem de novel florir," v. 47. "Bon Vezi," in "Ab la dolchor del temps novel," v. 26.

two codes—one, a dominant, masculine ideology, acknowledged by feudal custom, which asserts the right of men to exclusive access to their wives, and the other, a subversive, feminine creed, acknowledged only later by the legendary courts of love, which asserts the privilege of women to grant access to whomever they wish. While the clerics identify themselves with the one legitimate system of belief and express horror at whatever opposes this system, Guilhem identifies neither with the feudal code of the men nor with the courtly ethos of the women, pursuing, instead, his own idiosyncratic desires. It is insofar as he situates himself as a third party, outside the binary opposition of the dominant and the subordinate groups, that he is capable of experiencing the tension between them with pleasure rather than with anxiety.

TROBAR CLUS

During the same decades that the Manichaeans and the Cathars were said to be developing their secretive teachings, numerous troubadours were turning to the no less secretive poetics of *trobar clus*.[34] As we have seen, these heretics were believed to restrict their deepest mysteries to fully initiated members of their faith.[35] It was only after they had gained the sympathy of their auditors through the apparent holiness of their comportment that they were thought to introduce them to the basic dualism of the heterodox creed. And it was only after particular disciples had demonstrated an attachment to the heterodox faith and, even more, after they had completed the year-long *absentia* (or trial period of perfected life) that they were taught how the soul had come to be entrapped within the material body. Withholding their doctrines from their own believers, the heretics were said to withhold them all the more from Catholics and, especially, from Catholic clerics. Citing Christ's injunction not

---

34. On *trobar clus* in general, see Erich Köhler, "Zum 'trobar clus' der Trobadours," *Romanische Forschungen* 64 (1952): 71–101, rpt. *Trobadorlyrik und der höfische Roman* (Berlin: Rütten und Loening, 1962), pp. 133–52; Alberto del Monte, *Studie sulla poesia ermetica medievale* (Napoli: Giannini, 1953); Leo Pollmann, *"Trobar Clus": Bibelexegese und hispano-arabische Literatur* (Münster: Aschendorff, 1965); Aurelio Roncaglia, "Trobar clus—discussion aperta"; Ulrich Mölk, *Trobar clus, trobar leu: Studien zur Dichtungstheorie der Trobadors* (München: Wilhelm Fink Verlag, 1968); Linda M. Paterson, *Troubadours and Eloquence* (Oxford: Clarendon Press, 1975); Simon Gaunt, *Troubadours and Irony* (Cambridge: Cambridge University Press, 1989), especially the chapters on Raimbaut and Giraut; and Amelia E. Van Vleck, *Memory and Re-Creation in Troubadour Lyric* (Berkeley: University of California Press, 1991), especially pp. 133–63.

35. On the Cathars' instruction of their disciples, see Lambert, *Medieval Heresies*, pp. 118–21.

to give what is holy to dogs or to cast pearls before swine, the heretics were said to keep their beliefs hidden from the masses, who were not yet fully prepared to receive them and remained contemptuous of their truths. Even as the heretics were cultivating their esoteric dogma, the troubadours were cultivating an esoteric poetics. Guilhem de Poitiers, in the late eleventh century, had already set into place the distinction between the courtly audience, who understands and appreciates the troubadour's poems and the rustic audience, who fails to grasp the wisdom and joy that these verses offer, and Marcabru, in the early twelfth century, had already established himself as the first genuine practitioner of the closed style. It would not be until the final half of the twelfth century, however, that Peire d'Avernha, Giraut de Bornelh, and, especially, Raimbaut d'Auregna would develop the theory of *trobar clus* and that these poets, together with Arnaut Daniel, would put this theory into practice. Like the heretics as they are depicted in the pages of Catholic writings, the troubadours of the closed style pride themselves on a secretiveness identified not only with hidden places and hidden amorous acts but also with a knowledge imparted to a select few capable of understanding.

The troubadours envision *trobar clus* first of all as a secret space, one that is "closed" (*clus*) and "locked" (*serrat*) so that only the self possesses access to it. Peire d'Avernha writes in "Be m'es plazen," for example

> I prefer a locked, fortified garden,
> from which nothing can be stolen from me,
> to a hundred parcels of land
> up in the open plain,
> where another might own them and I only look at them.[36]

36. ". . . am un ort / serrat e fort / qu'hom ren no m'en puesca emblar / que cent parras / sus en puegz plas: / qu'autre las tenh'ez ieu las guar," in "Be m'es plazen," Peire d'Avernha, *Liriche,* ed. Alberto del Monte (Torino: Loescher-Chiantore, 1955), pp. 77–87, vv. 25–30. Manuscript M reads "claus ben" for v. 26. Del Monte comments, "questa è una tipica espressione del *trobar clus,* del poetare ermetico. . . . Il tema della canzone appare allora l'abbandono degli amori empirici e la dedizione alla propria solitudine spirituale, all'amore per l'amore, come pura nostalgia, culto interiore e norma di vita" (pp. 83–84). On these verses in particular, Del Monte notes that although the garden may be interpreted as an aristocratic, courtly class, contrasted with the people, it is better interpreted as a symbol of "la realtà sentimentale del poeta nella sua solitaria interiorità, dalla quale nessuno può sottrarre nulla e ch'è più vera degl'ingannevoli possessi nella realtà esteriore" (p. 85). In "Über die religiöse Lyrik der Troubadours," *Neuphilologische Mitteilungen* 38 (1937): 224–42, Dimitri Scheludko interprets the poet as expressing the topos of *contempus mundi*, while Köhler sees him as calling into question the courtly ethos. In *Troubadours and Eloquence,* Paterson writes of this poem

He writes in the same poem,

> To me it is well pleasing
> and fitting
> that one should undertake to sing
> with certain locked and closed words.[37]

With these verses, Peire imagines a space which contains within it something
desirable to others, like the fruits, vegetables, herbs, and flowers of a garden,
but which is "locked," "closed," and "fortified," and like a walled garden, so
that no one might enter and take these riches. Like Guilhem de Poiters, Peire
identifies this space with private property owned by one party and protected
against others. He claims that he prefers a "garden," a relatively small piece of
land, though one presumably filled with cultivated plants, which he owns and
locks up against potential intruders, to a large, wild territory that he does not own
and cannot enter. Like Guilhem, Peire associates this space with feminine sexuality, insofar as it is possessed by one party and protected against others. While
Guilhem has portrayed himself as the trespasser upon other men's sexual terrain,
Peire depicts himself as the guardian of his own particular plot, but both poets
take pleasure in a privileged access to the lady. More explicitly than Guilhem,
Peire connects this land or lady with poetry, insofar as it is possessed by one entity
and protected against others. Peire suggests that the meaning of his works resembles a piece of property or a woman in that it is desired by many but owned by
one, and that he, as the poet, resembles the possessor of these desired objects,
who alone enjoys the right to that which others covet. In order to reserve this
meaning to himself, its legitimate proprietor, he needs to sing "with certain
locked and closed words" and to make his poem resemble a "locked . . . garden"
which will defend this meaning against interlopers as locked and closed walls pro-

---

that "only the theme of love is expressed in blurred, and perhaps mystical terms; there is no
sense that [Peire] clarifies thought, he rather reaches into mystery for an esoteric meaning"
(pp. 210–11). She states, "He has chosen an aristocratic concept of poetry for a small élite: perhaps even solely for himself" (p. 83). In *Memory and Re-Creation*, Van Vleck reads Peire as
resisting the *mouvance* of medieval poetry, the process through which jongleurs and scribes
altered troubadours' words as they repeated them, through his use of the closed style (pp.
150–60).

37. "Be m'es plazen / e cossezen / que om s'ayzina de chantar / ab motz alqus / serratz
e clus," Peire d'Avernha, *Liriche,* vv. 1–5. MS A1 reads "cubertz" in v. 5. Del Monte writes, "Il
poeta è consapevole della singolarità della propria situazione sentimentale, della natura
eccezionale della propria 'rinuncia,' del suo destino lirico. Perciò inizia con un programma di
poesia 'chiusa,' inviolabile al volgo," ibid., p. 84.

tect the contents of a garden from thieves. Giraut de Bornelh describes his poetry with a similar special metaphor. "I join and bind together / finely-locked words [*Menutz motz serratz*]," he writes in "La flor el vergan," while in "Non puesc sofrir c'a la dolor" he also suggests that he has in the past employed "locked words [*motz serratz*]."[38] These poets identify *trobar clus* with entities—whether a walled garden, the female sex or female sexuality, or the meaning of a poem—which they alone possess, whether as proprietor, lover, or poet, and which all others, who do not enjoy this ownership, cannot attain.

The troubadours imagine *trobar clus* secondly as secret, amorous deeds, known to both the poet and his lady but not known to others outside the pair, or, more properly, as the secret, amorous language through which the poet can address the lady about his love without being understood by strangers. On one level, these poets resemble the vast majority of troubadours who recognize, as Guilhem did, that the lady forbids the poet to speak of their love openly and that the poet, if he is to be submissive to the lady, must bow to her will in this matter. Giraut de Bornelh, for example, declares of his lady in "Qan lo fretiz e·l glatz e la neus,"

> And let them call me a man of Béziers
> if I were ever heard to speak—
> and so anger her gracious self—
> of any secret she confided to me alone.[39]

Raimbaut d'Auregna similarly acknowledges, in "Una chansoneta fera," that he must find a "screen" with which he might hide his love and that "whoever finds love without a screen / ought not to complain if he loses / a fickle lady."[40] Were he to speak unguardedly about his lady, Raimbaut claims, he would be

---

38. ". . . ieu iong [e] latz / Menutz motz serratz," in "La flors el vergan," *The "Cansos" and "Sirventes" of the Troubadour Giraut de Borneil: A Critical Edition*, ed. and trans. Ruth Verity Sharman (Cambridge: Cambridge University Press, 1989), pp. 168–74, vv. 36–37; ". . . motz serratz," in "Non puesc sofrir c'a la dolor," ibid., pp. 216–222, v. 73, translation modified. It is true that *serrat* can mean not only "locked" but "pressed together," so that Sharman translates his expression in the second poem as "words that were dense with meaning." Yet, it is also true that Giraut's association of *serrat* with a garden, which is more likely to be "locked" than "pressed together," and with the adjectives "fortified [*fort*]" and "closed [*clus*]" indicate that it is this spatial metaphor which is most relevant here.

39. "E fos appellatz de Beders, / Qan ia parlar / M'auziri'hom de nuill celar / Q'ella·m disses privadamens, / Don s'azires lo sieus cors gens," in "Qan lo freitz e·l glatz e la neus," *The "Cansos" and "Sirventes" of the Troubadour Giraut de Borneil*, pp. 92–97, vv. 22–26.

40. "escrima," in "Una chansoneta fera," ibid., pp. 75–58, v. 90; "Qui trob'amor ses escrima / Ja non deu planher si pert / Domna qu'es vayra e griza," ibid., vv. 60–63.

committing a "mortal sin."[41] Both troubadours portray ladies who demand the poet's discretion about their love, whether by keeping a secret that the lady has told him or by using a "screen," such as a *senhal*, to disguise her identity, and who threaten to become angry and possibly dismiss the poet if he fails to exhibit such self-restraint. Yet, if both Giraut and Raimbaut resemble their lyric predecessors in their recognition of the necessity of the poet's silence about his love even as he speaks of it, Raimbaut, in particular, differs from them in his depiction of the closed poem as especially capable of at once concealing its meaning from the masses and revealing it to the lady. In "Un vers farai de tal mena," Raimbaut states of his love, "Since I cannot openly declare it to her, / may God give understanding [*entendensa*] of it / to her, so that she may make me joyous again."[42] He communicates that he will have the poem recited to her, and that, as he puts it, "I shall be exalted if she understands it [*l'enten*] in a joyous sense, / but I don't know why I should go on living / if she understands it [*l'enten*] and pays no heed."[43] Though Raimbaut establishes that his fear of his lady prevents him from making his love known to her, he prays God to grant "understanding" to the lady so that she might perceive his love all the same, and he hopes that she will "understand" it in such a way as to end by making him joyous. He makes "understanding" (*entendensa*) a substantive, something one does or does not possess though the grace of God and something his lady will, he hopes, possess upon hearing his poem. In "Assatz sai d'amor ben parlar," after chastising his tongue and resolving to keep his heart unopened, Raimbaut adds, "But my fine Joglar will easily comprehend [*sabra*] it; / for she . . . is of such worth and is so dear to me / that no evil will ever come to me from her."[44] Once again, although Raimbaut establishes that he cannot make his love known, he predicts that his lady, identified by the *senhal* "Joglar," will ascertain it nevertheless, not through God's grace but through her own excellence. In both poems, he contrasts indiscriminate masses, who cannot detect a secret love, and a special lady

41. "pechatz criminaus," ibid., v. 55.

42. "Pus no·ill o puesc a prezensa / Dir, Dieus l'en don entendensa / A lieys, tal que me torn en gaug!" in "Un vers farai de tal mena," *The Life and Works of the Troubadour Raimbaut d'Orange*, ed. Walter T. Pattison (Minneapolis: University of Minnesota Press, 1952), pp. 83–87, vv. 52–54. The *entendensa* Raimbaut hopes his beloved lady will possess anticipates the *entendement* heretical believers in Montaillou hope potential coreligionists will display.

43. "Ricx hom suy si l'enten en gaug, / Mas ieu no sai per que·m viva / Si l'enten e pueys non a sonh," ibid., vv. 57–59.

44. "Mas be·l sabra mos belhs Jocglars; / Qu'ilh val tant, e m'es tan coraus, / Que ja de lieys no·m venra maus," in "Assatz sai d'amor ben parlar," *The Life and Works of the Troubadour Raimbaut d'Orange*, pp. 134–37, vv. 57–59.

who, because of her special capacities, does grasp it. For Raimbaut and for other poets, *trobar clus* becomes the means through which a secret love is simultaneously kept from the crowd and communicated to the lady.

The troubadours conceive *trobar clus*, finally, as a secret, refined language through which the poet can address, not just his lady, but an elite of poetic connoisseurs without being understood by the masses. Peire's *vida* (or life) cites a *sirventes* where the poet says of himself, "If only he would make his words clear / Since one can hardly understand them."[45] Giraut's *vida* suggests similarly that those who cannot grasp "subtle words" fail to appreciate his compositions.[46] Arnaut's *vida* notes, "He developed a way of composing with rare rhymes, which is why his songs are not easy to understand or to learn."[47] All of these *vidas* connect the closed aspects of these troubadours' poems, whether their overall lack of "clarity," the "subtlety" of their words, or the "rarity" of their rhymes, with their difficulty in being understood or memorized. These troubadours' poems confirm the *vidas'* allegations that the poets resisted having their works lose their otherness through the processes of comprehension, memorization, and recitation, even if this resistance should ensure their lack of popularity. Raimbaut resolves ironically, for example, in "A mon vers dirai chansso," to compose "in simple words and simple tune / and in ordinary and common rhyme, for I am blamed / when I use words difficult for the fools."[48] Giraut, like Raimbaut, decides in "A penas sai comenssar" to compose

> on a theme
> which would be easy for everyone to understand
> and easy to sing,
> since I am composing it just to give pleasure.[49]

45. *The Vidas of the Troubadours,* trans. Margarita Egan (New York: Garland Publishing, 1984), p. 71. "Ab q'un pauc esclaris sos motz, / Qu'a penas nuillz hom los enten," *Biographies des Troubadours: Textes provençaux des XIIIe et XIVe siècles,* ed. Jean Boutière and A.-H. Schutz (New York: Burt Franklin, 1972), p. 219.

46. *The Vidas of the Troubadours,* p. 40; "subtilz ditz," *Biographies des Troubadours,* p. 191.

47. *The Vidas of the Troubadours,* p. 8; "pres una maniera de trobar en caras rimas, per que soas cansons no son leus ad entendre ni ad aprendre," *Biographies des Troubadours,* p. 14.

48. "Ab leus motz ez ab leu so / Ez en rima vil'e plana / (Puois aissi son encolpatz / Qan fatz avols motz als fatz)," in "A mon vers dirai chansso," *The Life and Works of the Troubadour Raimbaut d'Orange,* pp. 170–73, vv. 2–5.

49. ". . . de tal razo / Que l'entenda tota gens / E que·l fassa leu chantar, / Q'ieu fauc per plan deportar," in "A penas sai comenssar," *The "Cansos" and "Sirventes" of the Troubadour Giraut de Borneil,* pp. 196–99, vv. 4–7.

Both Raimbaut and Giraut identify a nonclosed poem's simplicity, ordinariness, and clarity as the qualities that make it capable of being recited and shouted by many people, including "fools," and therefore capable of being enjoyed by many, whereas they identify a closed poem's complexity, rarity, and obscurity with its corresponding difficulty and disagreeableness to the populace. If *trobar clus* is perceived as obscure, difficult, and therefore unpopular among the crowd, it is also, by the same token, perceived as learned, artistic, and appreciated among an elite. In "La flors el vergan," Giraut states that "[poetry deep with] meaning, rich and rare, / brings and bestows fine reputation, / just as unbridled nonsense / detracts from it."[50] Presumably referring to Raimbaut as his ally, he relates that after binding together "finely locked words" or words again associated with closed poetry,

> I am praised for it later
> when my fine theme
> appears and yields itself up;
> for a well-tutored man,
> who sees correctly in this
> and supports my case,
> in my opinion will not want me
> to sing for the vulgar herd.[51]

Raimbaut, as Giraut depicts him, scorns not only the foolish and easy-to-learn words that are associated with nonclosed poetry, but also the popularity of such poetry among fools, and he prefers the "finely locked words" associated with closed poetry, as well as the more limited "reputation" and "praise" which such words warrant. Closed poetry thus corresponds to a closed audience which, instead of singing songs by the public fountain, as Giraut depicts them at one point as doing, rewards high quality poems with the more aristocratic honor of high esteem. Indeed, while the *vidas* of the poets of the closed style complain of the difficulty and inaccessibility of these poets' verses, Giraut's *vida* states that not all fail to appreciate his works. Giraut is still known as "the master of the troubadours," the *vida* informs us, "by all those who truly understand subtle words in which love and reason are well expressed. He was greatly honored by the wor-

---

50. ". . . sens e cartatz / Adui pretz e dona, / Si cum l'ochaisona / Nonsens eslaissatz," in "La flors el vergan," ibid., pp. 168–74, vv. 23–26.

51. "Puois en sui lauzatz / Qan ma razos bona / Par ni s'abandona; / C'om ben enseignatz / Si be·i ve, / Ni mon dreich capte, / Non vol, al mieu escien, / C'a totz chant comunalmen," ibid., vv. 38–45.

thy men and by those who understand love, and by the ladies who understand the masterly words of his songs."[52] While those who cannot understand subtle verses do not value Giraut's poetry, "worthy men" and "ladies" who understand love and masterful words, though a minority in any audience, do appreciate him. The poets of the closed style, whose works are rare, dark, and obscure in their intertwined words, may be unpopular among the masses, but they find merit in the eyes of the cognoscenti.

The heresy described in ecclesiastical writings is related to *trobar clus* insofar as the practitioners of both ideologies define themselves as an elite which possesses a secret, whether that secret be the understanding of an obscure religious creed or the understanding of an obscure poetry, which the masses do not possess. Both the perfected heretics and the troubadours of the closed style define themselves as an elite which pursues an *askesis*, whether that *askesis* be a religion identified with inherent Christian virtue, arduousness of lifestyle, and a denial of the body, or with a poetics identified with inherent artistic value, difficulty of vocabulary and rhyme, and refusal to grant enjoyment to a general audience. Both groups replace the common pleasures the rabble is thought to enjoy, such those of the bed and the table or those of an easily understood poetry, with a sense of superiority to this rabble based upon the rejection of such sensual or literary indulgences. It is not that the elite to which the troubadours of the closed style address themselves consists of Cathars but, rather, that the structure under which Catharism is seen as operating, with its distinction between heretics and believers or, even more, between heretics and Catholics, parallels the structure inherent within *trobar clus*, with its opposition of the esoteric few who possess understanding and the exoteric many who do not. If, in Guilhem de Poitiers, one perceives a bemused, detached observer of subversives who resemble the heretics in their secret rebellion against a dominant class, in the poets of the closed style one perceives the subversives themselves in their pursuit of an occult and exclusive practice.

CARDINAL AND MONTANHAGOL

In the years during and after the Albigensian Crusade, when the Cathars of Toulouse were repressed first by military forces and then by mendicant inquisitors, two members of the last generation of important troubadours— Guilhem

---

52. *The Vidas of the Troubadours*, p. 40. "er toz aquels que ben entendon subtils ditz ni ben pauzants d'amor ni de sen. Fort fo honratz per los valenz homes e per los entendenz e per las dompnas qu'entendian los sieus maestrals ditz de las soas chansos," *Biographies des Troubadours*, p. 191.

de Montanhagol and Peire Cardinal—also found themselves embroiled in the affairs of Toulouse, including the clashes between the inquisitors and the heretics. Montanhagol is thought to have lived in the vicinity of this city between 1233 and 1249 as a member of Raimon VII's court, leaving for Spain only when his protector died.[53] Cardinal is likewise believed to have passed at least part of an extensive career, which ranged from 1216 to 1271, attached to Occitania's largest metropolis. If, in previous years, troubadours had oriented their poems around a secret, whether this secret concerned the lady's sex or sexuality or poetical language itself, now, as a distinct Occitan political and cultural life gave way to the dominant French forces and as heresy gave way to the Inquisition, this encrypted silence took on a new meaning. It is impossible to determine whether Montanhagol or Cardinal were heretics, as has, at times, been alleged, yet in their *sirventes* these poets speak of their own faith and the Inquisition then operative around them with an ambiguity that recalls the verbal tactics attributed to their heterodox neighbors in the same period. Like the citizens of Toulouse, as depicted in Guilhem Pelhisson's *Chronica*, the poets are reformist rather than radical in their criticisms of the Inquisition and focus on excesses rather than substance in their diatribes against it. Like these citizens, the poets employ a language that obscures their heretical identifications even as it reveals them and that thus recognizes the authority of those who would persecute heretics even as it struggles against that authority. In the context of Toulouse under the Inquisition, the ambiguity of troubadour poetry, once experienced as erotic or esoteric, now appears heretical in its evasiveness.

Like Pelhisson's Toulousans, Montanhagol and Cardinal deny that they are heretics. In "Del tot vey remaner valor," arguably his most anticlerical poem,

---

53. In "Ar ab lo coinde pascor," for example, Montanhagol writes, "from love comes chastity [*e d'amor mou castitatz*]," a remark which Rougemont has taken as evidence that the troubadours' ideology of love ultimately corresponded to the Cathars' ideology of celibacy (yet which others have read as proof that the poet subscribed to a common orthodox belief in the importance of moderation and self-restraint in such affairs). See *Les Poésies de Guilhem de Montanhagol, troubadour provençal du XIIIe siècle*, ed. and trans. Peter T. Ricketts (Toronto: Pontifical Institute of Mediaeval Studies, 1984), pp. 121–24, v. 18. Jules Coulet maintains that Montanhagol responded to the Inquisition's censure of courtly love as licentious by deciding to characterize it as chaste. See *Le Troubadour Guilhem Montanhagol* (Toulouse: Privat, 1898), pp. 44–55. It is with Montanhagol, Coulet maintains, that "cette poésie provençale, qui doit bientôt succomber sous l'inimitié du clergé, semble d'abord s'être efforcée de désarmer son adversaire. Accusée d'immoralité & poursuivie comme complice de l'hérésie, elle veut se conformer à l'orthodoxie & à la morale chrétiennes afin de conserver le droit de vivre" (p. 57).

Montanhagol asserts, "And God was truly man, I know it well."[54] While this statement may seem self-evident from the mouth of a professed Catholic, it is not so obvious from the mouth of someone who might be suspected of being a Cathar and, thus, of holding that Christ did not actually assume flesh and blood. The intensifiers "truly [*vers*]" and "I know it well [*qu'ieu o sai*]" reinforce the impression that the poet here speaks here in defense of his orthodoxy. In the same work, Montanhagol goes on to assert of the Dominicans, "Now they have made themselves inquisitors / and they judge as they please."[55] After offering this moderate reproach of the pursuers of the heretics, he adds quickly, "Nevertheless the making of inquests does not displease me, / but rather it pleases me that they pursue error."[56] As Montanhagol seems to defend himself against potential charges of dualism, he defends himself here against potential charges of opposition to the inquisitors' mission of suppressing heresy. As the intensifiers "truly" and "I know it well" add a defensive tone to his pronouncement of God's appearance as a man, the denial that the undertaking of inquests displeases him suggests, all the more, that he is protecting himself against a possible reproach.[57] Cardinal rejects heresy no less vehemently than Montanhagol. In "Un estribot farai, que er mot maïstratz," he writes,

> I hold belief in a God who was born of a mother,
> of a holy virgin, by whom the world is saved,
> and he is Father and Son and Holy Trinity,
> and he is in three persons and one unity.[58]

54. "e Dieus fo vers hom, qu'ieu o sai," in "Del tot vey remaner valor," *Les Poésies de Guilhem de Montanhagol,* pp. 43–48, v. 11.

55. "Ar se son fait enqueredor / e jutjon aissi com lur plai," ibid., vv. 19–20.

56. "Pero l'enquerre no·m desplai, / anz me plai que casson error," ibid., vv. 21–22.

57. Coulet rejects this reading, maintaining, "Ce n'est pas, croyons-nous, une déclaration d'orthodoxie de la part du poète, mais une formule sans grande valeur & qui est destinée surtout à finir le vers," *Le Troubadour Guilhem Montanhagol,* p. 91, n. 11. He compares this phrase to other similar phrases, such as "qui qu'o desvuelha" and "cui que plassa o greu sia," which perform a similar function in Montanhagol's poetry; see ibid., p. 85, n. 37. Ricketts, on the contrary, notes that however one interprets "qu'ieu o sai," the remainder of the verse continues to constitute a defense of Montanhagol against charges of heresy; see *Les Poésies de Guilhem de Montanhagol,* p. 47, n. 11. Coulet himself acknowledges that other passages in this poem, such as vv. 21–22, do constitute such a "déclaration d'orthodoxie," ibid., p. 93, n. 21–22.

58. ". . . ieu ai en Dieu crezensa que fon de maire natz, / D'una santa pieusela, per que·l mons es salvatz. / E es paire e filhs e santa trinitatz, / E es en tres personas e una unitatz," in "Un estribot farai, que er mot maïstratz," *Poésies complètes du troubadour Peire Cardenal (1180–1278),* ed. René Lavaud (Toulouse: Privat, 1957), pp. 206–15, vv. 3–6.

With these words, Cardinal seems to affirm a seemingly Catholic belief in the Incarnation, the Virgin Birth, the Redemption, and the Trinity and to deny a Cathar belief in the immateriality of Christ, which negated or radically altered these Catholic doctrines. In the course of his credo, he asserts, in addition, "And I believe in Rome and in Saint Peter to whom it was ordered / that he must judge penitence, regarding our good sense and our follies."[59] Here, the poet appears to affirm the authority of the Roman Catholic Church and the power of the keys and to deny Cathar scorn for this institution and its purported role as intercessor between Christians and God. As René Lavaud notes of this passage, "The poet protests . . . his perfect orthodoxy."[60] One could read such declarations of Catholic beliefs on the part of Montanhagol and Cardinal at face value as reflections of their true Catholicism, even though it remains unclear, if these poets were unequivocally orthodox, what suspicions of heterodoxy they felt the need to allay. Yet one could also read such declarations, as Varga suggests those of Cardinal's should be read, as an "alibi" which stands to help the poet "pass as a Catholic in order to avoid prosecution."[61] Varga recalls that the Cathars, as we have seen, are said to attend Catholic Mass because they can pray to God there as well as elsewhere and to make the sign of the cross because the gesture is helpful in chasing away flies, and she suggests that Cardinal, for one, could have made his apparent profession of orthodoxy out of a similar desire to pass as Catholic and a similar indifference to the deeper significance of such a profession. If Montanhagol and Cardinal reject certain heretical views, in doing so they merely resemble heretical figures in Pelhisson's chronicle, like del Soler, Tesseire, and Sans, who make similar denials.

Again, like Pelhisson's Toulousans, when Montanhagol and Cardinal do criticize the inquisitors, they reproach them not for the fact that they prosecute heretics but for the manner in which they prosecute them. As we have observed, Montanhagol has made clear that he is not displeased with the inquisitors. He affirms,

> It pleases me that they pursue error
> and that with fair, pleasant words, without anger,

---

59. "E cre Rom'e sant Peire a cuy fon comandatz / Jutge de penedensa, de sen e de foldatz," ibid., vv. 13–14.

60. Ibid., p. 208n.

61. Varga, "Peire Cardinal était-il hérétique?" p. 215.

they turn those who have erred, deviating, toward the faith,
and let him who has repented find fair mercy,
and thus let them do their work
so that penitents be treated with justice.[62]

Montanhagol may seem to commend the inquisitors here, to praise the gentle tone with which they address the heretics, the efforts they make to reconcile them with the Church, and the pardon they grant those who do so repent. He may seem to foreshadow Bernard Gui's later characterization of the ideal inquisitor as someone who is moderate in his temperament, compassionate in his ministrations, and just in his judgments.[63] At the same time, however, Montanhagol censures the inquisitors, both explicitly and implicitly. When he conveys that he is glad that the inquisitors turn those who have erred toward the faith and when he expresses hope that those who have repented will find mercy, he leaves it uncertain whether the inquisitors do bring about these conversions or whether the penitents do find pardon. His comment that "they have made themselves inquisitors and they judge as they please" suggests that the friars give verdicts according to their whim. If Montanhagol can be read as criticizing the friars here, it is not insofar as they prosecute heretics but, rather, insofar as they do so angrily, mercilessly, and capriciously. Cardinal gives no indication that he approves of the Inquisition either in its present or its future state, but he too voices objection, not to the fact that the friars pursue heretics, but to the manner in which they do so. In "Ab votz d'angel, lengue' esperta, non bléza," he states of the Friars Preachers, "And they have established a court

---

62. "anz me plai que casson error / e qu'ab bels digz plazentiers ses yror, / torno·ls erratz desviatz en la fe, / e qui·s penet que truep bona merce, / e enaissi menon dreg lo gazan / que tort ni dreg no perdan so que y an," "Del tot vey remaner valor," *Les Poésies de Guilhem de Montanhagol*, vv. 22–27. Coulet remarks both "la sévérité avec laquelle il y juge l'arbitraire de ces clercs qui se sont faits inquisiteurs 'Et jutjo aissi com lur plai'" and "les déclarations d'orthodoxie, de respect pour une Inquisition juste & charitable, dont il s'entoure pour désarmer les colères de ceux qu'il attaque," *Le Troubadour Guilhem Montanhagol*, p. 44.

63. "Primo videlicet, ut inquisitor . . . ferveat inter displicentia et occurrentia accidentia quod non furat indignationis aut iracundie furore, quia talis furor precipitat; nec etiam torpeat torpore cujuscumque ingavie vel accidie, quia talis torpor vigorem procedendi enervat. . . . Inquisitor igitur velut justus judex, sic teneat in condemnationibus penalibus rigorem justicie quod non solum in mente servet interius, set etiam in facie ostendat exterius compassionem, ut per hoc vitet notam indignationis et iracundie que argumentum et notam crudelitatis inducit," Bernard Gui, *Practica inquisitionis heretice pravitatis*, ed. Célestin Douais (Paris: Picard, 1886), pp. 232–33.

of inquiry, / and he is a Waldensian who deters them from it."[64] In "Clergia non valc anc mais tan," he states, similarly,

> The clerics are not worth much any more,
> for until now they have had the custom of preaching,
> but today they go throwing stones
> at other people,
> and they hold for the greatest publican
> him who defends himself against them.[65]

Cardinal attacks the logic under which any resistance to the Inquisition leads one to be suspected of heresy, but he refrains from defending the Waldensians and "publicans" (or Cathar heretics) who are accused, let alone identifying himself with these parties. Criticizing the difficulty of criticizing inquisitors, Cardinal complains of these friars, "And they want to know the secrets of men / so that they can better make them afraid."[66] It is not the inquisitors' prosecution of heretics that he protests but their arrogation of power over people in general through their investigation into their private lives. With this aside, he acknowledges that men possess "secrets," and he identifies these secrets with matters which, if known by the inquisitors, would make their holders fearful. Stressing the fear which makes people, in general, hesitate to stand up to the inquisitors, Cardinal acknowledges that he shares that trepidation. In "Qui volra sirventes auzir," he states, "Of the clerics I do not dare say bad things. / This could be bought dearly by me."[67] Likewise, in "Un sirventes fauc en luec de jurar," he confides, "I dare not say that which they dare to do, / for no one

64. "Et an de plaitz cort establia / Et es Vaudes qui·ls ne desvia," in "Ab votz d'angel, lengue'esperta, non bléza," *Poésies complètes du troubadour Peire Cardenal,* pp. 160–68, vv. 31–32.

65. "Clergia non valc anc mais tan: / Qu'ill solon anar prezicant, / Mas eras van peiras lansam / A l'autra gen, / E tenon per pus publican / Sel que·s defen," in "Clergia non valc anc mais tan," ibid., pp. 160–68, vv. 1–6. In "[Pels cleres es a]ppellatz herege qui ne jura," Cardinal appears to make a similar criticism of the Inquisition if he does affirm, as Lavaud reconstructs the sole mutilated manuscript, "[By the clerics is anyone] called a heretic who does not swear according to their system of trickery and falsity [Pels cleres es a] pellatz herege qui ne jura / [Segon la lor razon d'] engagn e de faussura; / [E tenen per nien] la santa escriptura, / [Qu'a tota hora mentem l] aidament ses mesura / [E volen qu'om los trob] figlos plens de dreitura." See "[Pels cleres es a] pellatz herege qui ne jura," ibid., pp. 184–90, vv. 1–5.

66. "E los secretz d'ome volon saber / Per tal que miels si puescan far temer," in "Ab votz d'angel, leng'esperta, non bléza," ibid., pp. 33–34, vv. 31–32.

67. "De clergues non auzi mal dir: / Car mi poiri 'esser comprat," in "Qui volra sirventes auzir," ibid., pp. 192–99, vv. 65–66.

with scalp disease likes being combed, / and no more do they like anyone who chastises them for their sin."[68] Though his references to the wicked habits of the clerics may well concern the vices for which he reproaches them elsewhere in general and not their actions against heretics in particular, Cardinal acknowledges having "secrets" himself which might place him under the power of these ecclesiastics. While both poets are circumspect in their criticism of the inquisitors, Cardinal indicates that their guardedness stems from the dangers they risk in making such criticism.

Finally, like the heretics in Pelhisson's chronicle, Montanhagol and Cardinal often speak vaguely of theological matters and thus leave uncertain their religious affiliation. Both poets seem to deny the existence of free will, as Cathars were known to do. In "On mais a hom de valensa," Montanhagol contends,

> . . . the wicked man, as far as I can see,
> does not commit a fault when he does something wicked,
> as it is out of necessity
> that the wicked do wickedness,
> just as the good do what is good.[69]

Similarly, in "Un sirventes novel vueill comensar," Cardinal claims that he expects to be saved despite any sins he may have committed during his life, for "I would not have committed them, if I had not earlier been born."[70] Both poets appear to argue, like Cathars and unlike Catholics, that the sinful should not bear responsibility for their sins because God created them as they are, in their capacity for sinfulness. Even if Montanhagol and Cardinal seem to reject free will, however, it is not clear that they do so under the influence of Catharism or, even if they do, that such an influence means that they themselves can be identified as Cathars. Cardinal is particularly ambiguous because in the very poem where he appears to express a Catharist determinism, he also expresses hope that God will save him "body and soul" at the hour of his death, though Cathars believed that salvation would entail escape from the material body, and he expresses fear lest he experience the torments of hell, though

---

68. "Jeu non aus dir so que el auzon far, / Car ans rascas non amet penchenar / Ni el home qui lor dan lur castia," in "Un sirventes fauc en luec de jurar," ibid., pp. 216–21, vv. 36–38.

69. ". . . malvatz, al mieu albir, / no falh, quam fai falhimen, / quar per dever yssamen / fan li malvat malestran / com fan bos fagz li prezan," in "On mais a hom de valensa," *Les Poésies de Guilhem de Montenhagol*, pp. 68–73, vv. 5–9.

70. "Qu'ieu no·ls fora si non fos natz enans," in "Un sirventes novel vueill comensar," *Poésies complètes du troubadour Peire Cardenal*, pp. 222–27, v, 40.

Cathars did not believe in the existence of hell. It may be, as Nelli suggests, that this poem and Cardinal's thought in general constitute a jumble of Cathar and Catholic beliefs, so that the troubadour cannot ultimately be located exclusively in either of the two religions. Yet it may also be, as Varga recommends, that this apparent adherence to Catholic beliefs itself constitutes part of Cardinal's Catharism. If Cardinal refers to the salvation of his body as well as that of his soul, it is possible that he does so, not because he adheres to the Catholic doctrine of the resurrection of the flesh, but, rather, because he is distinguishing between celestial human flesh and terrestrial human flesh, as some Cathars were said to do.[71] If he refers to the torments of hell, it is possible that he believes not in the Catholic conception of hell but in a Cathar conception of hell, where those persons who have not undergone the *consolamentum* suffer.[72] Similarly, if, in "Un estribot farai, que er mot maïstratz," Cardinal announces his belief in the Incarnation, the Virgin Birth, the Redemption, and the Trinity, it is possible that he holds to Cathar rather than Catholic views of these doctrines. As Varga recalls, while the Cathars may be considered heretics by the Catholics, they were also Christians who shared beliefs with Catholics and who and therefore shared a common vocabulary. In referring to their beliefs with a seemingly Catholic language, Cathars may purposefully employ such overlapping words and phrases so as to give the impression to their auditors that they are Catholics themselves. "Every Catholic thing had its 'true' equivalent, its Cathar equivalent," Varga writes.[73] If an author like Cardinal refers to the Son of Man, the Virgin Mary, and penance, she states, "these are technical terms of the secret Cathar language, abbreviations of their doctrine, which, for them, admit an entirely other content."[74] Varga concludes, "In order to hide themselves, in order to avoid a scandal, and even on account of the nature of their faith, they use orthodox formulas."[75] It is this ambiguity of the Cathars' language, which seems orthodox but is actually heretical in its meaning, that Gui warns his fellow inquisitors about and that Pelhisson illustrates through the condemned heretic Tesseire.

While Montanhagol and Cardinal, so far as we know, were never prosecuted as heretics, the satirical verse of the kind they wrote was identified with the Cathar faith by their heretical contemporaries. Both poets, and Cardinal in par-

71. See Varga, "Peire Cardinal était-il hérétique?" p. 215.
72. Ibid., p. 223.
73. Ibid., p. 228.
74. Ibid., p. 210.
75. Ibid., p. 212.

ticular, express an anticlericalism which, though common among medieval Catholics throughout Europe, assumes a particular resonance in a context as rife with heresy as Occitania was in the first half of the thirteenth century. In inquisitorial registers, accused heretics are said to quote *sirventes* against the inquisitors, which seem to them to justify their antipathy toward these clerics. After the murder of the inquisitor Guilhem Arnaut and his companions in Avignonet in 1242, for example, a certain Guilhem Audebert is said to have remarked to a companion, Estève Mazelier, in Castelsarrasin, "Do you want to hear a good *cobla* [or stanza or couplet] or *sirventes*?"[76] When Mazelier replied that he did, Audebert told him, "Friar Arnaut, who tracked us down, has been killed." Mazelier responded approvingly, "It is good, this *cobla*."[77] The line Mazelier cites cannot be attributed to any known poet, and the reference to it as a part of a *cobla* or *sirventes* appears to be ironic: the aesthetic appreciation the men express for this work is clearly a cover for their political appreciation of the inquisitor's death. Troubadour verse is evidently perceived here as the appropriate means of expressing dissident views, perhaps on account of its obliqueness. In the early fourteenth century, a suspected heretic by the name of Guilhem Saisset is said to have recited the first stanza of Cardinal's "Clergue si fan pastor," to which his interlocutor, Bertran de Taïx, replied that he would like to learn the poem. "Now the clerics have not only the defects contained in this *cobla*, but many others, in great number," Bertran stated.[78] Nelli concludes that such a diffusion of Cardinal's work among uncultivated audiences could only mean that even if he was not actually a heretic, he was believed to be one by his contemporaries. Even if such poets use denials, diversions, and double entendres when speaking of heresy and the Inquisition, the ambiguity of their remarks makes them seem, in this context, all the more typically heretical.

If the troubadours are responding to the anxiety about secretiveness evident in the prosecutions of heretics around them, as I suggest that they are, they are counterbalancing the clerics' fear of not controlling Christian souls subject to their jurisdiction with their own hope of escaping such surveillance. When a heretic withdraws himself from ecclesiastical view, clerics worry that they

76. Collection Doat, vol. 22, fol. 11. Cited in Yves Dossat, *Les Crises de l'Inquisition toulou-saine au XIIIe siècle (1233–1273)* (Bordeaux: Imprimerie Bière, 1959), p. 150.

77. Ibid.

78. "non solum modo . . . dicta mala que in dicta cobla erant contenta erant in clericis, set etiam multa alia, plura," *Le Registre d'Inquisition de Jacques Fournier, Evêque de Pamiers (1318–1325)*, ed. Jean Duvernoy (Toulouse: Privat, 1965), vol. 3, p. 320.

will no longer be able to apprehend, judge, and condemn his misdeeds. Troubled by the loss of this person's soul, they are even more troubled by the loss of the many other souls throughout the community at large, which would be caused by their failure to perceive the heretic's guilt and the ensuing lack of confidence in the Church's perspicacity. As a result of even one wily heretic's concealment of his sins, the clergy stands to lose its bearings and the Church to lose its hold on a neighborhood. When a troubadour withdraws himself from the dominant social gaze, however, he will not lose but, rather, will gain control over his environment, or so the poets dream. Women who belong to other men will grant access to him. Poems he has composed will resist being memorized, performed, and appropriated by the general public, and will thus preserve their lyric integrity. Religious beliefs he holds will escape categorization as heterodox or orthodox and, hence, will allow him freedom from the increasingly polarized Catholic and Cathar camps. For those with authority to rule over others, the secretiveness of others frustrates that command, but for those with no such authority and no hope of attaining it, darkness preserves their fragile autonomy.

4 THE STONING OF LADY GUIRAUDA
The Singularity of Noble Heretics

While Cathars, in general, were thought to escape prosecution on account of their reclusiveness, the noblemen and noblewomen among them eluded such a fate on account of their prominence. In 1177, as the dualist heresy was spreading throughout Occitania, Raimon V, count of Toulouse and Saint-Gilles and the most powerful lord in this area, wrote to Alexander, the abbot of Cîteaux, at the time of the General Chapter of the Cistercian order, informing him, "The more noble of my land cling to the withering pestilence of infidelity, and with them a great multitude of men, falling away from the faith, also adhere to it."[1] In the following decades, the heresy became so popular among the upper classes that the most important families of Occitania, including the counts of Toulouse, Foix, and Comminges and the viscounts of Béziers and Carcassonne, were all implicated in the sect, whether as adherents or as supporters, and the lesser clans were no less affected. Still, members of the aristocracy often refused to perceive other lords and ladies as erring in the faith. When Raimon VI, Raimon V's controversial son and heir, failed to repress the sectaries on his territory, Pope Innocent III appealed to the count's cousin and overlord, Philip Augustus of France, to embark on a crusade against him, but to little effect. In April of 1208, Philip replied to the pope, "As to the matter of your declaring the count's territory

---

1. Quoted in S. R. Maitland, *Facts and Documents Illustrative of the History, Doctrine, and Rites of the Ancient Albigenses and Waldenses* (London: C. J. G. and F. Rivington, 1832), pp. 145–49, at p. 145; "terrae meae nobiliores jam praelibata infidelitatis tabe aruerunt et cum ipsis maxima hominum multitudo a fide corruens aruit," ibid., pp. 487–88, at p. 487.

open to seizure, I must tell you that I have been advised by learned and eminent men that you cannot legally do this until he is condemned for heresy."[2]
Philip grumbles about Raimon's failure to support him in his wars, but he
reminds the pope that the count remains his vassal and his lands part of his
own domain; should these territories be transferred to a more orthodox ruler,
it is not certain that his successor would do the king homage. If Philip, from
the north, was lukewarm about the crusade, Peter of Aragon, Raimon's cousin
and brother-in-law from the south, was openly opposed to the endeavor.
Concerned about his own substantial holdings in Occitania, Peter championed the major southern lords, declaring that they were not heretics and had
never been condemned as such. If he speaks out in favor of Raimon Rogier,
the count of Foix, Peter affirms, it is only appropriate for him to do so, "since
the count is his dear kinsman and vassal, whose interest it would be shameful
of him to ignore."[3] Though the Church judges these noblemen, on the basis
of its interests, as defenders of the faith and condemns them as a result, their
fellow noblemen judge them, on the basis of their own interests, as defenders
of their families and subjects and excuse them for this reason.

To put the difficulty the Church was facing another way, members of the
nobility could not be perceived as heretics because their prominence made
them too distinguished, too distinctive, in a word, too singular to be absorbed
into any large social category. In the last half of the twelfth century, nobles were
increasingly consolidating as a class, defined by their military role and their
hereditary privileges, yet they continued to function in society as individuals.[4]

2. Quoted in Peter of Les Vaux-de-Cernay, *History of the Albigensian Crusade,* trans. W.
A. Silby and M. A. Silby (Rochester, NY: Boydell Press, 1998), appendix F, ii, p. 306; "De eo
autem quod vos predicti comitis terram exponitis occupantibus, sciatis quod a viris litteratis
et illustratis didicimus quod id de jure facere non potestis, quousque idem de heretica pravi-
tate fuerit condempnatur," *Histoire générale de Languedoc,* ed. Dom Claude Devic and Dom
Joseph Vaissète, vol. 8 (Toulouse: Privat, 1879), col. 559.

3. Peter, *History* (see n. 2 above), § 373, p. 175; "sicut pro consanguineo suo carissimo et
vassallo, cui sine verecundia in jure suo deesse non potest," Pierre des Vaux-de-Cernay,
Hystoria Albigensis, ed. Pascal Guébin and Ernest Lyon (Paris: Honoré Champion, 1926–39,
vol. 2, § 372, p. 71.

4. On the changing status of the French and Occitan nobility during these years, see Marc
Bloch, *La Société féodale* (Paris: A. Michel, 1939–40), trans. L. A. Manyon as *Feudal Society*
(London: Routledge & K. Paul, 1961; rpt. Chicago: University of Chicago Press, 1964); Jean
Flori, *L'Essor de la chevalerie, XIe–XIIe siècles* (Genève: Droz, 1986); Constance Brittain
Bouchard, *"Strong of body, brave and noble":* Chivalry and Society in Medieval France* (Ithaca:
Cornell University Press, 1998); and Linda M. Paterson, *The World of the Troubadour:
Medieval Occitan Society, c. 1100–c. 1300* (Cambridge: Cambridge University Press, 1993).

A duke, a count, or a viscount was powerful not because of his adherence to any corporate entity like a guild, a university, or a religious order but because of the lands he ruled, the wealth he possessed, and the alliances he enjoyed. Like celebrities nowadays, nobles were so well known as individuals, with their lineages, their marriages, and their political maneuvers, that it was difficult to consider them as members of a group, where only one of their many facets, such as their deviant religious beliefs, would be recognized. How can one perceive nobles as heretics when they possess an individuality that lifts them above social categories, let alone a category as infamous as unbelievers? How can one interpret their disobedience to the Church as heretical when they never cease to proclaim their independence of this institution, if not their power over it? Because nobles resemble heretics in their defiance of ecclesiastical power, they can seem to be either heretics denying the authority of Christ's representatives on earth or members of the upper class asserting their traditional autonomy.

With the categories of nobility and heresy overlapping, the two most important chroniclers of the Albigensian Crusade responded to this epistemological challenge in opposing ways. In his Latin chronicle, *Historia Albigensis*, Pierre, a monk at the Cistercian abbey of Les Vaux-de-Cernay in the Ile-de-France, identifies Raimon VI as a Cathar believer because his noble exceptionalism puts him in conflict with the Church's universalism. In contrast, in their Occitan chanson de geste, the *Canso de la Crozada*, Guilhem, a cleric from Tudela, and his anonymous continuator depict none of the noble characters who appear in their pages as heretical, despite external proof to the contrary, because their extraordinary status as nobles places them outside ordinary categorization. While the Latin, clerically oriented prose account of the crusade rejects the irreducible singularity of the nobility, the vernacular, popularly addressed verse telling of the war accepts that nobles remain inassimilable to the classifications used for the masses.

RAIMON VI

During his lifetime, the orthodoxy of Raimon VI was a matter of open dispute.[5] On the one hand, ecclesiastics repeatedly upbraided Raimon for his failure to rout his lands of heretics or to heed the Church's will in other matters. In April

---

5. On the counts of Toulouse at this time, see Laurent Macé, *Les Comtes de Toulouse et leur entourage, XIIe–XIIIe siècles. Rivalités, alliances et jeux de pouvoir* (Toulouse: Privat, 2000), and Jean-Luc Déjean, *Quand chevauchaient les comtes de Toulouse (1050–1250)* (Paris: Fayard, 1979). On Raimon's character, see Devic and Vaissète, *Histoire générale de Languedoc*,

of 1207, the papal legate Peire de Castelnau excommunicated Raimon for these misdeeds, and Innocent III later confirmed his act, informing the count, "Because you cherish heretics, you are yourself vehemently suspected of heresy."[6] After Innocent appealed to Philip Augustus for assistance in suppressing his recalcitrant vassal, Raimon sought to reconcile himself with the Church, yet his efforts to do so ended in disaster.[7] Raimon met with Peire in the abbey of Saint-Gilles, not far from Arles, in January of 1208 to amend their differences, but the negotiations between the two parties collapsed, and the legate took his leave. As Peire and his companions were preparing to cross the Rhône at Trinquetaille, a band of men said to be of the count's entourage approached them, and one of them drove his lance through Peire's back. The murder was roundly perceived as a gross defiance of the pope's authority, and the northern barons quickly rallied to his side to oppose this outrage. Despite Raimon's failure to curb the heretical activities of his subjects, however, other evidence suggests that the count was not so much a Cathar believer protective of his fellow sectaries as a Catholic lord unable to control his vassals. The chronicler Guilhem de Puylaurens, chaplain to Raimon's son, writes of Raimon that "even if he had wanted it, he could not have eliminated the heretics, who were so well rooted in the county, without the consent of his enemies."[8] While

---

vol. 5, pp. 303–5 for a helpful discussion. For a list of the troubadours Raimon supported, which includes Raimon de Miraval, Raimon Jordan, Guilhem Figueria, and Uc de Saint-Cyr, see ibid., vol. 5, pp. 305–8. Malcolm Lambert writes, "The evidence suggests that, disordered as his private life was and oppressive as he might be to churchmen, his piety was conventional," *The Cathars* (Oxford: Blackwell, 1998), p. 100. Jonathan Sumption observes, similarly, "What is known of his personal life suggests that he was a man of unexceptional, entirely conventional piety," *The Albigensian Crusade* (London: Faber & Faber, 1978), p. 65. Silby and Silby agree, remarking, "Raymond himself was certainly not a Cathar," but someone tolerant of the heretics (Peter, *History*, p. xxxvi). They reiterate, "Despite Peter's assertion and attempts to prove Raymond's personal heresy, there is ultimately no direct evidence of this" (ibid., p. 22, n. 38). Michel Roquebert, though acknowledging Raimon's Catholicism, finds in him "une secrète attirance" toward the heretics. He writes, "Sans jamais avoir adhéré positivement à la foi cathare, Raymond VI pouvait très bien éprouver pour elle une curiosité mêlée de sympathie" (*L'Epopée cathare*, vol. 1 [Toulouse: Privat, 1970–89], p. 138).

6. Peter, *History*, appendix F, p. 306; "quia . . . foves haereticos, suspectus de haeresi vehementer haberis," Innocent III, *Regestorum sive epistolarum*, PL 215, cols. 1–1194, *Epistola* 69, cols. 1166–68, at col. 1167.

7. On Innocent's role in promulgating the crusade, see Raymonde Foreville, "Innocent III et la croisade des Albigeois," *Cahiers de Fanjeaux*, vol. 4, *Paix de Dieu et guerre sainte* (Toulouse: Privat, 1969), pp. 184–217.

8. "Qui etiam si forte multum vellet, nec hereticos multum radicatos [iudicatos C] in terra sine adversantium sibi voluntate poterat extirpare," Guillaume de Puylaurens, *Chronique*,

Guilhem leaves uncertain whether it was "incapacity, negligence, or laziness" that prevented Raimon from taking action, he does not cite sympathy with the heretics as a possible motive.[9] Indeed, soon after the Albigensian Crusade was called, Raimon allied himself with the French side, opposing the very heretics he had once seemed to protect. Raimon is said to have kept a Catholic chaplain with him throughout his life and to have heard Mass from him every day, even when he was at war. Despite his normal series of conflicts with abbots and bishops over properties and jurisdictions, he supported several monasteries with grants of lands and privileges, and he funded the restoration of the Cathedral of Saint Stephen in Toulouse during the years of the crusade. Like his great-grandfather Raimon IV, who had distinguished himself as one of the heroes of the First Crusade, and his grandfather Anfos, who had made a name for himself during the Second Crusade, Raimon VI displayed special affection for the Holy Lands and the religious orders that defended them, requesting in his will that he should die in the garb of a Hospitaler of Saint John, as he did.[10] Though the Church was never to absolve Raimon of his excommunication and, hence, never to allow him to be buried in consecrated ground, his son was able to submit substantial proof of his father's orthodoxy to Rome in an attempt to bring about a reconciliation.[11] Whatever the value of this conflicting testimony, Pierre des Vaux-de-Cernay represents Raimon as committing a series of crimes which, while they may seem to reflect nothing more than the vices of his class, ultimately mirror the depravity of the believers of the heretics and thus reveal him to be a member of their sect.[12]

Like other noblemen, Raimon is said to resist the peace the Church is attempting to impose upon Occitania, especially through his reliance on noto-

---

1145–1275 / Chronica Magistri Guillelmi de Podio Laurentii, ed. and trans. Jean Duvernoy (Paris: CNRS, 1976; rpt. Toulouse: Pérégrinateur, 1996), § 6, p. 48.

9. "sive propter eius simplicitatem seu negligentiam, sive pigritiam," ibid., § 6, p. 48.

10. For precedent in using Anfos instead of Alfonso Jordan as Raimon's grandfather's name, see Macé, *Les Comtes de Toulouse.* On Raimon's end, see J. Delaville Le Roux, ed., *Cartulaire général de l'ordre des Hospitaliers de Saint-Jean de Jerusalem, 1100–1310* (Paris: E. Leroux, 1894), vol. 1, p. 246, n. 1617.

11. See Devic and Vaissète, *Histoire générale de Languedoc,* vol. 5, pp. 301–4. After his death, Raimon's body was consigned, in accordance with his wishes, to the house of the Hospitalers of Saint John of Jerusalem in Toulouse. By the mid-fourteenth century, his body was said to have been half eaten by rats, and by the sixteenth century only his skull had survived. In the late nineteenth century, the skull was still in the possession of this house.

12. On Raimon's very orthodox will, see Devic and Vaissète, *Histoire générale de Languedoc,* vol. 5, pp. 571–73.

riously disruptive paid soldiers. At this time, mercenaries, known as *ruptarii* in Latin and *rotiers* in the vernacular, consisted of independent bands of soldiers from northern Spain and the Low Countries for hire under the command of their own leader. The northern lords, including Philip Augustus and Simon de Montfort, had sufficiently strong affiliations with their vassals that they could rely primarily upon them for military service, but even these rulers turned to the troops known as "Flemings," "Brabantians," "Basques," "Aragonese," and "Navarrese" to supplement to their armies, especially to organize skilled assaults upon fortresses and to garrison these structures once conquered.[13] The southern lords, whose ties to their vassals were weaker than those of their opponents, depended more upon these roving bands to assist in their campaigns and, as a result, were thought to bear more of the responsibility for their crimes. Foreign to the lands in which they fought, mercenaries had little fear of the feudal authorities, who needed their services, or the ecclesiastical authorities, who had little power over them. With no normal social controls to restrain their behavior, they acquired a reputation as common brigands who pillaged wherever they went and perpetrated other acts of violence against civilians. As far back as 1179, the Third Lateran Council had condemned mercenaries for their depredations of the defenseless, including the clergy, the common people, women, and children. In canon 27, the council reproved "the Brabantians, Aragonese, Basques, Navarrese, and others who practice such cruelty toward Christians that they respect neither churches nor monasteries, spare neither widows nor orphans, neither age nor sex, but, after the manner of pagans, destroy and lay waste to everything."[14] It is within this context that Pierre writes of Raimon, "The count always had a remarkable liking for mercenaries, whom he employed to rob the churches, destroy the monasteries, and, wher-

---

13. See Peter, *History*, appendix D, "Mercenaries and the Crusade," pp. 299–301, and Philippe Contamine, *La Guerre au Moyen Age* (Paris: Presses Universitaires de France, 1980), trans. Michael Jones as *War in the Middle Ages* (Oxford: Blackwell, 1984), pp. 90–100 and 243–48.

14. "The Third Lateran Council, 1179," in Peters, pp. 168–70, at p. 169, translation modified; "De Brabantionibus et Aragonensibus, Navariis, Bascolis, Coterellis et Triaverdinis, qui tantam in Christianos immanitatem exercent, ut nec ecclesiis, nec monasteriis deferant, non viduis, et pupillis, non senibus, et pueris, nec cuilibet parcant aetati, aut sexui, sed more paganorum omnia perdant, et vastent," "Drittes Laterankonzil (1179), c. 27 De haereticis," in Kurt-Victor Selge, ed., *Texte zur Inquisition* (Gütersloh: Verlaghaus Gerd Mohn, 1967), pp. 23–25 at p. 24.

ever he could, deprive his neighbors of their possessions."[15] Indeed, Raimon
had been excommunicated in 1196 for relying upon hired soldiers to resolve his
conflicts with the abbeys of Saint-Gilles, Moissac, and Montauban over property rights and jurisdictions.[16] "You are retaining men from Aragon, treating
them in friendly fashion, and have joined them in devastating the land,"
Innocent charged in 1207.[17] When the count was briefly reconciled with the
Church in June of 1209, he agreed to expel mercenaries from his lands, but
again in 1213 and 1215 he was deemed guilty of still harboring these soldiers. By
refusing to curb his mercenaries, he was seen as undermining the social stabil-
ity of his lands, to the detriment of those—most especially the ecclesiastical
caste—who could not use force of arms to defend themselves.

If might appear that Raimon's resistance to keeping the peace was hardly
uncommon among feudal lords and thus hardly related to his alleged heresy,
yet in Pierre's chronicle, as in other clerical writings of this time, his involvement with mercenaries is regularly coupled with his involvement with heretics.
In condemning those who supported mercenaries, the Third Lateran Council
did so in the same canon in which it repudiated those who cultivated heretics,
and it assigned the same penalties to both groups of malefactors. When Peire
de Castelnau and Raoul de Fontfroide undertook "the business of the faith"
(*negotium fidei*) in Occitania, they attempted first to persuade the nobility in
Raimon's eastern territories to swear to agree to keep peace among themselves
in order to establish the environment within which heretics might be effectively
pursued. Similarly, when Urban II had initiated the First Crusade against the
Muslims in the Holy Land, he sought first to convince the nobility to cease their
internecine fighting.[18] One must turn one's aggression away from those within

15. Peter, *History,* § 42, pp. 24–25; "ruptarios mirabili semper amplexatus est affectu dictus comes, per quos spoliabat ecclesias, monasteria destruebat omnesque sibi vicinos quos
poterat exheredabat," Pierre, *Hystoria* (see n. 3 above), vol. 1, § 42, pp. 38–40.

16. See Pierre, *Hystoria,* vol. 1, pp. 38–39, n. 3 and p. 40, n. 1, for a list of the count's infractions and Sumption, *The Albigensian Crusade,* pp. 65–66 for a discussion of them.

17. Innocent III to Count Raimon VI of Toulouse, 29 May 1207. Quoted in "Translated
Extracts from Papal Correspondence," appendix F in Peter, *History,* pp. 304–5; "Aragonenses
familiariter tecum teneris, terram devastas cum ipsis," Innocent III, *Regestorum sive epistolarum,* PL 215, *Epistola* 69, col. 1168.

18. See Marie-Humbert Vicaire, "L'Affaire de paix et de foi du Midi de la France," *Cahiers
de Fanjeaux,* vol. 4, *Paix de Dieu et guerre sainte,* pp. 102–27. On the mercenaries, see H.
Géraud, "Les Routiers au XIIe siècle," *Bibliothèque de l'Ecole des Chartes* 3 (1841–42): 125–47.

the Church, namely, one's fellow orthodox Christians, if one intends to turn
it against those outside the Church, that is, heretics or Muslims. Indeed, given
the faith's reliance upon peace for its advancement, "the business of the
faith"(*negotium fidei*) which Peire and Raoul pursue in Occitania is regularly
coupled with "the business of peace" (*negotium pacis*), and the two goals are
often brought together as "the business of peace and the faith" (*negotium
pacis et fidei*).[19] When these legates turn against Raimon, it is not just for his
offense to the faith in protecting heretics, but also for his offense to the peace
in refusing to join the peace league.[20] As Pierre continually links faith and
peace, he continually links heretics and mercenaries, both of whom are
opposed to these paired conditions and supported by the count. With quotations from prelates, he complains of the inhabitants of Raimon's lands, for
example, that "heretics and mercenaries have each in turns violently assaulted
the clergy and the property of the Church," and of Raimon himself that "in
alliance with heretics, mercenaries, and other evil men, he attacked and subverted the Church of God and Christians, the faith, and peace."[21] Just as
heretics attack the Church through abstract denials of its institutional legitimacy, mercenaries attack representatives of the Church through assaults upon
their persons and their property. If heretics and mercenaries seem both to be
associated with these multiple levels of violence, some real and some symbolic,
it is because both thrive in a decentralized, disordered, violent society where
the rule of physical force prevails, like that of Occitania, which the clerics are
attempting to transform into a centralized, ordered, peaceful society where the
rule of law holds sway. In the former society, individuals, be they religious or
social deviants, can get away with what they would like, so long as they are
strong enough to do so, while in the latter all are obliged to conform to

19. Peter, *History,* § 59, p. 33; § 67, p. 38; § 74, p. 42; § 138, p. 76; and § 596, p. 268.
20. In the hands of the Church, peace seems to have become a means of attack. By uniting Raimon's eastern vassals in a peace league and by declaring Raimon *extra pacem* and liable
to attack for his refusal to join the league himself, the legates have set the count's vassals up
to defy him. As Vicaire writes in "L'Affaire de paix et de foi du Midi de la France," "La conjuration de paix entre barons est une arme offensive efficace contre quiconque ne veut pas
s'engager" (p. 114).
21. Peter, *History,* § 394, pp. 181–82; "in clerum et bona ecclesiastica hinc heretici inde ruptarii grassarentur," Pierre, *Hystoria,* § 394, vol. 2, p. 88; Peter, *History,* § 379, p. 176; "ecclesiam Dei et christianitatem, fidem et pacem, cum hereticis et ruptariis et aliis pestilentibus
fortius impugnavit et dampnificavit," Pierre, *Hystoria,* vol. 2, § 379, p. 75.

religious or social norms.[22] If Raimon is a supporter of both heretics and mercenaries, and if believers of the heretics in general are "given over to . . . pillage [and] murder," it is because they spurn a peace that would put an end to their disordered behavior.[23]

Indifferent to the peace, which he disrupts as he likes, Raimon is also said to be indifferent to oaths, which he breaks with regularity. At this time, members of the seigniorial class used oaths to call upon God as a witness to confirm utterances no mere human being could verify, such as assertions of their intention to perform certain acts. While lords took oaths seriously, given the dishonor attributed to those who broke them, they also tended to go back on their words when circumstances made it advisable to do so. Philip Augustus swore an agreement with the count of Flanders in 1197 which he later revoked, alleging that it had been made under coercion. John Lackland broke his allegiance with his brother Richard the Lion-Hearted when the latter was on crusade and, later, in captivity, affiliated himself with Philip; upon Richard's release from prison, John then returned to Richard, disregarding the oaths he had made to the French king. In like manner, Pierre charges, when Raimon swore to take

22. Walter Map refers to the Brabantines as "a sect of heretics [*secta hereticorum*]" in *De Nugis Curialium*, distinction 1, ch. 29, p. 118. Though Map acknowledges that these mercenaries confess Christ with their mouths as Catholics do, he maintains that they deny him with their acts. Their bands are composed of vassals who have rebelled against their lords and monks who have risen up against their abbots, he states. Having resisted the authorities to which they were subjected, they now destroy monasteries, villages, and towns. If these troops are to be understood not simply as pillagers but as heretics, Map suggests, it is because they "made themselves a law wholly against law [*legem sibi fecerunt, omnino contra legem*]" (p. 118) and because, by so disregarding the human order, they necessarily disregard the divine order. When Map attributes to these bands "hatred of God and man [*odio Dei et hominum*]" (p. 118), he indicates that the antipathy the mercenaries exhibit toward their fellow man implies an antipathy toward God, and when he terms them heretics, he indicates that this detestation of God implies heterodoxy. The Fourth Lateran Council also refers to the heretical aspects of mercenaries. See Bouquet 19, p. 598.

23. Peter, *History*, § 13, p. 13; "qui dicebantur credentes hereticorum dediti erant . . . rapinis, homicidiis," Pierre, *Hystoria*, vol. 1, § 13, p. 15. In "L'Affaire de paix et de foi du Midi de la France," Vicaire explains well in how a movement for peace on the part of the Church could turn so quickly to war. "La paix dont il est question ici n'est pas une oeuvre d'homme, c'est une paix transcendante, la Paix de Dieu, la Paix qui est Jésus-Christ" (p. 124), he writes. Because the peace consists of a blessed state that can be found in its full perfection only in heaven, a war against those who prevent us from attaining that beatitude can be an appropriate means of approaching it, in this fallen world. "Faire la guerre sainte, c'est pacifier une terre où la paix véritable avait péri avec la foi" (ibid., p. 125).

up arms against the heretics and their southern protectors and to support the crusaders in their similar actions, he spoke falsely, with no intention of ever fulfilling the spirit of his oath. Despite Raimon's professed ardor for the Church, Pierre writes, "I declare the count a false and most perfidious crusader. He took the cross not to avenge the wrong done to the crucifix but to conceal and cover his wickedness for a period."[24] In support of this assertion, Pierre alleges that Raimon played a double game as a crusader, seeming to assist the French invaders in their conquests but actually subverting their aims. Under "the mask of virtue," Raimon persuaded Simon to destroy several *castra* (or fortified villages) between his lands and the territories the crusaders had conquered, alleging that their elimination would be to Simon's benefit when it would actually strengthen his own position.[25] When the crusaders besieged the city of Lavaur, twenty-two miles from Toulouse, Raimon made a show of helping them by allowing provisions to be brought from Toulouse to the camp outside the walls, but at the same time he secretly undermined their efforts by sending a seneschal and several knights to contribute to the defense within. In other ways, Pierre relates, "the count of Toulouse continued surreptitiously to hinder Christ's business as much as he could."[26] With a play on words that seems to him telling, Pierre writes that "the Toulousan count" (*Tholosanus*) can be shown to be "deceitful" (*dolosanus*).[27] Raimon's mind goes in "twists and turns," Pierre asserts, and he is "like a man shifty and cunning, slippery and inconstant."[28] When Raimon weeps, the tears he sheds are "not tears of devotion and penitence, but of iniquity and deceit."[29] When he performs penance, his contrition is not sincere but "feigned."[30] By virtue of his natural "cunning," Raimon is

24. Peter, *History*, § 80, p. 45; "O falsum et perfidissimum crucesignatum, comitem dico Tholosanum, qui crucem assumpsit, non ad vindicandam injuriam Crucifixi, set ut suam ad tempus celare posset et tegere pravitatem!" Pierre, *Hystoria*, vol. 1, § 80, p. 80.

25. Peter, *History*, § 111, p. 61; "sub specie boni," Pierre, *Hystoria*, vol. 1, p. 116.

26. Peter, *History*, § 170, p. 91; "comes siquidem Tolose negotium Christi, quantum poterat, latenter impediebat," Pierre, *Hystoria*, vol. 1, § 170, p. 172.

27. Peter, *History*, § 68, p. 39; "comes Tholosanus, immo dicamus melius 'dolosanus,'" Pierre, *Hystoria*, vol. 1, § 68, p. 67.

28. Peter, *History*, § 71, p. 40; "versutias," Pierre, *Hystoria*, vol, 1, § 71, p. 71; Peter, *History*, § 57, p. 32; "sicut homo versipellis et callidus, lubricus et inconstans," Pierre, *Hystoria*, vol. 1, § 57, p. 53. See also Peter, *History*, § 68, p. 40; "sicut homo verspiellis et callidus," Pierre, *Hystoria*, vol. 1, § 68, p. 68.

29. Peter, *History*, § 164, p. 89, translation modified; "non . . . lacrime devotionis et penitentie, sed nequicie et doloris," Pierre, *Hystoria*, vol. 1, § 164, p. 169.

30. Peter, *History*, § 57, p. 32; Pierre, *Hystoria*, vol. 1, § 57, p. 53.

able to make oaths that he has no intention of keeping, to express atonement for sins he has no intention of abandoning, and, in doing so, to mislead secular and sacred authorities into thinking that he is not the opponent of the Church and the crusade that he is. Changing his position from one day to the next, Raimon, in Pierre's account, attempts to manipulate the papal legates and the crusaders, so that he might retain and, later, regain his lands.

It might appear that Raimon's faithlessness under oath, like his disruptiveness under peace treaties, is hardly unique to the heterodox, yet in Pierre's chronicle this fault betrays the count's heresy. Throughout the work, "faith" (*fides*) refers to the true faith, that is, to belief in the true God and, hence, to belief in orthodox Christianity, which alone recognizes that true God. The archbishopric of Narbonne, which included the bishoprics of Toulouse, Carcassonne, Béziers, and other important cities of the region, is described as a place "where once the faith had flourished" and where now "the enemy of the faith began to sow tares."[31] "The business of the faith" refers to an effort on the part of the Church to repair the damage sown by the devil, whether first through preaching or later through warfare.[32] If "faith" signifies the belief of the Catholics, "infidelity" (*infidelitas*) indicates the belief of the heretics, which is imagined only as an absence of faith. Peire de Castelnau and Raoul de Fontefroide, Pierre writes, combat not "the plague of heresy" but "the plague of infidelity" in Toulouse, even as neighboring cities were caught up in "the city's infidelity."[33] As his choice of this purely negative term might suggest, Pierre often insists that the supposed faith of the heretics is no faith at all. The heretics and their believers are described on more than one occasion as joined "in faith, or, rather, in infidelity."[34] If God is the one Being who truly is in its full perfection, as Catholic theology traditionally holds, those who believe in another god believe in a lesser or even nonexistent being. Since a true and

31. Peter, *History,* § 5, p. 7; "cepit Inimicus fidei superseminare zizania," Pierre, *Hystoria,* vol. 1, § 5, p. 5.

32. See Peter, *History,* p. 6, n. 9.

33. Peter, *History,* § 6, p. 8: "pestem infidelitatis," Pierre, *Hystoria,* vol. 1, § 6, p. 6; Peter, *History,* § 9, p. 9; "ejusdem infidelitatis," Pierre, *Hystoria,* vol. 1, § 9, p. 9.

34. Peter, *History,* §13, p. 13; "in fide (immo in infidelitate)," Pierre, *Hystoria,* vol. 1, § 13, p. 15. See also Peter, *History,* § 29, p. 22; "fidem (immo infidelitatem)," Pierre, *Hystoria,* vol. 1, § 29, p. 33, and Peter, *History,* § 54, p. 29; "fides (immo perfidia)," Pierre, *Hystoria,* vol. 1, § 54, p. 48. "Infidelity" also refers to an unwarranted violation of an oath sworn to one's lord. See *L'Ancienne coutume de Normandie,* ed. W. L. de Gruchy (Jersey: C. Le Feuvre, 1881), p. 42, and *Summa de legibus Normannie,* ed. E. J. Tardif (Rennes: Fr. Simon, 1906), pp. 38–39.

present Being can inspire only a true and present faith, a false or absent being would inspire a false or absent faith. While Pierre uses the language of "faith" and "infidelity" when speaking of his characters' orthodoxy and heterodoxy, he also uses this language when referring to their sincerity and insincerity in taking oaths. Having decried Raimon's "incredulity" or, later, his "infidelity" in speaking of his heresy, he then asserts, "The count, who had renounced the faith and was worse than any infidel, put no store by oaths. He gave his solemn word often enough, but perjured himself just as often."[35] Comparing Raimon's rejection of the faith which had once tied him to God, on one hand, and his rejection of the faith which had once tied him to his fellow man, on the other, Pierre explains the connection between these two betrayals. In the call for the crusade included in Pierre's chronicle, Innocent encourages the French lords to turn their backs on Raimon, whatever alliances they may have had with him, because "the canons of the holy Fathers provide that when one is dealing with a man who does not keep faith in God [*qui Deo fidem non servat*] and has therefore been excluded from communion with the faithful, faith need not be kept [*fides servanda non sit*]."[36] A man who keeps faith with his fellow men does so because he has faith in God, in whose name he has sworn his oath and from whom he expects punishment should he fail to keep it. Raimon, however, who breaks faith with his contemporaries, does so because he breaks faith with God, in whose name he has sworn only cynically, if at all, and from whom he expects no penalty should he deceive. If Raimon is, as Pierre claims, "a perjurer in all things" and if believers in the heretics are, in general, "given over to . . . all kinds of perjury," it is because they lack the faith—that is, the true faith—that would prevent them from acting in such a way.[37]

Chafing under the constraints of peace treaties and oaths, Raimon is, finally, said to resist the constraints of marriage. Between the early eleventh century and the early thirteenth, marriage was evolving from a purely secular arrangement, brokered by families desirous of establishing certain alliances with each other and terminated when other alliances became more attractive or other

35. Peter, *History,* § 27, p. 21; "qui fidem negaverat et erat infideli deterior, nunquam deferens juramento, juravit pluries, pluries pejeravit," Pierre, *Hystoria,* vol. 1, § 27, p. 30.

36. Peter, *History,* § 62, p. 36; "cum juxta sanctorum patrum canonicas sanctiones ei qui Deo fidem non servat fides servanda non sit, a communione fidelium segregato," Pierre, *Hystoria,* vol. 1, § 62, p. 61.

37. Peter, *History,* § 27, p. 22; "per omnia et perjurus," Pierre, *Hystoria,* vol. 1, § 27, p. 31; Peter, *History,* § 13, p. 13; "qui dicebantur credentes hereticorum dediti erant . . . perjuriis . . . universis," Pierre, *Hystoria,* vol. 1, § 13, p. 15.

brides seemed to promise a long-awaited heir, into a sacred union celebrated by a priest and ended only through formal annulment.[38] Despite the efforts of the Church to define marriage as a sacrament, instituted by God and indissoluble by man, other, more casual attitudes toward this institution persisted. In France, King Louis VII, troubled by the alleged infidelity of his wife, Eleanor of Aquitaine, and by her failure to give him a son, separated from her and wed Constance of Castile. Louis's son Philip Augustus, struck by repugnance for his wife, Ingeburga of Denmark, on their wedding night, repudiated her immediately thereafter and united with Agnès de Meran. In Occitania, Peter of Aragon convinced Bernart IV, the count of Comminges, to repudiate his wife, Maria de Montpellier, so that Peter could marry her himself and gain access to her considerable lands, which bordered on his own territories in Provence. Though Peter swore as part of his marriage vows never to repudiate Maria, in a few years he was already trying to get the alliance annulled in order to wed a daughter of Philip Augustus. During these years, as the Church was striving to strengthen marriages, it was also attempting to limit them to partners outside seven degrees of affinity, in the belief that *caritas*, or natural friendship, should already be uniting those within closer relationships. Even during Raimon's life, however, men and women regularly chose as spouses their distant cousins, whether because they were ignorant of these ties at the time of their weddings, because the advantages of the matches persuaded them to overlook the taint of incest, or even, for the most cynical, because an ambiguously legal marriage could prove useful later on, should a spouse wish to dissolve it.[39] After twelve years of wedlock, Louis was proved to be related to Eleanor in the fourth and fifth degrees; divorced, Eleanor then married Henry Plantagenet, the future Henry II of England, though she was rumored to have slept with his father. Philip Augustus's first wife, Isabella of Hainault, was said to be related to him

38. See Georges Duby, *Medieval Marriage: Two Models from Twelfth-Century France*, trans. Elborg Forster (Baltimore: Johns Hopkins University Press, 1978); *Le Chevalier, la femme, et le prêtre* (Paris: Librairie Hachette, 1981), trans. Barbara Bray as *The Knight, the Lady, the Priest: The Making of Modern Marriage in Medieval France* (New York: Pantheon, 1983); and Charles Edward Smith, *Papal Enforcement of Some Medieval Marriage Laws* (Baton Rouge: Lousiana State University Press, 1940).

39. Peter the Cantor cites a knight who remarked of his future wife, "I like her because she has a large dowry. She is probably related to me by an affinity of the third degree, but this is not close enough to require me to repudiate her. Still, if I find I do not like her anymore, because of that affinity I could be granted a divorce," quoted in Duby, *The Knight, the Lady, and the Priest*, p. 209.

within the forbidden degrees; his second wife, Ingeburga, was said to be linked to him in the fourth degree; and his third wife, Agnès, had a sister married to his nephew. Bernart de Comminges justified his repudiation of Maria de Montpellier by pointing out that they were related in the third and fourth degrees. It is within the context of such marriages, contracted with little concern for previous unions or incestuous affiliations, that Pierre takes Raimon to task for his wives. He writes: "Whenever his own wife displeased him, he sent her away and married another,"[40] so that he had had four wives, of whom three were still living. (The count in fact had had five wives: Aimersent de Pelet—whom Pierre overlooks—Béatris de Béziers, Bourguigne de Lusignan, Joan of England, and Eleanor of Aragon.)[41] Pierre protests that Raimon's fourth wife, Joan, was related to him in the third degree, and his fifth wife, Eleanor, in the third and fourth degrees. Even in his choice of concubines, Pierre claims, Raimon was not repelled but attracted by the possibility of incest. Of Raimon's consorts, Pierre writes, "None of them could please him unless he knew his father had previously slept with her."[42] Like many of his seigneurial peers, Raimon undermined the bonds established between people through lasting and exogamic marriages as well as through oaths and peace treaties.

Despite the frequency with which wives were repudiated and incestuous matches contracted among nobles in general during Raimon's day, Pierre traces the count's illicit amorous activity to his heresy. Summarizing the heretics' views of marriage, Pierre writes, "They preached that holy matrimony was mere harlotry, and that no one could find salvation in it by begetting sons and daughters."[43] Raimon sent his wives away, Pierre states, not just because he was succumbing to political ambitions or personal distaste but also because "he attached such little weight to the sacrament."[44] While Raimon may act like other, Catholic husbands in rejecting his wives, he is seen as especially prone to

<hr/>

40. Peter, *History*, § 38, p. 23; "quocienscunque ei displicuit uxor propria, ipsam dimittens, aliam duxit," Pierre, *Hystoria*, vol. 1, § 38, p. 35.

41. On Raimon's wives, see Devic and Vaissète, *Histoire générale de Languedoc*, vol. 5, pp. 400–404. Raimon's own daughter by Béatris, Constansa, was repudiated by Sancho VII the Strong, king of Navarre, only to marry Peire Bermond de Sauve, lord of Anduze.

42. Peter, *History*, § 41, p. 24; "vix enim aliqua ei placere poterat, nisi sciret patrem suum prius concubuisse cum ea," Pierre, *Hystoria*, vol. 1, § 41, p. 38.

43. Peter, *History*, § 12, p. 12; "sacrum matrimonium meretricium esse nec aliquem in ipso salvari posse predicabant filios et filias generando," Pierre, *Hystoria*, vol. 1, § 12, p. 13.

44. Peter, *History*, § 38, p. 23; "adeo parvipendebat matrimonii sacramentum," Pierre, *Hystoria*, vol. 1, § 38, p. 35.

behave in this manner because of his acceptance of a theology that dismisses the sanctity and even the value of lawful wedlock. In denigrating marriage, Pierre continues, the heretics go so far as to maintain that nonmarital sexual activity, including incest, is no worse than conjugal intercourse and thus to legitimize these illegitimate acts. "Some of the heretics declared that no one could sin from the navel downward," Pierre asserts.[45] "They said that it was no greater sin for a man to sleep with his mother or his sister than with any other woman."[46] If Raimon married women within prohibited degrees of kinship, if he slept with concubines already known to his father, if he slept even with his own sister, as Pierre too alleges, it was not just because he was succumbing to political inducements or carnal desires but because he held, in accordance with the heretics' theology, that it was no crime at all to engage in these acts. Indeed, when Pierre writes, "The count was a lustful and depraved man, to the extent that—we can take it as an established fact—he abused his own sister," he adds that he committed this crime "out of contempt for the Christian religion."[47] Far from being deterred by the Church's condemnation of his relationships with his father's consorts or his own sibling, Raimon is aroused by the thought of defying Catholicism's authority. If Raimon is "a lustful and depraved man" and if the believers of the heretics in general are said to be "given over to . . . carnal allurements,"[48] it is not only because they reject the Church's distinction between licit and illicit loves but because they take delight in rejecting this distinction.

It may be true that the same Raimon who dismisses peace treaties, oaths, and marriage can be, at times, gentle toward the weak, faithful to his word, and loyal toward his wife, but Pierre maintains that these seemingly contradictory aspects of his behavior are actually complementary. Raimon supports mercenaries who pillage the land, robbing churches and monasteries and abusing the weak and defenseless, but he also protects the heretics, who are not permitted

45. Peter, *History,* § 17, p. 14; "quidam heretici dicebant quod nullus peccare poterat ab umbilico et inferius," Pierre, *Hystoria,* vol. 1, § 17, p. 17.

46. Peter, *History,* § 17, p. 14; "dicebant quod non peccabat quis gravius dormiendo cum matre vel sorore sua quam cum qualibet alia," Pierre, *Hystoria,* vol. 1, p. 17.

47. Peter, *History,* § 41, p. 24; "etiam semper fuit luxuriosus et lubricus dictus comes quod, sicut pro certo didicumus, sorore propria abutebatur," Pierre, *Hystoria,* § 41, p. 38; Peter, *History,* § 41, p. 24; "in contemptum religionis christiane," Pierre, *Hystoria,* vol. 1, § 41, p. 38.

48. Peter, *History,* § 13, p. 13; "qui dicebantur credentes hereticorum dediti erant . . . carnis illecebris," Pierre, *Hystoria,* vol. 1, § 13, p. 15.

to kill any living creature. Far from glorying in his own strength as a feudal lord in contrast to these weak ministers of a minority religion, he is said to have claimed that "he would rather be like a certain heretic, a very evil man living at Castres in the diocese of Albi, who had lost his limbs and lived in wretchedness, than be king or emperor."[49] The same lord who shows himself to be unmoved by the sufferings of monks and priests at the hands of his mercenaries reveals himself to be affected by the situation of a heretic. Raimon breaks his word to the papal legates and the crusaders when he sees it to be in his best interest to do so, but he keeps faith toward the heretics, even to the point of self-sacrifice. Pierre quotes the count as having announced, "I know that I will suffer disin-heritance for the sake of these Good Men, but I am ready to suffer not just dis-inheritance for them, but even execution."[50] In accordance with this proclamation, Pierre observes, "None of the papal legates could ever persuade him to drive the heretics from his domain, even though the legates did very often compel him to denounce them."[51] As he would abandon a kingdom or an empire to be as holy as one of the heretics, so would he forsake his own lands and his own life for the sake of such men. Raimon repudiates his wives when-ever they begin to displease him, with an apparent indifference for their fates, but, Pierre relates, he encouraged one of these wives (identified elsewhere as Béatris) to become a heretic and promised that he would support her if she did so.[52] The chronicler records that "if she was willing to become a heretic, he

49. Peter, *History,* § 36, p. 23; "Dixit preterea aliquando sepedictus comes quod mallet assimilari cuidam pessimo heretico, qui erat apud Castras in Albiensi diocesi, detruncatus men-bris et habitu miserabilis, quam esse rex vel imperator," Pierre, *Hystoria,* vol. 1, § 36, pp. 34–35.

50. Peter, *History,* § 46, p. 25; "Scio me exheredandum fore pro bonis istis hominibus. Sed non tantum exheredationem, immo etiam decapitationem, pro ipsis paratus sum sustinere," Pierre, *Hystoria,* vol. 1, § 46, p. 41.

51. Peter, *History,* § 37, p. 23; "nunquam ab aliquo apostolice sedis legato potuit induci ad hoc ut sepedictos hereticos de terra sua depelleret, licet, compulsus ab ipsis legatis, eos mul-tociens abjuravit," Pierre, *Hystoria,* vol. 1, § 37, p. 35.

52. The *Cartulaire de Maguelone* confirms that Béatris was hereticated and that she received support from her former husband after entering into this state. It records of Raimon that "he had three living wives, of which one is a heretic to whom he has granted a certain prebend [*tres uxores vivas habet, quarum una est heretica, cui certam prebendam concessit*]" (vol. 2, no. 300). See Devic and Vaissète, *Histoire générale de Languedoc,* vol. 5, pp. 421–22. Jacques de Vitry tells an *exemplum* about Béatris as well, where the countess returns in a dream to her Catholic daughter Constansa and speaks ironically of the glory and honor she has received in heaven, after having believed "the Good Men and their doctrine [*bonis hominibus et eorum doctrine*]." See G. Frenken, "Die Exempla des Jakob von Vitry" in *Quellen und Untersuchungen zur lateinischen Philologie des Mittelalters* 1 (1914): 43–44.

would take care of all her needs," adding, "and this is how it turned out."[53] While Raimon's expression of concern for his wife's spiritual well-being may be interpreted as yet another means to be rid of a woman he has tired of, it is noteworthy that his wife appears to have consented to his plan without objection, as if she too found it attractive. Throughout his career, Raimon might seem to disregard the authority of the clergy and, especially, of the papal legates, but he consistently acknowledges the prestige of the Cathar heretics. When the count meets the heretics, Pierre relates, he genuflects before them, requests their blessing, embraces them, receives and cherishes gifts from them, and, most likely, listens to their sermons in his palace at night. When Raimon travels, he does so with heretics dressed as Catholics in his entourage, so that wherever he may be at the end of his life, he will be able to receive the *consolamentum* they offer. On the eve of Raimon's departure to fight in Provence, Pierre tells us, he arose in the middle of the night, went to a gathering of heretics, and informed them, "Masters and brothers, the fortunes of war are mixed. I commend my body and soul to your hands."[54] Interweaving his description of Raimon's his harshness, his infidelity, and his irreverence toward Catholics with his gentleness, faithfulness, and reverence toward Cathars, Pierre suggests that it makes sense that those who act badly toward the good will act well toward the wicked.

If Raimon errs in the eyes of the Church, Pierre makes clear, it is less as an individual, in his own personal beliefs, than as a lord, in his public dominion. As Innocent himself recalls in a letter to prelates in 1212 and at the Fourth Lateran Council of 1215, Raimon was never formally summoned before an assembly of ecclesiastics, never interrogated about his beliefs, and never convicted of heresy, as was customary with those suspected in matters of faith. He attracted Church disfavor not so much by practicing the Cathar religion as by refusing to respect the peace that the Church was attempting to impose upon his lands, which would have curbed his use of force in realizing his secular aims; by refusing to respect the oaths to combat heretics that the Church was attempting to impose upon the southern lords, which would have subordinated his feudal ties to his vassals to its religious ties to all Christians; and by rejecting the marriage that the Church was striving to institute among the nobility,

---

53. Peter, *History,* § 39, p. 24; "si vellet fieri heretica, ipse ei in omnibus provideret; et factum est ita," Pierre, *Hystoria,* vol. 1, § 39, p. 37.

54. Peter, *History,* § 44, p. 25; "Domini ac fratres! Bellorum varii sunt eventus. Quicquid de me contingat, in manus vestras commendo corpus et animam meam," Pierre, *Hystoria,* vol. 1, § 44, p. 40.

which would have transformed what had been a purely dynastic arrangement among members of this class into a holy sacrament. In all of these actions, Raimon set himself against a new vision of society that the Church had been attempting to implement since the mid-eleventh century. For Pierre, it stands to reason that society should be organized around God rather than around man and, hence, that it should be led by weak clerics, whose power derives from their representation of God through words, rather than by strong noblemen, whose power is rooted in their enforcement of men's will through warfare. It is self-evident, as he sees it, that the best nobles are those like Simon de Montfort, the hero to Raimon's antihero in Pierre's *Hystoria*, who, having much to gain from the Albigensian Crusade, shows himself to be as submissive to the Church that justifies this war as the count of Toulouse is rebellious to it. For Raimon, however, it is not surprising that this vision of society should be repugnant, coming, as it does, at the expense of his own power, and that the notion of sanctity espoused by the Cathar heretics, who radically renounce temporal ambition, should be preferable to that of the Catholic clerics, who are attempting to broaden their sphere of influence. Heresy, in Pierre's texts, though the provocation of the Church's action, is never a discrete, self-contained entity but always part of a more general disobedience to the Church's will, and it is for this reason that a powerful, independent nobleman like Raimon should fall prey to its charge.

RAIMON ROGIER OF FOIX

At first glance, it may seem that the two composers of the *Canso de la Crozada* remain almost entirely silent about the heretics who provoked the war of which they write.[55] Guilhem de Tudela, the pro-French author of the first part of the

---

55. Ever since Paul Meyer first distinguished the two authors of the *Canso de la Crozada* in his "Recherches sur les auteurs de la *Chanson de la croisade albigeoise*," *Bibliothèque de l'Ecole des chartes* 1 (1865): 401–22, scholars have devoted themselves to comparing these two poets. Guilhem is generally held to have been a cleric and jongleur who lived in Montauban for some time preceding the city's conquest by the crusading armies and later became a canon in Saint-Antonin, under the patronage of Baldwin, brother to Raimon VI of Toulouse. But Robert Lafont, "Guilhem de Tudela: Ses origines, les origines de son art," in *Les Troubadours et l'état toulousain avant la croisade (1209)*," ed. Arno Krispin (Actes du Colloque de Toulouse, 9 et 10 décember 1988) (Paris: CELO/William Blake & Co., 1994), pp. 219–28, and Jean-Marie d'Heur, "Sur la date, la composition et la destination de la *Chanson de la croisade albigeoise* de Guillaume de Tudèle," in *Mélanges d'histoire littéraire, de linguistique et de philologie romanes offerts à Charles Rostaing* (Liège: Association des romanistes de l'Université de Liège, 1974), pp. 231–66, both call into question some details of his biography. Though a partisan of

poem, devotes only 100 of his 2772 lines to these deviants in the faith, and his anonymous pro-Occitan continuator speaks of them even more succinctly, in 34 of his 6810 lines. This silence about the heretics can be traced, in large part, to the tradition of the chanson de geste, which encourages the two authors to focus upon the most powerful figures in the war, be they lay or ecclesiastical, at the expense of the many people affected by their actions. Given this generic orientation, Yves Dossat's words about the continuator's verses remain true for the work as a whole: "Heretics remain in the background. The war is a war of conquest, and heresy serves only as a pretext to justify the misdeeds of the crusaders."[56] Not one of the almost four hundred contemporary individuals who appear in the poem is identified as a heretic or a believer in the heretics, and insofar as these sectaries surface at all, it is only as part of the general, nameless population against which the specific, named characters emerge. In those few passages where these authors do address the heterodox masses, Guilhem speaks of them with conventional ecclesiastical disapproval, and the continuator gives no indication that he looks upon them more fondly. Yet if the poem gives the impression that heretics are base, plebeian masses, marginal to the events of the crusade, and that the nobly born and bred individuals central to this history are all orthodox, evidence both inside and outside the text suggests that this is not the case. Just as the tendency to transgress ecclesiastical strictures common to both nobles and heretics made Raimon seem, to Pierre, a Cathar believer, it also makes figures elsewhere identified as Cathar believers seem, to Guilhem

---

the crusaders' cause, Guilhem is praised by Martin-Chabot and others for his "impartialité" in depicting the two sides of the war, in Guilhem de Tudela and Anonymous Continuator, *Chanson de la croisade albigeoise*, ed. Eugène Martin-Chabot (vol. 1, Paris: Honoré Champion, 1931; vols. 2 and 3, Paris: Les Belles Lettres, 1957 and 1961), vol. 1, p. x. Yet he is also criticized by Yves Dossat, in "La Croisade vue par les chroniqueurs," *Cahiers de Fanjeaux*, vol. 4, *Paix de Dieu et guerre sainte en Languedoc au XIIIe siècle* (Toulouse: Privat, 1969), pp. 221–59, for his fearful prudence in the face of danger. The second, anonymous author, often commended for his greater poetic skill, is thought to have been a Toulousan cleric, and his contribution to the work, colored by his patriotic enthusiasm for his doomed land, is sometimes regarded as constituting the Occitan national epic. Rita Lejeune situates the poem within the context of other Occitan crusade epics in "L'Esprit de croisade dans l'épopée occitane," in *Paix de Dieu et guerre sainte en Languedoc au XIIIe siècle* (Toulouse: Privat, 1969), pp. 143–64, esp. pp. 15–60.

56. Dossat, "La Croisade vue par les chroniqueurs," p. 254. Simone Weil (alias Emile Novis) writes similarly in "L'Agonie d'une civilisation vue à travers un poème épique," in *Le Génie d'Oc et l'homme méditerranéen, Les Cahiers du Sud* 249, (1943): 99–107: "Ce qui frappe tout d'abord dans ce récit d'une guerre religieuse, c'est qu'il n'y est pour ainsi dire pas question de religion" (p. 100).

and the continuator, simply nobles, acting in accordance with the values of their caste. Their singularity as lords and ladies overshadows any group identity they might possess as adherents to the deviant faith.

In the first part of the poem, Guilhem represents the heretics, in general, as masses of people who have brought their unhappy fate upon themselves through their foolish and wicked behavior. From the very first verses, he recounts how most of the southerners from Béziers to Bordeaux subscribed to the heretical religion so adamantly that they refused to listen to the Cistercian preachers, dismissing their words as no more important than the buzzing of a bee or a rotten apple. In rejecting these preachers' words, Guilhem writes, the heretics showed themselves to be a "foolish [or mad] people" (*folas gens* or *fola gent*) because they underestimated the animosity their orthodox opponents bore toward them, a "hatred greater than that they bear toward the Saracen people,"[57] and because they underestimated the power these opponents wielded to act upon that animosity. When the Cistercian abbot and papal legate Arnaut Amalric traveled up and down this region, urging heretics to repent, Guilhem relates, "they mocked him and scorned him as a simpleton," though the poet remarks, "This was the legate to whom the pope gave so much power that he could destroy them, the misbelieving people."[58] Having covered their ears before those who attempted to reason with them, the citizens of Toulouse remained convinced that if they held together, no harm could come to them, yet they were deluding themselves about the forces they would soon face. Since the southerners rejected the abbot, Guilhem writes, "it is no marvel to me if men confound them, rob them, pillage them, and chastise them by force."[59] Just as many of those who turned away from such preachers have already perished, "others will still have the same fate, before the war is finished, for it cannot be otherwise."[60] Foolish or mad, the heretics showed themselves to be a "wicked" and "bad" people as well, for by ignoring the dangers to which their obstinacy in error exposed them, they sought their own destruction.[61] Even when the southern cities were taken by the crusaders and their inhabitants were

---

57. "folas gens," *Chanson de la Croisade albigeoise*, § 28, 2 and § 47, 11; and "fola gent," ibid., § 47, 11. ". . . felonia / Plus qu'a gent sarrazina!" ibid., § 7, 17–18.

58. "Eli plus l'escarnian e·l tenian per sot," ibid., § 3, 12; "Per so si era legatz, que l'apostolis l'ot / Donat tant de poder que·ls decaia per tot, / La mescrezuda jant," ibid., § 3, 13–15.

59. ". . . no m'em fas meravelha / Si om be los confon, ni los rauba, ni·ls pelha, / Ni per forsa·ls castia," ibid., § 46, 10–12.

60. "E o seran encara, tro la guerra er fenia, / Car als estre non pot," ibid., § 2, 29–30.

61. "felos," ibid., § 4. 4; § 49, 11; and § 107, 6; and "malvaza," ibid., § 17, 11.

given one last chance to repent of their errors and save their lives, the heretics spurned the raft cast out to them. After Casseneuil was taken, for example, many a male heretic and "many a fair female heretic" was thrown into the fire at this city, Guilhem states, "for they did not want to convert, however much one might entreat them."[62] As the southerners' rejection of the Cistercians' salutary words led inexorably to the declaration of the crusade against them, so their rejection of even such last-minute appeals to convert led inexorably to their annihilation. While Guilhem regrets the events that have come to transpire in Occitania, he sees the heretics and not the clerics or the crusaders as responsible for them.

In recounting the events that followed the crusaders' conquest of Lavaur, in particular, Guilhem shows little hesitation in condemning the masses of heretics who resided within this city and in approving their punishment. When the French armies took Lavaur on May 3, 1211, after a siege of five or six weeks, "they burned four hundred heretics of foul race in a fire and made a great pyre."[63] He adds, "There was a great massacre which will be spoken of, I believe, until the end of the world."[64] Commenting upon these heretics, Guilhem writes, "Lords, well should they be chastised. As I saw and heard, they suffered greatly, for they do not do what the clerics and crusaders ask them to do. In fine, they will end up, when they are pillaged, as those here did, and no one will have concern for them, neither God nor anyone in the world."[65] When Guilhem notes the size of the massacre and the fame it will thus acquire, he is admitting the remarkable and even terrible nature of this event, yet when he asserts that no one who hears of the heretics' plight will be troubled by it, he is defending what happened. As he has spoken of the sad fate of heretics in general as inevitable, given their rejection of orthodoxy, he speaks of the destruction of the heretics at Lavaur in particular as inevitable, given their refusal to obey the clerics and the crusaders. Sources outside the poem justify Guilhem's attitude toward the city. According to historical records, Lavaur had long been

---

62. "mota bela eretge," ibid., § 14, 8; "Car convertir no·s volon tan no·ls podon preir," ibid., § 14, 9.

63. "Ben quatre ens eretges de linage putnai / I arseron en un foc e si feron gran rai," ibid., § 71, 6–7.

64. ". . . fo lo faita aitant grans mortaldat / Qu'entro la fin del mon cug qu'en sia parlat," ibid., § 68, 29–30. Guilhem de Puylaurens states that three hundred, not four hundred, heretics were burned.

65. "Senhor, be s'en devrian ilh estre castiat / Qe, so vi e auzi, son trop malaürat, / Car no fan que·ls mando li clerc e li crozat / C'a la fi o fairan, can siran desraubat, / Aisi co aisels feiron, e ja non auran grat / De Dieu ni d'a quest mon," ibid., § 68, 31–36.

regarded as a principal source of heresy in Occitania and therefore had long served as an object of ecclesiastical concern. In 1178, a quarter century before the declaration of the Albigensian Crusade, Henri de Marcy, the abbot of Clairvaux, had resumed his predecessor Bernard's mission against the heretics of Toulouse by debating with two individuals in this meridional capital, both of whom hailed from Lavaur. Two and a half years later, Henri, now cardinal of Albano and a papal legate, marched on Lavaur with a small army, demanded to see his former disputants, and persuaded them in public to renounce their errors. Still, Lavaur continued to maintain numerous residences for heretics in its walls and to serve as the seat of a Cathar bishopric. At the time of the siege, Guilhem de Puylaurens would point to the high number of heretics in Lavaur as proof that Raimon VI had failed in his promise to rout his lands of these malefactors, terming the city a place "in which, through the heretics, the devil had established his seat and of which he had made a synagogue of Satan."[66] Pierre too depicts Lavaur as a city "in which was the source and origin of all heresies."[67] In describing hundreds of heretics "of foul race," Guilhem de Tudela leaves these people as an undifferentiated mass, known only by their heterodoxy, and hence as the embodiment of an abstract category of evil, and he shows little compassion for them.

When, however, Guilhem describes Aimeric de Montréal, the brother who defended Lavaur, and Guirauda de Lavaur, the sister who appears to have ruled the city after the death of her husband, he displays far different sentiments than he did when portraying the masses underneath them. Of Aimeric, Guilhem writes, "There was no more distinguished knight in Toulouse or in the county, nor a more generous spender, nor one of greater nobility."[68] While Guilhem scorns the four hundred heretics "of foul race" burned at Lavaur, he praises this lord of distinguished lineage. Disregarding the ignoble masses who exhibit none of the virtues of the aristocracy, he lauds this noble individual, who showed himself to be powerful in his society, liberal in his expenditures, and illustrious in his ancestors.[69] Though he commends the massacre of the anony-

66. "in quop per hereticos dyabolus sedem sibi paraverat et fecerat Sathanas synagogam," Guillaume de Puylaurens, *Chronique*, Prologue, p. 28.

67. Peter, *History*, § 220, p. 113; "in quo erat fons et origo tocius hereseos," Pierre, *Hystoria*, vol. 1, § 220, p. 219.

68. "N'ot plus ric cavaler en Tolza ni el comtat, / Ni plus larc depesaire, ni de major barnat," *Chanson de la croisade albigeoise*, § 68, 11–12.

69. For the knightly ethos which Aimeric is depicted as exemplifying, see Linda Paterson, "La *Chanson de la croisade albigeoise*: Mythes chevaleresques et réalités militaires," in *La*

mous four hundred, Guilhem is disturbed by the execution of Aimeric and his four score knights. "Lord Aimeric was hanged and many a knight with him," he writes. "Eighty were hanged there, as is done with thieves, and they were put on gibbets, one here and the other there."[70] He notes, "Never was such a great baron in Christianity, I believe, hanged with so many knights."[71] By juxtaposing the greatness of this baron with the base manner of his death, Guilhem intimates that the crusaders should have respected the nobility of his birth, position, and virtue instead of treating him like a common criminal. Of Guirauda, Aimeric's sister, Guilhem writes, even more sympathetically, that "no man in the world—know this truthfully!—left her without having received something to eat."[72] Having established Aimeric's munificence by describing him as "a generous spender," he establishes Guirauda's similar largesse by asserting categorically, with the confidence of a professional troubadour dependent upon the gifts of others, that every visitor benefited from her table. Having questioned the manner of Aimeric's execution, given his noble virtues, he deplores even more openly the form of Guirauda's demise: "Lady Guirauda was thrown into a pit. They covered her with stones, which was a misfortune and a misdeed."[73] In a second telling of the event, Guilhem provides the most detailed account of physical suffering in the work. "Lady Guirauda was taken

---

Croisade; Réalités et Fictions, ed. Danielle Buschinger, Actes du Colloque d'Amiens, 18–22 mars 1987 (Göppingen: Kümmerle Verlag, 1989), pp. 193–203, and "Knights and the Concept of Knighthood in the Twelfth-Century Occitan Epic," *Forum for Modern Language Studies* 17 (1981): 115–30, both reworked as chapter 4, "The Knight and Chivalry," in *The World of the Troubadours: Medieval Occitan Society, c. 1100–1300* (Cambridge: Cambridge University Press, 1993), pp. 63–84. René Nelli stresses the centrality of munificence, like that which Aimeric exemplifies, in thirteenth-century Occitan culture. When the Inquisition attacked the southerners' luxury and largesse, Nelli maintains, it was attacking the social conditions from which their courtly culture had emerged. See *L'Erotique des troubadours* (Toulouse: Privat, 1963), p. 239.

70. "N 'Aimericcs fon pendutz e mant cavaler lai: / Quatre vins n 'i penderon, com om los lairos fai, / E·ls meson en las forcas, l 'u sai e l 'autre lai," *Chanson de la croisade albigeoise*, § 71, 8–10. According to Pierre des Vaux-de-Cernay, after the crusaders hanged Aimeric, the gallows collapsed, obliging the soldiers in attendance to slay their prisoners with their swords.

71. "C'anc mais tant gran baro en la crestiandat / No cug que fos pendutz, ab tant caver de latz," ibid., § 68, 14–15.

72. "Que ja nulhs hom del segle, so sapchatz de vertatz / No partira de leis entro agues manjat," ibid., § 68, 23–24.

73. "Estiers dama Guirauda qu 'an en un potz gitat: / De peiras la cauferon; don fo dols e pecatz," ibid., § 68, 20–24. Martin-Chabot rejects the interpretation of the unusual *cauferon* as the third person plural of the perfect of *calcar* and proposes, instead, a derivation

crying and weeping and screaming," he states. "They threw her crosswise in a pit, well I know. They covered her with stones. There was great lamentation."[74] If the crusaders' treatment of Guirauda is even more reprehensible than their handling of her brother, as Guilhem suggests that it is, it is at least in part because the captors fail to act toward her as men are expected to act toward aristocratic ladies. Guilhem contrasts the crusaders' overall harshness toward Guirauda with one soldier's exceptional courtesy toward the other women of the castle. "And, as for the other ladies, a courteous and gay Frenchman had them all released, like a valiant and true man."[75] Men who are "courteous and gay," men who are "valiant and true," men who exemplify courtliness and chivalry, like this unique, unnamed Frenchman, do not bury noblewomen alive under piles of stones but, rather, grant them their freedom. Men who adhere to the courtly code do not treat ladies as they might treat other persons of a lesser rank or of the rougher sex but, rather, approach them more gently. As the object of violence shifts from an anonymous mass, characterized only by its members' adherence to heretical beliefs, to a named individual, male or female, defined through his or her possession of noble qualities, the violence ceases to be acceptable.

Despite Guilhem's positive depiction of Aimeric and Guirauda and his objection to the manner of their deaths, this brother and sister appear to have been no more orthodox than the rest of the city's inhabitants. Guilhem acknowledges that Aimeric was not unfamiliar with the Cathar heretics or the Waldensians: "To his misfortune [*mala*], he saw the heretics and the sandal-wearers."[76] Yet with the adverbial expression "to his misfortune," it is not the fact that Aimeric consorted with the heterodox that Guilhem deplores but the trouble that followed from this fact. He represents Guirauda as an aristocratic widow at a time when the females of her class were not infrequently hereticated after the deaths of their husbands and as the ruler of her city at a time when the most notable women of Occitania tended to be Cathar matriarchs.[77] Sources

---

from *caussar* whose meaning he glosses as "terrer (un arbre), c'est-à-dire accumuler de la terre autour de la base de son tronc, prise métaphoriquement et s'appliquant aux pierres entassés sur le corps précipité au fond d'un puits," ibid., pp. 172–73, note g.

74. "Na Guirauda fo preza que crida e plora e brai, / En un potz la giteron a travers, ben o sai; / De peiras la cauferon, trop om n'ac gran esmai," ibid., § 71, 11–13.

75. "E de las autras donas us Frances cortes gai / Las fe estorcer trastotas, com om pros et verai," ibid., § 71, 14–15.

76. "Mala vi los eretges e los ensabatatz," ibid., § 68, 13.

77. On the prevalence of Cathar matriarchs, especially in Aimeric and Guirauda's family, see Barber, *The Cathars: Dualist Heretics in Languedoc in the High Middle Ages* (Harlow, UK:

outside the poem confirm Guilhem's insinuation of these siblings' heterodoxy. We know Aimeric and Guirauda to be the children of Sicart II de Laurac—one of the most important rulers of Montréal, a *castrum* eighteen miles west of Carcassonne, and Laurac, a *castrum* another eighteen miles west of Montréal—and his wife Blanca. After Sicart died in 1200, Blanca established herself as a heretic in Laurac, along with her daughter Mabelia; two of her other daughters, Esclarmonda and Navarra, were also perfected.[78] Like Raimon VI and other southern lords, Aimeric had first allied himself with Simon, yet finding himself stripped of his lands, he too switched sides in the conflict, defending his sister Guirauda's city of Lavaur against the northern barons. While Aimeric's familial and political affiliations could render his orthodoxy suspect, apart from his evident frequentation of Cathars and Waldensians, Guirauda's situation was even more compromised. Pierre writes of her, "The lady of the castle, a widow by the name of Guirauda, was a heretic of the worst sort," and the chronicler Aubri de Trois-Fontaines agrees, likewise describing her as "an Albigensian of the worst sort."[79] Robert d'Auxerre, intensifying this negative portrait by attributing to this lady sexual as well as doctrinal deviations, claims that at the time of her death she was pregnant with her brother's or her son's child.[80] If Aimeric and Guirauda are not portrayed as heretics or believers in this poem and are therefore not subject to the same condemnation as their vassals, it appears to be because their noble qualities prevent them from being perceived and repudiated as such.

In the second part of the poem, the continuator, who says virtually nothing about heretics in general, displays an open and unambiguous affection for the seemingly orthodox Raimon Rogier, the count of Foix, who, along with Bernart IV, the count of Comminges, and Raimon Rogier Trencavel II, the viscount of Béziers and Carcassonne, was one of the most powerful lords of

---

Longman, 2000), pp. 34–43. On the attractiveness of Catharism to women, see Anne Brenon, *Les Femmes cathares* (Paris: Perrin, 1992), and René Nelli, *La Vie quotidienne des cathares du Languedoc au XIIIe siècle* (Paris: Hachette, 1969), pp. 79–94.

78. See Elie Griffe, *Le Languedoc cathare de 1190 à 1210* (Paris: Letouzey et Ané, 1971), pp. 109–13.

79. Peter, *History*, § 215, p. 111; "domina siquidem castri, vidua nomine Giralda, erat heretica pessima," Pierre, *Hystoria*, vol. 1, § 215, pp. 214–15; "pessima Albigensis," Aubri de Trois-Fontaines, *Chronica*, in MGH *Scriptores* 22, pp. 631–950, at p. 892.

80. "Domina castri Guirauda nomine, que de fratre vel filio se concepisse dicebat, proiecta est in puteum et acervus lapidum superiectus," Robert d'Auxerre, *Chronicon*, in MGH *Scriptores* 26, pp. 219–87, at p. 276.

Occitania after Raimon VI. In April of 1214, after years of combat with the crusaders, Raimon Rogier decided to reconcile himself with the Church. He met
with the cardinal and papal legate Pietro di Benvenuto in the archbishop's
palace in Narbonne, swore to oppose heretics, mercenaries, and the dispos-
sessed southern knights known as *faiditz*, and granted the castle of Foix to the
cardinal as a guarantee of his oath.[81] Given his submission to the Church,
Raimon Rogier was surprised to find this fortress transferred to Simon's guard
in May of 1215, as if it were being permanently alienated from him. In one of
the most famous passages in the poem, admired for its stylized but impassioned
dialogue as well as for the veracity of its historical details, Raimon Rogier arrives
at the Fourth Lateran Council in November of 1215 to argue for the restoration
of his lands. Here, in the old Lateran basilica, he declares, "I can justify myself
and take a true oath that never have I loved a heretic nor any believing man,
nor have I wanted their company, nor did my heart consent to it, and thus the
Holy Church finds me obedient."[82] He reiterates, later, "Never did I love
heretics, neither believers nor robed ones."[83] With these words, the count identifies the heterodox as those who personally bear affection for the heretics and
their believers, who personally seek out the companionship of these sectaries,
and who through this affection and companionship personally rebel against the
Church, and he denies that he has ever been such a man. Raimon Rogier cites
his financial support of the Cistercian abbey of Boulbonne in the Ariège, in
which his family members were traditionally interred and by whose monks he
has been well received. He affirms, "I rendered, gave, and offered rightly to
Boulbonne, where I was welcomed, where all my lineage is given and
buried."[84] The count cites, too, his current presence at the council, in recog-

---

81. For Raimon Rogier's statement of submission to the Church, see Devic and Vaissète,
Histoire générale de Languedoc, vol. 6, cols. 643–46.

82. "ieu me posc escondire e far ver sagrament / C'anc non amei eretges ni nulh home
crezent, / Ni volh ja lor paria ni mos cors no·ls cossent; / E pos la santa Glieza me troba obedient," *Chanson de la croisade albigeoise*, § 144, 12–15.

83. "Qu'anc no amei eretges, ni crezens ni vestitz," ibid., § 145, 36.

84. "Enans me soi rendutz e donattz e ufritz / Dreitamens a Bolbona, on ieu fui ben
aizitz, / On trastotz mos lhinatges es datz e sebelhitz," ibid., § 145, 37–39. Martin-Chabot
comments on the words "rendutz e donatz e ufritz": "Les mots . . . ont ici un sens spécial, à
peu près l'équivalent à celui d'oblat; ils sont synonymes et se rapportent à l'usage, fort répandu
en ce temps-là dans les contrées méridionales, de se faire accepter, moyennant une donation,
complète ou partielle de ses biens, comme 'donat' par une communauté religieuse; on était
ainsi agrégé à cette communauté et cela comportait des avantages d'ordre spirituel, dont celui
d'y recevoir la sépulture religieuse" (ibid., p. 51, no. 4).

nition of the pope as the legitimate arbiter of spiritual and temporal affairs, as further proof of his Catholicism. He opens his speech by addressing Innocent as "Right lord pope, to whom all the world is responsible, and who holds the place of Saint Peter and his government, in whom all sinners should find a protector and who must defend right and peace and justice, because you are placed here for our salvation."[85] By referring to the pope as the inheritor of the seat of Saint Peter, the count recognizes in him an authority which the heretics reject. By depicting him as the protector of all sinners, he acknowledges, moreover, not only the general, spiritual relationship between the pontiff and all Christians but also the specific, juridical relationship between the pope and himself that was established by his submission to the clerics and his absolution a year and a half before. If the heterodox are those who love the heretics and their believers and hate monks, cardinals, and popes, as Raimon Rogier suggests they are, the count himself, who supports the abbey of Boulbonne and submits to the Church, is clearly not among them.

Raimon Rogier does acknowledge that the presence of heretics in his family and in his neighboring lands might seem to implicate him in their error, but he attempts to separate these heretics from himself. At the time of the council, the count's sister, the now celebrated Esclarmonda de Foix, was living on an allodium of the canons regular of Saint Antonin in Pamiers—a city ruled jointly, though unhappily, by both the canons and the count—and, it appears, was disseminating the doctrine of the Cathar sect. "If my sister is evil or a sinful woman," the count declares (with an interesting use of hypothesis), "I should not suffer for her sin."[86] While the count refrains from arguing, in general, that lords are under no obligation to repress the heretics on their lands, he does argue that the presence of a heretic on his lands, even a heretic who happens to be his sister, does not diminish his own orthodoxy. He is a Catholic, Esclarmonda a Cathar, and, according to the count, the fact that he allows her to live in Pamiers and supports her in her lifestyle is no evidence that he is any less a Catholic: "To be on the land is how the law is interpreted. For the count my father said, before he died, that, if he had a child in any place who was afflicted, he should return into the land in which he had been raised and he

---

85. "Senher dreitz apostolis, on totz lo mon apent / E te·l loc de sent Peire e·l seu gover-nament, / On tuit li pecador devon trobar guirent, / E deus tener drechura e patz e judja-ment, / Per so car iest pauzatz al nostre salvament," ibid., § 144, 6–10.

86. "E si ma sor fo mala ni femna pecairitz, / Ges per lo sieu pecat no dei estre peritz," ibid., § 145, 42–43.

should have the means on which to survive and he should be welcomed."[87]
Citing this paternal dictate, the count suggests that his duty to his father and,
by extension, to his kinsmen takes precedence over his duty to the Church to
rout all heretics from his lands. At this time, moreover, the now famous mountain fortress of Montségur had recently been fortified and was well on its way
to becoming the principal refuge of the heretics.[88] "As for the peak of
Montségur," Raimon Rogier announces, "the law is clear, for never for one day
was I the proprietary lord."[89] While the count refrains from arguing, in general, that lords are under no obligation to repress the heretics on their lands,
he does argue that in this particular case he is under no obligation to repress
the heretics of this citadel because of his lack of title to this locale. As he had
cited "the law" of his father's will in defense of his tolerance of Esclarmonda's
presence in Pamiers, he now cites the law of land rights in defense of his tolerance of the heretics' presence at Montségur and thus suggests that his recognition of feudal law takes precedence over his recognition of ecclesiastical
commands.[90] Though the count does not deny his obligation to expel heretics
from his lands, he insists that his responsibility to his family and his vassals can,
at times, outweigh this obligation.

87. "estec en la terre es lo dreitz devezitiz / Car lo coms mos paire dih, ans que fos fenitz, /
Que si el efant avia qu'e nulh loc fos marritz, / Que tornes en la terra en que era noiritz / E
que i agues sos ops e i fos be reculhitz," ibid., § 145, 44–48.
88. At the beginning of the thirteenth century, the eagle's nest fortress of Montségur was
in ruins, yet around 1204 Fornieria de Péreille, a heretic separated from her husband, Guilhem
Rogier de Mirepoix, had the edifice restored so that it began to provide a refuge for other
heretics and *faiditz*. Around 1232, not long after the crusade had come to a close, Guilhabert
de Castres, the Cathar bishop of Toulouse, retreated here along with other members of the
Cathar hierarchy, making the site, in effect, the exiled capital of the persecuted religion. In
1242, a band of knights from Montségur traveled to Avignonet to assassinate a party of inquisitors and seize their registers, an act which prompted the siege and ultimately the conquest of
their *castrum*. On the complex network of families that ruled over Montségur—including
those of Péreille, Mirepoix, Foix, Trencavel, and Toulouse—see Michel Roquebert, *L'Epopée
cathare*, vol. 4, *Mourir à Montségur* (Toulouse: Privat, 1989), pp. 32–41, and Jean Duvernoy,
Le Dossier de Montségur: Interrogatoires d'Inquisition, 1242–1247 (Toulouse: Pérégrinatus,
1998).
89. "Del pog de Montsegur es lo dreg esclarzitz, / Car anc no·n fui un jorn senher poes-
taditz," *Chanson de la Croisade albigeoise*, § 145, 40–41.
90. Of the term *dreitz* Martin-Chabot comments, "Le mot du text signifie littéralement:
'droit': cette épithète s'applique à un souverain, à un seigneur ou supérieur, temporel ou spirituel, qui exerce un autorité légitime par doit de naissance ou d'élection, qui, par conséquent,
est le juge naturel de ses suject ou subordonnés, et dont il est juste et légal qu'ils respectent
les sentences et les décisions," ibid., p. 45, no. 1.

However forceful his words before the Fourth Lateran Council, Raimon Rogier finds a worthy antagonist in the figure of Folquet de Marseille, the Cistercian bishop of Toulouse. While the count distinguishes his own orthodoxy from the heterodoxy of those on his lands, the bishop refuses to make this distinction and, instead, interweaves assertions about the spiritual status of the count with assertions about the spiritual status of his subjects. "Lords," argues the bishop, "you have just heard the count affirm that he has held himself separated and removed from heresy. I say that his land was the greatest root of it, and that he loved and favored and welcomed them, and that all of his county was full and replete with them."[91] Through the paratactic structure of his syntax, the bishop suggests that however much the count protests his innocence of heresy, he must be considered guilty of protecting heretics because his lands contained so many of them. Far from allowing the count to contrast himself from his county, the bishop maintains that the character of the count is demonstrated by the character of his territory. Speaking of the oath which the count of Foix, along with the counts of Comminges and Toulouse, had taken at Narbonne to expel heretics and mercenaries from his domains, the bishop affirms to the pope, "I, who am your bishop, swear to you truthfully that none of them is a Catholic nor holds to his oath."[92] Again, through parataxis, the bishop suggests that, because these counts do not adhere to their promises to expel heretics from their lands, they are themselves heretical. Though the count excuses his tolerance of his sister Esclarmonda and the heretics of Montségur by citing feudal laws, the bishop faults him on both cases. Of Esclarmonda, the bishop relates, "And his sister was a heretic. When her husband died, she was then at Pamiers for more than three full years. To her evil doctrine she converted many."[93] Further, of Montségur the bishop relates, "The peak of Montségur was fortified so that it could defend [the heretics], and . . . [the count] consented to have them there."[94] Whatever feudal laws Raimon Rogier cites in defense of

---

91. "Senhors . . . / tug auzetz que·l coms ditz / Qu'el s'es de la eretgia delhiuratz e partitiz; / Eu dic que sa terra fo la mager razitz; /E el les a amatz e volgutz e grazitz / Et totz lo seus comptatz n'era ples e farsitz," ibid., § 145, 5–10.

92. "Eu, que so tos avesques, te jur be veramens / C'us d'els non es catholics ni no te sagramens," ibid., 148, 28–29. See Devic and Vaissète, *Histoire générale de Languedoc*, vol. 5, pp. 588–89 on the submission of these counts to the Church.

93. "E sa sor fo eretja cant moric sos maritz, / Es estec poih a Pamias plus de tres ans complitz / Ab sa mala doctrina n'i a mans convertitz," *Chanson de la Croisade albigeoise*, § 145, 13–15.

94. "E·l pog de Montsegur fu per aital bastitz / Qu'el les pogues defendre, e·ls hi a cossentitz," ibid., § 145, 11–12.

his toleration of Esclarmonda and Montségur, Folquet insists that ecclesiastical laws should take precedence over them. However pious Raimon Rogier may show himself to be in sacred matters, by donating to abbeys and submitting to the pope, and however virtuous he may show himself to be in secular matters, by respecting his father's will and a neighbor's property, none of this, Folquet maintains, can excuse the presence of heretics in his county.

Church decrees from the late twelfth and early thirteenth centuries justify Folquet's insistence that someone like Raimon Rogier, who tolerates heretics, is himself to be treated as one of their believers. A "receiver" (*receptor*) of heretics is understood to be someone who allows heretics onto personal property, a "defender" (*defensor*) of heretics to be someone who protects them from the actions of the Church against them, and a "favorer" (*fautor*) of heretics to be someone who in any way assists them. These decrees make clear that it is not only heretics and their believers but also their "receivers," "defenders," and "favorers" who are guilty of heresy. In 1179, for example, the ecclesiastics at the Third Lateran Council declared of the Cathars, "We decree that they and all those who defend and receive them are anathematized."[95] In 1184, Pope Lucius III similarly announced in the decretal *Ad Abolendum*, after condemning the Cathars and Waldensians, "We decree that their receivers and defenders, and, in like manner, all who show any countenance, or favor, to the aforesaid heretics, . . . shall be subjected to a similar sentence."[96] In 1212, Peter of Aragon protested to the prelates at the Council of Lavaur that "the count of Foix is not a heretic and has never been one," yet the prelates responded, "It has been proven that, for a long time, the count was a receiver of heretics and is still today their receiver and defender, for there is no doubt that the believers of heretics are themselves heretics."[97] A year later, Innocent informed Peter that the "protectors and defenders" of the heretics were "more dangerous than the heretics

---

95. "The Third Lateran Council," in Peters, p. 169; "eos, et defensores eorum, et receptores, anathemati decernimus subjacere," "Drittes Laterankonzil," in Selge, *Texte zur Inquisition*, p. 24.

96. "Pope Lucius III: The Decretal *Ad Abolendum*, 1184," in Peters, pp. 170–73, at p. 171, translation modified; "Receptores et defensores eorum, cunctosque pariter, qui praedictis haereticis ad fovendam in eis haeresis pravitatem patrocinium praestiterint aliquod vel favorem, . . . simili decernimus sententiae subiacere," Selge, *Texte zur Inquisition*, p. 27.

97. Peter, *History*, § 373, p. 175; "comes Fuxensis nec hereticus fuerit nec sit," Pierre, *Hystoria*, vol. 2, § 373, p. 71; Peter, *History*, § 381, p. 177; "constat de ipso quod hereticorum extitit a longo tempore receptator et impresentiarum etiam receptator est eorum et defensor, presertim cum non sit dubium quin credentes hereticorum heretici sint dicendi," Pierre, *Hystoria*, vol. 2, § 381, p. 77.

themselves."[98] Protecting the heretics, the count has failed to rout men from his lands, and that very failure has exposed him to accusations. In *Ad Abolendum* the pope demanded that all secular rulers swear to aid the Church in its struggle against the heretics and warned that if they did not do so, they would be excommunicated and their lands subject to interdict. In the proceedings of the Fourth Lateran Council, at which the count, in the *Canso de la Crozada*, pleads his case, the prelates reiterated the requirement that secular rulers take and keep such an oath and once again threatened that those who did not do so would find their lands taken from them and given to faithful Catholics. For both the bishop who speaks in this poem and for the clerics who composed Church directives during these years, an individual's orthodoxy is determined in large part by his willingness to support the Church in its prosecution of heretics, and a ruler's orthodoxy by his willingness to expel heretics from his or her lands.

If Church decrees affirm that the receivers and defenders of heretics are to be considered heretics themselves, other documents establish that Raimon Rogier was even guiltier of supporting these deviants than the poem supposes. Though he distances himself from Esclarmonda and her heresy at the Fourth Lateran Council, we know that Raimon Rogier was present at her *consolamentum* at Fanjeaux in 1204, which appears to have been an important and well-attended event. And though he and the bishop focus upon this one sister, we know that the count had another sister by the name of Cecelia, who was a Waldensian and lived with Esclarmonda at Pamiers. Raimon Rogier's wife Philippa was herself said to be a heretic, either a Cathar in residence at the castle of Dun or a Waldensian in residence with her sisters-in-law at Pamiers.[99] Pierre, who depicts Philippa as a Waldensian, asserts that "to the great displeasure of the canons, . . . these three women spread the poison of heresy in public and private meetings and seduced the hearts of the simple."[100] An aunt

---

98. Peter, *History,* § 409, p. 189; "plus ipsis hereticis sunt nocivi," Pierre, *Hystoria,* vol. 2, § 409, p. 104.

99. Pierre represents Philippa as a Waldensian, but Peire-Guilhem d'Arvigna testifies in the *Registre de Bernard de Caux (1246–47),* ed. Jean Duvernoy (Toulouse: Pérégrinateur, 1990), that she was a Cathar Perfect and lived in the castle of Dun, where Raimon Rogier visited her in 1206. Rogier Bernart, the son of Raimon Rogier and Philippa, testified to his mother's Catharism. See Devic and Vaissète, *Histoire générale de Languedoc,* vol. 8, deposition of March 12, 1241. See also Griffe, *Le Languedoc cathare,* pp. 154–55.

100. Peter, *History,* § 198, p. 104; "invitis predictis canonicis et . . . renitentibus publice et privatim venenum sue nequicie seminantes, corda simplicium seducebant," Pierre, *Hystoria Albigensis,* § 198, p. 199–200.

by the name of Faïs de Durfort was also reported to be a Cathar heretic, and as Pierre puts it, a "heresiarch" of this religion, [101] and she too was allowed to install herself at Pamiers. When the canons of Saint Antonin, already irritated by the presence of Raimon Rogier's heretical sisters and wife, expelled the aunt from the city, the count allowed his cousin to slay one of the canons and blind another, in anger at this show of disrespect. Building upon the religious diversity of his relatives at Pamiers, Raimon Rogier is said to have hosted a debate between Catholics and heretics in the city in 1207, in which one of his sisters took part.[102] Even outside his immediate family, the count is known to have consorted with heretics, meeting with Blanca and Mabelia in Laurac in 1200 and with Brunissen, the hereticated mother of a knight of his acquaintance, in Toulouse in 1209. Still, despite his attendance at heretical ceremonies and his visits to heretics, Raimon Rogier is said to have refrained from adoring the consecrated members of the sect and receiving their blessing on these occasions.[103] The count's relationship with the heretical citadel is no less ambiguous than that with his heretical female relatives. While he distances himself from Montségur at the council, we know that he possessed this mountain, not directly, as Raimon de Péreille did, but indirectly, as the latter's overlord, and that he would have had to give permission for the peak to be fortified.[104] As

101. Peter, *History,* § 199, p. 104; "heresiarcham," Pierre, *Hystoria,* vol. 1, § 199, p. 200.

102. The Spanish Cistercian Esteban de Mania is said to have told this sister at this time, "Go, madam, and work on your distaff! It is not appropriate for you to speak in a debate of this sort [*Ita, domina, filare colum vestram! Non interest vestra loqui in huiusmodi concione*]," Guillaume de Puylaurens, *Chronique,* § 8, p. 54. Though the sister who participated in this debate goes unnamed in this text, and though the heretics concerned are identified as Waldensians, not Cathars, it is often thought that the sister mentioned is Esclarmonda, and not the count's Waldensian sister, partly because manual labor like that which Esteban recommends would have been pursued by a Cathar Perfect but not by a Waldensian. It is on the basis of such slight and ambiguous allusions to Esclarmonda that Napoléon Peyrat, in *Histoire des albigeois* (Paris: Librairie Internationale, 1870–72), and his successors, such as Simone Coincy-Saint Palais, in *Esclarmonde de Foix, princesse cathare* (Toulouse: Privat, 1956), developed the legend of "la grande Esclarmonde," the great Cathar archdeaconness, patroness of troubadours, and ruler of Montségur. J. M. Vidal attacked this romantic view of Esclarmonda in "Esclarmonde de Foix," in the *Revue de Gascogne* n.s. 11 (1911): 52–79, as based on little evidence. Suzanne Nelli reemphasized the importance of the few facts we possess about this figure in "Esclarmonde de Foix," *Cahiers d'études cathares* 6, no. 24 (1955): 195–204. Krystel Maurin comments rightly of this Esclarmonde, "Il y a eut juste assez d'histoire pour créer l'illusion et juste assez d'absence pour permettre la mystification," *Les Esclarmonde: La femme et la féminité dans l'imaginaire du catharisme* (Toulouse: Privat, 1995), p. 119.

103. See Peyrat, *Histoire des albigeois,* vol. 1, p. 359.

104. A fourteenth- or fifteenth-century prose adaptation of the *Canso de la Crozada* cites the count as identifying the true owner of Montségur as his sister. The adaptation relates,

Pierre alleges, the count "allowed heretics and their supporters to stay in his territories and helped and encouraged them as much as he could," and, for this he was liable.[105]

Despite the evidence that Raimon Rogier was indeed a receiver and defender of heretics and, as such, blameworthy in the eyes of the Church, the continuator sides with him against Folquet. During their confrontation at the council, the count affirms his right to hold his lands. If he has fought crusaders, even massacring and mutilating them, as he was accused of doing on the field of Montgey, he claims to rejoice over those he has killed and to mourn over those who escaped his slaughter. He declares, "As for those brigands, those false traitors, those liars wearing crosses by whom I was destroyed, none has been taken by me or by my people who did not lose his eyes and feet and wrists and fingers."[106] He has acted brutally with these crusaders, he states, because they have acted brutally with him. As a result of their invading, pillaging, and appropriating the county of Foix, not only was his territory was ransacked but, as he puts it, "I was destroyed." So great is Raimon Rogier's identification with his lands that he speaks passionately of his desire to regain those territories and ironically of the missteps that led to their loss. "Let no man hold me for a simpleton or a fool if I want to recover the castle of Foix," he announces. "God knows, by my heart, how prudently I would hold it."[107] He speaks ardently about this topic to his fellow soldiers as well as to the ecclesiastics, urging his men, as they prepare to fight, "to think of the country and how it may be helped," and inciting them "to sell dearly our inheritances."[108] On the battlefield, as on the council floor, Raimon Rogier exemplifies what is known as *Paratge*, an Occitan word normally translated as "lineage" in which nobility of birth and character is linked with possession of ancestral lands. In a region

---

"Touchant lo dit pech de Montségur, que jamay el no era mestre ni senhor; car son payre quand morut, la donet a sadita sor, que ne fossa dona et senhoressa," Devic and Vaissète, *Histoire générale de Languedoc*, vol. 8, cols. 1–206, at col. 105.

105. Peter, *History*, § 197, p. 104; "hereticos et hereticorum fautores in terra sua tenuit, fovit, quantum potuit, et promovit," Pierre, *Hystoria*, vol. 1, § 197, p. 199.

106. "Mas d'aquels raubadors, fals trachors, fe-mentitz / Que portravan las crotz, per que eu fos destruisitz, / Per me ni per los meus non fo nulhs cosseguitz / Que no perdes los olhs e·ls pes e·ls punhs e·ls ditz," *Chanson de la Croisade albigeoise*, § 145, 54–57.

107. "E ja nulhs hom no·m tenga per nesci ni per fat / S'ieu lo castel de Foih volia aver cobrat, / Que Dieus ne sab mon cor co·l tendria membrat," ibid., § 146. 3–4.

108. "E pessem d'est lengatge, com sia milhoratz," ibid., § 210, 23; "car vendre las nostras heretatz," ibid., § 211, 4.

where the division of inheritance among siblings had produced numerous independent landholders with only the loosest of ties to their overlords, the attachment that these noblemen and noblewomen felt to inheritances had become
strong and, as we saw with Aimeric and Guirauda, the munificence that can
result from such autonomous wealth had become highly prized. As C. P. Bagley
writes, "the poet does not separate honor as a quality from the possession of
honor as land and authority. To lose one's fief is to be deprived of honor in both
senses, and so become a *faidit*."[109] While the *faidit* is regarded compassionately, his situation is regarded as worse than death because he has lost not only
his territory but his honor, his independence, and his capacity for generosity.
Though no character in the poem is ever said to possess *Paratge*, several are
said to desire it, and, states Bagley, "To desire *Paratge* is to desire the restoration of one's lands."[110] It is this restoration of *Paratge*, which is also a restoration of his lands, that the count seeks and believes to be his inalienable right.

   Even though Folquet was a pursuer of heretics extolled by the Church and
elevated to Dante Alighieri's Paradise, the continuator condemns him for his
actions against Raimon Rogier and other southerners. At the Fourth Lateran
Council, the bishop denies the count's right to hold his lands, given his defense
and protection of heretics. Far from viewing the crusaders as "liars wearing
crosses," as Raimon Rogier does, Folquet perceives them as "pilgrims, by
whom God was served."[111] He cries, "He who killed them and broke them and
tormented them should no longer hold land. This is what he deserves!"[112]
Whereas the count insists upon the ideal of *Paratge*, which Charles Camproux,
for one, views as defining the national identity of Languedoc, the bishop insists
upon the ideal of Orthodoxy, which can be seen as defining the universal identity of the Church.[113] Whereas the count insists upon the feudal law under

   109. C. P. Bagley, "*Paratge* in the Anonymous *Chanson de la Croisade albigeoise*," *French
Studies* 21 (1967): 195–204, at p. 200.
   110. Ibid., p. 199.
   111. "E los teus peregris, per cui Dieus fo servitz, / Que cassavan eretges et rotiers e
faizitz, / N'a tans mortz e trencatz e brizatz e partitz / Que lo cams de Montjoy ne remais si
crostitiz / Qu'encara·n plora Fransa e tu·n remas aunitz," *Chanson de la Croisade albigeoise*,
§ 145, 16–20.
   112. "E cel que los a mortz ni brizatz ni cruichitz / Ja no deu tenir terra, c'aitals es sos
meritz!" ibid., § 145, 25.
   113. Charles Camproux, *Histoire de la littérature occitane* (Paris: Payot, 1953), p. 224. Elie
Griffe also contrasts the attitude of the southern barons and the Church's prelates in *Le
Languedoc cathare*, pp. 53–59.

which he possesses an inalienable right to rule his land, the bishop insists upon the ecclesiastical law under which the count has forfeited that right through his toleration of heretics, mercenaries, and *faiditz*, whereas under that same law others, who serve God and the Church by opposing these subversives, have come to deserve this land in the count's stead. While Raimon Rogier stands by Raimon VI and his son and fights for the independence of Occitania from the French invaders, Folquet, though bishop of Toulouse, serves as one of Simon's closest counselors and uses his proximity to the crusade's leader to urge him regularly to destroy the city. The bishop advises Simon to slaughter all men, women, and children of the city, even those infants still suckling at the breast, because only by doing so will he know peace, and to strip them of all of their silver so that he can then vanquish Provence, Catalonia, and Gascony, as well as Languedoc. Taking advantage of the goodwill associated with his ecclesiastical office, Folquet tries to persuade the Toulousans that if they submit to Simon, he will treat them mercifully, though he knows that this conqueror will do no such thing. It is little surprise that the poet characterizes Folquet as "the wicked bishop" or that he describes Folquet and Simon as conspiring together "so that Worth and *Paratge* will lose their force."[114] While the count, despite his latent heterodoxy, is depicted as the epic hero of the chanson de geste, the bishop, as Bagley notes, is portrayed as the traitor.

According to Guilhem de Puylaurens, Folquet de Marseille once asked the knight Pons Azemar de Roudeille why he and his kind would not expel the heretics from their lands, even though he recognized the erroneousness of their beliefs, and the knight replied, "We cannot do it. We have been brought up among them, we have relatives among them, and we see them live honorably."[115] Pons Azemar and other Occitan noblemen may recognize that people around them are heretics, but they know them too well on account of the kinship and familiarity they share, and they respect them too much on account of the goodness of the heretics' lives, to persecute them for their creed. Like Pons Azemar and his companions, Pierre suggests, Philip Augustus, Peter of Aragon, and other noblemen are ready to overlook concerns about their kinsman Raimon Rogier's heterodoxy and his protection of heretics, perhaps

---

114. "l'avesque felon," *Chanson de la Croisade albigeoise*, § 200, 68. "E que Pretz e Paratges i perdra sa valor," ibid., § 175, 4.

115. "Non possumus; sumus enim nutriti cum eis, et habemus de nostris consanguineis inter ipsos et eos honeste vivere contemplamur," Guillaume de Puylaurens, *Chronique*, § 8, pp. 54–56.

dismissing his mercenaries, his broken oaths, and his multiple wives as no more than the typical behavior of a man of his class. Like these noblemen, Guilhem de Tudela and his continuator are inclined to disregard the heretical vices imputed to Aimeric, Guirauda, and Raimon Rogier because of their aristocratic virtues. These nobles and celebrators of the noble ethos all recognize an assortment of values, including honorableness, generosity, and gentleness, which are manifested in one's external comportment with others in the world. Yet Guilhem de Puylaurens comments, after recording Pons Azemar's remark, "It is thus that error, by the appearance of a pure life alone, tears unwary men from the truth."[116] As Pierre and his fellow ecclesiastics see it, the fact that people are heretics should negate whatever other virtues they possess and should even prompt one to reconsider the authenticity of those virtues. The clerics recognize only one value, that of orthodoxy, which is preserved in one's internal conscience, even at the expense of solidarity with one's vassals, loyalty to one's kinsmen, or protection of the weak. If one is to prosecute heretics and their believers, one must be able to reject any affiliation one may hold with these people and any virtues one may perceive in their behavior as deceptive illusions, and must concern oneself with their orthodoxy alone, as the sole significant truth about them.

If the ecclesiastical chroniclers of the affairs of Occitania at the turn of the twelfth and thirteenth centuries tend to identify the vices of noblemen and noblewomen with the vices of heretics, Pierre's *Hystoria Albigensis* and Guilhem and the continuator's *Canso de la Crozada* illustrate the dangers inherent in this association. When resistance both to the ecclesiastical campaign for "peace and faith" in these lands and to the extension of ecclesiastical power that comes with the campaign becomes evidence of heresy, all lords and ladies who assert their traditional seigneurial independence in the face of this movement begin to look heretical. When fidelity to kith and kin, including those of divergent religious beliefs, becomes proof of infidelity to the Church, all members of important families and networks will find the basis of their social standing tainted with error. The singularity of the noble individual, which makes this person irreducible to any broad social category such as that of heretics, paradoxically ensures that noble people will belong to this very category.

116. "Sic enim falsitas, sola nitide vite apparentia, subtrahebat incautos homines veritati," ibid., § 8, p. 56.

5

THE ROPES CUTTING INTO
ISEUT'S WRISTS

Heresy, Singularity, and the Romance of Tristan

One might expect, not only that the troubadours of the twelfth and thirteenth centuries would be heretics, as we saw in chapter 3, but that the courtly love of which the poets of the *lingua d'oc* as well as the *langue d'oïl* sang during this time period would have been regarded as heretical.[1] To begin with, courtly lovers often, if not always, seek the bodies as well as the hearts of the ladies they beseech. Occitan and French poets of this time period may differ from their Latin predecessors in the increasingly spiritual tenor of their amorous addresses, yet they continue to praise and

---

1. It has long been recognized that the term "courtly love" is highly problematic. Though medieval authors spoke of "love" (*amor*) or even "fine love" (*fin'amors*), it would not be until the late nineteenth century that the philologist Gaston Paris, in "Etudes sur les romans de la Table Ronde: *Lancelot du Lac*; *Le Conte de la Charrette*," *Romania* 12 (1883): 459–534, would coin the term *amour courtois* and identify the lover's social inferiority to his lady, his suffering as a result of his love, his purification through his suffering, and his awareness of the amorous code to which he adheres as the essential attributes of this phenomenon. While courtly love soon became seen as one of the primary themes of medieval Occitan and French literature, scholars such as D. W. Robertson Jr., "The Concept of Courtly Love as an Impediment to the Understanding of Medieval Texts," in F. X. Newman, ed., *The Meaning of Courtly Love* (Albany: SUNY Press, 1968), pp. 1–18, and John F. Benton, "Clio and Venus: A Historical View of Medieval Love," in ibid., pp. 19–42, put into question both the literary and the historical foundation of this perceived phenomenon. It is important to acknowledge the variety in depictions of love during the High Middle Ages and the possibility that a rigid adherence to the original definition of courtly love may prevent readers from recognizing that diversity. See, for example, René Nelli, ed., *Les Ecrivains anticonformistes du moyen âge Occitan*, vol. 2, *Hérétiques et politiques* (Paris: Editions Phébus, 1997), and Jean-Charles Huchet, *L'Amour discourtois: La "fin'amors" chez les premiers troubadours* (Toulouse: Privat, 1977). At the same time, it is important to acknowledge that medieval authors did make love

even to exalt the pleasures of the flesh. Such lovers often, if not always, direct their amorous attentions neither to women whom they have already married nor to young girls whom they might hope to wed but, rather, to the wives of other men. Andreas Capellanus goes so far as to assert in his *De Amore* that one cannot love one's spouse because love must be freely granted and freely withheld, in a manner impossible within the constraints of the marital bond, and because love must be pursued secretly and furtively, in a manner impossible within the openness and legitimacy of marriage. Enjoying carnal relations with ladies wedded to other men, such lovers approach these ladies as only God, the Virgin Mary, or saints should be approached. Bernart de Ventadour, for example, informs his beloved, "Lady, for your love, / I clasp my hands and worship you," and Chrétien de Troyes' Lancelot venerates a few of Guinevere's hairs as a relic and bows before her bed as before an altar.[2] If the Creator constitutes the only thing to be loved in and of itself, and if creatures constitute mere signs to be used in directing oneself toward this one thing, as medieval theologians believed, then clearly any practice which leads one to treat other human beings as things to be loved in and of themselves might be considered idolatrous, and any doctrine articulating and defending this practice might be regarded as heretical. In its refusal to respect the virtue of chastity over wantonness, the value of marriage over illicit intrigues, and the priority of the Creator over the creature, courtly love might seem to defy Christian teachings to the point where it represents, as Jeffrey Burton Russell puts it, "deviation from Christian principles, perversion of Christian ideals, and hostility to the Christian clergy and at least implicitly to the Christian Church"—and perhaps even, as Alexander Demony suggests, a full-fledged "heresy."[3]

---

a major theme in literary works of the time, differing in both the quantity and the quality of its expression from preceding centuries, even if they did not identify this theme with any technically precise label, as the French philologist did. I admit the difficulty of speaking of "courtly love," but, given the gap between what medieval authors represented and what they named, I fail to perceive a better alternative.

2. "Domna per vost'amor / jonh las mas et ador," in "Tant ai mo cor ple de joya," *The Songs of Bernart de Ventatorn,* ed. Stephen G. Nichols, Jr. (Chapel Hill: University of North Carolina Press, 1965), pp. 169–72, at p. 170.

3. Jeffrey Burton Russell, "Courtly Love as Religious Dissent," *Catholic Historical Review* 60 (April 1965–January 1966): 31–44, at p. 44. See also Russell, *Dissent and Reform in the Early Middle Ages* (Berkeley: University of California Press, 1965), p. 187; Alexander J. Denomy, *The Heresy of Courtly Love* (Gloucester, MA: Peter Smith, 1965), and "The *De Amore* of Andreas Capellanus and the Condemnation of 1277," *Mediaeval Studies* 8 (1946): 107–49.

No couple better exemplifies the proximity of heretics and courtly lovers than Tristan and Iseut, especially as they are depicted in Béroul's late twelfth-century "common" version of this romance.[4] Tristan and Iseut not only enter into a carnal relationship with each other, in defiance of their duties to King Mark—Tristan's uncle and lord and Iseut's husband—but rationalize this relationship in an almost heretical way. When Iseut explains to the hermit Ogrin how she and Tristan have come to be together, she asserts, "He does not love me nor I him except by a herbed wine from which he and I drank. That was a

4. For a good introduction to the basic problems of this text, see Alberto Vàrvaro, *Béroul's "Romance of Tristan,"* trans. John C. Barnes (Manchester: Manchester University Press, 1972), and Emmanuele Baumgartner, *Tristan et Iseut: De la légende aux récits en vers* (Paris: Presses Universitaires de France, 1987), along with Béroul, *"The Romance of Tristan": A Poem of the Twelfth Century,* ed. Alfred Ewert (Oxford: Basil Blackwell, 1929, rpt. 1970–72), and T. W. W. Reid, *The "Tristran" of Béroul: A Textual Commentary* (Oxford: Basil Blackwell, 1972). Pierre Jonin's *Les Personnages féminins dans les romans français de Tristan au XIIe siècle: Etude des influences contemporaines* (Gap: Ophrys, 1958), provides the most helpful contextualization of this work, and Rita Lejeune's review of it, "Les 'Influences contemporaines' dans les romans français de Tristan au XIIe siècle," *Le Moyen Age* 66 (1960): 143–62, is also of use. David J. Shirt's *The Old French Tristan Poems: A Bibliographical Guide* (London: Grant & Cutler, 1980) may also be consulted. For the distinction between Béroul's "common" and other "courtly" versions of this romance, see Jean Frappier, "Structure et sens du *Tristan*: Version commune, version courtoise," *Cahiers de civilisation médiévale* 6 (1963): 255–80, 441–54. It is a commonplace of medieval scholarship that Tristan and Iseut's love is not "courtly," as that of Lancelot and Guinevere or troubadour lovers and ladies is said to be, for several reasons: Tristan loves Iseut not because he has recognized her inherent merit but because he has drunk a love potion; Iseut responds to Tristan not with coldness and cruelty but with equal ardor because she has consumed an equal portion of this drink; and the relationship between the lovers leads not to the improvement as members of society but to their estrangement from society and ultimate death. The "common" versions of the legend, such as Béroul's poem, are considered particularly bereft of "courtly" resonances. At the same time, it is worth noting that medieval texts do not seem to have perceived the differences between Tristan and Iseut's relationship and those of more conventional lovers as sufficient to place the Celtic pair in a separate category. Chrétien de Troyes is said to have written a now lost *Tristan* alongside his *Chevalier de la Charrette,* and the heroine Fénice in his *Cligès* compares herself (favorably) with Iseut. As Keith Busby notes in "Le *Tristan* de Béroul en tant qu'intertexte," in *Continuations: Essays on Medieval French Literature and Language in Honor of John L. Grigsby,* ed. Norris J. Lacy and Gloria Torrini-Roblin (Birmingham, AL: Summa Publications, 1989), pp. 19–37 at p. 21, the troubadours mention Tristan and Iseut more than any other couple, comparing the love they experience with that of contemporary literary figures. The twelfth-century poets seem to stress not the distinction between free will and fate, idealization and mutual affection, or social integration and alienation but that between traditional, Germanic views of adultery, based on a coarse and exclusively carnal understanding of amorous relationships, and newer, romantic views of love, based on a more spiritualized comprehension of how a man and a woman can interact.

misfortune [*pechiez*]."[5] Tristan confirms Iseut's words, declaring, "If we have led [this life] for a long time, it was our destiny."[6] The lovers do what they do, they insist, not because they choose to do it but, rather, because they have been forced by a magic spell to act in this manner. With these declarations, Tristan and Iseut oppose Catholic doctrine, which has traditionally affirmed the freedom of the human will and the consequent responsibility of human souls for their deeds, in favor of a residually pagan belief in the helplessness of the human will before magical forces.[7] Like heretics, Tristan and Iseut encounter clerical opposition to their controversial views. Ogrin informs them, "He is dead who lives for a long time in sin [*en pechiée*], if he does not repent,"and "He who repents by faith and by confession, God pardons for his sin [*pechié*]."[8] While Iseut speaks of *pechié* as a misfortune she and Tristan have passively suffered,

5. "Il ne m'aime pas, ne je lui, / Fors par un herbé dont je bui / Et il en but. Ce fu pechiez," Béroul, *The Romance of Tristran*, ed. and trans. Norris J. Lacy (New York: Garland Publishing, 1989), vv. 1413–15.

6. "Si longuement l'avon menee, / Itel fu nostre destinee," ibid., vv. 2301–2.

7. One might be tempted to relate Tristan and Iseut's denial of free will to the Cathars' similar rejection of this Catholic doctrine. Indeed, much ink has been spilled connecting medieval romance to Catharism, though proponents of this affiliation have tended to focus the Grail legends more than on this love story. In the anonymous *Queste del Saint Graal*, Richard Hartman finds "nombreux éléments hétérodoxes," as he explains in "Les Eléments hétérodoxes de *La Queste del Saint Graal*," in *Marche romane: Mélanges de philologie et de littératures romanes offerts à Jeanne Wathelet-Willem* (Liège: Cahiers de l'A.R.U. Lg., 1978), pp. 219–37. In Wolfram von Eschenbach's *Parzival*, more importantly, the allusions to a hidden, seemingly religious knowledge have inspired countless readers to interpret this work as Cathar text, written covertly to escape the detection of persecutors. Wolfram speaks of having obtained his information about the Grail from a certain "Kyôt the Provençal" and, hence, for such readers, from a representative of a region famously infected with Catharism. In addition, Wolfram terms the Grail Castle "Muntsalvaesche," a name which, for these readers, recalls the fortress of Montségur, despite the linguistic problems this identification poses. The belletrists who argued for a connection between troubadour lyric and the Cathar religion—Aroux, Péladan, Rahn, and Rougemont—are also the major proponents of a connection between courtly romance and this heresy. James Westfall Thompson, in "Catharist Social Ideas in Medieval French Romance," *Romanic Review* 22, no. 2 (April–June 1936): 99–104, associates Catharism with the social mores evident in Arthurian legends. Once again, the rebutters of the Cathar thesis have tended to conclude the debate. Pierre Breillat, in "Le Graal et les Albigeois," *Revue du Tarn*, n.s. 10 (1944): 458–70 and n.s. 11 (1945): 99–169, and Michel Roquebert, in *Les Cathares et le Graal* (Toulouse: Privat, 1994), have identified the Grail myth not with Catharism but with the repression of Catharism. See also René Nelli, *Lumière du Graal: Etudes et texts* (Paris: Les Cahiers du Sud, 1951). The context of Tristan and Iseut's doctrinal deviation, however, appears to be more Celtic than Cathar.

8. "Assez est mort qui longuement / Gist en pechiée, s'il ne repent," vv. 1389–90; "qui se repent / Deu du pechié li fait pardon / Par foi et par confession," Béroul, *The Romance of Tristran*, vv. 1378–80.

Ogrin indicates with this word a misdeed they have actively committed.[9] With his Catholic conviction in one's capacity to change one's life, the hermit urges them to renounce the love they declare themselves incapable of ending. As if in recognition of Tristan and Iseut's differences with Catholic orthodoxy, Béroul represents them as sentenced to be burned alive, a punishment then reserved for heretics and a few other categories of malefactors but never, so far as we know, used for adulterers.[10] As the lovers approach the pyre, he describes the scene before them, with the pile of vine-shoots, hawthorns, and blackthorns set afire, the crackle of the flames spreading throughout the branches, and the cries of the crowds of spectators, in surprisingly realistic detail.[11] Escaping the death to which they are condemned, Tristan and Iseut undertake a life as furtive as that of any heretic. In 1157, the Council of Reims had complained of heretics who "hide among the poor and . . . move from place to place, and often change their names, accompanied by women sunk in sin."[12] Like the heretics of whom the council warned, Tristan conceals himself among the *menu peuple*, whether with a forester, as in Béroul's account, or with peasants, as in Marie de France's

9. See Janet H. Caulkins, "The Meaning of *Pechié* in the *Romance of Tristan* by Béroul," *Romance Notes* 13 (1971–72): 545–49; and Marie-Louise Ollier, "Le *Pechié* selon Yseut dans le *Tristan* de Béroul," in *Courtly Literature: Culture and Context*, ed. Keith Busby and Erik Kooper, Selected Papers from the 5th Triennial Congress of the International Courtly Literature Society, Dalfsen, The Netherlands, 9–16 August, 1986 (Amsterdam: John Benjamin Publishing Co., 1990) pp. 465–82.

10. See Jonin, *Les Personnages féminins*.

11. This realistic setting of the romance in all of its coarseness and brutality brings out the fundamental incompatability of love relationships and feudal society, as both Jean-Charles Payen and Joan M. Ferrante have noted, in contrast to the idealized environments of the romances of Chrétien and later authors, which attempt to reconcile love and service. In "Lancelot contre Tristan: La Conjuration d'un mythe subversif (Réflexions sur l'idéologie romanesque au Moyen Age), in *Mélanges de langue et de littérature médiévales offerts à Pierre le Gentil* (Paris: SEDES et CDU Réunis, 1973), pp. 617–32, Jean-Charles Payen speculates that only one, mutilated copy of Béroul's poem has survived to this day because it disturbed medieval audiences and, especially, medieval clerics in its depiction of the conflict between eros and faith, love and society, and divine clemency and ecclesiastical rigor. He writes, "Les oeuvres qui ont exercé un impact traumatisant ne sont pas celles dont survivent de nombreuses transcriptions, parce que toutes les vérités ne sont pas bonnes à dire" (p. 632). Joan M. Ferrante argues similarly in "The Conflict of Lyric Conventions and Romance Form," in *The Pursuit of Perfection: Courtly Love in Medieval Lyric*, ed. Joan M. Ferrante and George D. Economou (Port Washington, NY: Kennikat Press, 1975), pp. 135–77, that this poem was troubling for its audiences because it showed the incompatibility of romantic love and social duty.

12. Moore, "The Publicani: At Arras, 1162–3," p. 80; cf. 2 Tim. 3:6; "apud imperitissimos se occultans . . . qui saepe de loco fugiunt ad locum, nominaque commutarunt, captivas ducunt mulierculas oneratas peccatis," Mansi 21, col. 843.

lay; he moves from place to place and changes his name, disguising himself as a leper in Béroul's poem and feigning to be the fool Picolet or the minstrel Tantris in other accounts; he is accompanied at times in his exile by a woman sunk in sin, namely, the reputed adulteress Iseut. Heretics were traditionally compared to foxes, retreating to their lairs on byways, and the hero of this romance is likewise described, with reference to Renart the fox's home, as someone who "knows much about Malpertuis" and who slinks back to his den along "side-roads."[13] In their justification of their departure from Catholic morals, in their condemnation to the pyre, and in their itinerant and covert lifestyle, the lovers recall the heretics of Béroul's day.

Even as Béroul depicts Tristan and Iseut as acting and being treated like heretics, he emphasizes the nobility of their characters over the sinfulness of their alleged actions, as other celebrators of courtly love did at this time. The lovers' opponents, King Mark and the three barons Ganelon, Godoine, and Denoalen, are depicted as noble in birth but not in character. In an episode that occurred before the beginning of Béroul's fragmentary text, the barons shrank from defending Cornwall against the marauding Morholt, yet Tristan displayed the prowess for which noblemen are distinguished by defeating the Irish invader. Now, when the people hear that Tristan has been condemned to death, they cry out in protest of this sentence, "O Tristan, you are such a worthy knight,"[14] and they recall that he alone in the kingdom was brave enough to protect them in their hour of need. As Tristan personifies the valor commended in noblemen, Iseut exemplifies the beauty praised in noblewomen. The sentiment of the people when they see Iseut brought out to be burned, the ropes cutting into her wrists, is not that different in tone from the emotion Guilhem de Tudela expresses when Guirauda is thrown into the pit. "O noble and honored queen, in what land will there ever be born a king's daughter who is your equal?" the people exclaim.[15] If *vox populi* represents *vox dei*, as seems to be the case here, Tristan's character, as a valiant and courageous knight, and Iseut's character, as a beautiful and dignified queen, matter more than any actions imputed to the pair.[16]

---

13. "set molt de Malpertuis," Béroul, *The Romance of Tristran*, v. 4286; "destoletes," ibid., v. 2480.

14. "Ahi! Tristran, tant par es ber!" ibid., v. 833.

15. "Ha! roïne franche, honoree, / En qel terre sera mais nee / Fille de roi qui ton cors valle?" ibid., vv. 837–39.

16. It has been observed that in this text God too favors certain individuals over others not because of what they have done but because of who they are. Jean Larmat aptly observes,

In their nobility, Tristan and Iseut are essentially singular beings, to the point that even in the company of their servitors they seem irreducibly alone. In contrast, the lovers' nemeses, the three barons, are so fundamentally plural that when one of them is killed, they continue to be referred to as three barons. As comfortable placing others in groups as they are being members of a group, the barons accuse Tristan and Iseut of a crime for which, they claim, they should be punished no less than any other criminal. By charging the lovers with a common felony, the barons fail to acknowledge the unique passion these persons feel toward each other or the unique suffering they have endured as a result of that passion. If the framework within which the barons operate cannot begin to do justice to the exalted nature of Tristan and Iseut's love, it may well be because there exists no adequate category into which these lovers might be placed, precisely because their singularity eludes all categorization. Tristan and Iseut cannot speak of the magic potion to Mark, let alone to the barons, and when they do speak of it to Ogrin, they cannot make themselves heard because no one around them has shared their experience of the potion and, as a result, no one around them can understand what they have undergone. As with the noble heretics considered in chapter 4, Tristan and Iseut's singularity makes them at once more guilty, insofar as they are more likely to break rules established for society as a whole, and more innocent, insofar as these rules never reflected their individual experience in the first place. While Béroul does not declare, as a Cathar heretic might, that human beings in general lack free will and thus cannot be expected to conform to social and religious standards, he does suggest that this one couple, noble in lineage and in comportment, must be forgiven for their deviance.

Throughout this romance, Béroul can be seen to be responding to the epistemological challenges brought about by the pursuit of heretics during his day. With the barons and their ally the dwarf Frocin, he represents counterparts to clerics like Pierre des Vaux-de-Cernay, Folquet de Marseille, and Guilhem de Puylaurens, who propounded a kind of ecclesiastical universalism. For Tristan and Iseut's opponents, and for these Latinate authors, what matters is not who

---

"Dieu ne considère ni l'intention, ni l'acte, mais la personne," "La Religion et les passions dans le *Tristan* de Béroul," in *Marche romane: Mélanges de philologie et de littératures romanes offerts à Jeanne Wathelet-Willem*, p. 344. Barbara Nelson Sargent-Baur dismisses this tendency as immoral in "La Dimension morale dans le *Roman de Tristran* de Béroul," *Cahiers de civilisation médiévale* 31, no. 1 (1988): 49–56, but one might maintain that it simply reflects an alternate morality.

one is but what one has done. What beliefs do the inhabitants of Pons Azemar de Roudeille's lands hold? they ask. What activities do Tristan and Iseut indulge in behind closed doors? Because these parties are focused upon the single issue of the suspected "heresy" or "adultery" at the expense of all other information about the individuals said to commit these sins, they believe that truth can be clearly and simply ascertained through the consideration of objective evidence. With Tristan and Iseut, however, Béroul depicts counterparts to figures like Guilhem de Tudela and his anonymous continuator, who advocated what could be seen as a noble exceptionalism. For these lovers and for these vernacular authors, what matters is not what one has done but who one is. Do the heretics who reside on Pons Azemar's lands live honorably? Do Tristan and Iseut fulfill their roles as knight and queen? Because they allow their reaction to the suspected "heresy" or "adultery" to be influenced by consideration of the accused's other qualities, these parties believe that truth is never clear and never simple. Evidence is always subject to interpretation, and that interpretation is always prey to subjective biases. Ultimately, as we shall see, with their irreducible singularity and the aristocratic particularism which validates that singularity, Béroul shows that Tristan and Iseut cannot be perceived for who they are within the framework of any social or religious code but, rather, can only be appreciated within the context of a literary work.

THE BARONS

From the perspective of the feudal code dominant in the lands where the romance was composed and where it takes place, it is surprising that the three barons are so negatively portrayed. According to feudal customs, vassals have a duty to advise their lord about situations likely to dishonor him and to urge him to respond to those situations in a positive manner. As the barons remind Mark, "one should rightfully counsel one's lord . . . We, who are faithful to you, give you loyal counsel."[17] The barons have reason to believe that Mark's wife and nephew have entered into an adulterous liaison and have thus shamed their lord and master. They inform the king of the injury he has suffered and recommend that he take action against those who have harmed him. Again according to feudal customs, should a lord refuse to accept his vassals' advice and to follow their suggestions, to the detriment of his honor and status, the

---

17. "L'en devroit par droit son seignor / Conseillier . . . / . . . nos, qui somes ti feel, / Te donions loial consel," Béroul, *The Romance of Tristan*, vv. 3112–18.

vassals have a right to withdraw their fealty from him.[18] When Mark refuses to punish Tristan and Iseut, the barons threaten to retreat to their castles and wage war against him. Yet, though the barons exemplify the manner in which vassals would be expected to respond to such a crisis in the court at this time, they are regularly reproved in the course of the romance, while the instigators of the crisis are extolled. If Béroul judges the barons as harshly as he does, it is because he draws into question the supposed objectivity of the evidence they cite against Tristan and Iseut and the supposed altruism of their motivations in making their charges. As the clerics who wrote about heretics complained of the frequently ambiguous nature of the evidence against these malefactors, Béroul deems the proof against Tristan and Iseut to be similarly uncertain.[19] For the clerics, ecclesiastical authorities are able to overcome the epistemological difficulties they face and to prove heretics to be heretics through dispassionate investigation of the situation, yet for Béroul, if the barons believes

18. R. Howard Bloch, in "Tristan, the Myth of the State, and the Language of the Self," *Yale French Studies* 51 (1974): 61–81, reads the barons' actions as in accordance with feudal custom. He notes, "The feudal monarch swore, as part of the coronation ceremony, to uphold the customary law of the land. . . . The monarch who failed to recognize the practices of the past abrogated the contractual agreement between himself and his vassals. He forfeited the obedience of his subjects" (pp. 67–68). Bloch interprets the emphasis in the text upon Mark's subjectivity as the marker of a transition from a shame culture, where reality is defined by the group, to a guilt culture, where it is defined by the individual. According to Bloch, in refusing to accept that reality is what his barons declare it as being, Mark inaugurates a new epistemological order.

19. It has long been recognized that Béroul's romance is greatly concerned with the difficulty of interpreting ambiguous signs. See, for example, Brian Blackey, "Truth and Falsehood in the *Tristran* of Béroul," in *History and Structure of French: Essays in Honor of Professor T. B. W. Reid,* ed. F. J. Barnett et al. (Oxford: Blackwell, 1972), pp. 25–27; Norris J. Lacy, "Deception and Distance in Béroul's *Tristan:* A Reconsideration," *Journal of the Rocky Mountain Medieval and Renaissance Association* 6 (January 1985): 33–39; Jacques Ribard, "Le *Tristan* de Béroul: Un monde de l'illusion?" *Bulletin bibliographique de la Société internationale arthurienne* 31 (1979): 229–44; John L. Grigsby, "L'Empire des signes chez Béroul et Thomas: 'Le sigle est tut neir,'" *Mélanges de langue et de littérature du Moyen Age et de la Renaissance offerts à Charles Foulon* (Marche romane: Cahier des romanistes de l'Université de Liège) 30, no. 3–4 (1980): 115–25; Jean-Charles Huchet, "Les Masques du clerc," *Médiévales* 5 (1983): 96–116; Baumgartner, *Tristan et Iseut,* pp. 44–47; Douglas Kelly, "La Vérité tristanienne: Quelques points de repère dans les romans," in *Tristan et Iseut: Mythe européen et mondial* (Actes du colloque des 10, 11 et 12 janvier 1986), ed. Danielle Buschinger (Göppingen: Kümmerle, 1987), pp. 186–81; Marie-Louise Ollier, "Le Statut de la vérité et du mensonge dans le *Tristan* de Béroul," ibid., pp. 298–318; and Etienne Dussol, "A Propos du *Tristan* de Béroul: Du mensonge des hommes au silence de Dieu," in *Et c'est la fin pour quoy sommes ensemble: Hommage à Jean Dufournet, Littérature, histoire, langue du Moyen Age,* ed. Jean-Claude Aubailly et al. (Paris: Honoré Champion, 1993), vol. 3, pp. 525–33.

themselves able to overcome similar challenges, it is only through their resentful bias against the lovers.

At numerous points, the romance seems to indicate that Tristan and Iseut's love is of a carnal nature and, hence, that the barons' accusations against the lovers are valid, yet every time it does so, it conveys not so much an objective fact as a subjective perception. Of Ganelon, Denoalen, and Godoine, we are told, "They had seen the other day in a garden, under a grafted tree, the noble Iseut with Tristan in such a situation that no one should tolerate. And several times they saw them lying in King Mark's bed completely naked."[20] Of the dwarf Frocin, we are told that he looked into the king's chamber one night, and "by the moonlight he saw well that the two lovers were lying together. He trembled with joy."[21] Both of these passages affirm, in the clearest terms in which the poem speaks of this matter, that the lovers join in physical contact, yet both qualify these affirmations by attributing them to something *seen* by the barons or the dwarf. At the end of the fragment, an unnamed spy tells the barons that if they go to the back of the donjon, approach the window on the right-hand side, and pull back the curtain with a pointed stick, they will be able to see the banished Tristan enter the royal chamber wearing his sword and carrying his bow, with the presumed intention of uniting with Iseut. The lengthiness of the spy's account of what can be seen and how it may be done, the insistence of his offers to be killed if his report cannot be verified, and the intensity of the interrogation to which he is submitted all underscore the uncertainty surrounding such a subjective and, therefore, possibly dubious narration. When Godoine later follows the spy's instructions, the poem again stresses the subjective nature of his perceptions: "He saw [*vit*] the chamber, which was strewn with rushes. He saw [*vit*] all that was inside it. No man but Perinis did he see [*voit*]."[22] After Brangain enters with Iseut's comb in her hair, the poem adds, "The felon who was at the window watched and thus saw [*vit*] Tristan enter."[23] Again, the emphasis upon the verb *veoir* draws into

---

20. "Qar, en un gardin, soz un ente, / Virent l'autrier Yseut la gente / Ovoc Tristran en tel endroit / Que nus hon consentir ne doit; / Et plusors foiz les ont veüz / El lit roi Marc gesir toz nus," Béroul, *The Romance of Tristan*, vv. 589–94.

21. ". . . A la lune / Bien vit josté erent ensenble / Li dui amant. De joie en tremble," ibid., vv. 736–38.

22. "Vit la chanbre, qui fu jonchie, / Tot vit quant que dedanz avoit, / Home fors Perinis ne voit," ibid., vv. 4414–16.

23. "Le fel qui fu a la paroi / Garda, si vit Tristran entrer," ibid., vv. 4420–21.

question the ontological status of what is seen.[24] The point is not that Tristan and Iseut do not engage in carnal relations but, rather, that every representation of the pair engaging in such activity is mediated through their subjective perceptions of other characters and their subjective interpretations of what they have seen.

Throughout the romance, the barons, the dwarf, and a few other vassals attempt to transform their subjective apprehension of Tristan and Iseut's infraction into objective proof, yet they never succeed in doing so. If only they can enable Mark to see what they have seen, these characters think, the king's gaze will validate their own perceptions and render them actionable. Yet, whether they persuade Mark to climb into a tree in order to spy on the lovers' meeting, to return to the chamber at night in order to trap them in bed, or to track them down in their bower in the Morrois Forest where they are sleeping, there is always some ambiguity in what the barons and their cohorts show Mark, so that he never sees what they want and expect him to see and never passes a definitive verdict for or against the lovers. Whenever the king appears to be convinced

24. As Stephen G. Nichols Jr. points out, in "Ethical Criticism and Medieval Literature: The *Roman de Tristan*," in *Medieval Secular Literature: Four Essays*, ed. William Matthews (Berkeley: University of California Press, 1965), pp. 68–89, one can prove, on the basis of what we are told these people see, that Tristan and Iseut were together, but one cannot prove that anything culpable happened between them. Of the depiction of the lovers in Béroul's poem, Nichols remarks, "That they are lovers is clear from their own admission and the poet's, but we never see them engaged in conspicuous consumption, any more than does Mark" (p. 74), and "Of the six main scenes that constitute the episode, not one is solely concerned with analyzing the love they share, nor with recording how they share it" (p. 78). He observes of the scene with the flour, "Even though the couple has not actually been caught *en flagrant délit,* there is strong evidence to indicate that they have been together, or at least to prove that Tristan has made an improper advance, but there is no evidence to prove the Queen's complicity" (p. 75). Writing of the scene that seems to provide the clearest evidence against the lovers, Barbara Nelson Sargent-Baur notes, in "Truth, Half-Truth, Untruth: Béroul's Telling of the Tristan Story," in *The Craft of Fiction: Essays in Medieval Poetics*, ed. Leigh A. Arrathoon (Rochester, MI: Solaris Press, 1984), pp. 393–421, "The lovers have not actually been caught *in flagrante delicto,* that is to say that no one—not even the reader—can be sure beyond a shadow of a doubt that on this particular occasion Tristan and Iseut committed adultery." Denis de Rougemont, in *Love and the Western World,* trans. Montgomery Belgion (New York: Harcourt Brace and Co., 1940; rpt. New York: Schocken Books, 1983), especially pp. 39–48, long ago interpreted the tendency of Tristan and Iseut to seek separation rather than union as proof that they ultimately love love itself, which is best preserved precisely through separation, rather than each other. Michel Cazenave, in *Le Philtre et l'Amour: La Légende de Tristan et Iseut* (Paris: Librairie José Corti, 1969), has argued against Rougemont's loose association of the lovers' askesis with Catharism, though he has not addressed the heart of Rougemont's interpretation of the romance.

that Tristan and Iseut are guilty, he soon comes to suspect that they are innocent. He arrives quickly in the chamber after Frocin has seen the lovers in bed,
yet by the time he enters, Tristan has already returned to his own bed, and the
king can no longer be said to have caught them *in flagrante delicto*. It is with
the law on his side that Tristan will demand to defend himself in battle against
his accusers, as was the right of those who were not caught red-handed in a
crime, and it is in recognition of this law that the king ultimately concedes that
the evidence against the lovers was not absolute.[25] Mark follows the forester
into the wood with the intention of killing Tristan and Iseut, and he finds them
in each other's arms underneath the bower. Because they are both clothed,
because their lips and bodies are not touching, and because a sword lies
between them, he concludes, however, "They have no heart for foolish love."[26]
Frustrated by Mark's refusal to see the lovers' guilt on account of his sympathy
for his wife and his nephew, the barons declare, "He can know it who wants
to,"[27] but if perception is, indeed, contingent upon the desire to perceive, it is
possible that they themselves believe they know the lovers' guilt only because
they want to know it.

Indeed, the romance itself suggests that despite the persuasiveness of the
barons' claims, Mark may have reason to think that the lovers' intercourse is
more verbal than physical. Béroul exclaims, "Oh, God! Who can keep love for
a year or two without being discovered? For love cannot conceal itself. Often
one partner nods to the other. They often come together for speech [*a parlement*], both in hiding and before people."[28] If lovers inevitably reveal the
secret of their love, he suggests, it is not because they want to make love but
because they want to communicate and, especially, to speak with one another.
When Frocin persuades Mark to tell Tristan that he must leave on a mission the
next morning, the dwarf assures him, "I know that he will want to speak [*parler*] to her tonight," and "if Tristan loves her foolishly, he will come to her for
speech."[29] Likewise, the spy who informs on Tristan and Iseut to the barons
promises them only that they "will see the interior clearly, when he comes to

25. See Bloch, "Tristan, the Myth of the State," p. 64.
26. "De fole amor corage n'ont," Béroul, *The Romance of Tristran*, v. 2013.
27. "Savoir le puet qui c'onques veut," ibid., v. 608.
28. "Ha, Dex! Qui puet amor tenir / Un an ou deus sanz descovrir? / Car amors ne se
puet celer: / Sovent clin l'un vers so per, / Sovent vienent a parlement, / Et a celé et voiant
gent," ibid., vv. 573–78.
29. ". . . en ceste nuit, / Sai que voudra a lui parler," ibid., vv. 656–67. "Se Tristran l'aime
folement, / A lui vendra a parlement," ibid., vv. 661–62.

speak with her," and he offers to be hanged "if I do not show you openly Tristan there where he waits at his ease to speak with his dear mistress."[30] In fulfillment of these predictions, Béroul writes of Tristan, after he has received his assignment, "In his heart he said that he would speak to the queen, if he could,"[31] and he represents the lovers, when seen in the chamber, as doing no more than talking. It is true that at this time the desire to speak with a lady often masked the desire to enter into another sort of interaction with her and that *parler* could thus serve as a euphemism for other acts. When Mark wants to slip away from the court privately, for example, he tells his men that a maiden has asked that he "go quickly to speak to her,"[32] with presumably erotic connotations. Similarly, when Chrétien de Troyes' contemporaneous Lancelot asks Guinevere for permission to come to her one night, he informs her, "I would willingly speak with you," though after some discussion he manages to pull apart the iron bars over her window and join her in carnal solaces.[33] Nevertheless, it is striking that whereas Chrétien writes of his amorous pair that "her loveplay seemed so gentle and good to him, both her kisses and caresses, that in truth the two of them felt a joy and wonder the equal of which has never been heard or known," and refers to even greater delights that he will not describe, Béroul never portrays Tristan and Iseut as engaging in anything nearly as sexually explicit or, indeed, as doing anything with each other except talking.[34] The poet writes that "whenever the king went into the woods, Tristan would say, 'Sire, I am leaving.' Then he would remain behind and enter the chamber. They would be together for a long time."[35] Tristan's decision to remain behind in the castle when the king goes out, his false promise to soon

---

30. ". . . tu voies la dedenz cler, / Qant il venra a lui parler," ibid., vv. 4329–30. "Se ne vos mostre apertement / Tristran, la ou son aise atent / De parler o sa chiere drue," ibid., vv. 4281–83.

31. "En son cuer dist qu'il parleroit / A la roïne, s'il pooit," ibid., vv. 697–98.

32. "Que j'aille tost a lié parler," ibid., v. 1933.

33. Chrétien de Troyes, "Lancelot, or The Knight of the Cart," trans. William W. Kibler, in *The Romance of Arthur: An Anthology of Medieval Texts in Translation*, ed. James J. Wilhelm, rev. ed. (New York: Garland Publishing, 1994), p. 173; "volantiers a vos parleroie," *Les Romans de Chrétien de Troyes édités d'après la copie de Guiot (Bibl. nat., fr. 794),* vol. 3, *Le Chevalier de la Charrette,* ed. Mario Roques (Paris: Honoré Champion, 1983), v. 4504.

34. Chrétien de Troyes, "Lancelot," p. 173; "Tant li est ses jeus dolz et buens, / et del beisier, et del santir, / que il lor avint sanz mantir / une joie et une mervoille / tel c'onques ancor sa paroille ne fuoïe ne seüe," *Le Chevalier de la Charrette,* vv. 4674–79.

35. ". . . quant li rois en vet el bois, / Et Tristran dit: 'Sire, g'en vois,' / Puis se remaint, entre en la chanbre, / Iluec grant piece sont ensemble," Béroul, *The Romance of Tristran,* vv. 595–98.

quit the enclosure himself, and his withdrawal behind closed doors with the queen certainly all raise suspicions, yet Béroul leaves the door shut behind the lovers and does not specify what they do together.

Mark and his barons believe that if only they can break the periphery of Tristan and Iseut's secret and behold the activity at its core, they will know the truth about their liaison, yet they appear misled in this assumption. When Mark comes upon Tristan and Iseut in the Morrois Forest, where they have been living in circumstances most conducive to the physical expression of their love, there is no indication that they have been engaging in any wanton conduct. It may seem to be happenstance that Mark finds the lovers asleep, with their clothing on and their bodies separated by a sword. Béroul remarks, "If [Iseut] had been naked that day, disaster would have befallen them,"[36] as if she had, in fact, been unclothed on other days. Yet, throughout their stay in this forest, the lovers are portrayed as spending their time sleeping rather than engaging in carnal solaces. From the very beginning of their exile, we are told that that "the queen was greatly wearied because of the fear that she had experienced. Drowsiness took her. She wanted to sleep. She wanted to sleep beside her friend" and that "at night, they lay down on a hill."[37] When Governal returns from killing one of the barons, brandishing the enemy's head on the end of a branch, it is said that "Tristan was lying in his bower. He had closely embraced the queen, for whom he had been put in such pain, in such trouble. Both were asleep."[38] Still later, after Tristan has come back exhausted from hunting a stag and finds Iseut also fatigued from the heat, we are told that they lie down under the bower. "Thus the lovers fell asleep, expecting no trouble."[39] Not only the apparent frequency of the lovers' slumber but their apparent persistence in dozing through many of the most dramatic moments of their exile, including Governal's decapitation of the baron, the forester's penetration of the bower, and Mark's exchange of their rings and swords, give the impression that when they are finally free to be together undisturbed, they pass their days unconscious. Though it may seem at times to Mark, to the barons, to the dwarf, and even to us that there is some positive and illicit core to their love that constitutes the focus of their

36. "Se ele fust icel jor nue, / Mervelles lor fust meschoiet," ibid., vv. 1808–9.
37. "La roïne ert forment lassee / Por la poor qu'el ot passee; / Somel li prist, dormir se vot, / Sor son ami dormir se vot," ibid., vv. 1299–1302. "La nuit jurent desor un mont," ibid., v. 1276.
38. "Tristran gesoit en sa fullie, / Estroitement ot enbrachie / La roïne, por qu'il estoit / Mis en tel paine, en tel destroit; / Endormie erent amedoi," ibid., vv. 1673–77.
39. "Eisi s'endorment li amant, / Ne pensent mal ne tant ne quant," ibid., vv. 1829–30.

desire, it is not a presence but an absence, not an action but an inaction, not carnal fervor but somnolent haze that is finally uncovered here. Far from discovering an objective truth about the lovers, all of these interlopers affect what they see through their very act of seeing. When Mark beholds the couple underneath the tree, he does not realize that the seemingly unwary lovers are crafting their dialogue for his ears, and when he finds them in the bower, he does not apprehend, according to some versions of the legend, that the seemingly sleeping Tristan is actually aware of his presence. When Frocin espies the lovers together in the chamber, he does not know that Tristan has already taken action to avoid falling prey to the dwarf's trap. When Godoine peers at the lovers through the window, he does not grasp that his own silhouette is the "thing that weighs upon me" of which Iseut complains to Tristan and to which she advises him to turn his bow.[40] All three onlookers think they are peering from the periphery into the center of the secret, and all three err because they do not realize that the center is staring back at them—that the pair's secret *is* the secret which their gaze has all along been helping to constitute. However much it may seem that Tristan and Iseut love and are forced by circumstances to conceal their love, it is the secretiveness with which they conceal their love from their observers that brings them together and creates their bond.

The barons and their allies interpret Tristan and Iseut's contact as unfavorably as they do, not because of what they see of this contact, which remains ambiguous, but because of what they themselves are, which is ignoble. As the lovers and the people recall, when the dreaded Morholt was ransacking the Cornish coast, the barons were not brave enough to stand up to him, let alone defeat him in battle.[41] They hate Tristan, Béroul maintains, "because of his prowess,"[42] that is, because he has consistently shown them up and made them seem lesser men than they wish they were. They are "full of envy" of him for

---

40. "tel chose dont moi poise," ibid., v. 4455.

41. Throughout the poem, Béroul refers to the barons as *felons* or as "cruel," "wicked," or "perfidious" men and, to a lesser extent, as *losengiers*, that is, "false flatterers" or "devious informers." One of the barons, Ganelon, is named after the famous Frankish traitor of the *Chanson de Roland*, who brings about the destruction of Roland and the twelve peers, and another, Godoine, is named after the Saxon traitor Godwin, who died after being exiled in 1053. See F. Lot, "Godoine," *Romania* 35 (1906): 605–17. If the barons are accused of felony and treason, it is not because they actually betray Mark in any recognizably feudal manner but because, like such contemptible criminals, they are too cowardly and weak to attempt to promote themselves through more properly knightly endeavors.

42. "Por sa prooise," Béroul, *The Romance of Tristran*, vv. 774.

his superiority.[43] Even now the barons do not dare accuse Tristan openly, for if they did so, they would be obliged to meet him in a trial by combat to prove their accusation. They attack Iseut only because she is a foreigner, far from the kinsmen who could champion her against them, and only on those occasions when Tristan is exiled from court and thus hindered from defending her himself. While the barons are cowardly and weak, Frocin is not even a knight. He advances himself not by wielding a sword but by knowing many fields, including astronomy and astrology. He is described as a "divine" because of his powers of divination and as someone "full of craftiness," and it is on account of this cunning, with its nefariously supernatural connotations, that he almost succeeds in catching the lovers.[44] As someone who relies upon his learning and intelligence to uncover alleged malefactors, Frocin more than any other character in the romance resembles the ecclesiastics who also depend upon such skills in pursuing heretics. At the same time this romance was being composed, in which the dwarf and the barons insist upon the quality of the crime rather than that of the alleged criminal as the appropriate basis of judicial inquiry, such ecclesiastics, under the influence of the revival of Roman law, were no less stressing what people do and not who they are as the determinant of how they should be judged. Despite their resemblance to these clerics, the dwarf and the barons pursue Tristan and Iseut not out of an impersonal concern for justice but out of an all-too-personal *ressentiment* toward those superior to them. Blinded by their belief in the existence of an objective truth, the lovers' enemies fail to recognize the degree to which subjective bias, such as their *a priori* hatred of the lovers, inevitably shapes what they see.

Insofar as Béroul is responding to the epistemological crisis associated with heretics in late twelfth- and early thirteenth-century France and Occitania, he is countering the perspective on this dilemma offered by Catholic clerics like Pierre des Vaux-de-Cernay. As Pierre sees it, Raimon VI can be proved a heretic by the evidence mounted against him, which includes his predilection for the disorder of warfare, the breaking of oaths, and the repudiation of wives. As Béroul sees it, however, the accused cannot always be proved guilty of the crimes with which they are charged because the motivations of the accusers are often not as pure as they may seem. Just as it is impossible, in the context of the *Roman de Tristan*, to dissociate the barons' perception of Tristan and Iseut's

43. "plan d'envie," ibid., v. 1061.
44. "devin," ibid., vv. 635 and 646; "plains de voisdie," ibid., v. 328.

guilt from their resentment of Tristan's valor in defending Cornwall against the Morholt, Béroul seems to suggest that Catholic clerics' perceptions of southern lords' heresy cannot be dissociated from their anger at these lords' defiance of ecclesiastical power. It is not that Raimon VI or Tristan and Iseut are innocent of the charges against them but, rather, that any seemingly impersonal desire on the part of the clerics or the barons to lodge complaints against them is inevitably tainted by the accusers' personal interests.

THE LOVERS

As the barons, it appears, want only to inform their lord of the true nature of Tristan and Iseut's relationship, so the lovers seem intent only on concealing that information from the king. In the first scene of Béroul's fragmentary text, Tristan and Iseut meet under a tree in whose branches they know Mark is lurking, and their dialogue appears deliberately to mislead their eavesdropper about the situation between them. After complaining that the king suspects she loves Tristan, Iseut declares, "But may God guarantee my loyalty, who may set a scourge upon my body if ever anyone had my love except him who had me as a maiden."[45] While Mark, hearing these words in the branches above, may believe that Iseut was deflowered when he slept with her on their wedding night and that she has just attested her fidelity to him, the lovers below him know that she took Tristan as her first lover on the boat to Cornwall.[46] Later,

---

45. "Mais Dex plevis ma loiautée, / Qui sor mon cors mete flaele, / S'onques fors cil qui m'ot pucele, / Out m'amistiée encor nul jour," ibid., vv. 22–25.

46. Similarly, Iseut later affirms, "I would like better to be burned and to have the wind scatter my ashes than to have any man but my lord any day that I live [*Mex voudroie que je fuse arse, / Aval le vent la poudre esparse, / Jor que je vive que amor / Aie o home qu'o mon seignor*]," ibid., vv. 35–38. While Mark may believe Iseut to understand himself as that "lord," it is not altogether clear that Iseut does not regard Tristan as occupying that seigneurial role on account of her prior relationship with him. In "L'Esprit celtique dans le roman de Béroul," in *Mélanges de langue et de littérature médiévales offerts à Pierre le Gentil* (Paris: Société d'Edition de l'Enseignement Supérieur et Centre de Documentation Universitaire Réunies, 1973), pp. 409–20 at p. 410, Pierre Jonin interprets *seignor* as an allusion to Tristan rather than to Mark, suggesting that Iseut recognizes him who took her virginity as her lord. In "Sur le climat social, moral, religieux du *Tristan* de Béroul," *Le Moyen Age* 82 (1976): 219–61, Jean Subrenat argues that Iseut may well consider Tristan rather than Mark to be her true husband, given that a promise to wed and a consummation of the relationship were often considered sufficient at this time to establish matrimony. We have no indication that Tristan and Iseut ever intended to marry each other or that they believed their connection legitimate, yet Subrenat is right to stress the apparent ambiguity of Iseut's phrase. Iseut's earlier, more

as Iseut is about to travel with the rest of the court to the White Heath so that
she might swear her innocence over relics, she sends word to Tristan to appear
dressed as a leper by a muddy ford which the court will be obliged to cross.
While the other members of her entourage founder in the filth, she mounts her
disguised lover and orders him to carry her across the ford on his back.
Afterwards, when she is undergoing the judgment of God, she is able to vin-
dicate herself by swearing truthfully that "no man has ever entered between my
thighs except the leper who made himself a beast of burden, who carried me
over the ford, and my husband King Mark."[47] In both situations, underneath
the tree or at the White Heath, Iseut cites a referent which her audience believes
that it knows but of which it actually remains ignorant, and she exploits this
confusion to her advantage.[48] Still, as the barons' apparent desire to expose the
truth about Tristan and Iseut's relationship was ultimately not as pure as it
seemed, the lovers' apparent desire to conceal their truth may not be as corrupt as one may think.

In their dialogue underneath the tree and in their later discussions with
Mark about this encounter, Tristan and Iseut may not, in the end, be misrepresenting what has happened between them. Iseut informs Tristan, "Sire, you
have no desire, nor do I, by almighty God, have heart for wantonness [*druërie*]

---

obvious equivocation about the man who had her as a maid cannot but ready the reader for
further equivocations, so that any indirect phrasing, such as she employs here, seems suspect,
even if it is not. Sargent-Baur, however, observes in "Truth, Half-Truth, Untruth," at p. 417,
note 18, that *seignor* is commonly used to designate a woman's husband, and in "Between
Fabliau and Romance: Love and Rivalry in Béroul's *Tristran*," *Romania* 105 (1984): 292–311
at p. 297, she points out other problems in Subrenat's thesis.

47. "entre mes cuises n'entra home, / Fors le ladre qui fist soi some, / Qui me porta outre
les guez, / Et li rois Marc mes esposez," Béroul, *The Romance of Tristan*, vv. 4205–8.

48. Iseut's ability to manipulate signs to her advantage has been compared to that of other
literary Irishwomen, such as Grainne in "The Pursuit of Diarmaid and Grainne," Maeve in
"The Cattle Raid of Cooley," and Becfola in "The Wooing of Becfola." See Gertrude
Schopperle Loomis, *Tristan and Isolt: A Study of Sources of the Romance* (Frankfurt: J. Baer,
1913; rev. ed., New York: Franklin, 1970); Helaine Newstead, "The Tryst beneath the Tree: An
Episode in the Tristan Legend," *Romance Philology* 9 (1955): 269–84; and Jonin, "L'Esprit celtique dans le roman de Béroul." In *Les Personnages féminins,* Jonin compares Iseut's ambiguous oath at the White Heath to similar *juramenta dolosa* in the *Roman de Renart* and the
Miracles de Saint Benoît, contrasting it to the equivocations used by early Christian martyrs
who sought to highlight rather than obscure their defiance of the law (see pp. 104 and 370).
See also Helaine Newstead, "The Equivocal Oath in the Tristan Legend," in *Mélanges offerts
à Rita Lejeune* (Gembloux: J. Duculot, 1969), vol. 2, pp. 177–85, and Gérard Fransen, *Le dol
dans la conclusion des actes juridiques: Evolution des doctrines et systèmes du Code canonique*
(Gembloux: J. Duculot, 1946), pp. 146–47 and 200–209.

which leads to any baseness [*vilanie*]."⁴⁹ Tristan confirms her words when he
tells Mark, "Never did I have a desire for such raving" and "Of such great disorder, such crime [*felonie*], we never thought, God knows."⁵⁰ If one considers
the literal meaning of these words, is it not true that Tristan and Iseut do, in
fact, lack desire for an amorous relationship? When they are speaking with
Ogrin in the Morrois Forest, Tristan informs the hermit, "If she loves me, it is
on account of the potion. I cannot separate myself from her, not she from
me."⁵¹ He adds, "I would not have anyone speak of my leaving her, certainly,
for I cannot do it."⁵² When the lovers insist that they have no desire for love,
they may be merely affirming, accurately, that they would never have entered
into this liaison were it not for the potion that compelled them to do so. In
addressing Tristan under the tree, Iseut criticizes those who think "that I have
loved you . . . foolishly [*par folie*]" and "that you love me with a base love
[*d'amor vilaine*]," and in addressing Mark in their later conference she censures those who think "that I love Tristan out of whorishness [*puterie*] and
trickery."⁵³ Tristan in turn scorns those who believe "that I have been taken in
wantonness [*druërie*] with the queen out of foolishness [*par folie*]."⁵⁴ Is it not
true, however, that Tristan and Iseut do not perceive their relationship as

49. "Sire, vos n'en avez talent; / Ne je, par Deu omnipotent, / N'ai corage de druërie /
Qui tort a nule vilanie," Béroul, *The Romance of Tristan*, vv. 31–33. Ewert interprets *vilanie*
here, as in vv. 1090, 2230, 3044, and 4165, as "dishonorableness," though he elsewhere identifies this word as "blameworthiness" or "wickedness." In translating *vilanie* as "baseness," I
hope to evoke somewhat the association between this characteristic and the vulgar classes.
    50. "Onques n'oi talent de tel rage," ibid., vv. 253; "Si grant desroi, tel felonie, / Ainz nu
pensames, Dex le set," ibid., vv. 560–62.
    51. "Q'ele m'aime, c'est par la poison. / Ge ne me pus de lié partir, / n'ele de moi . . . , "
ibid., vv. 1384–86.
    52. "De lié laisier parler ne ruis, / Certes, quar faire ne le puis," ibid., vv. 1407–8.
    53. ". . . que par folie, / . . . vos aie amé," ibid., vv. 20–21; "Que vos m'amez d'amor
vilaine," ibid., v. 57. There is some debate as to how *folie* might best be translated in this text.
While Ewert interprets *folie* here and in vv. 661, 1655, 2007, 3042, and 4155 as "sinfulness" or
"wickedness," I hesitate to follow, given the importance of the word *pechié*, the more precise
term for "sin," in the poem. I am reluctant also to translate *folie* as "wickedness" because it
does not necessarily carry the connotation of "wickedness" and because the complexity of
what the text actually believes "wickedness" to be makes a less categorical term more desirable. Lacy notes, "*Folie* (literally folly, foolishness, or insanity) is a very common word in
courtly texts and a most difficult one to translate adequately. In ecclesiastical contexts it often
referred to a failure to obey God's law; adopted to courtly vocabulary it most often reflected
a disregard for the rules of courtliness," *The Romance of Tristan*, p. 227. Given these nuances,
I have translated *folie* by its closest English equivalent, "folly." ". . . que j'aim Tristran /
Par puterie et par anjen," Béroul, *The Romance of Tristan*, vv. 407–8.
    54. "Que pris eüse druërie / O la roïne par folie," ibid., vv. 801–2.

principally distinguished by "wantonness" (*druërie*) and "whorishness" (*put-erie*)?[55] Mark and his barons may imagine that an illicit liaison between a man and a woman, such as that between Tristan and Iseut, must necessarily be centered around sexual contact and that this sexual contact must necessarily be understood as "base love" (*amor vilane*) on account of its defiance of traditional conceptions of honor, as a "crime" (*felonie*) on account of its rupture of the legal codes of this society, and as an act of "folly" (*folie*) on account of its seemingly irrational rupture of social bonds. Yet Tristan and Iseut do not seem to share these views. It is true that Iseut tells Ogrin, after the effect of the love potion has presumably subsided, "I will never again any day of my life have heart for folly" and that "of the commerce of our bodies we are entirely free,"[56] yet even if she acknowledges, in retrospect, that they may have once been engaged in "folly" or that there has once been commerce of their bodies, she never positively affirms that this is the case, nor does the text do so. Instead, she speaks of them as continuing to love each other "with good love" (*de bone amor*),[57] a phrase that could be translated nowadays as "with courtly love," as if she were contrasting their primarily spiritual bond with others lovers' more exclusively carnal connection. However Iseut may seem to be opposing the past and present forms of her and Tristan's relationship, the events that follow make clear that the pair continue to pursue an amorous liaison, little different from the one they have pursued earlier. Like the heretics who deny to their interrogators that they are heretics because they believe that their faith is not heresy, the lovers deny to Mark and others that they have ever engaged in the base and foolish love of which they stand accused because they do not regard their love as base or foolish.

55. As Roger Dubuis has demostrated, the lovers do depict themselves as acting out of *druërie*, but they imply by this word a far more spiritual love than that which their accusers can imagine. In "'Dru' et 'druërie' dans le *Tristan* de Béroul," in *Mélanges de langue et littérature française au Moyen Age offerts à Pierre Jonin* (Aix-en-Provence: Publications de CUERMA, 1979), pp. 223–31, Dubuis has shown that while *druërie* can evoke the sexual act in all of its carnal crudeness, it can also designate an amorous gift, such as the ring and the dog that Tristan and Iseut exchange, in all of their symbolic delicacy. Dubuis attributes the former, pejorative sense of the term, which the lovers reject as inappropriate in depicting their relationship, with the barons, and the latter, positive sense of the word, which the lovers do use in describing their rapport, with them. If these two parties in the romance risk misunderstanding each other, Dubuis rightly asks, "Le *Tristan* n'est-il pas, dans une large mesure, l'illustration dramatique de cette incompréhension?" (p. 226).

56. "Qar ja corage de folie / Nen avrai je jor de ma vie," Béroul, *The Romance of Tristran*, vv. 2323–24; "De la comune de mon cors / Et je du suen somes tuit fors," ibid., vv. 2329–30.

57. ". . . de bone amor," ibid., vv. 1365 and 2327.

If Tristan and Iseut can be said to deceive Mark and others about their relationship, it is only insofar as they distance themselves from the one form the
king can imagine their love as taking. Watching the lovers' encounter under the
tree, Mark tells himself, "Now I can finally know it. If [the dwarf's allegations]
were true, this meeting would not have ended this way. If they loved each other
with foolish love [*de fol amor*], they had enough leisure. I would have seen
them kiss each other. I have heard them lament. Now I know well that they
have no heart for it."[58] According to Mark, if a man and a woman love each
other in the only way he can conceive of their loving, they will spend their time
together not lamenting but, rather, making love. According to Tristan and
Iseut, however, who alone in this romance appear familiar with the courtly tradition, if a man and a woman love each other in this more refined manner, they
will indeed pass their time lamenting. Echoing the language of the troubadour
poets before him, Tristan addresses Iseut as "Lady" (*Dame*), and he appeals for
her mercy and pity. He begs, "Lady, for the love of God, mercy. . . . Hear a little my prayer!"; "Lady, now I want to implore your mercy, so that you remem-
ber this unhappy man [*chaitif*] who undergoes travail and bitter sorrow"; and
"Lady, in your great nobility, are you not taken by pity? Lady, I implore mercy
from you."[59] Within the immediate context of his speech, Tristan is entreating
Iseut to listen to his request, to reconcile him with Mark, who has banished
him from the court, and to settle the debts he has accumulated while forced to
live in town. Within the wider literary context of his speech, however, he is presenting himself as an "unhappy man" (*chaitif*) seeking "mercy" (*merci*) from
his lady, not unlike the lover in Bernart de Ventadorn's famous *canso* "Can vei
la lauzeta mover," who also portrays himself as an "unhappy man" (*chaitius*)
demanding "mercy" (*merces*) from his beloved.[60] Again recalling the language
of troubadour poets, Iseut responds to her lover's entreaty by expressing fear

58. "Or puis je bien enfin savoir. / Se feüst voir, ceste asenblee / Ne feüst pas issi finee. /
S'il s'amasent de fol'amor, / Ci avoient asez leisor, / Bien les veïse entrebaisier. / Ges ai oï
gramoier. Or sai je bien n'en ont corage," ibid., vv. 298–305.

59. "Dame, por amor Deu, merci! / . . . Entent un poi a ma proiere," ibid., vv. 93–95;
"Dame, or vos vuel merci crïer, / Qu'il vos menbre de cest chaitif / Qui a traval et a duel vif,"
ibid., vv. 106–8; "Dame, por vostre grant franchise, / Donc ne vos en est pitié prise? / Dame,
je vos en cri merci," ibid., vv. 157–59.

60. *The Songs of Bernart de Ventadour*, pp. 167–68, translation modified. Andreas writes
that such refined amorous figures, in general, experience love as "an inborn suffering" (*pas-
sio quaedam innata*) and seek from their ladies mercy and pity, *Andreas Capellanus on Love*,
ed. and trans. P. G. Walsh (London: Duckworth, 1982), pp. 32–33.

that she has already compromised herself by meeting with him and reluctance to perform any other actions which might compromise her further. As Tristan repeats his appeal for her mercy, crying, "Lady, for the love of God, mercy," "Lady, now I want to implore your mercy," and "Lady, I implore mercy from you," she repeats her wish to flee the encounter, warning in her own almost lyrical refrain, "Too long have I stayed here," "Too long have I stayed here," and "Too long have I been here."[61] She resembles the lady in Bernart's *canso* who also repulses her servitor, indifferent toward his pleas and the suffering that has prompted them. After this exchange, where the lover appeals to the lady and the lady refuses his request, Tristan prepares to depart for an unknown destination, leading Iseut to later declare three times, "Tristan is going away [*Tristan s'en vet*]."[62] Their conversation thus ends like that in Bernart's *canso*, where the lover concludes,

> Thus I part from her and I give it all up.
> Death she has given me, and with death I respond.
> And I go away [*vau m'en*], because she does not retain me,
> An unhappy man, in exile, I know not where.
> Tristan, you will have nothing more from me,
> For I go away [*eu m'en vau*], an unhappy man, I know not where.[63]

Tristan's name is generally thought to appear in this poem as a *senhal* rather than as an allusion to the legendary character, but as Don Alfred Monson surmises, it is perhaps not accidental that the romance and the poem so resonate in their themes of mercy, unhappiness, departure, and exile.[64] As the comparison with Bernart's verses suggests, Tristan and Iseut's preference for laments

61. "Trop demor ci . . . ," Béroul, *The Romance of Tristran*, v. 64; ". . . trop i demor," ibid., v. 92; "trop sui ci longuement," ibid., v. 196.

62. "Tristran s'en vet," ibid., v. 429; "Tristran s'en vet," ibid., v. 442; "Povre, s'en vet," ibid., v. 455.

63. "Aissi·m part de leis e·m recre. / Mort m'a, e per mort li respon, / e vau m'en pus ilh no·m rete, / chaitius, en issilh, no sai on. / Tristrans, ges no·m auretz de me, / qu'eu m'en vau, chaitius, no sai on," *The Songs of Bernart de Ventadour*, "Can vei la lauzeta mover," pp. 166–68, at vv. 53–58, translation modified.

64. Don Alfred Monson, "Bernart de Vendadorn et Tristan," in *Mélanges de langue et de littérature occitanes en hommage à Pierre Bec* (Poitiers: CESCM, 1991), pp. 385–400, writes, "Quelle meilleure association pour cette fin de poème, le nadir d'une oeuvre toute imprégnée de mélancholie où, comblé de désespoir, le poète se livre à une réconciliation totale?" See also Irénée Cluzel, "Les plus anciens troubadours et la légende amoureuse de Tristan et d'Iseut," in *Mélanges de linguistique et de littérature romanes à la mémoire d'Istévan Frank* (Saarbrücken: Universität des Saarlandes, 1957), pp. 155–70.

over embraces, far from indicating that they do not love each other, indicates that their love is not base but courtly, not carnal but refined, and not pleasurable but sorrowful. If these lovers lament rather than kiss, they can be seen to be deceiving Mark not so much by concealing the true nature of their love as by revealing the true nature of this love, when he is incapable of recognizing it as such.

Likewise, it is not altogether clear that Iseut is misleading her audience in alluding to her encounter with the leper at the ford. The many people, including King Arthur and King Mark, who witness her dealings with the leper do not perceive them as erotic, yet this does not mean that they are not. Before Iseut crosses the ford, she prepares the palfrey she has been riding to cross, knotting the fringes of his saddle-cloth better than "any squire or serving boy" would have done,[65] tucking the stirrup-straps under the saddle, and removing the harness and reins. With her dress in one hand and her whip in the other, she then strikes the horse until he crosses to the other bank. Turning from the palfrey to the leper, she informs him that he will take the horse's place. She appears to enjoy thinking of him not merely as a human being who carries her across a ford but as an actual beast of burden. She declares to him, "You will be an ass to carry me quite gently across the plank," and, later, during her oath, she refers to him as "the leper who made himself a pack-animal."[66] As Tristan becomes, in Iseut's imagination, an ass or pack-animal, she becomes the lad who mounts and rides such a beast. Already compared to a squire or a serving boy, she tells the leper, "I will mount you like a valet," and, the text relates, "Iseut the fair rode one leg on this side, the other on that side," using the verb *chevaucher,* normally used for humans riding animals, to signify her riding of this human being.[67] If Tristan becomes a sumpter and she the boy who rides this creature, she makes sure to handle this beast with a verbal whip. She addresses the leper roughly, dismissing his protests against carrying her across the ford with a series of curt orders. "Hurry, . . . take up position," she orders him.[68] "Turn your face there and your back here."[69] After he has transported her to the other bank, she refuses to reward him for his services, claiming that

---

65. "Nus escuiers ne sus garçons," Béroul, *The Romance of Tristran,* v. 3888.

66. "Asne seras de moi porter / Tot souavet par sus la planche," ibid., vv. 3918–19; "le ladre qui fist soi some," ibid., v. 4206.

67. "Ge monterai conme vaslet," ibid., v. 3931; "Yseut la bele chevaucha, / Janbe deça, janbe dela," ibid., vv. 3939–40.

68. "Cuite . . . t'arenge," ibid., v. 3923.

69. "Tor la ton vis et ça ton dos," ibid., vv. 3929–31.

he is "a worthless fellow" and "a real vagabond" who has already received more than enough alms that day.[70] While Iseut casts Tristan plays the role of a pack-animal and herself in the role of the serving boy who rides and abuses the beast, she does not limit the eroticism implicit in this interaction to fantasy. When she first addresses the leper, she tells him, "I want to have business with you," about which T. B. W. Reid comments, "These words of Iseut are deliberately ambiguous: *avoir a faire* can mean 'have sexual relations with.'"[71] As she prepares to mount him, she exclaims, "Leper, you are big!" without making clear which part of his anatomy she is observing.[72] The text notes that "she held her thighs over his crutch" and that those who watch the pair's progress from the bank remark, "He holds his crutch underneath her hip," in a linguistic context where "crutch [*puiot*]" could often indicate the male member.[73] When Iseut tells Arthur that the leper has already earned too much that day, she explains that when she was riding on his back, she could feel loaves, half-loaves, quarter-loaves, and pieces of bread on his person. She adds, "I felt his pouch under his cloak. King, his purse does not diminish," and "I felt well through his bag" in a linguistic context where "pouch" (*guige*), "purse" (*aloiere*), and "bag" (*sac*) often signify a man's testicles.[74] Later, on the White Heath, when Iseut openly admits to those who realize the leper's identity that she has had Tristan between her legs, she may well be referring to no other scene of erotic contact than that of the crossing of the ford, during which she appears at once to have played out a sadistic fantasy with her lover and to have fondled his body to her satisfaction.[75]

If Mark and his companions cannot recognize what has taken place between Iseut and the leper as an erotic scene, it may well be because, as they are familiar only with amorous relationships characterized by "wantonness" (*drüerie*),

---

70. "herlot," ibid., v. 3977; "Fors truanz," ibid., v. 3963.

71. "Ge vuel avoir a toi afere," ibid., v. 3913; Reid, *The "Tristran" of Béroul*, p. 75.

72. ". . . Malades, molt es gros!" Béroul, *The Romance of Tristran*, v. 3929.

73. "Ses cuises tient sor son puiot," ibid., v. 3936; "Son puiot tien desoz sa hanche," ibid., v. 3946.

74. "Soz sa chape senti sa guige. / Rois, s'aloiere n'apetiche," ibid., vv. 3964–65; "Ai bien parmi le sac sentu," ibid., v. 3969.

75. For another reading of the eroticism present in this scene, see E. Jane Burns, "How Lovers Lie Together: Infidelity and Fictive Discourse in the *Roman de Tristan*," *Tristania* 8, no. 2 (Spring 1983): 15–30; rpt. in Burns, *Bodytalk: When Women Speak Out in Old French Literature* (Philadelphia: University of Pennsylvania Press, 1993), pp. 203–50, and in *Tristan and Isolde: A Casebook*, ed. Joan Tasker Grimbert (New York: Garland Publishing, 1995), pp. 75–93.

they comprehend only amorous relationships that take place on a literal rather than a metaphorical level. As a point of comparison to Béroul's account of Iseut the Blond's experience crossing the ford, Thomas of Britain's contemporaneous account of Iseut of the White Hand's similar experience of horseback riding can be illuminating. One day, Thomas relates, while Tristan's neglected wife is riding with her brother Caerdin, her palfrey stumbles against that of her companion and rears up, so that in order to control her mount, she is forced to prick him with her spurs, raise herself up on her stirrups, and open her thighs slightly to steady herself. The horse bolts into a nearby body of water, and when she opens her thighs again to spur him on, the water splashes up against her. The text relates, "Iseut was startled by the cold, emitted a cry, and said nothing. She laughed so deeply that even if she had been a widow, she could have hardly stopped herself."[76] Caerdin is shocked by this laugh and worried that she has found "folly or wickedness or baseness" in something he has said,[77] so he demands that she explain to him why she has laughed. Iseut responds, "This water, which burst here, mounted higher on my thighs than any man's hand ever has or than Tristan has ever sought me."[78] In both romances, Iseuts find sexual pleasure not in conventional sexual relations but in horseback riding. While this activity provided a common medieval metaphor for sexual relations, the women in these tales reject the traditional, phallically oriented uses of this metaphor, where the man plays the role of the rider in mounting, agitating, and dominating the woman, and the woman the role of the horse, mounted, agitated, and dominated. Though they are women, these Iseuts position themselves as the riders who mount their steeds and strive to master them, if not with physical whips and spurs, then with verbal rebukes. They are active, not passive, dominant, not submissive, and violent, not victimized, in these sexual experiences. Courtly love is characterized not only by the lover's appeals to the lady for mercy and the lady's rejection of those appeals but, more generally, by the lover's attempt to serve and please the lady through his actions and the lady's tests and even torments of the lover. If Mark and the others at the ford cannot perceive the leper's submissive service to the queen and her abusiveness

76. "De la fraidur s'esfroie Ysodt, / Getë un cri, e rien ne dit, / E issi de parfont cuer rit / Que, si ere une quarantaigne, / Oncore astenist donc a paigne," Thomas of Britain, *Tristran*, ed. and trans. Stewart Gregory (New York: Garland Publishing, 1991), vv. 1164–68.

77. ". . . folie / ou mauvaisté ou vilannie," ibid., vv. 1171–72.

78. "Ceste aigue, que ci esclata, / Sor mes cuisses plus haut monta / Quë unques main d'ome ne fist, / Ne que Tristran onques me quist," ibid., vv. 1193–96.

to him as erotic, it is because they are ignorant of amorous situations where the customary roles of men and women are reversed and where fantasy and role playing take the place of sex acts. While Mark can conceive of literal sexual relationships like that between the wife of the emperor Constantine and the dwarf Segoncin to which he alludes at one point, neither he nor his companions can conceive of more metaphorical erotic experiences like that of Iseut the Blond with the pack-animal or Iseut of the White Hands with the bold water, where the pleasure is due less to the physical sensation of bodily contact than to the mental idea of the leper's substitution for the beast or the water's substitution for the man.

In both of these scenes, under the tree or by the ford, it becomes clear that the moments of greatest intimacy between Tristan and Iseut are to be found not in alleged acts of sexual intercourse but, rather, in actual acts of mutual recognition, where the lovers understand each other's messages to the exclusion of the others around them. After Tristan joins Iseut underneath the tree, uneasy about the king whose presence he has noted over their heads, Béroul reports, "When he heard his mistress speak, he knew that she had realized it."[79] Later, when he arrives at the ford disguised as a leper, the text acknowledges that this was a strange place to beg for alms. "But . . . when he saw his friend Iseut, who has the blond hair, pass by, he wanted her to have joy from this in her heart." [80] At the moment she appears, Tristan has just persuaded the barons to enter the deepest part of the marsh, so that they are immersed in mud up to their saddle-bows. "She saw her enemies in the mud. On the hill sat her friend. She had great joy from this. She laughed and rejoiced."[81] After Iseut then commands the leper to get into position to take her on his back, Tristan exclaims, "Ah, God! . . . What will come of this? I never tire of talking with her," and the text then notes, "the leper smiled about it."[82] As Iseut laughs at Tristan's capers at the ford, knowing the sadism that underlies his apparently innocent efforts to aid the barons, Tristan smiles at Iseut's mounting of him, knowing the eroti-

---

79. "Qant out oï parler sa drue, / Sout que s'estoit apercüe," Béroul, *The Romance of Tristran,* vv. 97–98.

80. "Mais . . . / Qant or verra passer s'amie, / Yseut, qui a la crine bloie, / Que ele an ait en son cuer joie," ibid., vv. 3692–96.

81. "Et taier vit ses ainemis, / Sor la mote sist ses amis. / Joie en a grant, rit et envolse," ibid., vv. 3825–27. Barbara Nelson Sargent-Baur discusses the various medieval states that *rire* can suggest in "Medieval *ris, risus:* A Laughing Matter?" *Medium Aevum* 43 (1974): 87–96.

82. "A, Dex! . . . ce que sera? / A lui parler point ne m'ennoie," Béroul, *The Romance of Tristran,* vv. 3926–27; ". . . s'en sorrist li deget," ibid., v. 3932.

cism that underlies her apparently innocent efforts to preserve her clothes from the mud. With their laughs and smiles, the lovers establish a small, secretive community of those who know within a large, open crowd of those on the banks, watching them, who do not know. Braingain and Governal, who are told of the lovers' ambiguous words underneath the tree and who rejoice with them in their escape from peril through this speech, and Dinas, the lord of Dinan, who witnesses the lovers' interaction by the ford and rejoices with them in their antics, belong to this secretive community and reinforce its exclusivity by their covert participation in it. Dinas sees Tristan pretend to help Denoalen out of the mud but suddenly release the baron from his grasp so that he falls back into the muck. Dinas, we are told, "realized what was happening and winked at him. He knew well that Tristan was underneath the cloak. He saw the three felons in the trap. It was very fair and pleasing to him that they were in such dire trouble."[83] In discussing with Iseut how she might best cross the ford, Dinas saw the queen wink at him and give him a look, so that "he knew the thought of the queen."[84] Whether for their own amusement or for that of their friends, Tristan and Iseut delight in revealing the truth about the nature of their love, without being recognized as revealing that truth. They do so in part because the ambiguity of their actions prevents them from suffering the consequences that would ensue if their actions were clearer to their audience, but also, in part, because what appears ambiguous is, in fact, perfectly clear to those who have eyes to see it.

If Béroul is read as responding to the epistemological challenges identified with heretics during his lifetime, he can be seen as showing that people may be unable to defend themselves against accusations brought against them, not because they are guilty, but because their self-justifications are inaudible to their accusers. In the *Canso de la Crozada*, Raimon Rogier of Foix responds to Folquet de Marseille's charges at the Fourth Lateran Council in a manner not unlike that in which Tristan and Iseut reply to Mark and his barons. The count speaks indirectly about his protection of heretics. "Never did I love heretics, neither believers nor robed ones," he states, emphasizing unverifiable emotions over verifiable actions. Whatever Raimon Rogier felt toward heretics, there is no indication that he ever used his authority in his family to reform his heretical wife, aunt, and sisters or his authority in his lands to repress his heretical

---

83. "Aperçut soi, de l'uiel li cline. / Bien sout Tristran ert soz la chape, / Les trois felons vit en la trape; / Molt li fu bel et molt li plot / De ce qu'il sont en lait tripot," ibid., vv. 3854–56.

84. "Le penser sout a la roïne," ibid., v. 3875.

subjects. He speaks equivocally of Esclarmonda. "If my sister is evil or a sinful woman, I should not suffer for her sins," he affirms, leaving unclear whether he himself deems her to act badly. His presence at the ceremony of her hereti-cation, his hosting of debates among Catholics and heretics in which she seems to have participated, and his financial support of her heretical household all suggest that he does not disapprove of her activities as much as he might like the ecclesiastics at the council to believe. Finally, the count espouses values incomprehensible to those around him. Throughout the *Canso de la Crozada*, Raimon Rogier champions *Paratge* (that is, familial lineage), the property which helps perpetuate that lineage, and the noble virtues which derive from a propertied status, yet, as we have seen, clerics exhibit little respect for this value, especially when it comes into conflict with orthodoxy. Again, the real issue is not whether Raimon Rogier is a supporter and defender of heretics and, hence, a heretic himself, as members of the Church allege, or whether Tristan and Iseut are lovers, as Mark and the barons maintain. The issue is, rather, that what Raimon Rogier perceives as *Paratge* ecclesiastics perceive as heresy, and what Tristan and Iseut perceive as a spiritual union Mark and his barons understand as a carnal bond. If accused heretics and accused lovers cannot defend them-selves effectively, it is because they attempt to do so in terms unrecognizable to the authorities who charge them.

THE KING

Torn between the barons' accusations of Tristan and Iseut and the lovers' efforts to exculpate themselves, Mark wavers, uncertain whom to believe. When those around him appeal to him as a king, demanding that he act in accordance with his public role, he responds with extraordinary harshness. Only because the barons threaten to withdraw their fealty from him if he con-tinues to tolerate the behavior of Tristan and Iseut does he grant their request and agree to the dwarf's plan to entrap the lovers. Only because the barons cry out, "Sire, now avenge yourself!"[85] when they break into the chamber and behold Iseut's bed sheets bloody from Tristan's wound does Mark condemn the lovers to be burned without a trial. As ruler, Mark functions as the corner-stone for the vast social edifice that structures the relations between kings and subjects, husbands and wives, and uncles and nephews, so that if he, in his per-sonal life, allows the subordinate members in these relations to abuse the dom-

---

85. "Sire, or te venge," ibid., v. 786.

inant members, he allows the entire hierarchy to be overturned. The forester who finds Tristan and Iseut asleep in the Morrois Forest warns Mark, "King, if you do not now take harsh vengeance, you have no right to the country, without doubt,"[86] linking his potential reluctance to punish the lovers to the loss of his authority as monarch. Just as the presence of his vassals requires Mark to act in accordance with his public role, their absence, at times, allows him to function as a private person. Seemingly conscious of this distinction, he instructs the forester to whisper his message in his ear and then orders him to leave the court without telling anyone what he knows. Despite the objections of his courtiers, who fear for his safety, he insists upon following the forester into the woods without an entourage. When they arrive at the bower where the lovers are sleeping, he bids the forester to let him enter by himself. It is only because Mark beholds Tristan and Iseut alone, unobserved by companions who would be expecting him to act as the enforcer of the law, that he is able, once having raised his sword, to set it down. In his solitude, Mark begins to feel "pity" for the lovers and to act compassionately toward them. He observes the thinness of Iseut's finger as he draws his ring from it "gently," and he notes the brightness of the sunshine on her face, so that he shades her "simply" with his fur glove.[87] He will later remark of his wife, "She has suffered too much in her youth," and of his nephew, "If he has done wrong, he is distressed about it,"[88] as if their travails have begun to outweigh their possible misdeeds in his mind. Mark may be misled about the relationship between Tristan and Iseut at this moment, as he may be misled about it at other moments, but it is also true that just as the lovers are able to speak the truth about their love only when they deceive, Mark is able to hear this truth only when he is deceived.

Later in the text, when he arrives at the muddy ford, Mark is again mistaken in thinking the beggar before him to be a leper and the discussion he has with him to be about leprosy, but he is right in thinking that the man is afflicted with a condition that causes him to suffer through little fault of his own. When under the influence of the barons, Mark believes that if Tristan and Iseut are involved in an amorous relationship, it is because they have intentionally chosen to initiate and pursue such a liaison. The lovers have been condemned to be burned

---

86. "Rois, s'or n'en prens aspre venjance, / N'as droit en terre, sanz doutance," ibid., vv. 1903–94.

87. "souef," ibid., v. 2044; "molt bonement, "ibid., 2042.

88. "Trop a mal trait en sa jovente," ibid., v. 2644; "S'il se mesfist, il est en fort," ibid., v. 3073.

in a pyre and banished from society, he believes, because they deserve to undergo retribution for their misdeeds. Now, however, Mark asks the leper, "How many years have you been outside of society?"[89] With this question, he presumably alludes to his interlocutor's leprosy, a state which, though commonly said to be the result of sexual contact and hence a punishment for lechery, was also recognized to be an experience of unparalleled suffering that almost no one would want to share.[90] With this reference to the leper living "outside of society," Mark also alludes to the custom of segregating lepers from their neighbors by forcing them to reside in separate communities outside the walls of cities and castles, like that which the leper Yvain and his companions were described as inhabiting earlier in the romance, and by refraining from touching, eating with, or even talking downwind with healthy people. In reply to Mark's question, Tristan states, "Sire, it has been three years, and I do not lie."[91] With this response, he alludes not to the onset of his literal leprosy, because he is no literal leper, but to the onset of his love of Iseut, which took place when they first drank the love potion on the boat to Cornwall three years ago and which has, in some sense, exiled him from society ever since. As Tristan suggests through his elliptical speech, love is like leprosy in that it too is a sickness that affects people through no will of their own, and it too banishes them from society. For those who had enjoyed the pleasures of court, this exile to the outskirts of civilization would be particularly distressing. When Yvain had proposed that Mark give Iseut to himself and his companions so that she might receive a punishment worse than death, he had contrasted the great halls of dark marble in which she resided with their "low hovels," the fine foods and wine that she consumed in the palace with the "pieces" and "quarter-loaves" of bread they receive at the gates,[92] and the furs she has worn so far with the clothes that stick to their bodies. In the Morrois Forest, Tristan had echoed this leper's description of degradation, complaining not only that he had been forced to abandon chivalry and his knightly life because of his love for Iseut, as lepers of his social status would have to abandon their noble customs because

89. "Qanz anz as esté fors de gent?" ibid., v. 3759.

90. For a study of twelfth-century leprosy and its connection to this passage of the romance, see Jonin, *Les Personnages féminins,* pp. 109–38. Some medieval holy people did pray for leprosy, primarily as a form of mortification of the flesh that would enable them to do their penance on earth rather than in Purgatory, as Jonin discusses. See also Saul Nathaniel Brody, *The Disease of the Soul: Leprosy in Medieval Literature* (Ithaca: Cornell University Press, 1974).

91. "Sire, trois ans i a, ne ment," Béroul, *The Romance of Tristran,* v. 3760.

92. "bas bordeaus," ibid., v. 1204; "pieces . . . quartiers," ibid., v. 1208.

of their illness, but that Iseut had been obliged to exchange her "fair chambers
. . . draped with silk cloth" for a "hut" because of her passion for him,[93] as lepers of her rank would, again, be obliged to do because of their disease. As love
is an illness no less than leprosy, Tristan here indicates that the social ostracism
and degradation that results from love is a source of anguish for its victims, no
less than the similar conditions that result from this other sickness. Mark does
not detect the metaphorical level that Tristan is casting over their dialogue, but
he acknowledges the passive affliction that the leper undergoes all the same.

Mark is mistaken in attributing the leper's sufferings to leprosy instead of to
himself, but he is right, again in the terms of the romance, in pitying him for
his sufferings. Under the influence of the barons, Mark thinks of his own role
in Tristan's alleged involvement with Iseut, becomes resentful, and wishes to
punish the perpetrator of this injury. Focusing upon himself, he looks at Tristan
from the outside and perceives only the external, physical acts of lust and infidelity. He condemns Tristan to be burned alive, thus compelling him to flee to
the Morrois Forest and to live in exile from the court. Now, faced with the
leper, Mark is ignorant of any role he has played in the leper's situation and thus
free to consider the situation apart from himself. Focusing upon the other, he
looks at the leper from the inside and appreciates his internal, emotional experience of suffering, which he recognizes could only be passively and unwillingly
endured. When the leper begs alms from him, Mark removes his hood and says,
"Here, brother, put this on your head. Many a time has the weather caused you
grief."[94] Whereas earlier he has been indignant, angry, and violent, now he is
sympathetic, gentle, and generous. The Mark here recalls the Mark in the
branches of the tree, who, when beholding Tristan and Iseut's encounter,
alone, unobserved, and free from the obligation to fulfill his social role, "was
so overcome by the pity that took him by the heart that he could not keep from
crying." Later he would say of himself, "Pity took me up there in the tree. I
smiled softly to myself but did nothing more."[95] In the tree, Mark did not realize that Tristan and Iseut had caught sight of him and were tailoring their words
to his ears, just as here he does not realize that the exposed head he now seeks

---

93. ". . . beles chanbres, . . . / Portendues de dras de soie," ibid., vv. 2183–84; "loge," ibid.,
v. 2180.

94. ". . . Tien, / Frere, met la jus sus ton chief: / Maintes foiz t'a li tens fait grief," ibid.,
vv. 3749–52.

95. "De la pitié q'au cor li prist, / Qu'il ne plorast ne s'en tenist / Por nul avoir . . ." ibid.,
vv. 261–63. "Pitié m'en prist a l'arbre sus. / Souef m'en ris, si n'en fis plus," ibid., vv. 49–92.

to protect from the elements is the one he once bared, but in both cases he rec-ognizes the suffering of those he witnesses and pities them for that suffering, as the author of the romance does and as the audience is expected to do as well.

Mark is deluded in failing to perceive that the lady of whom the leper speaks is, in fact, his wife, but he is right, once more, in refusing to take offense at the connection Tristan makes between his beloved and the queen. When acting in accordance with his social role, Mark grows irate at any insinuation that Tristan has had carnal relations with his wife, for such relations would constitute an affront to his power in his kingdom, his marriage, and his family. Here, however, the text reports that, after the leper blames his "courtly lady" for his disease,

> The king said to him, "Do not conceal from me how your lady gave this to you." "Lord king, her husband was a leper. I had my pleasure with her, and the illness came to me from our union. Only one woman was fairer than she." "Who is that?" "The fair Iseut! She even dresses as the other one did." The king listened and went away laughing.[96]

Since the narrative does not seem to implicate Mark, it leaves him free to iden-tify with characters other than the cuckolded spouse. Indeed, by sharing this story, the leper encourages him, as he encourages us, to share his happiness with such a courtly lady and his sorrow with the suffering that ensued. If Mark laughs even when the leper does overtly involve Iseut in his tale, it is because his near equalization of his lady and the queen and, hence, of himself and the king, so threatening when performed by Tristan himself, becomes comic when performed by a leper. In the *Folie de Berne,* Tristan gets away with similarly dar-ing remarks before Mark because he has disguised himself as the fool Picolet and because fools, like lepers, are not to be taken seriously. When the fool becomes agitated from recounting his life in the forest with his lady, Mark attempts to soothe him by suggesting, "Rest yourself now, Picolet. It grieves me that you have done so many things. Leave your jesting now for today." Picolet replies angrily, "What do I care if it grieves you? It's not worth a lump of clay to me!"[97] The barons remind Mark, as if to prevent him from becom-

---

96. "cortoise amie," ibid., v. 3761; "Li rois li dit: 'Ne celez mie / Conment ce te donna t'amie.' / 'Dans rois, ses sires ert meseaus, / O lié faisoie mes joiaus, / Cist maus me prist de la comune. / Mais plus bele ne fu que une.' / 'Qui est ele?' 'La bele Yseut: / Einsi se vest con cele seut.' / Li rois l'entent, riant s'en part," ibid., vv. 3769–77.

97. "Or te repose, Picolet. / Ce poise moi que tant fait as. / Lai or huimas ester tes gas," *Les deux poèmes de la Folie Tristan,* ed. Félix Lecoy (Paris: Honoré Champion, 1994), vv. 187–89; "A moi que chaut s'il vos en poise? / Je n'i donroie un po de gloise," ibid., vv. 190–91.

ing irritated, "No one heeds a fool or argues with him."[98] Like the fool, the leper seems to enjoy the privilege of speaking the truth, even when it is offensive, without being seen as speaking the truth and thus without causing offense. As Mark's sense of detachment from the leper's personal situation allows him to sympathize with the other's sufferings, so his sense of detachment from the leper's social situation makes him laugh at his impudence.

Mark responds to the leper the way that we respond to Tristan and Iseut. When we are confronted with a fact, such as the assertion that our wife is having an affair with our nephew, we respond as people with a stake in the situation at hand. We think of the effects that this experience will have upon us and not of the effects it may have upon others, and we are thus prevented from recognizing a certain truth about that experience. When we are confronted with a fiction, such as the account of the liaison between Tristan and Iseut, however, we respond as people who have nothing to gain or lose from these accounts. Identifying with people whose experiences we share vicariously, we gain access to a certain truth we would not otherwise have. Within the confines of our own reality we may decree that adultery is always a wicked act, willfully chosen by its practitioners and deserving of punishment, but within the realm of an alternate, imaginary reality, such as that of the Tristan poems, we can acknowledge that a specific instance may differ from the general rule, that passion may, on occasion, seem to overwhelm free will, and that tears or laughter may sometimes be more appropriate than condemnation. But just as the fool can speak an otherwise unendurable truth only because his speech is seen to be mere "jesting," fiction can tell a truth contrary to mainstream morality only because it is seen as mere fiction. When Tristan receives Mark's sympathy in the *Roman de Tristan* and, even more, in the *Folie de Berne,* he appears to grow angry with the king, as if impatient with the contradiction between the king's hostility toward a truth presented as fact and his delight in a truth presented as fiction. He then allows the literal truth to shine more and more brightly through his metaphors and metonymies, as if taunting his uncle to see through the beautiful veil of his fiction to the appalling reality of fact behind it. Yet this tendency to reject in history the truth that one embraces in literature is precisely what underlies the difference between social responses to adultery and literary responses to courtly love during this period.

Ecclesiastics of the twelfth and thirteenth centuries appear to have responded to the literature of courtly love, despite its heretical undertones,

98. "N'a fol baer, n'a fol tancier!" ibid., v. 193.

with the same tolerance that Mark shows to the leper. It is true that members
of the clergy and even members of the laity who shared clerical concerns could,
on occasion, voice suspicion of vernacular literature and the love of which it so
often sang. Folquet de Marseille is said to have repudiated the songs he had
composed once he became a Cistercian monk and bishop of Toulouse, going
so far as to fast on bread and water whenever he happened to hear one of them
performed. While the early contributors to the legend of Lancelot and
Guinevere depict the love between this adulterous couple favorably, the
unknown Cistercian author of the *Queste del saint Graal* represents a Lancelot
now recognizant of the sinfulness of his relationship with the queen and repentant of it. Though ecclesiastics could, on occasion, perceive courtly literature
as depicting lust, adultery, and idolatry in a deceptively positive light and, in
doing so, as promoting vice, they did not appear to consider it doctrinally as
well as morally problematic. At the end of the thirteenth century, Etienne
Tempier, the bishop of Paris, would cite Andreas's *De Amore* as blameworthy
for professing "manifest and execrable errors," such as the beliefs that fornication is not a sin and that sexual continence is not a virtue, yet it is not inconsequential that the text Tempier chooses to attack is written in Latin, rather than
the vulgar tongue, and takes the form of a treatise, rather than that of a poem
or prose tale.[99] Harsh toward the authors and defenders of heresy, with their
threatening dogmas, medieval clerics were lax toward the poets of courtly love,
with their entertaining fictions.

If Béroul is read as reacting to the epistemological challenges forefronted by
the pursuit of heretics during this time period, he can be seen as calling into
question the ecclesiastics' distinction between didactic works, which, being
taken seriously, are expected to condemn those who break the law, and literary
works, which, not being taken seriously, are free to seek to understand these
malefactors and, in doing so, to sympathize with them. By juxtaposing, more
than any other medieval romance, to my knowledge, the harshness of judicial
prosecution and the beauty of noble love, Béroul's text causes us to contem-
plate the pain undergone by individuals we might normally be quick to condemn. Could one imagine a Pierre des Vaux-de-Cernay returning from his
travels in Occitania to his monastery in the Ile-de-France and hearing, at some
point in his journey, the tale of a nobleman and a noblewoman expelled from

99. "manifestos et execrabiles errors," Pierre Mandonnet, *Siger de Brabant et l'averroïsme
latin au XIIIme siècle. Etude critique et textes inédits*, 2nd ed. (Louvain: Institut supérieur de
philosophie de l'Université, 1908–11), 2 vols, pt. 2, pp. 175–91, at p. 175.

their lands, stripped of their social status, and threatened with the stake, like the heretical believers in the region from which he has come, and pitying them for their suffering? Could one imagine Guilhem de Tudela lending a sympathetic ear to the story of two people who, whatever misdeeds they might have committed, demonstrate, like Aimeric de Montréal and Guirauda de Lavaur, a nobility of birth and character that outweighs their crimes? Despite the pyres these clerics may well have beheld during the Albigensian Crusade, would they agree with Béroul (and Scripture) that "God . . . does not want a sinner to die"?[100] Literature, as Béroul deploys it, is that which enables us to transcend the limits of our social position and apprehend truths in conflict with our interests—truths we otherwise would never see.

---

100. "Damledé . . . ne vieat pas mort de pecheor," Béroul, *The Romance of Tristran*, vv. 909–11; cf. "nolo mortem impii sed ut revertatur impius a via sua et vivet," Ez 33:11.

6 PROTEUS TEACHING IN THE FIELDS

The Duplicity of the Waldensians

While other heretics are characterized in clerical writings as secretive, hiding from others what they are, or as singular, resisting categorization as a group, the Waldensians are portrayed as duplicitous, pretending to be what they are not.[1] At times the Waldensians are said literally to assume the clothing and accoutrements of different ways of life. The Anonymous of Passau affirms that they present themselves as merchants, hawking rings and jewels to members of the courts through which they pass, and then, when customers express interest in their merchandise, offering them gems of far greater value, which they ultimately reveal to be their doctrines.

---

1. For the history of the Waldensians, see Peter Biller, *The Waldenses, 1170–1530: Between a Religious Order and a Church* (Aldershot, UK: Ashgate Publishing, 2001); Euan Cameron, *Waldenses: Rejections of Holy Church in Medieval Europe* (Oxford: Blackwell, 2000), esp. pp. 11–206; Gabriel Audisio, *The Waldensian Dissent: Persecution and Survvial, c. 1170–c. 1570*, trans. Claire Davison (Cambridge: Cambridge University Press, 1999); Jean Gonnet and Amedeo Molnar, *Les Vaudois au Moyen Age* (Torino: Claudiana, 1974); Kurt-Victor Selge, *Die ersten Waldenser, mit Edition des Liber Antiheresis des Durandus von Osca* (Berlin: De Gruyter, 1967), esp. vol. 1, *Untersuchung und Darstellung*; and Grado Merlo, *Identità valdesi nella storia e nella storiographica* (Torino: Claudiana, 1991), pp. 71–92. For shorter accounts, see Christine Thouzellier, *Catharisme et valdéisme en Languedoc à la fin du XIIe et au début du XIIIe siècle: Politique pontificale—Controverses* (Paris: Presses Universitaires de France, 1969), and *Hérésie et hérétiques: Vaudois, Cathares, Patarins, Albigeois* (Roma: Edizioni di storia e letteratura, 1969); Malcolm Lambert, *Medieval Heresy: Popular Movements from the Gregorian Reform to the Reformation*, 3rd ed. (Oxford: Blackwell, 2002), pp. 70–96; and Herbert Grundmann, *Religious Movements in the Middle Ages: The Historical Links Between Heresy, the Mendicant Orders, and the Women's Religious Movement in the Twelfth and Thirteenth Century, with the Historical Foundations of German Mysticism*, trans. Steven Rowan (Notre Dame, IN: University of Notre Dame Press, 1995), pp. 40–55.

Adopting new personae in order to insinuate themselves among potential converts, the Waldensians also adopt such guises in order to elude potential persecutors.[2] David von Augsburg testifies of the Waldensians, "These wanderers go about in outfits of different clothing, so that they are not recognized. Whenever they go from one house to another, they remove some part of their mantle or headdress. They go in the darkness, so that no one considers what they are doing."[3] Etienne de Bourbon describes the Waldensians, in a similar manner, as people given to "transfiguring themselves under various clothes and occupations."[4] He cites one such sectary who carried about with him the emblems of various crafts, presenting himself now as a cobbler, now as a barber, and now as a harvester. "Like Proteus, he would transfigure himself," Etienne writes. "If he were sought in one appearance and realized the fact, he would transmute himself into another."[5] Most dangerously, the Waldensians are described as taking on not just the sartorial appearance of different tradesmen but the social role of clerics. Like ecclesiastics, the Waldensians studied Scripture and the Church Fathers, so that they could know the foundation of their faith. Like

2. As Jean Gonnet writes, "Les Vaudois, non contents de se présenter partout sous les dehors de la foi et de la sainteté sans cependant en posséder la vérité, étaient d'autant plus dangereux qu'ils se dissimulaient sous les déguisements les plus divers. . . . Cette forme marquée de nicodémisme, cette technique spéciale de propagande, unie à la practique toujours plus suivie de l'itinérantisme, caractérise bien la période qui fait suite à la condamnation de Vérone," "La Figure et l'oeuvre de Vaudès dans la tradition historique et selon les dernières recherches," *Cahiers de Fanjeaux*, vol. 2, *Vaudois languedociens et Pauvres Catholiques* (Toulouse: Privat, 1976), pp. 88–109, at p. 98.

3. My translation; "Vadunt autem i diversis habitibus vestium isti circatores, ne agnoscantur, et cum transeunt quandoque de domo forte in domum, aliquod onus deferunt in capite palee vel vasis, et in obscuro vadunt, ne quis perpendat quid agant," David von Augsburg, *De inquisicione hereticorum*, in "Der Tractat des David von Augsburg über die Waldesier," ed. Wilhelm Preger, *Abhandlungen der historischen Classe der königlich bayerischen Akademie der Wissenschaften* 13, no. 2 (1878): 204–35, p. 210. A short section of this text has been translated as "David of Augsburg: On the Waldensians of Bavaria, 1270," in Peters, pp. 149–50.

4. "Stephen of Bourbon on the Early Waldenses," in Wakefield and Evans, pp. 208–10, at p. 210, translation modified (the translation is, again, partial); "se sub diversis hominum habitibus et artificiis transfigurantes," Etienne de Bourbon, *Anecdotes historiques, légendes et apologues tirés du recueil inédit d'Etienne de Bourbon, dominican du XIIIe siècle*, ed. A Lecoy de la Marche (Paris: Renouard, 1887), p. 293. On Etienne de Bourbon, see Jacques Berlioz, "La Prédication des cathares selon l'inquisiteur Etienne de Bourbon (mort vers 1261)," *Heresis* 31 (n.d.): 9–35, and "Etienne de Bourbon, l'inquisiteur exemplaire," *L'Histoire* 125 (1989): 24–30.

5. "Stephen of Bourbon on the Early Waldenses," p. 210, translation modified; "quasi Proteus se transfigurabat: si quereretur in una similitudine et ei innotesceret, in alia se transmutabat," Etienne de Bourbon, *Anecdotes historiques*, p. 293.

ecclesiastics, they preached publicly, so that they could share their understanding of what they had read with others like themselves. While the Waldensians would gradually develop doctrinal differences with Catholic clerics, it was originally only this desire to study and preach, like men of the Church, that distinguished them from their orthodox peers. As the clerics saw it, in reading theological works and preaching about the faith to others, at a time when the word *clericus* was synonymous with "learned" and the word *laicus* with "unlearned," the Waldensians deceived onlookers as to who they were no less than if they had donned a scapular and tunic.[6] Even as, for most people, identity functioned as what one had been born into being, for the Waldensians it functioned as what one made of oneself or, better, what one convinced others one had made of oneself. While other heretics were perceived as annulling their identity through their secretiveness or rendering it unique and uninterpretable through their singularity, the Waldensians were understood as doubling who they were through their duplicity, deceiving others as to the truth even before they began to spread their errors.

Like other chroniclers of heretics, the clerics who provide accounts of the Waldensians are troubled by their deceit because the epistemological confusion it causes makes it difficult for authorities to identity them and to convict them of their crimes. Time and again, the clerics depict these authorities as aware of the existence of the Waldensians among them yet frustrated in their attempts to establish their guilt to their communities. How can people be exposed as heretics when they seem more learned than the local priest? How can they be convicted when they appear to preach more eloquently than visiting friars? How can they be condemned when, seized and brought before inquisitors, they respond so cunningly to the questions set to them that they seem to be simple people harassed by malicious clerics? Insofar as the clerics succeed in unmasking the Waldensians, as we shall see, it is only because their duplicity becomes, in the clerics' hands, evidence of their heresy.

---

6. M. T. Clanchy argues that, just as every bachelor of arts knew that evil, by definition, is not good, despite the numbers of cases which complicate the opposition of these categories, every bachelor would also know that clerics, by definition, are learned and laymen unlearned. "Scholastic axioms derived their validity not from individual experience but from universal rules, which were superior and prior to particular cases because they were part of a divine order of things," *From Memory to Written Record, England 1066–1307*, 2nd ed. (Oxford: Oxford University Press, 1993), p. 182.

SCHOLARS

In 1173, the anonymous chronicler of Laon tells us, a wealthy burgher of Lyon by the name of Valdès happened upon a minstrel who was recounting the life of Saint Alexis to a crowd, and he found himself moved by the story he heard.[7]

7. On the life of Valdès, see an *exemplum* from the *Liber visionum et miraculorum* from the abbey of Clairvaux (Bibliothèque municipale de Troyes, ms 946), ed. Olivier Legendre and Michel Rubellin, in "Valdès: Un 'exemple' à Clairvaux? Le plus ancien texte sur les débuts du Pauvre de Lyon," *Revue Mabillon*, n.s., t. 11 (=t. 72) (2000): 187–95, at p. 188, which was probably composed circa 1174; the Anonymous of Laon, "The Origins of the Waldensian Heresy," in Wakefield and Evans, pp. 200–202, and *Ex chronico universali anonymi Laudunensis*, in MGH, *Scriptores* 26, pp. 442–57, which was written around 1220; "Stephen of Bourbon on the Early Waldenses" and Etienne de Bourbon, *Anecdotes historiques*, which was drafted between 1250 and 1261; and Richard de Poitiers, *Vita Alexandri Papae III*, in Gonnet, ed., *Enchiridion fontium Valdensium: Recueil critique des sources concernant les Vaudois au moyen âge du IIIe Concile de Latran au Synode de Chanforan (1179–1532)*, vol. 1 (Torre Pellice: Claudiana, 1958), pp. 164–66. As Rubellin maintain in "Au temps où Valdès n'était pas hérétique: Hypothèses sur le rôle de Valdès à Lyon (1170–1183)," in Monique Zerner, ed., *Inventer l'hérésie? Discours polémiques et pouvoirs avant l'Inquisition* (Nice: Z'éditions, 1998), pp. 193–217, Valdès is not depicted as a heretic in the first account of his life but, rather, as a legitimate holy man. Legendre and Rubellin speculate that Valdès was championed by Guichard de Pontigny, the Cistercian archbishop of Lyon, who is known to have supported the spiritual aspirations of such laymen. It may well have been Guichard who passed on Valdès's story to Jean, the prior of Clairvaux, when he visited this monastery in 1174 for the celebration of Bernard of Clairvaux's canonization, and who thus provided the material for the *exemplum* from this abbey. When Valdès and his followers appeared at the Third Lateran Council in 1179, Legendre and Rubellin suggest, it was with the approbation of Guichard. It was only when Jean de Bellesmains replaced Guichard as archbishop that the church of Lyon repudiated the Waldensians, as it did in 1183, and only when Lucius III replaced Alexander III as pope that they were condemned, as happened in 1184. See Olivier Legendre, "L'Hérésie vue de Clairvaux: Témoinage inédit d'un recueil cistercien d'*exempla* sur les movements hérétiques de la fin du XIIe siècle," *Heresis* 33 (décembre 2000): 69–78. Other scholars have argued that Valdès was at first perceived more as a saint than as a heretic. Kurt-Victor Selge, for example, suggests that the Anonymous of Laon follows an alternative, positive tradition about the life of Valdès in his depiction of this individual, one perhaps identified with Fontevrault, where Valdès's daughters were said to have been nuns. See Selge, *Die ersten Waldenser*, pp. 227–42, and "Caractéristiques du premier mouvement vaudois et crises au cours de son expansion," *Cahiers de Fanjeaux*, vol. 2, *Vaudois languedociens et Pauvres Catholiques*, pp. 110–42. Grado G. Merlo concurs with Selge's estimation of this chronicle: "Il *Chronicon universale* procede per stereotipe agiografici, profilando il ritratto di un futuro santo la cui conversione all' Evangelo avviene—non può non avvenire—nella piena sottomissione alle autorità ecclesiatiche e alla cultura chiericale," *Identità Valdesi nella storia e nella storiografia*, p. 72. See also Merlo, "Le mouvement vaudois des origines à la fin du XIIIe siècle," in *Les Vaudois des origines à leur fin (XIIe–XVIe siècles)*, ed. Gabriel. Audisio (Colloque international, Aix-en-Provence, 8–9 avril 1988) (Torino: A. Meynier, 1990), p. 18. Christine Thouzellier has likewise termed the Anonymous's account of Valdès's life a "légende," like those of more canonical saints, *Catharisme et valdéisme*, p. 16.

Whether Valdès heard the famous eleventh-century version of the life of Saint
Alexis, a poem of 625 lines that has long been considered one of the founding
works of Old French literature, or the lesser-known twelfth-century account
of the saint's life, which, with its additional 731 lines of psychological embel-
lishment and more popular orientation, would more likely have been sung on
a Lyonnais street, he would have learned that Alexis was a wealthy nobleman
of Rome who turned to prayer rather than to reading in order to understand
how he might best live a holy life.[8] Alexis's lack of recourse to texts is all the
more striking given that both narratives of his life make clear that he knew well
how to read. In the earlier version, the narrator relates, "he so learned letters
that he was well furnished with them," and in the later work, the holy man
himself asserts, "I was a cleric [i.e., a learned man], well learned in letters."[9]
The only book Alexis was explicitly said to read was the Psalter, one of the few
religious texts laymen were encouraged to peruse because of its emphasis on
devotion rather than on theology.[10] The eleventh-century life states, "Holy
Scripture was his counsel," yet it does not specifically state that the saint read
this text; with lay study of Holy Writ being discouraged by the Church, Alexis
might be understood to be guided by this text without having read it.[11] Even
if we are to assume that Alexis did read Scripture, the poem places his consul-
tation of this work within the context of his restriction of his diet, his attendance at Mass, and his taking of Communion, as if holy reading were just one
more devotional practice.[12] Insofar as Alexis reads, he does so not specula-

8. On the connection between Valdès and Alexis, see Alison Goddard Elliott, "The
Triumphus Sancti Remacli: Latin Evidence for Oral Composition," *Romance Philology* 22, no.
3 (February, 1979): 292–98, and Ulrich Mölk, "La *Chanson de Saint Alexis* et le culte du saint
en France aux XIe et XIIe siècles," *Cahiers de civilisation médiévale* 21 (janvier–mars 1978):
339–55. For the eleventh-century version of Alexis's life, see *La Vie de Saint Alexis*, ed.
Christopher Story (Genève: Droz, 1968). For the twelfth-century version, see "C'est li
Roumans de Saint Alessin," in Alison Goddard Elliott, *The "Vie de saint Alexis" in the Twelfth
and Thirteenth Centuries: An Edition and Commentary* (Chapel Hill: University of North
Carolina Department of Romance Languages, 1983), pp. 93–150.
9. "Tant aprist letres que bien en fut guarnit," "C'est li Roumans de Saint Alessin," v. 34;
"jou fui clers, de letre bien apris," ibid., v. 561.
10. On the Psalter, see Margaret Deanesly, *The Lollard Bible and Other Medieval Biblical
Versions* (Cambridge: Cambridge University Press, 1920; rpt. 1966), pp. 36–37, and "The
Council of Toulouse, 1229," in Peters, Canon 14, pp. 194–95, at p. 195.
11. "Sainte escriture ço ert ses conseilers," *La Vie de Saint Alexis*, v. 258. On such prohibitions, see Deanesly, *The Lollard Bible*.
12. Alexis recognizes, as Evelyn Birge Vitz puts it, that "God is the subject here, in the
sense that it is his will that guides the action, that pulls Alexis where he goes, making him do
what he does"; if Alexis functions as the subject here at all, it is only insofar as he freely

tively, not as a means of inquiry into the truth, but piously, as a means of meditating upon a truth which is already revealed to him.[13] Even after he has died, Alexis discourages lay reading, refusing to release the letter he has composed when his father attempts to take it from his hand and permitting only the pope to remove it. Alive or dead, Alexis makes clear that the study of important texts should remain the privilege of clerics appointed to such tasks. Despite the model of the saint to whom he was so drawn, neither Valdès nor the Waldensians imitated Alexis's alexia. On the contrary, both the founder of the sect and his followers attempted to make themselves learned people, with controversial results.[14]

Although Valdès was not "well learned," as Alexis was, his spiritual awakening made him aspire to this state. Etienne de Bourbon describes Valdès as "a rich man . . . who, on hearing the Gospels, although he was not very learned [*non . . . multum literatus*], was curious [*curiosus*] to understand what they

acknowledges God's will as greater and more determinative than his own. See Evelyn Birge Vitz, "*La Vie de saint Alexis*: Narrative Analysis and the Quest for the Sacred Subject," in *Medieval Narrative and Modern Narratology: Subjects and Objects of Desire* (New York: New York University Press, 1989), ch. 5, pp. 126–48, at p. 133.

13. As Brigitte Cazalles comments, "The pope, representing doctrinal and scriptural authority, serves as a mediator between the written world of the saint and the oral world of his family; he treats Alexis' letter as a sacred text that belongs to those who have mastered learning. By contrast, the inability of Alexis' father to take the letter symbolizes his ignorance and illiteracy, which are compensated by the chancellor's reading the document aloud. The layman's access to knowledge, then, is indirect, through an oral narrative orchestrated by Church dignitaries," Cazalles, "Saints' Lives," in *A New History of French Literature*, ed. Denis Hollier et al (Cambridge, MA: Harvard University Press, 1992), pp. 13–18, at p. 14.

14. The literacy or illiteracy of the Waldensians has been amply addressed. See Peter Biller, "The Topos and Reality of the Heretic as *illiteratus*," in *The Waldenses*, pp. 169–90 and Peter Biller and Anne Hudson, eds., *Heresy and Literacy, 1000–1530* (Cambridge: Cambridge University Press, 1994), esp. Alexander Patschovsky, "The Literacy of Waldensiansism from Valdes to c. 1400," pp. 112–36; Anne Brenon, "The Waldensian Books," pp. 137–59; Pierette Paravy, "Waldensians in the Dauphiné (1400–1530): From Dissidence in Texts to Dissidence in Practice," pp. 160–75; and Gabriel Audisio, "Were the Waldensians more Literate than their Contemporaries?" pp. 176–85. See also Deanesly, *The Lollard Bible*, esp. pp. 25–42. On literacy at this time period in general, Clanchy, *From Memory to Written Record*, esp. pp. 175–201, and Herbert Grundmann, "*Litteratus-illitteratus*: Der Wandel einer Bildungsnorm vom Altertum zum Mittelalter," *Archiv für Kulturgeschichte* 40 (1958): 1–65. See also Yves Congar, "Les laïcs et l'ecclésiologie des 'ordines' chez les théologiens des XIe et XIIe siècles," in *I Laici nella "societas Christiana" dei secoli XI e XII* (Atti della terza settimana internazionale di studio, Mendola, 21–27 agosto, 1965) (Milano: Vita e pensiero, 1968), pp. 83–117, and Paul Zumthor, "*Litteratus/illiteratus*: Remarques sur le contexte vocal de l'écriture médiévale," *Romania* 106 (1985): 1–18.

said."[15] The day after hearing about Alexis, the Anonymous of Laon relates, "The said citizen hastened to the school of theology seeking counsel for his soul's welfare."[16] He hired a grammarian by the name of Etienne d'Anse, a prebendary of the cathedral of Lyon, to dictate translations for him, and a scribe known as Bernard Ydras, a young priest, to take down Etienne's words. Together, these clerics provided Valdès with vernacular versions of numerous books of the Bible and passages from the Church Fathers, arranged by topic. "This citizen . . . read often these texts and learned them by heart," Etienne de Bournon reports.[17] On the one hand, neither the Anonymous of Laon nor Etienne de Bourbon, our only two sources for this episode in Valdès's life, explicitly condemns Valdès's efforts to read the central texts of the Christian tradition, though they do express disapproval of his and his followers' actions later on.[18] The concern Valdès shows for his soul seems only laudable, as does his desire to learn through study the best way to bring about his salvation. Pope Innocent III himself acknowledged in speaking of the Waldensians, "The desire to understand Holy Scripture . . . is not to be reprehended but rather to be commended."[19] At the same time, however, the "curiosity" (*curiositas*) Etienne de Bourbon attributes to Valdès implicitly suggests a desire for learning beyond what is appropriate for one's status and, hence, beyond what is needed for one's salvation. Scripture warns, "Seek not the things that are too high for thee, and search not into things above thy ability."[20] If studiousness was commonly regarded as praiseworthy insofar as it led the seeker to truths, it was thought to become blameworthy and to harm him insofar as it led him

15. "Stephen of Bourbon on the EarlyWaldenses, p. 209, translation modified; "Quidam dives . . . , audiens evangelia, cum non esset multum litteratus, curiosus intelligere quid dicerent," Etienne de Bourbon, *Anecdotes historiques,* p. 16.

16. "The Origins of the Waldensian Heresy," p. 201, translation modified; "Facto mane, civis memoratus ad scolas theologie consilium anime sue quesiturus properavit," *Ex chronico universali anonymi Laudunensis,* p. 447.

17. "Stephen of Bourbon on the Early Waldenses," p. 209; "sepe legeret et cordetenus firmaret," Etienne de Bourbon, *Anecdotes historiques,* p. 294.

18. The *Liber visionum et miraculorum* depicts Valdès as inspired by visions rather than by Scripture and the writings of the Church Fathers. The text cites Valdès as informing his fellow citizens, "Si . . . vobis datum esset videre et credere, que vidi et credo tormenta futura, forsitan et vos similiter faceretis. Verum modo abscondita sunt ab oculis vestris, sed veletis nolitis, per experientiam noveritis, que nunc credere et formidare recusatis," Legendre and Rubellin, "Valdès: Un *exemple* à Clairvaux?" p. 188.

19. "Licet autem desiderium intelligendi divinas Scripturas . . . reprehendendum non sit, sed potius commendandum," Innocent III, *Regestorum sive epistolarum,* PL 215, col. 595.

20. "altiora te ne scrutaveris et fortiora te ne exquisieris," Ecclus. 3:22.

to falsehoods.[21] According to Thomas Aquinas, the desire for truth is good in itself, yet it becomes evil "when a person applies himself to grasp truths beyond his capacity; by doing so he may easily slip into error."[22] With his reliance upon theological learning instead of prayer and devotional practices as a means of access to God, Valdès departs radically from the tradition of Alexis and other holy laymen before him.

Even though the Waldensians were no more learned than their founder, they too sought the education they lacked. Walter Map, an associate of King Henry II, archdeacon of Oxford and chancellor to the bishop of Lincoln, encountered a group of Waldensians at the Third Lateran Council of 1179, six years after Valdès's conversion, and described them as "ignorant, unlearned men" (*homines ydiotas, illiteratos*) who aspire to a knowledge of Scripture beyond their native capacity.[23] When he calls them *illiterati*, he characterizes them, according to the meaning of this term at this time, as people who cannot read Latin, even if they can read the vulgar language; he observes, for example, that the codex they offer the pope is composed of religious texts "in the French tongue."[24] When he terms them *idiotae*, he portrays them, by the same token, as people who lack a certain specialized knowledge—in this case the knowledge clerics attain through study of theology in a university. In the years that followed the council, virtually all clerics writing about the Waldensians, including

21. For a useful survey of late antique and medieval attitudes toward curiosity and its connection with heresy, see Edward M. Peters, "Transgressing the Limits Set by the Fathers: Authority and Impious Exegesis in Medieval Thought," in Scott L. Waugh and Peter D. Dieh, eds., *Christendom and Its Discontents: Exclusion, Persecution, and Rebellion, 1000–1500* (Cambridge: Cambridge University Press, 1996), pp. 338–62, at p. 339. As Peters writes, "Although *curiositas* never became one of the major vices that, with the virtues, stand at the root of Christian moral theology and palaeopsychology, it was frequently discussed by early Christian writers, sometimes attached to a major vice such as pride, avarice, or sloth, and built into the characterization of certain kinds of dissent, notably heresy and the practice of magic. From Tertullian on, it was regularly applied to heterodoxy."

22. "inquantum aliquis studet ad cognoscendam veritatem supra proprii ingenii facultatem, quia per hoc homines de facili in errores labuntur," Thomas Aquinas, *Summa Theologiae*, vol. 44, *Well-Tempered Passion (2a 2ae. 155–70)*, ed. and trans. Thomas Gilby, Qu. 167, Art. 1, Reply, pp. 204–5.

23. Walter Map, *De Nugis Curialium / Courtiers' Trifles*, ed. and trans. M. R. James, rev. C. N. L. Brooke and R. A. B. Mynors (Oxford: Clarendon Press, 1983), pp. 118, 124.

24. "lingua . . . Gallica," ibid., p. 124. Map could also be depicting the Waldensians as people who cannot understand Latin texts, even if they can make sense of their words, because they are unfamiliar with the intellectual context from which they emerged. Given Map's reference to the French tongue, however, he seems to be referring at this moment to their linguistic incompetence instead of their interpretive failings.

Etienne de Bourbon, the Anonymous of Passau, Alain de Lille, David von Augsburg, Bernard Gui, and Nicholau Eymerich, repeat Map's description of them as *illiterati* and *idiotae*.[25] On one level, these authors marvel at the zeal the Waldensians exhibit for learning and the feats of memorization they achieve, despite the disadvantages of their class, sex, and age. The Anonymous of Passau writes of the Waldensians, "Men and women, great and lesser, day and night, do not cease to learn and teach; the workman who labors all day teaches or learns at night."[26] In Occitania and Lombardy, he claims, "there are more schools of heretics than of theologians, and they have more hearers; they debated publicly, and they convoked the people to solemn disputations in fields and forums, and they preached 'from the rooftops.'"[27] Etienne de Bourbon tells of a young plowman who, after spending a year among the Waldensians, could recite forty Sunday Gospels, and David von Augsburg speaks of "little girls" who are schooled in the Gospels and the Epistles.[28] On another level, however, these authors express dismay at the Waldensians' ambition, because these seekers will never be able to achieve genuine learning on account of the disadvantages of their lowly social position. While the Waldensians may commission translations of Latin texts into the vernacular, their ignorance of the Church's language impedes any true comprehension of the texts they read. The Anonymous of Passau complains that their edition of Scripture mistakes "his own" (*sui*) for "pigs" (*sues*) and "reeds" (*harundis*) for "swallows" (*hirundis*).[29] David von Augsburg points out that despite all the Waldensians' efforts, a Catholic schoolboy of twelve is more learned than any of their grown

25. As Alexander Patschovsky observes, "The characterization of Waldensians—*all* of them, without distinction—as illiterate idiots begins with Walter Map, and there is scarcely a single 'Catholic' author who does not join the chorus when he has occasion to speak of the Waldensians," "The Literacy of Waldensianism," p. 127.

26. "The Passau Anonymous: On the Origins of Heresy and the Sect of the Waldensians," in Peters, pp. 150–63, at p. 150; "viri et femine, parvi et magni, nocte et die non cessant discere et docere: operarius in die laborans, nocte discit vel docet," "Auszüge aus dem Sammelwerk des Passauer Anonymous," in Alexander Patschovsky and Kurt-Victor Selge, eds., *Quellen zur Geschichte der Waldeser* (Gütersloh: Verlagshaus Gerd Mohn, 1973), pp. 70–103, at p. 70.

27. "The Passau Anonymous," p. 152, translation modified; "plures erant scole hereticorum quam theologorum. Et plures auditores habebant, publice disputabant, et populum convocabant ad staciones sollempnes in foro et in campo, et predicabant 'in tectis," "Auszüge aus dem Sammelwerk des Passauer Anonymous," p. 72. Cf. Mt. 10: 27

28. David von Augsburg, "On the Waldensians of Bavaria," in Peters, pp. 149–50, at p. 149; "puellas parvulas," David von Augsburg, "De inquisicione hereticorum," p. 213.

29. "The Passau Anonymous," p. 151; "Auszüge aus dem Sammelwerk des Passauer Anonymous," p. 71.

men because he has access to vast numbers of Latin works of which these adults must necessarily remain ignorant. The very juxtapositions these authors set up between plowmen and the Gospels, little girls and the Epistles, suggest an inherent contradiction between who the Waldensians are and what they are attempting to achieve, as well as an inherent danger in their failure to recognize this contradiction.

By reading Scripture on their own, unaided by the exegetical tradition of the Church, the Waldensians grasp the most obvious, literal level of the text without suspecting the existence of more subtle, figurative layers. As David von Augsburg writes, "Because they presumed to interpret the words of Gospel in a sense of their own, not perceiving that there were any others, they said that the Gospel ought to be served altogether according to the letter [*iuxta literam*], and they boasted that they wished to do this and that they alone were the true imitators of Christ."[30] Elsewhere, David reinforces this point, adding that the Waldensians "boasted that they lived entirely according to the doctrine of the Gospel and that they served it perfectly to the letter [*ad literam*]."[31] As we recall, heresy had long been identified with excessively literal interpretations of Scripture. Saint Paul had warned that "the letter killeth, but the spirit quickeneth," and later exegetes, like Augustine, had explained that those who grasp the literal level of a text and not the figurative level perceive only its surface at the expense of its deeper truth.[32] Though Jews were the first population seen as susceptible to this superficial reading, heretics were also judged guilty on this score.[33] It was this literalness of their interpretations of Scripture which, according to these clerics, led to many of the errors of their doctrine. If the Waldensians claim, heretically, that one is never permitted to swear, this is because, according to Bernard Gui, they read the apparent injunctions against

---

30. David von Augsburg, "On the Waldensians of Bavaria," p. 149, translation modified; "quia sensu proprio verba ewangelii interpretari presumpserunt, videntes nullos alios ewangelium iuxta literam omnino servare, quod se favere velle iactaverunt, se solos Christi veros imitatores esse dixerunt," David von Augsburg, *De inquisicione hereticorum*, p. 206.

31. "omnino vivere secundum ewangelii doctrinam et illam ad literam perfecte servare," David von Augsburg, "De inquisicione hereticorum," p. 205.

32. "littera enim occidit, Spiritus autem vivificat," 2 Cor. 3:6. See Augustine, *On Christian Doctrine*, trans. D. W. Robertson Jr., Library of the Liberal Arts (New York: Macmillan, 1958; rpt. 1988), bk. 3, ch. 5, p. 84.

33. When Paul lists "dissensions" (*dissensiones*) and "sects" (*sectae*) as "works of the flesh" in Gal. 5:20, he was understood by later exegetes to be placing heretics within the category of such carnal misreaders. See Benoît Jeanjean, *Saint Jérome et l'hérésie* (Paris: Institut d'Etudes Augustiniennes, 1999), esp. pp. 275–76.

swearing in the Gospel of Matthew and the Epistle of James too literally, "with
an interpretation as extravagant as it is erroneous," and thus ignore "the sound
teaching of the saints, of the doctors of the Church, of the tradition of the same
Holy Catholic Church" that the taking of oaths is permitted.[34] If the Waldensians claim that one is never allowed to judge or to condemn a man to death,
this is because they read the apparent prohibitions against judging and killing
in the Gospel of Matthew, again too literally, "without the proper explanation
essential to their interpretation," and thus ignore "the signification or explanation which the Holy Roman Church wisely perceives and transmits to the
faithful in accordance with the teachings of the Fathers, the doctors, and the
canonical decrees."[35] It is because the Waldensians overlook the body of
exegetical works by late antique and medieval theologians, which has determined that these passages should not be read "to the letter," that they read
these passages in so literal a fashion. Ignorant of their exegetical predecessors,
the Waldensians are ignorant of the deeper levels of Scripture revealed by these
predecessors, and therefore they fail to detect the subtleties inherent in the
Scripture they presume to study.

During the Third Lateran Council, Map had occasion to expose the
Waldensians' unfamiliarity with clerical modes of thought and, as a result, their
inadequacy in interpreting Scripture. Examining two Waldensians present at
the council, he asked them, "Do you believe in God the Father?"[36] When they
replied, "We believe," he asked, "And in the Son?"[37] When they again responded, "We believe," he demanded, "And in the Holy Spirit?" and they
asserted once more, "We believe."[38] Finally, Map inquired, "And in the

---

34. Mt 5:34; Jas. 5:12; "Bernard Gui's Description of Heresies," in Wakefield and Evans,
pp. 373–445, at p. 388; "tam insamo quam devio applicando," Bernard Gui, *Manuel de l'inquisiteur*, vol. 1, pp. 38–40; "Bernard Gui's Description of Heresies," p. 388; "sanam doctrinam sanctorum et doctorum Ecclesie et traditionem ejusdem sancte Ecclesie catholice,"
Bernard Gui, *Manuel de l'inquisiteur*, vol. 1, p. 40. On Bernard Gui, see *Cahiers de Fanjeaux*,
vol. 16, *Bernard Gui et son Monde* (Toulouse: Privat, 1981), and Bernard Guenée, *Entre l'Eglise
et l'état: quatre vies de prélats français à la fin du Moyen Age, XIIIe–XVe siècle* (Paris: Gallimard,
1987), trans. Arthur Goldhammer as *Between Church and State: The Lives of Four French
Prelates in the Late Middle Ages* (Chicago: University of Chicago Press, 1991).
35. Mt 7:1 and 5:21; "Bernard Gui's Description of Heresies," p. 389; "sine expositione deb-
ita ad hec applicans," Bernard Gui, *Manuel de l'inquisiteur*, vol. 1, p. 40; "Bernard Gui's
Description of Heresies," p. 389; "nec . . . recipiens intellectum nec expositionem eorum, sicut
sancta Romana ecclesia ea sane intelligit et tradit fidelibus secundum doctrinam Patrum et
doctorum et canonicas sanctiones," Bernard Gui, *Manuel de l'inquisiteur*, vol. 1, p. 40.
36. "Creditis in Deum patrem?" Walter Map, *De nugis curialium*, p. 126.
37. "Credimus," ibid.; "Et in Filium?" ibid.
38. "Credimus," ibid.; "Et in Spiritum sanctum?" ibid.; "Credimus," ibid.

Mother of God?" to which they stated for the fourth time, "We believe."[39] After this last answer, Map recounts, "they were hooted down with universal clamor by everyone present, and they went away ashamed."[40] As Map sees it, the first three questions, with their focus upon the Father, the Son, and the Holy Spirit, establish that he is examining them on their views of the Trinity, and the use of the same verb, "Do you believe" (*Creditis*), to link these questions with the following one on the Mother of God indicates that he has not yet left this topic. Although the Waldensians seem to think he is asking them if they believe in the existence of the Mother of God, Map believes it obvious from this context that he is asking if they believe in her divinity. In approaching this complex issue so indirectly, through the parallel structure of his questions and the repetition of the same verb, he might seem to be using semantics to set up the Waldensians instead of substance to plumb their views. Yet Map evidently believes his tactic with these sectaries to be justified because it succeeds in showing, if not *what* the Waldensians think, then *how* they think. These Waldensians reveal themselves capable of grasping only the superficial value of Map's questions and incapable of grasping the latent meaning, indicated by his parallel structures and repeated verbs. Earlier, Map asserted that even learned, literate men face difficulties when attempting to fathom the mysteries embedded in Holy Writ. After describing the complexities within Scripture, Map praised those "who engage all their days in subtle discourse, who can entrap and only with difficulty be entrapped," and who, as a result of their vocation, can escape the "fine snares or nets" set within these pages.[41] Now Map suggests that through their single answer to his questions the Waldensians show that they would be unable to recognize and evade the "fine snares or nets" in Scripture, just as they are unable to recognize and evade them in their examiner's speech. Entrapped with such ease, they manifest their difference from clerics in general, "who can only with difficulty be entrapped"; from the clerics at the council, who laugh at the sectaries in apparent confidence that they themselves would have escaped such humiliation; and from Map himself, who, as a cleric, proves able to entrap them so easily. The Waldensians lack the hermeneutic skills necessary, Map maintains, for reading Scripture and, hence, deserve the jeers with which they are met.

39. "Et in matrem Christi?" ibid.; "Credimus," ibid.

40. "Et ab omnibus multiplici sunt clamore derisi, confusique recesserunt," ibid.

41. "qui capciosis exercitantur tota vita sermonibus, qui capere et capi vix possunt," ibid., p. 124; "subtiles . . . laqueos aut rete," ibid.

Ultimately, the Waldensians err in their desire for learning, these clerics suggest, because they do not really desire learning itself but only the reputation of learned people. When discussing theology, the Waldensians are said to use quotations from Scripture and the writings of the Church Fathers manipulatively, in order to support their points, without concern for the meaning of these passages within their original contexts. David von Augsburg complains, "They do not receive the Old Testament as of faith, but they learn only certain passages from it, in order to attack us and defend themselves. . . . And similarly they pluck out the words of the saints Augustine, Jerome, Gregory, Ambrose, John Chrysostom, Isidore, and truncated passages from their books, in order to prove their illusions and to resist us."[42] He adds, "They pass over in silence those passages of the saints which seem to contradict them and by which their error is refuted."[43] The Waldensians treat authoritative texts not as a means to attain truth but, rather, as the means to convince others of a truth they have already attained. For them, the words in sacred texts constitute not the source of their faith but the justification of a faith that little to do with those words. Bernard Gui protests that "in order to have their words accepted by their listeners when they preach from the Gospels, the Epistles, and the *exempla* and passages of the saints, they say, by way of proof, 'This is said in the Gospel,' or 'in the Epistle of Saint Peter, or of Saint Paul, or of Saint James,' or they say, 'this saint or this doctor.'"[44] Gui reinforces David's suggestion that the Waldensians approach Scripture and the Church Fathers, not reverentially, for the purpose of the truth, but instrumentally, for their own purpose. As other authors put it, these sectaries exploit these texts as they do because they seek not salvation in heaven but glory on earth. The Anonymous of Passau writes, "Since [Waldensians] see learned men honored in the Church, they wish to be

---

42. "David of Augsburg," pp. 149–50; "Vetus testamentum non recipiunt ad credendum, sed tantum aliqua inde discunt, ut nos per ea impugnent et se defendant. . . . Sic et verba sanctorum Augustini, Ieronymi, Gregorii, Ambrosii, Johannis Crisostomi, Isidori et auctoritates ex libris eorum truncatas decerpunt, ut sua figmenta inde approbent vel nobis resistant," David of Augsburg, *De inquisicione hereticorum,*" p. 209.

43. "David of Augsburg,"p. 150; "Illas autem sanctorum sentencias, quas sibi vident esse contrarias, quibus error suus destruitur, tacite pretermittunt," David of Augsburg, *De inquisicione hereticorum,*" p. 209.

44. "Bernard Gui's Description of Heresies," p. 396; "quandoque predicant de evangeliis et de epistois vel de exemplis et auctoritatibus sanctorum, dicendo et allegando: 'Istud dicitur in evangelio vel in epistola sancti Petri aut sancti Pauli aut sancti Jacobi,' vel [imo] dicunt: 'Talis sanctus aut talis doctor,' ut magis dicta eorum ab auditoribus acceptentur," Bernard Gui, *Manuel de l'inquisiteur,* vol. I, p. 62.

honored for learning themselves."[45] Etienne de Bourbon concurs with the Anonymous: "They affirm these words from the Gospels so that they may be held masters of error among the people."[46] Whatever knowledge of the divine other the Waldensians claim to seek, the clerics conclude, an aggrandizement of the human self is their final goal.

PREACHERS

Though Saint Alexis provided the prototype for Valdès's conversion, it is noteworthy that this saint shows no more inclination for preaching than he does for learning. Immediately after he "remembers God," he flees his native city for the East, distributes his money to the poor, and sits down beside them on the street to beg. When two of his father's servants are sent to find him, they fail to recognize him because of the alteration his flesh has undergone, and merely give him alms as they pass by. The legend relates, "He was their lord, now he is their beggar. I do not know how to tell you how happy he was about it."[47] Later, when the people in the city where Alexis lives begin to honor him as a holy man, he flees them as he has fled his family. For the last seventeen years of his life, he resides under the steps to his parents' house, overhearing his mother, his father, and his bride bemoan his absence and delighting in their inability to recognize the beggar on their grounds as the man they miss. Concealed by his apparent status as one poor, wasted wretch among many, Alexis shuns any recognition of his identity, whether social, spiritual, or personal, because such recognition would attach him to the world and thus hinder the loss of selfhood necessary for his spiritual ascent. As part of his efforts to efface himself, Alexis remains silent throughout most of the works written about him. In neither the eleventh- nor the twelfth-century texts does he speak out in public, and in the earlier version of his life he allows himself no more than five lines of direct discourse, even in private. When people mistake his holiness for foolishness, he does not correct them, and when they pour dirty water over his head and throw cups and dishes at him, he does not protest. "Everyone mocked him and held him to be a fool," we are told, but Alexis welcomes all perceptions of himself

45. "Quia enim vident doctores in ecclesia honorari, ideo et ipsi appetunt per doctrinam honorari," "Auszüge aus dem Sammelwerk des Passauer Anonymous," p. 70; "The Passau Anonymous," p. 150.

46. "Hec autem verba evangelica affirmant, ut apud suos magistri habeantur erroris,"Etienne de Bourbon, *Anecdotes historiques*, p. 309.

47. "Il fut lur sire, or est lur almosners; / Ne vus sai dire come il s'en firet liez," *La Vie de Saint Alexis*, vv. 124–35.

that contribute to his self-abnegation.[48] The text relates, "He did not become angry, this most holy man."[49] Far from preaching to others about the spiritual path he has chosen, Alexis refuses to justify himself even when he is misunderstood. Though Valdès and the Waldensians would imitate Alexis's pursuit of a life of poverty, neither party would preserve his silence, but, on the contrary, both would publicize their views in sermons, again to controversial results.[50]

If Alexis hides himself in his new, holy lifestyle, the same cannot be said of Valdès. While Alexis flees Rome in order not to be recognized, and distributes his money to the poor anonymously, Valdès remains in Lyon and disposes of his money "in the streets" of his native city, where he is recognized by all.[51] He acknowledges, "I know that a great many will find fault with me for having done this publicly."[52] Alexis suffers mockery silently, but Valdès exhibits no such patience with those who misunderstand him. After the burgher began to distribute his offerings, the Anonymous of Laon reports, "all the citizens hurried to him, supposing that he had lost his senses."[53] As the crowd assembled, the chronicler continues, "he climbed up to a commanding spot and addressed them thus, 'My friends and fellow townsmen, indeed, I am not, as you think, insane.'"[54] Alexis conceals who he is, so that he is either unrecognized or misrecognized,[55] yet Valdès publicizes himself, speaking out to a crowd. As part of his self-defense against others' criticism, he begins to criticize the behavior of those around him. Addressing his distribution of money

48. "Tuz l'escarnissent, sil tenent pur bricun," ibid., v. 266.

49. "Ne s'en corucet giens cil saintisme hom," ibid., v. 268.

50. On the Waldensians' preaching, see Jean Gonnet, "La Prédication vaudoise à ses origines," *Heresis* 30: *La Prédication sur un mode dissident: Laïcs, femmes, hérétiques . . . (XIe–XIVe)* (Actes du 9e Colloque du Centre d'Etudes Cathares/René Nelli, Couzia, 26–30 août 1996), ed. Beverly M. Kienzle (Carcassonne: Centre d'Etudes Cathares, 1999), pp. 93–121, and Jean Duvernoy, "La Prédication des vaudois en Languedoc aux XIIIe et XIVe siècles, d'après les registres de l'Inquisition," in ibid., pp. 123–35.

51. "The Origins of the Waldensian Heresy," p. 201. "per vicos," *Ex chronico universali anonymi Laudunensis*, p. 448.

52. "The Origins of the Waldensian Heresy," p. 201; "Scio, quod me reprehendent plurimi, quod hoc in manifesto feci," *Ex chronico universali anonymi Laudunensis*, p. 448.

53. "The Origins of the Waldensian Heresy," p. 201; "Tunc accurentes cives arbitrati sunt, eum sensum perdidisse," *Ex chronico universali anonymi Laudunensis*, p. 448.

54. "The Origins of the Waldensian Heresy," p. 201; "Et ascendens in loco eminenciori, ait: 'O cives et amici mei! non enim insanio, sicut vos putatis,'" *Ex chronico universali anonymi Laudunensis*, p. 448.

55. On Alexis' silence, see Alexandre Leupin, "Naming God: *La Vie de Saint Alexis*," in *Barbarolexis: Medieval Writing and Sexuality*, trans. Kate M. Cooper (Cambridge, MA: Harvard University Press, 1989), ch. 2, pp. 39–58.

among the poor, Valdès explains to the people before him, "But I did it for myself and also for you: for myself, so that they who may henceforth see me in possession of money may think I am mad; in part also for you, so that you may learn to fix your hope in God and to trust not in riches."[56] Far from seeking the darkness and silence that Alexis so cultivates, Valdès wishes to be seen and heard by all.

The Waldensians established themselves as no more self-effacing than Valdès. The Anonymous of Laon notes that soon after Valdès had distributed his money, he began to gather companions in his voluntary poverty and that, "little by little, both publicly and privately, they began to declaim against their own sins and those of others."[57] Like Valdès, who begins his speech to the public by condemning his own actions and ends by condemning the actions of others, the Waldensians begin by censuring themselves and end by censuring their neighbors. It was not long before the ecclesiastics of Lyon began to object to these unauthorized and unregulated holy people, with their often anticlerical sermons, and that the archbishop Jean de Bellesmains, in particular, took them to task. Even at the Third Lateran Council, where Valdès and his companions were embraced by Pope Alexander III, they were warned against preaching in territories where they had not received the permission of the priest to do so. According to the chronicle of Laon, "this injunction they observed for a short time; then, from the day they became disobedient, and they were the cause of scandal to many and disaster to themselves."[58] At times, ecclesiastics acknowledged the good intentions of such laymen's desire to preach and even admitted

56. "The Origins of the Waldensian Heresy," p. 201; "Sed propter me ipsum et propter vos hoc egi: propter me, ut dicant qui me viderint possidere deinceps pecuniam, me amentem esse; set et propter vos hoc feci in parte, ut discatis in Deum spem ponere et non in diviciis sperare," *Ex chronico universali anonymi Laudunensis*, p. 448. On Saint Alexis and poverty, see Alexander Gievsztor, "*Pauper sum et peregrinus*: La Légende de saint Alexis en occident: un idéal de pauvreté," in *Etudes sur l'histoire de la pauvreté (Moyen Age–XVIe siècle)*, ed. Michel Mollat (Paris: Publications de la Sorbonne, 1974), vol. 1, pp. 126–39. On Valdès and poverty, see Etienne Delaruelle, "Le Problème de la pauvreté vu par les théologiens et les canonistes dans la deuxième moitié du XIIe siècle," *Cahiers de Fanjeaux*, vol. 2, *Vaudois languedociens et Pauvres Catholiques*, pp. 48–63.

57. "The Origins of the Waldensian Heresy," p. 202; "Ceperunt paulatim tam privatis quam publicis ammonicionibus sua et aliena culpare peccata," *Ex chronico universali anonymi Laudunensis*, p. 449.

58. "The Waldenses at the Third Lateran Council: A Report in the Chronicle of Laon," in Wakefield and Evans, p. 203; "Quod preceptum modico tempore observaverunt, unde extunc facti inobedientes, multis fuerunt in scandalum et sibi in ruinam," *Ex chronico universali anonymi Laudunensis*, p. 449.

that their sermons could lead to good results. Guichard de Pontigny, who preceded Jean de Bellesmains as archbishop of Lyon, appears to have supported
Valdès and other lay preachers, so long as they restricted themselves to moral
exhortation and left doctrinal instruction to clerics.[59] Innocent III remarks of
the Waldensians, "The zeal for exhorting in accordance with [Holy Scriptures]
is not to be reprehended but, rather, to be commended."[60] More often, however, clerics expressed regret that the Waldensians sought to preach when they
were unequipped for this task. Etienne de Bourbon relates that "persons even
of the basest occupations, . . . men and women alike, ignorant and unlearned
people, . . . wandered through the villages, entered houses, preached in the
squares and even the churches, and induced others to do likewise."[61] If the
Waldensians encourage laymen as well as clerics, women as well as men, and
laborers as well as leisured persons to become learned and even to preach, it is
clear that, for Etienne and his like, they are expanding the educated and edu-
cating classes beyond their customary and appropriate members. Alain de Lille
decries the prevalence among heretics of "ignorant people who do not know
what should be preached, or to whom, when, and where there should be
preaching," thus showing themselves to be unaware of the conventions of the
ars praedicandi.[62] While clerics spend years of their lives preparing to preach,
the brevity of the Waldensians' instruction alone ensures that they do not pos-

59. In "'Vox clamatis in deserto?' Pierre le Chantre et la prédication laïque," *Revue
Mabillon*, n.s. 4 (1993): 5–47, Philippe Bec argues that although clerics like Alain de Lille and
Bernart de Fontecaude insisted that laymen should never be allowed to preach, others, like
Peter the Cantor, recommended that they be permitted to address the public about morals,
but not about doctrine. Given Guichard's reformatory impulses, Michel Rubellin surmises in
"Au temps où Valdès n'était pas hérétique" that the archbishop hoped the sermons of Valdès
and his followers would be effective in touching other laymen's hearts. It is noteworthy that
at the Third Lateran Council, Alexander III, another Cistercian and an admirer of Guichard's,
did not forbid the Waldensians to preach, though he did order them to obtain ecclesiastical
approval before doing so.

60. "Licet autem desiderium intelligendi divinas Scripturas, et secundum eas, studium
adhortandi reprehendendum non sit, sed potius commendandum," Innocent III, *Regestorum
sive epistolarum*, PL 215, col. 595.

61. "Stephen of Bourbon on the Early Waldenses," p. 209, translation modified; " . . . vilis-
simorum quorumcumque officiorum. Qui eciam, tam homines quam mulieres, idiote et
illiterati, per villas discurrentes et domos penetrantes et in plateis predicantes et eciam in ecclesiis, ad idem alios provocabant," Etienne de Bourbon, *Anecdotes historiques*, p. 292.

62. "Alan of Lille: A Scholar's Attack on Heretics," in Wakefield and Evans, pp. 214–20,
at p. 219, translation modified; "idiotis, qui nescient quod praedicandum, quibus praedicandum, quomodo praedicandum, quando praedicandum, ubi praedicandum," Alain de Lille, *De
Fide Catholica*, PL 210, cols. 305–430, at col. 379.

sess the proper training. According to the Anonymous of Passau, "When someone has been a student [of theirs for as little as] seven days, he seeks someone
else to teach, 'as one curtain draws another.'"[63] As the clerics suggest a contradiction between the social and, hence, intellectual origins of the Waldensians
and their efforts to study Scripture and the Church Fathers, they invoke a similar contradiction between who the Waldensians are, as unlearned and ignorant
laymen, and what they are attempting to do as preachers.

Just as the Waldensians go wrong in interpreting Scripture "in a sense of their
own" instead of in the sense of orthodox Catholic exegesis, the clerics agree,
they go wrong in preaching on their own initiative and not at the bidding of the
Church hierarchy. Virtually all the authors who address the Waldensians'
preaching recall Saint Paul's question to the Romans, "How shall they preach,
unless they be sent?"[64] recalling that one must not actively and independently
assume the office of preaching but must passively receive it from an outside
party. Alain de Lille recalls that "Christ was sent by the Father and came to
preach only at God's good pleasure. . . . Likewise, Christ's disciples are called
Apostles as though, beyond others, they were sent."[65] Etienne de Bourbon
agrees with Alain that the Apostles "did not presume to preach until they had
been clothed with power from on high, until they had been illuminated by the
best and fullest knowledge, and until they had received the gift of tongues."[66]
Alain continues, "By the fact that Christ sent the Apostles and others to preach
is signified that lesser persons in the Church of God ought not to preach unless
they are sent by superiors. . . . No one ought to undertake the function of a
preacher on his own authority."[67] If Christ the Son preached, these authors
agree, it was only because he was sent by God the Father; if the Apostles

---

63. "The Passau Anonymous," p. 151; "Item discipulus septem dierum alium querit quem
doceat, 'ut cortina cortinam trahat,'" "Auszüge aus dem Sammelwerk des Passauer
Anonymous," p. 70.

64. "Quomodo praedicabunt nisi mittantur?" Rom 10:15.

65. "Alan of Lille," p. 218; "Nam et Christus a Patre missus est, nec venit ad praedicandum nisi secundum Patris beneplacitum. . . . Similiter et discipuli Christi dicti sunt apostoli,
quasi super alios missi," Alain de Lille, *De Fide Catholica*, cols. 378–79.

66. "Stephen of Bourbon on the Early Waldenses," p. 210; "predicare non presumpserunt
usquequo induti virtute ex alto fuerunt, usquequo perfectissime et plenissime sciencia per-
lustrati fuerunt, et donum linguarum omnium susceperunt," Etienne de Bourbon, *Anecdotes
historiques*, p. 292.

67. "Alan of Lille," p. 218; "Per hoc etiam quod Christus misit apostolos et alios ad praedicandum, signatum est, quod minores in Ecclesia Dei praedicare non debent, nisi a majoribus
mittantur. . . . nec aliquis ad officium praedicatoris sua auctoritate accedere debet," Alain de
Lille, *De Fide Catholica*, col. 379.

preached, it was only because they were sent by Christ and inspired by the Holy Spirit; and if "lesser persons in the Church of God" have preached and still preach, it is only because they were and are sent by the successors of the Apostles. Tracing a chain of authority from the Father to the Son, to the Apostles, to the Catholic clerics, these authors stress the necessity that all those who preach be authorized by one link along this chain. According to their paradigm, authority resides in an other outside the self, whether that other be God, from whom all privileges ultimately derive, or God's representatives on earth, who mediate his will to their fellow humans. Authority is, by definition, the other, which legitimizes the self; the objective, which legitimizes the subjective; or the impersonal, which legitimizes the personal. Because authority is always transcendent, a human being, whether pope, prelate, or ordinary cleric, never possesses authority but merely channels that authority which flows through him. The Waldensians, however, are said to refuse to acknowledge the necessity of being sent before they preach. Alain protests, "These persons proceed against divine authority and against the proclamation of Holy Writ because they preach, being sent neither by a superior nor by God."[68] Without this human or divine approval, the Waldensians are alleged to "usurp the office of preaching," assuming a power which is not theirs to receive, as a pretender might assume a throne which it is not his to occupy.[69] Usurping the position of rightful descendents of the Apostles by preaching "on their own authority"—as if there were such a thing as "one's own authority"—the Waldensians assert the self in the place of the other, the subjective in the place of the objective, and the personal in the place of the impersonal. Their preaching is problematic not only because they fail to rely upon a tradition of patristic and medieval interpreters in their own exegesis but also because they fail to recognize a tradition of apostolic succession in their sermons and insist, instead, upon their own self-sufficiency.

Just as Map shows the Waldensians to read badly because of their isolation from the exegetical tradition of the Church, he shows them to preach badly because of their isolation from the pastoral authority of this institution. Having

---

68. "Alan of Lille," p. 218; "Qui . . . in hoc navigant contra divinam auctoritatem, et contra sacrae Scripturae praeconia, quod praedicant non missi a superiori praelato, aut a Deo," Alain de Lille, *De Fide Catholica*, col. 378.

69. See, for example, "Alan of Lille," p. 218, translation modified; "officium usurpavit," Alain de Lille, *De Fide Catholica*, col. 379; "Stephen of Bourbon on the Early Waldenses," p. 209; "officium apostolorum usurpavit," Etienne de Bourbon, *Anecdotes historiques*, p. 291; and "Bernard Gui on Heresies," p. 387; "apostolorum sibi officium usurparunt," Bernard Gui, *Manuel de l'inquisiteur*, vol. 1, p. 34.

contrasted "those who engage all their days in subtle discourse" with the Waldensians, who can so easily be trapped in semantic nets, Map contrasts the "many thousands" in attendance at the Third Lateran Council—among whom he numbers "the supreme pope," "a great prelate" to whom the supreme pope had committed the charge of confessions, and "many lawyers and skilled men"— with "two Waldensians who figured as leaders in their sect" who appeared before that body.[70] The vast multitude of Catholic clerics, who are distinguished within the universal Church by their authority and experience, are set against the two Waldensian laymen, who serve merely as representatives of a small sect. As the Waldensians showed themselves to be inferior to the Catholic clerics in their claim to learning, they show themselves to be inferior to them in their claim to authority as well. Map reports that the Waldensians at the council "pressed very earnestly that the right [*auctoritatem*] to preach be conferred upon them, for in their own eyes they were experts, though in reality they were hardly beginners."[71] It was well that their two leaders were hooted down, Map deems, "for they were governed by none and yet desired to become governors, like Phaethon, who 'knew not even the names of his steeds.'"[72] Map suggests that just as the Waldensians consider themselves learned only because they fail to perceive the snares set up to entrap them, they consider themselves deserving of the authority to govern others only because they fail to respect the authority of those who should govern them. The contrast between Map himself and the Waldensian leaders illustrates the difference between clerics within the Church who, governed by others, possess the right to speak out, and laymen outside the Church who, refusing that governance, possess no such right. If Map examines these leaders, it is not, he makes clear, because he considers himself worthy to represent the Church in this matter; on the contrary, he characterizes himself as "the least of the many thousands who were called" to the council.[73] He assumed this role only because he was summoned to do so by "a great prelate" who in turn, had been charged with confessions by the "supreme pope." Authority is not

---

70. "qui capciosis exercitantur tota vita sermonibus," Walter Map, *De nugis curialium*, p. 124; "multorum milium," ibid., p. 126; "maximus papa," ibid., "magno pontifice," ibid.; "multisque legis peritis et prudentibus," ibid.; "due Valdesii, quia sua videbantur in secta precipui," ibid.

71. "Hii multa petebant instancia predicacionis auctoritatem sibi confirmari, quia periti sibi videbantur, cum vix essent scioli," ibid., p. 124.

72. "quia a nullo regebantur et rectores appetebant fieri, Phetontis instar, qui 'nec nomina novit equorum,'" ibid., p. 126. Cf. Ovid, *Metamorphoses*, bk. 2, v. 192.

73. "multorum milium qui vocati fuerunt minimus," Walter Map, *De nugis curialium*, p. 126.

something to be demanded actively by those proudly convinced of their worthiness but, rather, something to be received passively, even under protest, by those humbly convinced of their unworthiness. And if Map succeeds in unmasking the Waldensians' ignorance of theology and consequent unworthiness to preach, it is not, he also makes clear, because he is so clever. He expresses the hope that, as he puts it, "the grace of speech should [not] be denied me."[74] Since the prelate and, by extension, the pope authorize Map to speak, the Holy Spirit enables him to speak well. Authority is bestowed by an other, here in the person of the Church dignitaries, and the ability to use authority well is bestowed by an other, namely, the Holy Spirit. The Waldensians, who seem to have authorized themselves, in contrast to Map, reveal their own lack of any outside support for their demand for the right to preach.

Finally, just as the Waldensians seek learning not in order to know the truth but in order to be regarded as knowing the truth, so they seek to preach not because they desire to share the truth as they perceive it with other souls but because they hope to be considered the new leaders in the Church. Map acknowledges that these sectaries seem humble. He writes, "These people have no settled abodes. They go about two and two, barefoot, clad in woolen, owning nothing, but having all things in common, like the Apostles nakedly following the naked Christ."[75] With their itinerancy, their lack of possessions, and their meanness of dress, they seem to resemble the immediate successors of Christ. At the same time, Map warns, the Waldensians' meekness is deceptive, hiding their true ambition. He affirms, "They are now beginning in a humble manner, because they cannot get their foot in, but if we let them in, we shall be turned out."[76] Though the sectaries claim merely to pursue the *vita apostolica*, they implicitly aspire to replace the true successors of the Apostles. The conflict between the Waldensians' apparent religious inspiration and their real political motivation is evident even in Map's interaction with them at the council. The two Waldensians who come forth to dispute with him about the faith do so, he writes, "not for love of ascertaining the truth, but that I might be put to shame."[77] These representatives of the sect are ultimately directed not by a

74. "gracia negaretur sermonis," ibid., p. 126.

75. "Hii certa nusquam habent domicilia, bini et bini circueunt nudi pedes, laneis induti, nichil habentes, omnia sibi communia tanquam apostoli, nudi nudum Christum sequentes," ibid., p. 126.

76. "Humillimo nunc incipiunt modo, quia pedem inferre nequeunt; quos si admiserimus, expellemur," ibid., p. 126.

77. "non amore veritatis inquirende, sed ut me convicto," ibid., p. 126.

desire to discern the truth for their own personal, spiritual purposes but by a desire to defeat and disgrace Map for public and political ends, just as the Waldensians overall are stirred not by a longing to follow a lifestyle in accordance with the Gospel but by a longing to duplicate and thus supplant the clergy in the Church. Whatever humble aims the Waldensians attribute to their desire to preach, their actions betray their proud ambition.

SOPHISTS AND SIMPLETONS

When a Waldensian is brought before an inquisitor, clerical authors affirm, he does not present himself as a learned preacher, let alone one of heterodox views, but, rather, insists upon his simplicity. "I am a simple and unlearned [*illiteratus*] man," he announces in David von Augsburg's treatise.[78] "I am a simple man, and I am not familiar with these questions," he declares in Etienne de Bourbon's work.[79] "I am a simple and unlearned man, and I am not familiar with these questions, these subtleties," he professes in Bernard Gui's tract.[80] As the Waldensian presents himself, *quaestiones*, the controversial matters about which medieval scholastics debated, and *subtilitates*, the distinctions these scholastics used in resolving their debates, are entirely foreign to him and beyond his understanding. If the inquisitor perceives such academic nuances in the Waldensian's speech, it is only because this cleric is projecting his own learning onto his interlocutor's meaning. The inquisitor may question the sincerity of his humble speech or the straightforwardness of his professions of orthodoxy, but the respondent expresses frustration at such suspicions of duplicity on his part. He protests, "If you want to interpret all that I say, which I proffer reasonably and simply, otherwise, I do not know how I should respond. . . . Do not catch me in my words."[81] He complains, "It is easy for you to catch me and to induce me into error."[82] At times, these authors note, the Waldensian

78. "Simplex homo sum et illiteratus," David von Augsburg, *De inquisicione hereticorum*, p. 230.

79. "Ego sum homo simplex, . . . et nescio istas questiones," Etienne de Bourbon, *Anecdotes historiques*, p. 313.

80. "Bernard Gui's Description of Heresies," p. 401; "Ego sum homo simplex et illiteratus et nescio istas questiones, subtilitates," Bernard Gui, *Manuel de l'inquisiteur*, vol. 1, p. 74.

81. "Bernard Gui's Description of Heresies," p. 401; "si omnia que dico vultis aliter interpretari, que sane et simpliciter profero, tunc nescio quid debeam respondere," Bernard Gui, *Manuel de l'inquisiteur*, vol. 1, p. 74; "Bernard Gui's Description of Heresies," p. 401; "nolite me capere in verbis meis," Bernard Gui, *Manuel de l'inquisiteur*, vol. 1, p. 74.

82. "Bernard Gui's Description of Heresies," p. 401; "de facili caperetis me et induceretis in errorem," Bernard Gui, *Manuel de l'inquisiteur*, vol. 1, p. 74.

will seem miserable, will weep, and will fawn over his examiners, in apparent despair at the power the learned inquisitor has to turn his words against him and to find error in them where none was meant. At other times, Bernard Gui observes, the Waldensian will appear a "simpleton" or a "madman" who mixes a confession of heresy with "irrelevant, ridiculous and seemingly idiotic statements," so that it seems that he should be dismissed because of this folly.[83] Yet with their claims to simplicity, the clerical authors argue, the Waldensians manifest yet another form of duplicity by assuming yet another disguise. Relying upon "their own sense" in their interpretations of these texts and upon "their own authority" in preaching to their followers, the Waldensians depend, in their responses to inquisitors, not upon the common system of reference, where a certain signifier indicates a known signified, but upon their own sectarian code, which reconfigures the relations between those two components of the sign.

On one level, the Waldensian appears to aver an orthodox Christianity before the inquisitor. He seems calm and he smiles as if he is innocent of the wrong of which he is accused and confident that his innocence will soon be demonstrated. Asked about his faith, he affirms that he believes all that a good Christian should believe. Asked what a good Christian should believe, he replies that such a person should believe all that the Holy Church teaches. When the inquisitor then demands to know what the Waldensian means by the Holy Church, he answers that he means what the inquisitor himself means by this term. When the inquisitor then asserts that he believes the Holy Church to be that institution over which the pope and the other prelates preside, the Waldensian appears to agree with him, stating, "That I do believe."[84] In response to an inquiry whether he knows the Gospels and the Epistles, as Waldensians normally do know these texts, the heretic asserts, "They ought to learn this who are great and profound of intellect or who are leisured and suitable."[85] In response to an inquiry whether he believes that everyone who takes

83. "Bernard Gui's Description of Heresies," p. 401–2; "fatuos," Bernard Gui, *Manuel de l'inquisiteur*, vol. 1, p. 74; "Bernard Gui's Description of Heresies," p. 402; "alienatos," Bernard Gui, *Manuel de l'inquisiteur*, vol. 1, p. 74; "Bernard Gui's Description of Heresies," p. 402; "verba impertientia et irrisoria et quasi fatua," Bernard Gui, *Manuel de l'inquisiteur*, vol. 1, p. 76.

84. "Bernard Gui's Description of Heresies," p. 398; "Et ego credo," Bernard Gui, *Manuel de l'inquisiteur*, vol. 1, p. 64.

85. "Bernard Gui's Description of Heresies," p. 401; "Hec debent discere, qui sunt magni vel profundi intellectus vel qui ad hoc sunt ociosi et ydonei," Bernard Gui, *Manuel de l'inquisiteur*, vol. 1, p. 74.

an oath sins, as Waldensians normally do believe, the heretic maintains, "He who speaks the truth does not sin " and "He who swears does not sin in telling the truth."[86] In these answers to the inquisitor's questions, the Waldensian seems to demonstrate that he shares Catholic views on the nature of the faith and the Holy Church, as well as proper attitudes regarding biblical studies and oath taking. So orthodox does the Waldensian present himself as being that he occasionally professes astonishment at the points of dogma about which the inquisitor interrogates him, as if the latter were expressing doubt about the points himself. Asked, for example, if he believes that the bread and the wine are transubstantiated during the Mass, the heretic answers with surprise, "In truth, should I not believe this?"[87] Asked if he subscribes to other articles of the faith, he likewise responds, "What else should I believe? Is this not what I ought to believe?"[88] Far from insisting upon his own views, as heretics are held to do, he seems to submit to the judgment of both God and the inquisitor. He tells his interrogator, when asked about various Catholic teachings, "If it please God, I truly believe this or that."[89] He informs him that if he is taught something good for his soul, he will believe it, and if he is found to believe what he should not, he will repent of this error. "Lord, if I have done wrong in anything, I will willingly undergo penance," he assures his questioner.[90] He consents to swear, should the inquisitor desire him to do so, declaring, "If I must swear, I will do so willingly" and "If you command me to swear, I will swear."[91] In all of these utterances, the Waldensian appears to reside within the boundaries of Catholic orthodoxy.

On another level, however, the Waldensian speaks craftily and deceptively, in order only to seem to aver an orthodox Christianity. When he declares that he believes all a good Christian should believe or all the Holy Church teaches us to believe, he may seem to use the expression "good Christian" to designate an orthodox Catholic and the expression "Holy Church" to designate the

---

86. "Qui dicit verum non peccat," Etienne de Bourbon, *Anecdotes historiques*, p. 313; "Qui jurat dicendo verum non peccat," ibid.

87. "nonne deberem hoc credere?" David von Augsburg, *De inquisicione hereticorum*, p. 229.

88. "Bernard Gui's Description of Heresies," p. 401; "Quid crederem ego aliud, numquid debeo ego ita credere?" Bernard Gui, *Manuel de l'inquisiteur*, vol. 1, p. 74.

89. "Si Deo placet, ego bene credo hoc et hoc," Etienne de Bourbon, *Anecdotes historiques*, p. 313.

90. "domine, si in aliquo deliqui, protabo libenter penitenciam," David von Augsburg, *De inquisicione hereticorum*, p. 231.

91. "si debeo iurare, libenter iurabo," ibid., p. 230. "si iubetis me iurare, iurabo," ibid.

Roman Catholic Church, yet the inquisitors affirm that he is actually using "good Christian" to indicate a Waldensian and "Holy Church" to indicate his sect. When, after the inquisitor has defined the Holy Church, the Waldensian states, "That I do believe," he may seem to state that he believes the inquisitor's definition, yet he means only that he believes the inquisitor to believe it. According to the Anonymous of Passau, the Waldensians signify a church by the words "stone house," clerics by the word "scribes," and monks by the word "Pharisees," and, when they suspect a Catholic to be present at one of their gatherings, they warn, "Beware, lest there be a curved stick among us."[92] The Anonymous comments, "Some of them speak by signs, which no one knows but themselves."[93] The inquisitors term this technique, variously, "the equivocation of words," the use of "duplicities of words," and "the cloaking of words," as does David von Augsburg when he entitles one section of his treatise on the Waldensians "On the cloaking of words."[94] David notes, "Modern heretics seek more to cloak their errors covertly than to profess them openly."[95] With this vocabulary these inquisitors suggest that while the orthodox use words with one meaning, immediately perceptible to their interlocutor, the heterodox use words with two meanings, one that is immediately perceptible to their interlocutor but does not reflect the truth of what they hold, and one that is "cloaked" or "covered," so that it cannot be apprehended but does reflect that truth. They suggest that, while the orthodox speak on a single, open level, the heterodox speak on two levels, one open and one closed.

In addition to equivocation, the Waldensian is seen to resort to indirection in order to conceal the meaning of his words. Replying to the question about his knowledge of the Gospels and the Epistles with the claim, "They ought to learn this who are great and profound of intellect or who are leisured and suitable," the Waldensian may seem to imply that those who are not great or profound of intellect or who lack the leisure for such study should not undertake to learn these

92. "The Passau Anonymous," p. 151; "Cavete, ne inter nos sit lignum curvum," "Auszüge aus dem Sammelwerk des Passauer Anonymous," p. 71.

93. "The Passau Anonymous," p. 151; "sicut quidam per signa locuntur, que nullus intelligit nisi ipsi," "Auszüge aus dem Sammelwerk des Passauer Anonymous," p. 71.

94. "verborum equivocacionem," Etienne de Bourbon, *Anecdotes historiques*, p. 312; "Bernard Gui's Description of Heresies," p. 397; "dupplicitates," Bernard Gui, *Manuel de l'inquisiteur*, vol 1, p. 64; "Bernard Gui's Description of Heresies," p. 397; "duplicitates," Bernard Gui, *Manuel de l'inquisiteur*, vol 1, p. 72; "De palliacione verborum," David von Augsburg, *De inquisicione hereticorum*, ibid., p. 212.

95. "moderni heretici magis querunt latenter palliare errores suos quam aperte profiteri," David von Augsburg, *De inquisicione hereticorum*, p. 228.

texts. He may seem to imply that because he himself is not distinguished by this intellectual and social status, he should not and, therefore, does not seek this learning. Similarly, when the Waldensian replies to the question about the sinfulness of taking an oath by stating, "He who speaks the truth does not sin" and "He who [swears] does not sin in telling the truth," he may seem to imply that he who speaks the truth in swearing does not err. Yet however close the Waldensian may appear to be to making these orthodox claims and thereby denying his heterodox beliefs, he does not actually make these claims and, indeed, says nothing out of harmony with his heresy. The Waldensians "do not respond directly,"[96] says the Anonymous of Passau. "When asked about one thing, they respond obliquely about another,"[97] states David von Augsburg. The latter author complains of their "billowing circumlocutions [*fluctuosas ambages*] of responses," employing a term which suggests, etymologically, that they go around that which they are supposed to address.[98] These inquisitors thus imply that unlike the orthodox, who orient their discourse in a straight line toward the one, stable point to which they are supposed to turn, the Waldensians veer away from this single point. With a different vocabulary, Etienne de Bourbon asserts that "they hide their doctrine with sophistries and involutions of words [*involutionibus verborum*]" and that "they "envelop [*involvunt*] themselves in many sophistries"; they "roll up [*volvent*]" their meaning within their utterances, so that it is no longer visible underneath the folds.[99] David von Augsburg asserts that "they dupe their auditors cunningly [*versute*]" and that they use "cunning tricks [*versucias*]," as if they "turn around [*vertent*]" that which they address and transform it by turning it around.[100] As the Waldensians differ from the orthodox in the double rather than single layer of their speech, they also differ from them in the orientation of the line which connects their speech to that which it is meant to address, a line which is indirect rather than direct, rolled up rather than flat, and twisted around rather than smooth.

Equivocal and indirect, the Waldensian is, finally, seen to respond with interrogative and conditional phrases which again conceal his meaning. When he

---

96. "The Passau Anonymous," p. 151, translation modified; "Directe non repondent," "Auszüge aus dem Sammelwerk des Passauer Anonymous," p. 71.

97. "ut, cum de uno requiritur, de alio oblique respondeant," David von Augsburg, *De inquisicione hereticorum*, p. 212.

98. Ibid., p. 228.

99. "doctrinam suam sophismatibus et involucionibus verborum occultant," Etienne de Bourbon, *Anecdotes historiques*, p. 311; "multis sophismatibus se involvunt," ibid., p. 312.

100. Ibid., pp. 228–29.

gives such responses as "In truth, should I not believe this?" or "What else should I believe? Is this not what I ought to believe?" or "If it please God, I truly believe this or that," he appears to avow his agreement with the inquisitor. Yet with the interrogative, which makes the ontological status of that of which he speaks determined by his interlocutor, he does not state that he believes in the matters about which he is questioned but he merely expresses the idea of such beliefs, leaving their existence obscure. With the conditional, which makes the ontological status of that of which he speaks dependent upon a qualification, he does not state that he believes this or that but merely expresses the idea of such stances, leaving the existence of these stances contingent upon other factors. Etienne de Bourbon complains of the way in which the Waldensians "meet question with question in order to blunt one nail on another" and of the way in which they respond to questions "by adding a condition."[101] While the orthodox speak affirmatively, responding to a question with an answer in the constative mode, the Waldensians hope that their nonaffirmative and therefore nonprobatory sentences will pass for genuine answers.

Acknowledging the Waldensians' sophistication in deflecting inquisitors' questions, the clerics employ a logical terminology to describe the heretics' verbal techniques. Etienne de Bourbon, as we have seen, writes that the Waldensians may be identified by the fact that they "hide their doctrine with sophistries."[102] He elaborates, "They envelop themselves in many sophistries, by which they endeavor to escape and deceive their interrogators" and, again, "The heretic . . . runs to sophistries . . . , so that he belabors his words, lest he be seen."[103] Bernard Gui devotes a section of his discussion of the Waldensians to "the sophistries . . . of their statements," in which he asserts, echoing Etienne, that these heretics resort "to sophistries . . . lest they be detected in their errors."[104] When not describing the Waldensians as relying upon *sophis-*

---

101. "obieciendo questionem contra questionem, ut ut clavum clavo retundant," ibid., p. 313; "per condicionis addicionem," ibid., pp. 312–13.

102. "doctrinam suam sophismatibus . . . occultant," Etienne de Bourbon, *Anecdotes historiques*, p. 311. On the connection between heresy and sophistry, see Le Boulluec, *La Notion d'hérésie*, vol. 1, pp. 136–57, and vol. 2, pp. 280–88.

103. "multis sophismatibus se involvunt, per que conantur effugere et decipere interrogantes," Etienne de Bourbon, *Anecdotes historiques*, p. 312; "Hereticus . . . currit ad sophismata . . . , ut operiat verba sua, ne videatur," ibid.

104. "Bernard Gui's Description of Heretics," p. 400; "De sophismatibus . . . ipsorum," Bernard Gui, *Manuel de l'inquisiteur*, vol. 1, p. 72; "Bernard Gui's Description of Heretics," p. 400; "ad sophismata . . . ne deprehendantur in suis erroribus," Bernard Gui, *Manuel de l'inquisiteur*, vol. 1, p. 72.

mata, these inquisitors describe them as relying upon *fallaciae*, a term which, when it first appears in their manuals, can be translated, as do Walter L. Wakefield and Austin P. Evans, as "deceptions" or "tricks," or, as does Guillaume Mollat, as "tromperie[s]," "fourberie[s]," "astuce[s]," and "réticences," but which by the 1260s could increasingly be rendered as "fallacies," or deductions made from invalid reasoning.[105] It is this interpretation that Mollat follows when he translates this word as "fallacieuses . . . réponses."[106] David von Augsburg uses the term when he speaks of a prostitute who, because she knew "the fallacies of the heretics," was able to bring about the conviction of an associate of hers more readily "than a great theologian who presided by day from his chair in Paris."[107] Bernard Gui also uses this term when he devotes another section of his discussion of the Waldensians to "the tricks and fallacies in which they take refuge when questioned" and when he complains, "It is very difficult to examine and question Waldensians and to get the truth from them about their errors. This is due to the fallacies . . . they use in their testimony, behind which they hide in order to avoid being detected."[108] Insofar as the inquisitors' terminology of *sophismata* and *fallaciae* resonates with that of Aristotle's *De Sophisticis Elenchis* and other logical works these friars would have studied as bachelors of arts, it suggests that the Waldensians, like the ancient sophists, pursued not truth but, to use the Philosopher's phraseology, "the appearance of truth without the reality."[109] With their reliance upon equivocations, indirect answers, and interrogative

105. "Bernard Gui's Description of Heresies," p. 397–98; Bernard Gui, *Manuel de l'inquisiteur*, vol. 1, pp. 65, 66, and 77.

106. "Bernard Gui's Description of Heresies," p. 397. Bernard Gui, *Manuel de l'inquisiteur*, vol. 1, p. 65.

107. "hereticorum fallacias, . . . quam magnus theologus qui Parisus diu in cathedra rexisset," David von Augsburg, *De inquisicione hereticorum*, p. 228.

108. "Bernard Gui's Description of Heretics," p. 397, translation modified; "De astuciis et fallaciis quibus se contegunt in respondendo," Bernard Gui, *Manuel de l'inquisiteur*, vol. 1, p. 64; "Bernard Gui's Description of Heretics," p. 397; "Valdenses sunt valde difficiles ad examinandum et inquirendum et ad habendum veritatem ab eis de erroribus suis propter fallacias et dupplicitates verborum quibus se contegunt in responsionibus suis ne deprehendantur," Bernard Gui, *Manuel de l'inquisiteur*, vol. 1, p. 228.

109. Aristotle, *Sophistical Refutations*, trans. W. A. Pickard-Cambridge, in *The Complete Works of Aristotle, the Revised Oxford Translation*, ed. Jonathan Barnes (Princeton: Princeton University Press, 1984), vol. 1, pp. 278–314, at p. 279; "est . . . sophistica apparens sapientia, non existens autem," *De Sophisticis Elenchis, translatio Boethii, Fragmenta Translationis Iacobi, et Recensio Guillelmi de Moerbeke*, ed. Bernardus G. Dod, in *Aristoteles Latinus*, ed. Gérard Verbeke (Leiden: E. J. Brill, 1975–90), vol. 6, p. 6.

and hypothetical phrases in eluding their inquisitors' grasp, the Waldensians provide seemingly convincing, but actually fallacious responses, no less than their philosophical predecessors.

Whereas other heretics disconcerted clerics by their secretiveness and their singularity, the Waldensians prove no less troubling in their duplicity. Doubling their meanings with ambiguities of speech, as they doubled their identities with pretensions of dress and manner, the Waldensians seem to speak the same language as the inquisitors but ultimately do not do so. With their plays on words, they undermine any conception of a common system of reference, where signifiers always indicate a known signified. The threat they pose is not purely symbolic. If the Waldensians did not appear to speak the same language as the orthodox but instead introduced terms altogether foreign to the inquisitors, or if they spoke gibberish to them, they would be less threatening. It is because the Waldensians appear to speak the same language when they do not, because they operate on two opposing levels, one open, the other hidden, one orthodox, the other heterodox, that they resemble the moles, grubs, and foxes to whom heretics are so often compared, which destroy without being noticed. And because the Waldensians speak to the inquisitor not as an other but as the same, because they attack not as wolves but as small, furtive creatures, they are far more difficult to oppose. When people argue openly against the faith, claims David von Augsburg, following Bernard of Clairvaux, they can easily be deemed heretics because they condemn themselves by their own mouths. When people hide their errors with their speech, however, as the Waldensians do, David continues, "the learned cannot convict them by their knowledge of letters and writings because they do not proceed by that path, and, instead, learned men are confounded by them, and the heretics grow stronger, seeing that they dupe our learned persons."[110] As the heretics who trick the inquisitors grow more powerful, gaining confidence in their superiority to those they have fooled, the faithful laity grow weaker, losing confidence in the clerics they once trusted. The confusion of the inquisitors before the Waldensians suggests to them the confusion of Catholicism before a possibly superior faith. With their ambiguities of speech, the Waldensians undermine not only, symbolically, the shared system of reference which creates a community but also, politically,

---

110. "literati per scienciam literarum et scripturam non possunt eos convincere, qui non procedunt per viam illam, et pocius confunduntur ab eis viri literati, et heretici roborantur per hoc, videntes quod nostris literatis ita illudent," David von Augsburg, *De inquisicione hereticorum*, p. 228.

the Church itself, or *Ecclesia*, which is supposed to constitute that community for all Christians, and the faith with which the Church is identified.

Confronted with the challenge of the duplicitous Waldensians, the clerics respond, as they have done with other heretics, by making the means of the sectaries' escape from their clutches the means of their capture. Etienne de Bourbon cites "the sophistries and duplicities of words" of the heretics as a "sign . . . by which they can be known."[111] Bernard Gui, following Etienne, asserts even more boldly, "It is a plain sign by which they can be known to be heretics that they respond with duplicities."[112] If, as Bernard alleges, "it is very difficult to examine and question Waldensians to get the truth from them about their errors" because of the ambiguous speech that they use to hide that truth, so the inquisitors respond to that ambiguity by making the ambiguous speech itself proof of their heresy. If the form of these heretics' speech impedes the inquisitors' access to its true content, then the form itself becomes sufficient proof of what that content must be. Just as physical flight from an accusation of heresy is considered proof of guilt, so "flights of words," like those with which these Waldensians are associated, are also considered incriminating.[113]

The dangers of identifying Waldensians through their perceived verbal duplicities are obvious. It is not clear how a genuinely simple Catholic, appearing before the inquisitors, might avoid being taken for one of the falsely simple Waldensians. He, too, might protest his simplicity and complain that his interrogators are seeing complexities in his words that are not there. Just as it may be impossible for suspected Manichaeans and Cathars to prove that they did not indulge in incestuous and cannibalistic rituals at night, behind closed doors, it may be impossible for suspected Waldensians to use words which cannot be interpreted as equivocal, indirect, or otherwise ambiguous. If every claim to believe what the Holy Church believes and every offer to swear, if ordered to do so, can be read as evidence of heresy, it is hard to see what an innocent party might say to exculpate himself. Bernard Gui, for one, acknowledges these dangers, but he insists upon greater hazards which outweigh them. He writes of the inquisitor, "On the one hand, his conscience troubles him if an individual is punished who has neither confessed nor been proven guilty; on

---

111. "sophismat[a] et duplicitat[es]," ibid., p. 311; "[signum] . . . per quod maxime cognosci possunt," ibid.

112. "Bernard Gui's Description of Heresies," p. 400, translation modified; "Et hoc est unum signum evidens per quod cognosci possunt esse heretici in duplicitatibus respondendo," Bernard Gui, *Manuel de l'inquisiteur*, vol 1, p. 72.

113. "fugas . . . verborum," Etienne de Bourbon, *Anecdotes historiques*, pp. 311–12.

the other, it causes even more anguish to the mind of the inquisitor, familiar through much experience with the falsity, cunning, and malice of such persons, if by their wily astuteness they escape punishment, to the detriment of the faith, since thereby they are strengthened, multiplied, or rendered more crafty."[114] The inquisitor, here, may never ultimately know whether his last accused Waldensian seemed to speak duplicitously because he was covering his heresy or because all words, when considered with sufficient skepticism, can seem to have another level of meaning, but, Gui maintains, this is a necessary risk to run. In taking duplicity as evidence against the Waldensians, these clerics agree, they protect the Church by turning the sectaries' weapons against themselves, even if these weapons might now be being used against an innocent person.

114. "Bernard Gui's Description of Heresies," p. 377; "Angit enim conscientia, ex una parte, si non confessus nec convictus puniatur; ex altera vero parte, angit amplius animum inquirentis informatum de falsitate et calliditate et malitia talium per experientiam frequentem, si evandant per suam vulpinam astutiam in fidei nocumentum, quia ex hoc ipsi amplius roborantur et multiplicantur et callidiores efficiuntur," Bernard Gui, *Manuel de l'inquisiteur*, vol. 1, p. 6.

7 THE HERETIC IN THE POULTRY YARD

Heresy, Duplicity, and Medieval Comic Tales

In the comic literature composed in France between the mid-twelfth and mid-thirteenth centuries, a cluster of characters emerge who prove no less duplicitous in their ways than the Waldensians were said to be. The prostitute Richeut, who gives her name to an anonymous fabliau of the last third of the twelfth century, disguises herself at different points as a nun and as a gentlewoman, while her similarly lecherous son Samson passes himself off as a cleric and a gentleman.[1] The simpleton Trubert, to whom

1. *Richeut* has been edited by D. M. Méon in *Nouveau Recueil de fabliaux et contes inédits des poètes français des XIIe, XIIIe, XIVe et XVe siècles* (Paris: Chasseriau, 1823), vol. I, pp. 38–79; by Irville Charles Lecompte in "*Richeut*: Old French Poem of the Twelfth Century, with Introduction, Notes, and Glossary," *Romanic Review* 4, no. 3 (July–September 1913): 261–305; and by Philippe Vernay as *Richeut: Edition critique avec introduction, notes et glossaire* (Berne: Editions Francke, 1988). This last edition is the one that will be cited here. The poem has been addressed by Joseph Bédier, "Le Fabliau de Richeut," in *Etudes romanes dédiées à Gaston Paris le 29 décembre 1890 (25e anniversaire de son doctorat ès lettres)* (Paris: Emile Bouillon, 1891), pp. 23–31; rpt. in Bédier's *Les Fabliaux: Etudes de littérature populaire et d'histoire littéraire du Moyen Age* (Paris: Emile Bouillon, 1893), pp. 265–70; Lucien Foulet, "Le Poème de *Richeut* et le *Roman de Renard*," *Romania* 42 (1913): 321–30; Edmond Faral, "Le Conte de *Richeut*: Ses rapports avec la tradition latine et quelques traits de son influence, in *Cinquantenaire de l'Ecole des Hautes Etudes* (Paris: Champion, 1921), pp. 253–70; Alberto Vàrvaro, "Due Note su *Richeut*," *Studi mediolatini e volgari* 9 (1961): 227–33; Janis L. Pallister, "Forms of Realism in *Richeut*," *L'Esprit Créateur* 5 (1965): 233–39; Franz Rauhut, "Sanson in der *Richeut*: Ein Don Juan des Mittelalters," *Archiv für das Studium der neueren Sprachen und Literaturen* 207 (1970): 161–84; Donald Eugene Ker, "The Twelfth-Century French Poem of *Richeut*: A Study in History, Form, and Content," Ph.D. Dissertation, Ohio State University, 1976; and André Vernet, "Fragments d'un *Moniage Richeut?*" *Etudes de langue et de littérature du Moyen Age offertes à Félix Lecoy* (Paris: Honoré Champion, 1973), pp. 585–97. Ker has also provided an

Douin de Lavesne devotes a fabliau in the first half of the thirteenth century, takes on the roles of a carpenter, a physician, a knight, and a woman.[2] The fox Renart, who inspires the animal epic *Le Roman de Renart*, composed by Pierre de Saint-Cloud and his followers between the late twelfth and mid-thirteenth centuries, presents himself at various points as a jongleur, a pilgrim, a monk, a physician, and an emperor.[3] Though possessing separate literary traditions, all

---

English translation of the poem in "The Twelfth-Century French Poem of *Richeut*, pp. 185–239. Most of these studies have addressed how Richeut might be situated within the history of medieval literature.

2. *Trubert* has been made available, most recently, in Guy Raynaud de Lage, ed., *Trubert, fabliau du XIIIe siècle* (Genève: Droz, 1974); and Willem Noomen, ed., *Nouveau recueil complet des fabliaux* (Assen, Netherlands: Van Gorcum, 1983–98), vol. 10, pp. 143–262 and 360–75. My citations are from Raynaud de Lage's edition. For commentary, see Guy Raynaud de Lage, "Trubert est-il un personnage de fabliau?" in *Mélanges d'histoire littéraire, de linguistique et de philologie romanes offerts à Charles Rostaing* (Liège: Association des romanistes de l'Université de Liège, 1974), pp. 845–53; Jean-Charles Payen, "*Trubert* ou le triomphe de la marginalité," in *Exclus et systèmes d'exclusion dans la littérature et la civilisation médiévales* (Aix-en-Provence: CUERMA, 1978): 119–33; Pierre Badel, *Le Sauvage et le sot: Le fabliau de "Trubert" et la tradition orale* (Paris: Champion, 1979); L. Rossi, "*Trubert*: il trionfo della scortesia e dell'ignoranza. Considerazioni sui *fabliaux* e sulla parodia medievale," *Studi francesi e portoghesi*, 1979, pp. 5–49; Massimo Bonafin, "La Parodia e il briccone divino: Modelli letterari e modelli antropologici del *Trubert* di Douin de Lavesne," in *L'Immagine riflessa: Rivista di sociologia dei testi* 5 (1982): 237–72; Jean Batany, "*Trubert*: progrès et bousculade des masques," in *Masques et déguisements dans la littérature médiévale* (Montréal: Presses de l'Université de Montréal, 1988), pp. 24–34; Kathryn Gravdal, "Trubert: The *Courtois Trompé*," in *Vilain et Courtois: Transgressive Parody in French Literature of the Twelfth and Thirteenth Centuries* (Lincoln: University of Nebraska Press, 1989), pp. 113–40 and 166–72; Jean-Pierre Bourdier, "Pathelin, Renart, Trubert, Badins, Décepteurs," *Le Moyen Age* 98, no. 1 (1992): 71–84; and Carlo Dona, *Trubert, o la Carriera di un furfante: Genesi e forme di un antiromanzo medievale* (Parma: Pratiche, 1994).

3. Caesarius von Heisterbach cites a priest, learned in theology, by the name of "Pierre de Saint-Cloud," among the members of an Amalrician heretical sect uncovered in Paris around 1210. He affirms that this Pierre entered a monastery in order to escape the pyre, and the records of the abbey of Saint-Denis confirm the presence of such a monk. See "The Amalricians: The Condemnation of the Amalricians at Paris," in Wakefield and Evans, pp. 258–62, and Caesarius von Heisterbach, *Dialogus miraculorum*, ed. Joseph Strange (Köln: J. M. Heberle, 1851), vol. 1, pp. 304–7. Though there is no evidence to link this Pierre de Saint-Cloud with the originator of the *Roman de Renart*, Jelle Koopmans notes justly, "Si c'est l'auteur des plus anciennes branches du *Roman de Renart*, cela pourrait avoir des conséquences pour l'étude et l'interprétation de l'épopée animale," *Le Théâtre des exclus au Moyen Age: Hérétiques, sorcières et marginaux* (Paris: Editions Imago, 1997), p. 91, n. 111. For a summary of the branches and manuscripts of the *Roman de Renart*, see Kenneth Varty, ed., *The Roman de Renart: A Guide to Scholarly Work* (Lanham, MD: Scarecrow Press, 1998), pp. 1–14. MS A has been edited by Ernest Martin as *Le Roman de Renart* (Strasbourg: Trübner et Leroux, 1882–87), MS B by Mario Roques as *Le Roman de Renart, édité d'après le manuscrit de Cangé* (1948–63), and MS C by Naoyuki Fukumoto, Noboru Harano, and Satoru Suzuki as *Le*

of these characters are interrelated.[4] In certain of the twenty-seven branches of the *Roman de Renart*, each of which provides a different assortment of tales about the vulpine hero and his companions, Renart's wife is known as "Richeut," and throughout this compilation Isengrin the wolf's wife (and the object of Renart's amorous attentions) is called "Hersent," the name of Richeut's companion in vice. As the *Roman de Renart* refers to *Richeut*, so *Richeut* cites the *Roman de Renart*: Samson is described at one point, with an

---

Roman de Renart, édité d'apres les manuscrits C et M, 2 vols. (Toyko: France Tosho, 1983–85). Martin's edition, from which my citations will be taken, has also been prepared by Jean Dufournet and Andrée Méline as *Le Roman de Renart*, 2 vols. (Paris: Garnier-Flammarion, 1970). My translations here have borrowed from *The Romance of Reynard the Fox*, trans. D. D. R. Owen (Oxford: Oxford University Press, 1994). It is impossible to summarize the modern criticism on this work, given its abundance, but probably still the most useful intro-ductions to the work are Lucien Foulet, *Le Roman de Renart* (Paris: Honoré Champion, 1914); Robert Bossuat, *Le Roman de Renart* (Paris: Hatier-Bouvin, 1957); John Flinn, "*Le Roman de Renart*" *dans la littérature française et dans les littératures étrangères au Moyen Age* (Toronto: University of Toronto Press, 1963); and Jean Batany, *Scènes et coulisses du "Roman de Renart*" (Paris: SEDES, 1989). Also helpful are the collections Edouard Romabauts and Andries Welkenhuysen, eds., *Aspects of the Medieval Animal Epic: Proceedings of the International Conference* (Louvain, May 15–17, 1972) (The Hague: Martinus Nijhoff, 1975); *Proceedings of the First International Animal Epic, Fable, and Fabliau Colloquium* (University of Glasgow, September 22–25, 1975) (Glasgow: n.p., 1976); Nico van den Boogaard and Jacques de Caluwé, eds., *Epopée animale, fable et fabliau* (Actes du colloque de la Société internationale renardienne, Amsterdam, 21 au 24 octobre 1977), *Marche Romane* 28 (1978); Jan Goosens and Timothy Sodmann, eds., *Third International Beast Epic, Fable and Fabliau Colloquium* (Münster, 1979, Proceedings) (Cologne: Bohlau, 1981); Danielle Buschinger and André Crépin, eds., *Comique, satire et parodie dans la tradition renardienne et les fabliaux* (Actes du colloque, Université de Picardie, 15 et 16 janvier 1983) (Göppingen: Kummerle, 1983); and Gabriel Biancotto and Michel Salvat, ed., *Epopée animale, fable, fabliau* (Actes du IVe Colloque de la Société internationale renardienne, Evreux, 7–11 sepembre 1981) (Paris: Presses Universitaires de France, 1984). See also Alison Williams, *Tricksters and Pranksters: Roguery in French and German Literature of the Middle Age and Renaissance* (Amsterdam: Rodopi, 2000), esp. pp. 85–110.

4. All of these characters were sufficiently well known for their names to become bywords, whether for a "whore" or "bawd" as happened with Richeut, a "naïf" or "trickster" as hap-pened with Trubert, or a "fox" or "trickster" as happened with Renart. Richeut and Trubert were well-known figures, despite the fact that their fabliaux both survive in single manuscripts. For *Richeut*, see MS 354 of the Bibliothèque de la Bourgeoisie de Berne as well as a few brief fragments from a Sotheby's catalogue of 1859 and MS 1511 of Troyes, discussed in Vernet, "Fragments d'un *Moniage Richeut*." Bédier termed *Richeut* the first fabliau and, indeed, the model for this genre, yet despite this identification, the poem was not reprinted in Anatole de Montaiglon and Gaston Renaud, eds., *Recueil général et complet des fabliaux des XIIIe et XIVe siècles* (Paris: Librairie des Bibliophiles, 1872–90; rpt. New York: Burt Franklin, n.d.), which limits itself to these later dates, nor in van den Boogaard and Noomen, eds., *Nouveau recueil complet des fabliaux*. Foulet argued that the work derived from the *Roman de Renart*, where, in Branch XXIV, the fox's wife is identified as "Richeut," but Faral and others have maintained

allusion to one of Renart's adventures, as "more tricky than the fox who took the crow by guile."[5] While Trubert is not explicitly affiliated with Renart, he too is described as vulpine, wreaking havoc at court and then slinking back to his sylvan "den."[6] In his tendency to attack a population center and then retreat along byroads to an isolated lair, Trubert recalls the movements attributed to foxes in general and to Renart in particular during the Middle Ages. With their predilection for disguises and other forms of duplicity, Richeut, Samson, Trubert, and Renart behave, like the contemporaneous Waldensians, as if identity were not what one is made but, rather, what one makes of oneself, and they never cease to baffle those around them with their self-transformations.

Even as these comic characters resemble the Waldensians in their duplicity, they differ from them in the judgment their authors make of their actions. On the most explicit level of these texts, all of these characters are condemned for their assaults upon the social organization of the world in which they live. Like the Waldensians, who were stereotypically ignorant and insignificant laymen who usurped the position of learned and authoritative clerics, these comic characters are members of the lower echelons of society who rise up against those of the upper levels. In *Richeut*, a prostitute exploits a priest, a knight, and a merchant; in *Trubert*, a *vilain* torments the duke and duchess of Burgundy;

---

that this name was already a byword for a bawd and that, if anything, it was accounts of Richeut that influenced the animal epic. While Faral, Pallister, and Rauhut have treated the poem as an isolated text, Bédier and Vàrvaro hypothesized, to the contrary, that there at one time existed a cycle of treatments of the prostitute, and Vernet has reinforced this thesis with his research. For *Trubert*, see MS 2188 of the Bibliothèque Nationale. On the word "trubert," see Frédéric Godefroy, *Dictionnaire de l'ancienne langue française et de tous ses dialectes du IXe au XVe siècle* (Paris: F. Viewes, 1881–1902), 8:96a; Alfred Tobler and Erhard Lommatzsche, *Alfranzösisches Wörterbuch* (Weisbaden: F. Steiner Verlag, 1927–76), 10:702; and Walther von Wartburg, *Französisches Etymologisches Wörterbuch* (Leipzig: B. G. Teubner, 1940–65), 13(2):324b. Pierre-Yves Badel writes in *Le sauvage et le sot*, "Dans la littérature médiévale ce nom est aussi celui du personnage de la *Farce de Maistre Trubert et l'Antrongnart* d'Eustache Deschamps. Par ailleurs, 'trubert' est un nom commun substantif ou adjectif, relevé une quinzaine de fois aux XIVe et XVe siècles. A. Couson a enregistré 'trubert' dans sa liste de 'noms épiques entrés dans le vocabulaire commun' à côté de 'renart' et 'richeut' [*Romanische Forschungen* 23 (1907): 412]; mais le fabliau de Douin ne parait pas avoir eu une large diffusion et l'on peut bien aussi admettre que Douin et Deschamps, indépendamment l'un de l'autre, ont fait d'un nom commun, peut-être régional (champenois et picard) un nom propre" (p. 23). He concludes, "le mot, par les associations que son signifiant suggère, note l'ambivalence du sot médiéval; niais ridicule, mais dangereux à cause de sa conduite imprévisible" (p. 24).

5. ". . . trechieres / Plus que gorpille / Qui par engin prant la cornille," *Richeut*, ed. Vernay, vv. 939–41.

6. "repere," *Trubert*, ed. de Lage, v. 2254.

and in the *Roman de Renart*, a fox defies a lion and his court. Like the Waldensians, these characters seek mastery over their social superiors, not through force, because they are not strong, nor through the law, because they are not in the right, but through guile, because that is the only recourse left for the weak and illegitimate. They do not strive to overthrow their superiors any more than heretics strive to unseat ecclesiastics, but they do attempt to subvert them by beating the men or having them beaten, by seducing the women or having them seduced, and by letting everyone know that whatever power others may enjoy within the social structure, it is they who dominate its interstices. On a more implicit level of these texts, however, Richeut, Trubert, and Renart are celebrated for the ingenuity with which they carry out their attacks. Men may have power over women, dukes over peasants, and lions over foxes, yet the success of these characters in upsetting social hierarchies draws into question the ability of their superiors and, hence, the rightfulness of the superiors' authority over them. Other characters may protest the tricksters' tendency to seem to be what they are not, yet these texts show they do so not because they are attempting to preserve some naturally or divinely ordained order but because they are simply trying to maintain their own social position, as parties who benefit from seeming to be what they are. Insofar as the comic authors are responding to the characterization of the Waldensians in the air at this time, they are acknowledging that there are people who assume new personae in order to improve their rank in society, but they are also challenging the supposedly transcendental basis of identity, which would make such self-transformations improper.

RICHEUT

Like the Waldensians, Richeut and Samson behave as if they have no natural social roles, and so no social roles seem unnatural to them. At a time when secular women are defined socially as the daughters, wives, or widows of particular men, Richeut is attached to a thousand men and, hence, to no man at all; she consorts with priests, knights, and burghers, as well as with bachelors, vagabonds, and laborers, her status fixed by all and by none of them. With no masculine guarantor of her social identity, Richeut travels throughout the world, adopting different manners of dress and behavior. At a time when children are defined socially as the offspring of particular men, Samson has no certain father and thus no certain male foundation of his identity. Instead of being trained to assume the occupation of a single, known progenitor, as most youths of his time would be, he is educated to assume the occupations of members of each of the three estates who may have begotten him and encouraged to decide which of their lives he would like to pursue. "Of these three, go to the most attractive," his mother urges him. "Make your choice."[7] Instead of a supposedly natural identity, passively received from his actual sire, Samson is to assume an artificial identity, actively chosen and assumed on his own initiative. Because Samson has not inherited the nature of any father, but only that of his mother, it is no surprise that he becomes a trickster himself, passing himself off as a denizen of both courts and abbeys. In their absence of fixed identities, Richeut and Samson may resemble the heretics condemned in clerical pages, but their author criticizes Richeut only to celebrate her triumph at the end of the fabliau, and he refrains from criticizing Samson at all. He does not label their disregard of the transcendental level of reality heretical, though he does make clear the degree to which it threatens the orthodox worldview.

Richeut and Samson undermine their society by defying the assumption that women and men love each other and enter into carnal relations with each other as a result of that love. Within this fabliau, Richeut sleeps with a "thousand"[8] men merely in order to profit from them, however much she claims to have acted out of tenderness. She tells the priest, for example, "Surely I do not love you just a little, but very much indeed, if God Almighty help me," and when he begs her to keep silent about his siring of her child, she states, "If I did not love you so much I would not conceal this at all."[9] She has become pregnant purposely, in order to profit from her lovers, yet she claims to have done so by chance so that they will sympathize with her condition and contribute to her welfare. She visits the men, weeping, sighing, and holding her hand to her cheek, only in order to make them pity her and pay her off. Far from feeling any genuine affection for these men, she elicits all the food, clothes, and money she can from them, leaving them impoverished in her wake. "Have you ever heard of such a wicked woman who always reaps and never sows?"[10] asks the author. In opposition to the biblical dictum cited in the text, Richeut gets more from men than she gives and even gets from them without having given at all. As the male counterpart of his mother, Samson professes to love countless women, addressing one object of his affection as "love" and "my fair one"; telling her, "Your love

---

7. "De ses .iii. va au plus menant; / Met t'an à chois," *Richeut*, ed. Vernay, vv. 672–73.

8. "mil," ibid., v. 666.

9. "Certes ne vos ain pas petit; / Mout durement, se Dex m'aït, / Le tot puissant," ibid., vv. 211–12; "Se je ne vos enmasse tant / Ne'l ceslasse ne tant ne qant," ibid., vv. 211–15.

10. "Oïstes mais si male fame, / Qui totjors quialt et rien ne seme?" ibid., vv. 396–97. Cf. Lk 19:22.

greatly speaks to me. My heart constricts in my chest for your love"; and warning her, "If I lose you, I will have no remedy for it. I will never again have any joy."[11] Though he claims to bear tender emotions for the girl, the pattern of his previous behavior and the evidence of his ensuing actions make clear that he feels only crude physical desire for her and that his effusions serve only as a means to satisfy that desire. Both mother and son act as if social interaction is a game where the point is to triumph over others and even to cause their destruction, for doing so, more than anything else, establishes their own sovereignty. The mother is described as "Richeut who takes all and ravages all," and it is observed of the son, "He ravishes everywhere, he spends everywhere."[12] If bonds of love traditionally tie the sexes together, Richeut and Samson, by counterfeiting love, debase those bonds and thus debase their society.

Richeut and Samson do not themselves destroy members of the opposite sex but, rather, induce them to bring about their own ruin. Of Richeut the author writes, "More does she conquer by her ruses and flattery than he who takes and seizes and steals," and of Samson, "A knife with which he skins them is flattery."[13] Some, like thieves and murderers, may gain power over others through force, but Richeut and Samson gain power through speech. Richeut intoxicates the men who fall prey to her. "Few are the men whom she does not make drunk and from whom she does not receive something,"[14] we are told. Of the burgher, it is added, "Now Richeut leads him like a drunkard."[15] As for her son, the author relates, "Samson enchants all those whom he frequents" and "he knows spells well."[16] The author adds, "He went so much here and there that he made more than a hundred mad" and, more generally, "He drives women mad."[17] The young noble girl he believes himself to be seducing at the end of the tale confesses that, in granting Samson her friendship, "I am bold in

11. "amie," ibid., v. 1229; "ma bele," *Richeut*, ed. Vernay, v. 1230; ". . . vostre amor mout me favele; / Li cuers m'estraint desoz l'aisselle / Por vostre amor," ibid., vv. 1231–33; "Se je pert vos, n'en ai retor; / Ja n'avrai mais joie nul jor," ibid., vv. 1234–35.

12. "Richeut qui tot prant et tot gaste," ibid., v. 1255; "Par tot ravist, par tot despant," ibid., vv. 909.

13. "Plus conquiert el par sa boidie / Et par sa lobe / Que cil qui prant et tost et robe," ibid., vv. 366–68; ".I. cotel a don les escorce, / C'est la losange," ibid., vv. 832–33.

14. "Po sont des homes qui n'enboive / Et don que que soit ne reçoive," ibid., vv. 523–25.

15. "Or lo moine Richeut con ivre," ibid., v. 360.

16. "Sanson . . . enchante / Trestotes celes o il ante," ibid., vv. 932–33; "Mout set caraudes," ibid., v. 634.

17. "Tant a alé et ça et là / Que plus de .c. en afola," ibid., vv. 927–28; "Fames afole," ibid., v. 792.

daring to do it. I have really become mad."[18] With their intoxicating, enchant-
ing, or maddening speech, Richeut and Samson cause people to enter alternate
states where they are no longer aware of what they are doing and can therefore
be "led" (*mene*) to act to their disadvantage. We are told of Richeut that "she
leads a man at a walk and then she makes him run," and of Samson that "he
led more than seven hundred of them" and that "there is none so prudent that
he does not lead her."[19] Altering their victims' mental state, mother and son
induce these men and women to trust them, so that they will follow them wherever they are led. In this approach they resemble not so much ordinary malefactors, who get from people what they do not want to give, as the devil, who
gets from people what he makes them want to offer. Like the devil, these two
appeal to others' weakness, whether it be men's wantonness or women's vanity, and thus enter into illicit carnal relations with them. "He who believes
Richeut and fucks her is very miserable,"[20] we are told, but one must believe
her and have sex with her in order to become this wretched. Once they have
compromised their victims, Richeut and Samson reduce them to poverty, thus
illustrating the Christian belief that sin inevitably brings about its own punishment, as God even works through the limbs of the devil to bring about justice.
Richeut and Samson persuade their victims to love them for their own financial well-being, but, as is the case with the devil, the ultimate goal of mother
and son is not monetary profit but harm to others, as it is this harm that most
clearly reflects their ascendancy over them.

Failing to respect the social bond that connects men and women, Richeut
and Samson fail to respect the divine bond that connects God and human
beings. Both mother and son enter abbeys, but both break their vows and
depart when they choose to do so. Of Richeut, the narrator informs us simply,
"She no longer wanted to be there."[21] Of Samson it is explained, "When it
pleased him, he escaped from [the monastery]."[22] He steals the house's crosses
and chalices because "he does not make up his mind to serve God."[23] If Richeut
chooses to pursue her own will at the expense of her obligations to God, her
irreverence appears to be related to her lack of a formal, clerical education,

18. "Hardie sui qant fare l'ox, / Mout par sui fole," ibid., vv. 1244–45.

19. "Lo pas moine home et puis l'acorse," ibid., vv. 381; "Plus de .Vii.c. en a menees,"
ibid., vv. 846; "N'i a si cointe qu'il n'en moine," ibid., v. 842.

20. "Qui croit Richeut et qui la fot / Mout est chaitis," ibid., vv. 613–14.

21. "N'i vost plus estre," ibid., v. 42.

22. "Qant lui plaist, bien s'an set estordre," ibid., v. 915.

23. ". . . il ne s'asanse / De Deu servir, tant ne se panse," ibid., v. 906.

which would have instructed her in her responsibilities, but the same cannot be said of the well-schooled Samson: "He knows well that that this [life] leads to sin, but the delights of the world, which greatly please him, vanquish him,"[24] we are told. Samson has learned his lessons about the ephemerality of this world, but his nature is so debauched that transitory pleasures overwhelm his reason. He fails to serve God, we are told, because "he does not think that he will ever leave this life" and because "he does not concern himself much with it but [has his mind on] the present."[25] Without trepidation for the afterworld and the punishment it might bring, it is said, "he fears neither sin nor opprobrium."[26] An Epicurean in his religious beliefs, he seems to hold that he will live forever and this world is the only one he will ever experience. Richeut and Samson are not accused of heresy, but by preferring this world to the next, putting their own desires before their duties toward God, and exploiting their victims rather than helping their neighbor, they place themselves on the side of religious deviants and are applauded for doing so.

TRUBERT

Like the Waldensians and also like Richeut and Samson, the simpleton Trubert possesses no natural definition, so he experiences no natural limits upon his behavior. Living alone in the forest of Pontarlie with his mother and sister, he comes from a household with no paternal figure. As a result of his fatherless isolation, he has no sense of the social hierarchy operative in the Burgundian capital he visits, where vassals are subject to lords and rustic *vilains* to courtly aristocrats, and no sense of the deference expected of him, as a rough woodsman interacting with noblemen and noblewomen. Having inherited no fixed social role, he is free to assume different guises and able to act so convincingly in all of them that he deceives everyone he encounters. The ecclesiastics who opposed the Waldensians intimated that these heretics acted like clerics, reading Scripture and the writings of the Church Fathers and preaching to the people about what they had learned, not because they genuinely sought to know more about their religion or to share what they knew with others, but because they hoped to acquire the reputation of wise and important people and, in doing so, to supplant the clerics who legitimately enjoyed this reputation.

24. "Ce set il bien qu'en pechié maint, / Mais li deliz do mont lo vaint / Qui mout li plaist," ibid., vv. 886–88.
25. ". . . ja ne cuit qu'il laist / Iceste vie," ibid., vv. 890–91; "De Deu servir, tant ne se panes, / Mais des presant," ibid., vv. 905–9.
26. "Pechié ne dote në oprobre," ibid., v. 918.

When Trubert acts like a carpenter, a physician, a knight, or a woman, presenting himself to the duke and duchess in these various guises, Douin makes
clear that his ultimate goal is not to adopt any of these social positions but,
rather, to gain the confidence of this noble court and thus to rule over his lawful ruler. Though Douin does not describe the rejection of all transcendental
authority implicit in Trubert's ambitions as heretical, he does represent his pro-
tagonist as challenging the orthodox world around him.

Trubert unsettles his society by defying the assumptions implicit in the relations between nobles and plebeians. He does so not by feigning a respect for the
duke and duchess of Burgundy, as Richeut and Samson feign an affection for the
objects of their seduction, but by appearing to be ignorant of the respect this
noble couple is due. When Aude, the duchess's maid-in-waiting, informs him
that her lady commands him to come speak with her, he asks, "Commands?. . .
What does she want with me?"[27] Aude explains, "Sir, . . . you should have great
joy from it when my lady wants to see you."[28] Only after she counsels him for
some time does he agree, "I will go there to see truly what she wants with me."[29]
In this interaction, Trubert shows no recognition of the fact that he is a *vilain*
and the duchess a duchess and, hence, no appreciation of the honor the duchess
is doing him by ordering him into her presence. When he arrives before the
duchess and hears her request to buy his painted goat, he responds, "Lady, . . .
if God save me, I will sell it to you willingly for one fuck and five sous *de
deniers.*"[30] The duchess admonishes him, "Friend, be silent about sex and keep
yourself from speaking more of it. Take so many of our deniers that you will lose
nothing from it."[31] In this encounter, again, Trubert shows no recognition that
a lady of such high rank as the duchess is supposed to be sexually inaccessible,
especially to someone of such low rank as himself, and no recognition that such
a lady should be addressed gently, without mention of sex, let alone without
repeated and obstinate demands for the act and, least of all, without the use of
crude expressions such as *foutre* to indicate his desire. In all of this boorish
behavior, however, Trubert can be seen, on another level, as someone not so

---

27. "Mande?. . . que me velt ele?" *Trubert,* ed. de Lage, v. 139.

28. "Sire, . . . / mout en devez grant joie avoir / quant ma dame vos velt veoir," ibid., vv.
140–43.

29. ". . . G'irai la / por savoir mon qu'elle me velt," ibid., vv. 144–45.

30. "Dame, . . . se Deus me saut, / je la vos vandrai volentiers; / un foutre et cinc sous
de deniers / la faz," ibid., vv. 154–57.

31. "Amis, du croistre voz taisiez / et gardez que plus n'en pleidiez! / De nos deniers en
prenez tant / que vos n'i perdez ja neant," ibid., vv. 159–62.

much unfamiliar with the customs of courtliness as deliberately rejecting them. If he appears startled when told that the duchess "commands" an audience with him, it is because, having grown up in rustic independence, he does not automatically accept that anyone should so quickly assume a position of authority over him. If he demands "a fuck" from the duchess in exchange for his goat, it is because he does not automatically accept that any woman should behave to him as haughtily as this lady assumes she has the right to do. He seeks to drag her down from above and to push her below him, literally as well as figuratively, putting his arm around her neck, throwing her on the bed, and having his way with her, as he is then said to do. With this behavior, Trubert shows himself to understand that courtliness—a code that insists upon gentle and even deferential behavior toward noblewomen—reinforces the power of the nobility over *vilains* like himself, so that in defying that code, he defies that power. While Richeut and her son destabilize social bonds by feigning a love for members of the opposite sex, Trubert unsettles them by denying the class boundaries meant to protect women of the aristocracy from the advances of men like himself. All three characters triumph over their sexual partners because they focus exclusively upon the power struggle inherent within such liaisons.

Like Richeut and Samson, Trubert undermines society not by attacking nobles directly but by inducing them to contribute to their own downfall. He does so by inciting their imaginations and, by extension, their desires. As the fabliau begins, Trubert appears foolish in arranging to have his goat painted. He seems to reveal his ignorance in confusing a farm animal, valued for its usefulness, with a church sculpture, valued for its beauty. The narrator explains, "He was naive and foolish. Never in all his life had he sold or bought."[32] Yet while exposing his ignorance of the conventions of the marketplace, Trubert also reveals his grasp of a deeper level of the economy than that reflected by these conventions. In producing a painted goat, for example, he creates what people in this text call a "marvel" and what we might nowadays term a pure commodity. Upon seeing the goat outside her window, the duchess of Burgundy cries, "By my faith, I marvel greatly at it. Never in my life have I seen anything equal to it."[33] Nor had others at court seen anything like it. "All of them laughed, marveling at it."[34] Those who see the painted goat are attracted

32. ". . . cil estoit nices et fous, / n'onques mes en tout son aé / n'avoit vendu ne acheté," ibid., vv. 38–40.

33. "Par ma foi, j'en ai grant merveille! / Onques men ne vi la pareille," ibid., vv. 126–27.

34. "Tuit s'en rient a grant merveille," ibid., v. 30.

to it precisely because it constitutes, in its uniqueness, the ultimate object of desire. In later episodes, when Trubert reappears in disguise—as a carpenter, promising to build the duke a house without a quarrystone, a cornerstone, rafters, or pegs; as a physician, promising to cure him of the wounds he has himself caused; and as a knight, promising to defend the realm against the invading King Golias—he gains power over the ducal pair not by force but by "enchantment." When the duchess confesses her infidelity to her husband, she tells him, "So much did he say to me and so much did he enchant me—I know not how nor with what—that he lay in bed with me and did his will with me."[35] Admitting that he too has been mysteriously overcome by Trubert, the duke informs his wife, "Lady, in the presence of all my people, he so treated me—I know not how—that I cannot remain on my feet."[36] Trubert "enchants" the duchess and duke and gains a disconcerting power over them by casting them into states like those produced by magical spells, where they believe themselves to be living in an alternate and more desirable reality. He makes them believe in the possibility of what is impossible or, at best, improbable, and, in doing so, makes them yearn for it so ardently that they consent to place themselves in positions they would otherwise never accept. He ignites their imaginations, inflames their appetites, and dampens their reason so that they cannot see, until too late, the dangers to which they are exposing themselves. Because Trubert seems supernatural in his ability to perform marvels, to bedazzle people through these phenomena, and thus to lead them into temptation, and because he seems maleficent in his penchant to visit abuses upon those who have done him no harm, he is identified overtly with the devil. The duke protests to his wife, "He is not a man but a demon who has enchanted us so," and to Trubert's alleged sister, "Your brother has acted badly. He has the Enemy in his body because I have done nothing to him and he does the worst he can to me."[37] Immune to the secondary desires—for painted goats, remarkable houses, medical cures, and champions at arms—that blind the duchess and duke, Trubert

---

35. "Tant me dit et tant m'enchanta, / je ne sai coment ne a quoi, / qu'en un lit se coucha o moi / et de moi fit ses volentez," ibid., vv. 380–83.

36. "Dame, voiant toute ma gente / m'a si mené, ne sai coment, / que ne puis sor mes piez ester," ibid., vv. 391–93.

37. "Ce n'est pas hom, ainz est malfez / qui ainsi nos a enchantez," ibid., vv. 2361–62; "Vostre frere m'a mal bailli; / il a bien ou cors l'anemi, / que je ne li ai riens forfet / et dou pis que il me puet me fet," ibid., vv. 2344–46. When Trubert prepares to thrash the duke at one point, the lord protests, "How, devil, are you such? I have never done any wickedness to you [*Coment, deable, estes vos tes? / Ja ne vos ai ge riens forfet*]," ibid., vv. 802–3.

concentrates only upon the primary desire for power over others, a power most fully experienced when the other is abused, and he triumphs because of his concentration upon this exclusive goal. To the duke he gloats, "You have fallen into my power."[38]

Neglecting the social bond between members of the upper and lower classes, Trubert neglects, as well, the divine bond between God and human beings. Like the Waldensians, who can be recognized, according to Bernard Gui, by their tendency to use duplicities of words, Trubert takes advantage of what he knows to be the arbitrary relation between signifier and signified. As he lies in bed with the duke and duchess's daughter Rosette, the supposedly female Trubert explains that what his companion feels against her thigh is "a bunny rabbit" (*connetiaus*),[39] which he places in his *con* from time to time and which gives him much pleasure. He instructs Rosette how to pet the animal so that it responds to her, how to let it enter and play inside her to their mutual delight, and how to let it rest when it is fatigued. The irreverence with which Trubert disengages the object, as people understand it, from the term conventionally used to indicate this object recalls the Waldensians' irreverence toward the stable system of reference that necessarily underlies a community, a church, and a faith. When Rosette becomes pregnant, Trubert (still in the guise of a woman) convinces her parents, to their great delight, that a dove appeared at night and impregnated her with angels. He shows no qualms about using a sacrilegious parody of the Annunciation to conceal his own act of seduction. Douin does not attribute to Trubert the developed Epicurean beliefs ascribed to Samson, but he depicts the rustic, too, acting as if he rejects the immortality of the soul. Trubert takes such pure, untroubled, and unstudied delight in tormenting others that he gives no indication of believing he will ever be held accountable before any celestial tribunal for his wicked actions. As the duke complains, "He fears neither God nor man."[40] Without fear of death or damnation, Trubert values the here and now, not the there and then, the physical, not the metaphysical, the immanent, not the transcendent, and, as a result, the carnal pleasure of his current existence, not the spiritual blessedness of any future one.

38. "Cheüz estes en mon dangier," ibid., v. 1290.
39. Ibid., v. 2487. This use of an alternate language for sexual organs and sexual acts is common among the fabliaux and the novelle. See Guillaume de Blois' *Alda*, *La Damoisele qui ne pooit oïr parler de foutre*, and *L'Esquiriel*.
40. "il ne doute ne Dieu ne gent," ibid., vv. 2360.

RENART

Of the set of characters we have been considering, Renart enjoys the most defined social position, being both male and seigniorial, with a well-fortified castle into which he can retreat and a wife and children by whom he is tended. If, despite these advantages, Renart proves as eager to adopt new social roles as Richeut, Samson, and Trubert are, it is only because, in the animal kingdom in which he resides, he occupies the position of a fox. As Jacques Voisenet has demonstrated, before the twelfth century the fox had been the animal most universally condemned in Western literature—even more so than the dragon or the serpent—on account of its predilection for fraud and ruses. During the years when the various branches of the *Roman de Renart* were being composed, Voisenet writes, the fox increasingly came to be celebrated for the tricks he employed to get the better of those stronger than himself, as well as for the cleverness, the ingenuity, and the gaiety these ruses seemed to imply. Diagonal in his traversal of society as well as in his traversal of terrain, the fox resembled the mercantile classes burgeoning at this time, Voisenet argues, in that he incarnated "the *novitas*, the new state of mind, which, in order to overturn old structures, can only impose itself through ruses" and which, in doing so, necessarily contested the social order.[41] As a fox, Renart represents all those who, whatever their rank in society, perceive themselves as smaller and weaker than those above them and who rely upon cleverness rather than strength to establish their ground. With the fox being the dominant symbol of the heretic during these years, it is not surprising that in the *Roman de Renart* the comic characters' disregard of a transcendental order, whether natural or divine, becomes explicitly linked with heresy.

As Richeut and Samson disrupt the bond between men and women, and Trubert that between nobles and plebeians, so Renart disrupts the bond between lords and vassals. The other animals in King Noble the lion's domain have agreed to refrain from harming those who, like themselves, have submitted to this ruler. They have consented to limit their liberty by renouncing assaults they might otherwise have committed in order to enjoy safety from others' attacks upon them. They have forsaken some of their autonomy as individuals in order to benefit from the protection of a group. Renart, though also

---

41. Jacques Voisenet, "Le Renard dans le bestiaire des clercs médiévaux," *Reinardus* 9 (1996): 179–88, at 188. For additional texts on the image of the fox in the Middle Ages, including the animal's association with heretics, see chapter 2 note 62.

one of Noble's vassals, is unwilling to curtail his own impulses in order to benefit from such peace. While he exhibits attachment to his wife and children, whom he supplies with food and speaks of with affection, and to his cousin Grimbert the badger, whom he refrains from tormenting as he torments other emissaries of Noble, Renart delights in harming all the other beasts. Most often he plays tricks upon the animals, who end up with their tails cut off, their coats shorn, and their limbs broken. As the animals represent the situation in repeated appeals to Noble, the damage Renart causes is not just to them, through their various physical sufferings and mental humiliations, but to society as a whole, through the destruction of the kingdom's tranquillity. The barons decry "this thief who . . . has broken the peace so often," and Noble denounces the fox for "the shame he has brought upon me and the peace he has broken."[42] Renart does not openly rebel against Noble and his rule, but by causing harm and even death to his vassals and by refusing to obey summonses to appear for his crimes he defies the kingdom's centralized power. It is not that Renart opposes Noble and his court for any injustices they have performed, or that he would prefer any other sovereign or fellow barons to those he knows, but simply that he, as an individual, opposes all groups, along with the restriction such groups place upon his liberty. With the "pride" that both Noble and his barons lament, Renart holds himself aloof from the feudal structures that subsume other beasts into a peaceful, ordered whole, regarding the loss of individual autonomy, implicit in bringing about the group's peace and order, as an infringement upon his essential liberty.[43]

Like the other tricksters, Renart upsets his society not so much by force as by guile. Most often, he tempts his fellow animals by firing their imaginations with promises of food, to the point where they forget his reputation for deceit in their hope for the nourishment he has depicted to them. He persuades Isengrin to fish by dipping his tail into a hole in a frozen pond, only to have the ice close in upon this extremity. He convinces Brun to wedge his head into an oak tree in order to find honey, though the bear will end up stuck and exposed to the beatings of a forester and his companions. He incites Tibert to enter a priest's house in order to find mice and rats, though the cat will get trapped in a snare and subjected to similar abuse. At other times, Renart appeals to the beasts' vanity, flattering them so that they will again drop their guard before

---

42. "cel laron . . . qui tantes pes a enfretes," *Le Roman de Renart*, ed. Martin, I, 436–38; "Et de la honte qu'il m'a fete, / Et de la pes qu'il a enfrete," ibid., I, 394–96.

43. "orgueil," ibid., I, 27 and 394.

him. After praising their voices, he urges Tiecelin the crow to caw so that he
will drop the cheese he holds in his mouth and gets Chantecler the cock to sing
with his eyes closed so he will fail to protect himself from Renart's approaching jaws. As Renart reminds the animals, when their imaginations are ignited
and their appetites inflamed, it is their own weakness that leads to their downfall. He asks the wolf, who has fallen for one of his tricks, "Isengrin, do you
really claim that I caused these misfortunes of yours? I swear you don't know
what you are saying: your gluttony was responsible."[44] While Richeut, Samson,
and Trubert were all described as diabolic for their tendency to lead others
astray and then punish them for their divagations, Renart is even more explicitly identified with the devil for this habit. In the Middle Ages, Satan was often
imagined as a fox and a "redhead" (*roux*), as Renart is described as being, and
his behavior was often assimilated to that of a trickster, like this animal.[45] Across
the different branches, the *Roman de Renart* returns to the phrase, "Renart,
who . . . [*Renart, qui . . .*]," which allows the text to shift from the narration
of the plot, occurring within specific times and places, to the exposition of character, surfacing across time and place. Renart represents not just a particular
fox who exists in time, the text makes clear, but a universal principle of *renardie*
which will survive for eternity. He is described as "Renart, who tricks the
world," "Renart, who deceives the whole world," and "Renart, who ensnares
the whole world."[46] Not only a concrete figure but an abstract force, Renart is
depicted repeatedly as "a living demon" and "a living devil," and his deeds are

44. "Ysengrin, dis le tu a certes / Que tu oüs par moi ces pertes? / Par foi tu paroles a
force, / Ta lecherie te fist force," ibid., VI, vv. 673–75.

45. See Jeffrey Burton Russell, *Lucifer: The Devil in the Middle Ages* (Ithaca: Cornell
University Press, 1984), pp. 67 and 69.

46. ". . . Renart qui le monde engagne," *Le Roman de Renart*, ed. Martin, I, 482; "Renars
qui tot le mont deçoit," ibid., II, 430; "Dans Renars qui le siecle engigne," ibid., I, 1873; ". . .
Renars qui tot siecle abeite," ibid., I, 34. On the vocabulary of trickery in the *Roman de
Renart*, see Gaston Zink, "Le vocabulaire de la ruse et de la tromperie dans les Branches X et
XI du *Roman de Renart*," *L'Information grammaticale* 43 (octobre 1989): 15–19. Zink defines
engignier as "tromper en faisant preuve d'intelligence inventive" (p. 15), *deçoivre* as "induire
volontairement en erreur, dans sa plus large extension" (p. 15), and *abeter* as "prendre à
hameçon" (p. 16). On trickery in the *Roman de Renart* in general, see Roger Bellon, "Trickery
as an Element of the Character of Renart," *Forum for Modern Language Studies* 22, no. 1
(January 1986): 34–52, where the author distinguishes three aspects of Renart's deceptive disposition, and André Villeneuve, "Renart, ou le risque de la séduction (*Le Roman de Renart*,
Branche II)," *Reinardus* 6 (1993): 185–202, where the author stresses the degree to which
Renart brings about the victim's collaboration in his or her undoing. "La stratégie du goupil
dans la branche II consiste à faire naître chez l'autre, avec la plus grande intensité, le désir,"
writes Villeneuve (p. 191).

characterized as "devilry."[47] A trickster, Renart is also the Arch-Trickster, who incarnates the very principle of trickery, to the detriment of all mankind. Insofar as the *Roman de Renart*, like the texts discussed earlier, is responding to the persecution of Waldensians and other heretics at this time, it is agreeing with them that there do exist diabolical characters like these unbelievers, determined to undo social bonds and spread disorder.

Disregarding the social bond that links lords and vassals, Renart also disregards the divine bond that brings together God and man, and this irreverence is explicitly linked with heresy. In Branch I, after Grimbert the badger summons him to Noble's court to be tried, Renart asks to confess his sins to his cousin so that if he does die, his soul will be saved.[48] Grimbert hears the fox's confession and warns him, as confessors were wont to warn penitents at the time, that if God helps him out of his current fix he must not relapse into evil. The next morning, however, as the two animals are trotting back to court alongside a monastery farm, Renart suggests that they go by way of the poultry yard. Grimbert cries out, "Renart, Renart, . . . God knows why you say this. Son of a whore, stinking heretic [*heirites*], wicked and cruel trickster, have you not confessed to me and cried mercy?"[49] Renart claims to have forgotten his confession and agrees to continue on their way, though he looks back sadly at the chickens. In another incident, in Branch XV, Tibert has grabbed a chitterling that Renart has caught and is sitting atop a cross with this booty. When Renart begs him to throw his share of the prize down to him, the cat objects that a chitterling is a "sanctified thing" which must be eaten on a cross or church in order to exalt it.[50] Renart then offers to take the sin upon himself if Tibert will toss him some of the chitterling, but Tibert replies, "I will not do this, by faith. Companion Renart, you speak marvelously. You are worse than a heretic

---

47. "un vis maufés," *Le Roman de Renart*, ed. Martin, II, 743, and X, 9; "le vis dïable," ibid., V, 10; "dïablie," ibid., I, 564; ibid., I, 923; ibid., I, 1779 et passim.

48. On the circumstances under which a layman might quite properly replace a priest in accepting an individual's confession, see Jean Subrenat, "Les Confesssions de Renart," *Epopée animale, fable, fabliau*, ed. Gabriel Biancotto and Michel Salvat (Actes du IVe Colloque de la Société Internationale Renardienne, Evreux, 7–11 septembre 1981) (Paris: Presses Universitaires de France, 1984), pp. 625–40. Since Grimbert here, and Hubert the Kite later on, indicate that they are hearing confession only because of the absence of a priest, their actions do not seem unorthodox.

49. "Renart, Renart, . . . / Dex set bien por qoi vos le dites. / Filz a putein, puanz heirites, / Malvés lecheres et engrés, / N'estieés vos a moi confés / Et avïez merci crïe?" *Le Roman de Renart*, ed. Martin, I, 1162–67. While MS A, the basis of Martin's edition of the *Roman de Renart*, reads "puanz heirites" as above, MS B reads "leres traitres."

50. "chose saintefiee," ibid., XV, 205.

[*herites*], who want me to throw down something one must not dishonor."[51] Gerald Herman has stressed the degree to which the word *herite* could function as a common expletive at this time, meaning no more than "wretch" or "scoundrel," but both animals use the term with specifically religious connotations.[52] Grimbert speaks of a heretic as someone who does not respect Catholic rites, such as penance, and Tibert refers to him as someone who does not venerate sanctified objects, such as the chitterling.[53] Both identify a heretic as a person who fails to exhibit a genuine belief in the sanctity of Catholic observances and a genuine concern for the status of his soul. While a strict clerical text might sympathize with the accuser of an alleged heretic, the *Roman de Renart* sympathizes with the accused party in these instances. Again, if Renart seeks to go by the poultry yard or to procure his share of the chitterling, it is only because it is his nature, as a fox, to eat chickens and chitterlings. Where a divine order seems to conflict with a natural order, as is the case here, the implication is that the divine order must be misguided if it would lead an animal to self-starvation. In accordance with this view, the Cathars argued that sinful impulses, such as gluttony, were the result of the malign god's creation of our bodies and the physical world they inhabit and that sinners who succumbed to those impulses were thus not responsible for their deeds. Other heretics, condemned by Etienne Tempier, the bishop of Paris, in 1277, maintained that whatever is natural, such as a desire for food with which to sustain oneself, is good. If Renart is termed a heretic on account of his reversion to his vulpine nature, the text implicitly refrains from condemning him for his heresy.

It is not only when Renart gives in to his own nature but when he gives in to his tendency toward unnaturalness, at the expense of divine commands, that he is identified as a heretic. In Branch VI, when attempting to persuade Isengrin that he has not mounted his wife Hersent, Renart declares, "May it

---

51. "Non feré, . . . par foi. / Conpains Renart, merveilles dites. / Pires estes que uns herites, / Qui me rouvés chose geter / Que l'en ne doit deshonnourer," ibid., XV, 225–28.

52. Gerald Herman, "Old French *herite*," *Romance Notes* 17 (1976–77): 328–34.

53. Interestingly enough, both Grimbert and Tibert make their accusations of heresy not after Renart has revealed his sinful inclinations, whether his cruel intention toward the chickens or his irreverence toward the chitterling, but after he has attempted ineffectively to conceal these inclinations. Renart recommends not that he be allowed to steal a hen but merely that they travel by the poultry yard, and he does not deny the sanctity of the chitterling (as dubious as it may seem) but offers to assume the guilt of its desecration upon himself. It is possible that Renart is termed a heretic less because of his impiety toward a sacrament and a presumed holy object than because of his efforts to conceal that impiety, as heretics were known to conceal their similar deviations from the faith.

not please God the Creator that he should so hate me that the thing should happen thus—that I should touch my gossip lower than her eyes—for which I would be worse than a heretic [*erites*]."[54] Similarly, in Branch VII, when confessing his sins to Hubert the kite, Renart avows, "Sire, I have been a sodomite and an utter heretic [*herites*]. I have been a publican, and I have denied Christians."[55] Shortly thereafter, he adds, "Sire, I have been very perverse [*pervers*]. I have done many things in reverse [*a envers*] that I should not have done."[56] During an extensive description of his sexual exploits, he states, "I have fucked the daughter and the mother and all the children and the father and afterwards all the household."[57] In these passages, Renart accuses himself or says that he would accuse himself of heresy in the context of mentioning certain sexual infractions, as is not unusual at a time when the word *herite* could signify a sodomite and when the word *bougre* was heading toward the modern "bugger." Herman has maintained that so complete was the identification of the word *herite* with *sodomite* at this time that the term should be translated in these instances not as "heretic" but as "sodomite" or even "abuser of animals." He cites the fabliau *Le sot chevalier*, where the character imagined as given over to sodomy is referred to as "this *erite*," and the poem *Witasse le Moine*, which states, "Wistasse says he is not a *herites*, not a fuck-in-the-ass or a sodomite," as evidence that this term could indicate a sodomite without any resonance with heresy. Yet Renart's linkage of being "a sodomite and an utter heretic" with being a "publican" or Cathar heretic and denying Christians suggests that he is locating sexual deviance within the framework of religious deviance.[58] Within the context of this discussion of heresy and sodomy, Renart speaks of doing

54. "Ja Dex ne place / Le crëator que tant me hace / Que la chose soit si corue / Que ma conmere aie ferue / Plus bas de l'ueil si con vos dites. / Dont seroie je plus qu'erites," *Le Roman de Renart*, ed. Martin, VI, 577–82.

55. "Sire, g'ai esté sodomites, / Encore sui je fins herites, / Si ai esté popelicans / Et renaié les cristïens," ibid., VII, 349–52. Other manuscripts read "hermites" instead of "herites" in this passage.

56. "Sire, j'ai esté molt pervers, / Meinte chose ai fete a envers / Que je ne doüsse pas fere," ibid., VII, 681–83.

57. "J'ai fotu la fille et la mere / Et toz les enfanz et le pere, / Et aprés tote la mesnie," ibid., VII, 707–9. On the progression from Renart's confession of sin to his exultation in his sinful nature, see Batany, *Scène et coulisses du Roman de Renart* (Paris: SEDES, 1989), pp. 245–47.

58. The connection between sodomy and heresy has not gone unobserved. John Boswell, for example, notes in *Christianity, Social Tolerance, and Homosexuality: Gay People in Western Europe from the Beginning of the Christian Era to the Fourteenth Century* (Chicago: University of Chicago Press, 1980), "It became a commonplace of official terminology to mention

things "perverse[ly]" and "in reverse." With these phrases, he may be referring to the sodomy he appears to have performed with Hersent, entering her from behind as he does in Branch II, or the sodomy he presumably practiced with the "father" with whom he claims to have had sex. Yet with these phrases he may also be suggesting that heresy, like sodomy, is something perverse, something done backwards, something, if one may use an anachronism, queer. To be a heretic, to be a sodomite, is to disregard the straight, authorized path of orthodoxy or the straight, authorized path of a sexuality that leads to the supposedly natural telos of conception and to choose, instead, an alternate, forbidden path that leads off into deviant and unproductive directions.

If Renart is termed a heretic for engaging in sodomy and for thus acting perversely, it is not because he is acting naturally, as he is when craving chickens and chitterlings, but, on the contrary, because he is acting unnaturally, yet he continues to be depicted sympathetically for doing so, as were his contemporaneous tricksters in similar circumstances. Neither Richeut nor Samson was said to limit sexual intercourse to supposedly natural positions. Of Richeut's relations with her lovers, we are told, "she did it on top and underneath," and, of Samson's relations with his paramours, that he enters them in front and in back; from above, from below, and from the side; with their bodies folded over and with their knees on their chests.[59] Trubert, masquerading as a woman, plays the feminine role in a sexual encounter with King Golias, though he is motivated by malice rather than by desire and hurts rather than gives pleasure to his partner. In the *Roman de Renart*, as in these texts, the choice of unnatural sexual positions is associated with the overall excessiveness of the protag-

---

'traitors, heretics, and sodomites' as if they constituted a single association of some sort" (p. 284), exactly as we see in the *Roman de Renart*. Boswell acknowledges that heretical groups like the Cathars, which prided themselves on the rigor of their moral codes, were no doubt disinclined to indulge carnal appetites, whether heterosexual or homosexual, and that the accusations of sodomy levied against heretics are mostly formulaic in nature. Even as Boswell states that the association of sexual and religious deviance appears to have been made more in orthodox minds than in heterodox practices, he speculates that homosexuals may have been attracted to the perhaps more tolerant environments of heretical circles and that Cathars in particular may have been drawn to homosexual acts because they did not lead to procreation and, hence, to the imprisonment of yet more souls within material bodies. See also Robert Lerner, "Heresy and Fornication: A Topos of the Thirteenth Century," in *The Heresy of the Free Spirit in the Later Middle Ages* (Berkeley: University of California Press, 1972), ch. 1, pt. 3, pp. 20–25; Mark Jordan, *The Invention of Sodomy* (Chicago: University of Chicago Press, 1997); and Michael Goodich, *The Unmentionable Vice: Homosexuality in the Later Medieval Period* (Santa Barbara, CA: ABC-Clio, 1979).

59. "Tant a alé desus desoz," *Richeut*, ed. Vernay, v. 149.

onist's sexual appetite. Richeut couples with a thousand men of all social classes. Samson, it is said, "fucks the niece and the aunt, then the sisters. . . . He fucks the mother and the daughter and the cousins."[60] Trubert unites with the mother and the daughter, the master and the maidservant. Renart, as we have seen, joins with the mother and the daughter, the father and the whole household. Excessive in whom they have sex with, these characters are also excessive in how long they have sex for. Trubert informs the duchess that in the land he comes from, people put an entire month into the act, and he has intercourse with this lady thirteen or fourteen times before midnight one evening. Renart boasts of having performed this deed fifteen or even nineteen times in one night. Surpassing rather than falling short of nature in how, with whom, and for how long he has sex, he is described as "Renart who is so deviant and who works against nature."[61] Once more, the rhetorical force of these passages, which stress the quantity rather than the quality of what Renart does and the vitality rather than the virtue of his character, offsets the moral force of the text's condemnation of him. While we are led to view Renart's "heresy" as the result of a natural need for food, we are also led to view it as the result of a desire for sexual pleasure that, by its very forcefulness, will inevitably exceed all boundaries, including those of nature, and we tend to excuse or even admire it as such.

If the authors of these texts show themselves to be torn in their judgments of the trickster characters, condemning them explicitly while they celebrate them implicitly, it is because they write both didactically and literarily. Didactically, they present these stories as *exempla*, which instruct us about tricksters who, like the devil, can appear as angels of light and lead us to our destruction, so we may learn how best to avoid such predators. Richeut shows how women conspire to deceive and exploit men for their own gain, Trubert how rustic simpletons can get the better of even the highest nobility, and Renart how ingenious vassals can disrupt a kingdom. It is from this didactic perspective that the authors speak up in their texts, allying themselves with the dominant if dull masses, always in danger of being duped by subordinate if clever individuals, and with the orthodox doctrine associated with those masses. Insofar as they

---

60. "Il fout la niece e puis la tante / Puis les serors . . . / La mere fout et puis la fille / et les coisines," ibid., vv. 934–44.

61. "Renart qui tant est desvez / Et qui ovre cntre nature," *Le Roman de Renart*, ed. Martin, VII, 71–72.

express themselves literarily, however, these authors present their stories as fictions, which entertain us by creating alternate realities into which they invite us to enter. As poets and jongleurs intoxicate or enchant their audiences with their tales, so all of these tricksters are storytellers who recount at length and in detail the love they feel for their sexual partners, the marvelous benefits they will provide for their lord or lady, and the outstanding foodstuffs they have found for their companions. As poets and jongleurs assume the characters of the persons they depict, so all of the tricksters assume various personae, imitating the appearance and speech patterns of the figures they pretend to be. At times, these tricksters become literally the composers and performers of poems. It is said of Samson that he "knew how to compose good poems. . . . He made so many verses that he could compose a number of types" and, in particular, that he could sing with expertise *rotruanges, conduiz,* and *sons.*[62] At the end of the fabliau Trubert recounts all of his adventures to an amazed maidservant, just as Douin has recounted them to us. As we have noted, Renart at one point appears as a jongleur, advertising the various lays, romances, and other works he can sing. "Renart knows well how to amuse people . . . through his speech,"[63] the poet asserts. If these tricksters are storytellers, it is because storytellers are themselves tricksters. The authors of these texts tell us untrue tales about prostitutes, simpletons, and talking foxes, which, through their fantastical and often humorous details, appeal to our imagination and appetite rather than to our reason. They intoxicate and enchant their hearers, no less than their heroes and heroines do, so that we are lulled into a state foreign to that in which we normally confront the world. It is from this literary perspective that the authors allow their tricksters to preside over their texts and, hence, that they give voice to subordinate, clever individuals and to the deviant ethos identified with these individuals. The conflict between the explicit and the implicit levels of these texts reflects, ultimately, the conflict between philosophy and literature, truth and fantasy, reason and appetite, moral judgment and visceral pleasure, and, by extension, orthodoxy and heresy.

62. "Et .i. sot bon ditié faire. / . . . / Tant a fait vers / Qu'il en set faire de divers," *Richeut,* ed. Vernay, vv. 564–67.
63. "Bien set Renart gent amuser / . . . par parole . . . ," *Le Roman de Renart,* ed. Martin, X, 430–32.

CONCLUSION

It was with the development of the
Dominican and Franciscan orders that the heretical sects we have been considering finally met their match. The mendicant friars vanquished the heretics
by resembling them, whether intentionally or not. Like the heretics, they
focused not upon administering ecclesiastical realms, as bishops did, nor upon
praying and weeping for their sins, as monks did, nor upon saying the Mass
and celebrating the Eucharist, as priests did, but upon tending to the spiritual
needs of the people. At the beginning of the thirteenth century, Diego, the
bishop of Osma, and his companion Dominic de Guzmán wandered through
the towns and villages of Occitania, debating publicly with heretics and
preaching to crowds under their influence in order to persuade them to return
to the Catholic faith. During the same years, Francis of Assisi and his followers traveled through central Italy, also addressing the people in churches and
town squares about their religion in a way in which few had spoken to them
before. Though the Franciscans were less focused upon heretics than the
Dominicans were, they too arose in a region deeply affected by alternative
creeds, and they too defined themselves, at least in part, by their opposition
to these sects.[1] Like the heretics, in addition, the mendicant orders saw them-

---

1. See Adolf Holl, *The Last Christian* (Garden City, NJ: Doubleday, 1980), on Francis's
connection to heresy. Holl speculates that Francis's father was a Cathar believer and suggests,
as other readers have done, that his "Canticle of Brother Sun" is an anti-Cathar polemic,
affirming the divine origin and goodness of the physical world against heretical beliefs in its
Satanic source and wickedness.

selves as preaching to the people not only in word but in deed. They espoused poverty, not only individually, as monks already did, but corporately as well, gaining the confidence of their audiences through their holy behavior. When Diego learned that the people of Occitania scorned the Catholic prelates because of their sumptuous lifestyles, he abandoned his horses and baggage train and set out to speak to them on foot, as the Cathars had already done. When Francis's merchant father brought him before a judge and accused him of having stolen his cloth in order to restore a local church, Francis stripped off his garments and offered them as repayment for the theft, thus embracing poverty as publicly and dramatically as did the heretical Valdès. In their efforts to supplant the heretics, the Dominicans and Franciscans did not limit themselves to imitation alone. It was the Dominicans and, later, the Franciscans who served as the first inquisitors, an office they would dominate throughout the Middle Ages. Educated in theology and canon law, trained in verbal disputation, and oriented toward the *cura animarum*, the friars were better qualified to pursue heretics than the sacred and secular rulers who had attempted to do so before them, and they succeeded in this task as none of their predecessors had done. By the first decades of the fourteenth century, the last Cathar heretic had been burned at the stake, and the last believers of the dualist sect faded away soon thereafter. While so-called Waldensians would resurface in the Dauphiné in later years, the Poor of Lyon were suppressed by this date as well. Whether by imitating or by opposing them, the mendicants displaced the heretics in medieval culture.

Given the close connection between heretics and their mendicant pursuers, it is not surprising that, after the mid-thirteenth century, literary works identified epistemological instability not so much with Cathars and Waldensians as with Dominicans and Franciscans. Both Rutebeuf, in his eighteen or so poems on the "Jacobins" and "Cordeliers," and Jean de Meun, in his lengthy contribution to the *Roman de la Rose*, take the side of the secular masters at the University of Paris in their ongoing conflict with their mendicant rivals, and they do so by criticizing the latters' seeming sanctity. As these poets put it, the friars wear simple, rough habits, yet they show their nature no more truthfully in this costume than does Renart when he is dressed in a gray, belted tunic or Isengrin when he is shielded by a round cape. Rutebeuf is describing these religious when he warns about those "who wear wool against the skin because they have something else under the belt," and Meun is speaking of them when his allegorical False Seeming asserts, "I prefer to pray in front of people and cover my Renart-like nature under a cloak of *papalardie* [or religious hypocrisy]."[2] In their conduct as well as in their clothing, the friars are not what they seem. They are said to consort with female companions and, in particular, with Béguines, women who devote themselves to religious life outside the supervision of the Church. Rutebeuf echoes Bernard of Clairvaux's censure of the Cathars when he writes of the dialogues between the Jacobins and these seemingly holy ladies: "I do not say that they are up to anything more than this, but it seems that they do not hate each other. Saint Bernard says, it seems to me, 'For a man and a woman to converse together, without doing anything more according to nature, this is virtue as clear and pure . . . as what Jesus Christ did with the leper.'"[3] Meun similarly portrays False Seeming, dressed as a Jacobin, as visiting Constrained Abstinence, attired as a Béguine, and hearing her confession so intimately that their two heads are hidden underneath one headdress. Even the friars' celebrated learning is perceived more as appearance than as reality. Having taken over the secular clergy's privileges, they are said to justify this usurpation with a dubious scholastic logic. Rutebeuf describes them as people "who do not like truth and who have attributed such things to authority that they should not have."[4] Meun shows False Seeming to so harangue another character that the latter "did not know how to reply to his argument, since he saw the semblance of logic in every case."[5] The friars' dialectical arguments, though appearing to rest upon rational and biblical foundations, are devised

---

2. " . . . qu'au lange se froie / Qu'autre chose a souz la corroie," *Oeuvres complètes de Rutebeuf,* ed. Edmond Faral and Julia Bastin (Paris: A. et J. Picard, 1959–60), vol. 1, "Du Pharisien," pp. 249–55, vv. 89–90; "J'aime mieux devant les gens orer, / Et afubler ma renardie / Du papelardie," *Le Roman de la Rose,* ed. Daniel Poirion (Paris: Garnier Flammarion, 1974), vv. 11523–25. A *papelard* was originally a clergyman but by this time had become a layperson who showed excessive religious devotion in public, as Béguines, Beghards, mendicant tertiaries, and anchoresses were said to do, and who earned a widespread, if contested, reputation for sanctity as a result. Ultimately, this term came to designate any religious hypocrite. For an intriguing defense of hypocrisy—at least in liberal society—see Ruth W. Grant, *Hypocrisy and Integrity: Machiavelli, Rousseau, and the Ethics of Politics* (Chicago: University of Chicago Press, 1997).

3. "Je ne di pas que plus en facent, / Més il samble que pas ne hacent, / Et sains Bernars dist, ce me samble: / 'Converser homme et fame ensemble / Sanz plus ouvrer selonc nature, / C'est vertu si nete et si pure, / . . . / Com de Ladre fist Jhesuschriz,'" "Des Règles," *Oeuvres complètes de Rutebeuf,* vol. 1, pp. 267–76, vv. 163–70.

4. ". . . qui n'aiment verité, / Qui ont mis en auctorité / Tels choses que metre n'i doivent," ibid., vv. 5–6.

5. "Cis ne set respondre a la prueve, / Et voit iluec tel aparance," *Le Roman de la Rose,* vv. 12329–30.

more to advance their interests than to establish the truth, these poets imply. With their seemingly ascetic dress, their seemingly chaste interactions with women, and their seemingly learned discourse, the friars, like the heretics before them, appear to be one thing when they are, in fact, another.

The connection between the Dominicans and Franciscans and the heretics they were supposed to seek out did not escape the poets' notice. We have observed how heretics were seen to present themselves as new apostles, but now Rutebeuf alleges that the Jacobins, with their white robes and black mantles, also pass themselves off as holy men. He writes, "There is in this world neither *bougre*, nor heretic, nor publican, nor Waldensian, nor sodomite who, if clothed in the habit to which a *papelard* is accustomed, would not be held to be a saint or a hermit."[6] If the hypocritical Jacobins take after heretics, the poet alleges, it is because Hypocrisy, in general, is "first cousin to Heresy,"[7] inducing her followers to mistake falsity for truth, wickedness for goodness, and sin for sanctity and, thus, leading them into perdition. Given the friars' resemblance to heretics, it is hardly surprising that, according to Rutebeuf and Meun, they have ceased to pursue actual deviants in the faith. Rutebeuf depicts the Jacobins as promising to unlock the gate of paradise for heretics in exchange for donations to their order. He claims that the friars offer heaven to those "who give enough for them to drink and get drunk with and who grease their palms" and to those "who are, perhaps, perfected *bougres*."[8] Elsewhere, he refers to the money the friars have received from "the wills of *bougres* held to be loyal."[9] Meun's False Seeming likewise suggests that those who inhabit "a castle or city where *bougre* may be spoken of" may deter the friars inquisitor if they offer them sufficient foodstuffs.[10] While failing to pursue their heterodox friends, the friars are nonetheless said to accuse their orthodox enemies of het-

---

6. "Il n'a en tout cest mont ne bougre ne herite / Ne fort popelican, vaudois ne sodomite, / Se il vestoit l'abit ou papelars abite, / C'on ne le tenist ja a saint ou a hermite," "Des Jacobins," *Oeuvres complètes de Rutebeuf,* vol. I, pp. 313–17, vv. 49–52. The word *bougre* originally appears to have designated Cathars, whose religion is, in fact, linked to that of the Bulgarian Bogomils, but it soon began to apply to heretics in general and, by extension, to sodomites, usurers, and other malefactors. See J. Orr, "*Bougre* as Expletive," *Romance Philology* I (1947–48): 71–74.

7. "Cousine germaine Heresie," "Du Pharisien," *Oeuvres complètes de Rutebeuf,* vol. I, v. 8.

8. "Qui les aboivrent et enyvrent / Et qui lor engressent les pances / . . . / Qui sont, espoir, bougre parfet," "Des Règles," ibid., vv. 20–23.

9. "De bougres por loiaus tenuz," "La Complainte de Constantinople," ibid., vol. I, pp. 428–32, v. 112.

10. ". . . chatiau ne cité / Ou bougre soient recité," *Le Roman de la Rose,* v. 11724.

erodoxy. "Now no man who does not bow before them is a good believer," Rutebeuf relates ironically; "rather, he is a *bougre* and a miscreant."[11] If anyone declines to take a friar as his confessor, he adds, "such a *bougre* has never been born."[12] A "heretic" is here not someone who maintains heterodox views but, rather, someone who withholds from the friars the veneration and confidence they believe to be their due. In their cynicism, the friars not only assume a guise of sanctity in order to gain influence over others, as the heretics did before them, but tolerate the existence of heretics in their midst in order to ensure their own financial well-being.

As the figure of epistemological instability in literature shifts from the Cathar and the Waldensian to the Dominican and the Franciscan, it shifts from the heretic to the hypocrite and, hence, from a positive to a negative valuation. In the High Middle Ages, when this figure was identified with the heretic, he appeared as the underdog, taking the form of a lover threatened by his lady's husband or guardians, a poet belittled by advocates of easy verse, or a fox embattled by stronger animals. In deceiving and thus getting the better of others more powerful than they, these protagonists were applauded for their ingenuity. In the Late Middle Ages and the Renaissance, however, when this figure is associated with the hypocrite, he appears as the master. If one considers the Franciscan friars in Boccaccio's *Decameron*, Chaucer's *Canterbury Tales*, or Marguerite de Navarre's *Heptaméron* and their descendant in Molière's *Tartuffe*, to take only the best-known examples, this figure uses his religious habit and manner to gain the confidence of innocent men and, especially, innocent women, to obtain access to their households, and to satisfy his appetites at their expense. While the heretic and his literary counterparts use trickery to compensate for their social disadvantages, as members of stigmatized or disfavored groups, the hypocrite employs similar means to capitalize upon his social advantages as a friar. If the duke of Burgundy is harmed because he trusts Trubert, it is because his own imprudence has led him to place confidence in an unknown rustic, but if a woman is raped because she trusts a Franciscan, it is because the Church and Christian society have encouraged her to confess her sins to such religious men. The heretic and his confrères harm because they betray a confidence they should not have been given, yet the hypocrite abuses

---

11. "Or n'est més hom qui ne l'encline / Ne bien creanz, / Ainz est bougres et mescreanz," "Du Pharisien," vv. 22–24.

12. "Tels bougres ne nasqui," "La Chanson des ordres," *Oeuvres complètes de Rutebeuf,* vol. 1, pp. 330–33, v. 28.

because he betrays a trust it is his right to receive. As the destabilizer of the epistemological order becomes not someone outside the Church but someone inside this institution, literature takes the lead in criticizing him. When Renart was depicted as a heretic in the *Roman de Renart*, he was praised for his cleverness and audacity, but now, when described as a hypocrite in later versions of his legend, such as Rutebeuf's *Renart le Bestourné*, Jacquemart Giélée's *Renart le Nouvel*, and the anonymous *Renart le Contrefait*, he is condemned for his maliciousness. Ultimately, it was only for a finite period, roughly corresponding to the years during which heretics were being most pursued in France and Occitania, that literature affirmed the epistemological confusion with which the heretic was associated.

Insofar as the medieval heretic and his literary career are still of interest to us nowadays, despite the limited historical period of their efflorescence, it is because they remind us that there exist some truths that cannot be told except through literature. During the decades surrounding the turn of the twelfth and thirteenth centuries, it was unthinkable for anyone, of whatever Christian persuasion, to acknowledge any merits in heretics. Even those considered heretics by the Catholic Church agreed that heretics should be prosecuted, and some of them conducted their own campaigns against those they perceived as heterodox. One might claim that those accused of heresy were not, in fact, guilty or that those convicted of this crime should be allowed to repent, but one could not deny that they were wicked and deserving of punishment. At a time when heretics were, by definition, people living in error and sin, to defend heretics as heretics (and not as wrongly accused Catholics) would be as outrageous as it would be in our day to defend gang members as gang members (and not as disadvantaged youths). It was only in literature, as we have seen, that the epistemological instability with which heretics were identified could be perceived not as troubling but as delightful. Lyric poems, romances, and comic tales constituted the media in which the heretics' secretiveness could be read, not as concealing depravity for fear of recrimination, but as concealing purity for fear of contamination; in which their singularity could be interpreted, not as a failure to conform to appropriate standards of behavior, but as a transcendence of those standards; and in which their duplicity could be viewed as the result not of malice but of overflowing vitality. By the same token, it is only in cinema today that gang wars, shoot-outs, and vigilante justice are regarded not as social pathologies, suffered by people unable to find good jobs and become productive members of society, but as social strengths, cultivated by people who value honor, loyalty, and courage more than middle-class comforts. Fictional discourses, whether literary or cinematic, are capable of affirming deviant value systems and, hence, deviant populations in a way in which factual discourses cannot.

In all of the literary genres we have considered, an image of a private and secure space, closed off from the hero's or heroine's pursuers, keeps resurfacing. Troubadours sing of withdrawing to a locked garden, where no one but they can enter. Tristan and Iseut flee to the Morrois Forest, where they live in anxiety but relative security from Mark's court. Renart retreats to Maupertuis, his well-fortified and well-stocked den. These spaces constitute sanctuaries where these characters can live free from the surveillance and prosecution of authorities, yet they offer this security only so long as their inhabitants remain within their confines, which they can never do. If the motif of the sanctuary occurs so repeatedly and prominently in literary works of this period, it may be because it represents, ultimately, the space of literature, which allows us the safety within which to pursue our desires, but only so long as we remain within its boundaries.

SELECTED
BIBLIOGRAPHY

GENERAL

Bibliographies

Berkhout, Carl T., and Jeffrey B. Russell. *Medieval Heresies: A Bibliography, 1960–1979.* Toronto: Pontifical Institute of Medieval Studies, 1981.

Duvernoy, Jean. "La Contribution des ouvrages critiques récents à l'histoire de l'hérésie mériodionale." *Bulletin de la Société ariégoise des sciences, lettres et arts* 1969: 231–47.

Grundmann, Herbert. *Bibliographie zur Ketzergeschichte des Mittelalters (1900–1966).* Roma: Edizioni di storia e letteratura, 1967.

———. "Bibliographie des études récentes." In Jacques Le Goff, ed., *Hérésies et sociétés dans l'Europe pré-industrielle, 11e–18e siècles.* Paris: Mouton, 1968, pp. 408–67.

Modern Criticism

Arnold, John. "Inquisition, Texts and Discourse." In Caterina Bruschi and Peter Biller, eds. *Texts and the Repression of Medieval Heresy.* Woodbridge, Suffolk, UK: York Medieval Press, 2003, pp. 63–80.

Biller, Peter. "The Historiography of Medieval Heresy in the United States of America and Great Britain, 1945–1992." In *The Waldenses, 1170–1530: Between a Religious Order and a Church.* Aldershot, UK: Ashgate Publishing, 2001, pp. 25–47.

———. "The Topos and Reality of the Heretic as *illitteratus.*" In ibid., pp. 169–90.

Biller, Peter, and Anne Hudson, eds. *Heresy and Literacy, 1000–1530.* Cambridge: Cambridge University Press, 1994.

Borst, Arno. *Medieval Worlds: Barbarians, Heretics, and Artists in the Middle Ages.* Trans. Eric Hansen. Chicago: University of Chicago Press, 1992.

Bruschi, Caterina, and Peter Biller, eds. *Texts and the Repression of Medieval Heresy.* Woodbridge, Suffolk, UK: York Medieval Press, 2003.

Chenu, Marie-Dominique. "Orthodoxie et hérésie. Le point de vue du théologien." *Annales* 18 (1963): 75–80.

Copeland, Rita, ed. *Criticism and Dissent in the Middle Ages.* Cambridge: Cambridge University Press, 1996.

Conformité et déviance au Moyen Age. Ed. Marcel Faure. Actes du 2e Colloque international de Montpellier, Université Paul Valéry (1993). Montpellier: Association CRISIMA, 1995.

De Salvio, Alfonso. *Dante and Heresy.* Boston: Dumas Bookshop, 1936.

Dondoine, Antoine. "Le Manuel de l'inquisiteur (1230–1330)." *Archivum fratrum praedicatorum* 17 (1947): 85–194.

Dontenville, Henri. "Hétérodoxies médiévales et souterrains refuges." *Bulletin de la société de mythologie française* 64 (1955): 143–49.

Evans, A. P. "Hunting Subversion in the Middle Ages." *Speculum* 33 (1958): 1–22.

Fichtenau, Heinrich. *Heretics and Scholars in the High Middle Ages, 1000–1200.* Trans. Denise A. Kaiser. University Park: Pennsylvania State University Press, 1998.

Grundmann, Herbert. *Religious Movements in the Middle Ages: The Historical Links Between Heresy, the Mendicant Orders, and the Women's Religious Movement in the Twelfth and Thirteenth Century, with the Historical Foundations of German Mysticism.* Trans. Steven Rowan. Notre Dame, IN: University of Notre Dame Press, 1995.

———. "*Oportet et haereses esse*: Das Problem der Ketzerei im Spiegel der mittelalterlichen Bibelexegese." *Archiv für Kulturgeschichte* 45, no. 2 (1963): 129–64.

———. "Der Typus des Ketzers in mittelalterlicher Anschauung." In *Kultur- und Universalgeschichte: Walter Goetz zu seinem 60. Geburtstage.* Leipzig and Berlin: B. G. Teubner, 1927, pp. 91–107.

Koopmans, Jelle. *Le Théâtre des exclus au Moyen Age: Hérétiques, sorcières et marginaux.* Paris: Editions Imago, 1997.

Lambert, Malcolm. *Medieval Heresy: Popular Movements from the Gregorian Reform to the Reformation.* 3rd ed. Oxford: Blackwell, 2002.

Lea, Henry C., *History of the Inquisition in the Middle Ages.* 3 vols. New York: Harper & Bros., 1887.

Le Goff, Jacques, ed. *Hérésies et sociétés dans l'Europe pré-industrielle, 11e–18e siècles.* Paris: Mouton, 1968.

Lourdaux, W. and D. Verhelst, eds. *The Concept of Heresy in the Middle Ages, 11th–13th Centuries.* Proceedings of the International Conference, Louvain (May 13–16, 1973). The Hague: Martinus Nijhoff, 1976. Rpt. Leuven: University Press, 1976.

Manselli, Raoul. *Studie sulle eresie del secolo xii.* Roma: Istituto storico italiano per il medio evo, 1953.

Molinier, Charles. *L'Inquisition dans le Midi de la France au XIIIe et au XIVe siècle: Etude sur les sources de son histoire.* Paris: Sandoz & Fischbacher, 1880.

Moore, R. I. *The Formation of a Persecuting Society: Power and Deviance in Western Europe.* Oxford: Blackwell, 1987.

———. "Heresy as Disease." In W. Lourdaux and D. Verhelst, eds. *The Concept of Heresy in the Middle Ages, 11th–13th Centuries*. Proceedings of the International Conference, Louvain (May 13–16, 1973). The Hague: Martinus Nijhoff, 1976. Rpt. Leuven: University Press, 1976, pp. 1–11.

———. "New Sects and Secret Meetings." *Studies in Church History* 23, *Voluntary Religion* (1986): 47–68.

———. *The Origins of European Dissent*. London: Allen Lane, 1977. Rpt. Toronto: University of Toronto Press, 1994.

Patschovsky, Alexander. "Heresy and Society: On the Political Function of Heresy in the Medieval World." In Caterina Bruschi and Peter Biller, eds. *Texts and the Repression of Medieval Heresy*. Woodbridge, Suffolk, UK: York Medieval Press, 2003, pp. 23–41.

Peters, Edward. *Inquisition*. New York: Free Press, 1988. Rpt. Berkeley: University of California Press, 1989.

———. "Transgressing the Limits Set by the Fathers: Authority and Impious Exegesis in Medieval Thought," in Scott L. Waugh and Peter D. Diehl, eds. *Christendom and its Discontents: Exclusion, Persecution, and Rebellion, 1000–1500*. Cambridge: Cambridge University Press, 1996, pp. 338–362.

Robert, Ulysse. *Les Signes d'infamie au Moyen Age: Juifs, sarrasins, hérétiques, lépreux, cagots et filles publiques*. Paris: Honoré Champion, 1891.

Russell, Jeffrey Burton. *Dissent and Reform in the Early Middle Ages*. Berkeley: University of California Press, 1965.

———. "Interpretations of the Origins of Medieval Heresy." *Mediaeval Studies* 25 (1963): 26–53.

———. *Religious Dissent in the Middle Ages*. New York: Wiley, 1971.

———. "Witchcraft and the Demonization of Heretics." *Mediaevalia* 2 (1976): 1–21.

Stock, Brian. *The Implications of Literacy: Written Language and Models of Interpretation in the Eleventh and Twelfth Centuries*. Princeton: Princeton University Press, 1983.

Thijssen, J. M. M. H. *Censure and Heresy at the University of Paris, 1200–1400*. Philadelphia: University of Pennsylvania Press, 1998.

Zerner, Monique, ed. *Inventer l'hérésie? Discours polémiques et pouvoirs avant l'Inquisition*. Nice: Z'éditions, 1998.

LATE ANTIQUE HERETICS

Late Antique Texts

Augustine of Hippo. "Against Lying." In *Treatises on Various Subjects*. Trans. Harold B. Jaffee. New York: Fathers of the Church, pp. 125–79.

———. *La Cité de Dieu*. Ed. G. Combes. *Oeuvres de saint Augustin*. Vol. 35. Sources chrétiennes. Paris: Desclée & Brouwer, 1959.

———. *The City of God*. Trans. Gerald G. Walsh and Daniel J. Honan. New York: Fathers of the Church, 1954.

———. "Contra mendacium ad consentium." PL. Vol. 6, cols. 517–48.

———. *De Haerisibus.* CC Lat. Vol. 46, pp. 236–345.

———. *The "De Haerisibus" of Saint Augustine.* Trans. Liguori G. Müller. Washington, DC: Catholic University of America Press, 1956.

———. *Epistolae.* PL. Vol. 33.

———. *In Iohannis Evangelium Tractatus CXXIV.* CC Lat. Vol. 31.

———. *Letters.* Trans. Wilfrid Parsons. New York: Fathers of the Church, 1953.

———. "De moribus Manichaeorum." PL. Vol. 6, pp. 550–80.

———. "On the Morals of the Manichaeans." *The Writings against the Manichaeans and against the Donatists.* Nicene and Post-Nicene Fathers of the Christian Church. Grand Rapids, MI: Wm. B. Eerdmans Publishing Co., 1974, pp. 69–89.

———. *Tractates on the Gospel of John 55–111.* 5 vols. Trans. John W. Rettig. The Fathers of the Church. Washington, DC: Catholic University of America, 1988–95.

Clement of Alexandria. *Stromata.* Ed. Otto Stählin and Ludwig Früchtel. 4 vols. Berlin: Akademie Verlag, 1970.

———. *The Writings of Clement of Alexandria.* Trans. William Wilson. Ante-Nicene Christian Library. Vols. 4 and 12. Edinburgh: T. & T. Clark, 1867–69.

Cyprian. "De ecclesiae catholicae unitate." In *Opera.* CC Lat. Vol. 3, pp. 249–68.

———. "The Unity of the Catholic Church." In *Early Latin Theology: Selections from Tertullian, Cyprian, Ambrose, and Jerome.* Library of Christian Classics. Ed. and trans. S. L. Greenslade. Louisville: Westminster Press, 1956, pp. 31–64.

Hilary of Poitiers. *De Trinitate.* CC Lat. Vol. 62.

———. *The Trinity.* Trans. Stephen McKenna. New York: Fathers of the Church, 1954.

Hippolytus. *Refutatio omnium haeresium.* Ed. Miroslav Marcovich. Berlin: W. De Gruyter, 1986.

———. *The Refutation of All Heresies, with Fragments from His Commentaries on Various Books of Scripture.* Trans. S. D. F. Salmond. Ante-Nicene Christian Library. Edinburgh: T. & T. Clark, 1868.

Hultgren, Arland J., and Steven A. Haggmark, eds. *The Earliest Christian Heretics: Readings from their Opponents.* Minneapolis: Fortress Press, 1996.

Irenaeus of Lyons. *Contre les hérésies: Edition critique d'après les versions arméni-enne et latine.* Ed. Adelin Rousseau and Louis Poutreleau. 10 vols. Paris: Editions du Cerf, 1969–90.

———. *Against the Heresies.* Trans. Dominic J. Unger with John J. Dillon. Ancient Christian Writers. 2 vols. Mahwah, NJ: Paulist Press, 1992.

Isidore of Seville. *Etymologiarum sive Originum Libri XX.* Oxford: Clarendon Press, 1911.

———. *Opera Omnia.* PL. Vol. 82.

Jerome. *Opera.* CC Lat. Vol. 79.

Justin Martyr. *The First Apology, The Second Apology.* Trans. Thomas B. Falls. Washington, DC: Catholic Universityh of America Press, 1948.

———. *Opera Quae Exstant Omnia.* PG. Vol. 6.

Minucius Felix. *Octavius.* Ed. Jean Beaujeu. 2nd ed. Paris: Les Belles Lettres, 1974.
———. *Octavius.* Trans. Rudolph Arbesmann, Emily Joseph Daly, and Edwin A. Quain. Fathers of the Church. Washington, DC: Catholic University of America Press, 1950.
Origen. *Contre Celse.* Ed. Marcel Borret. 5 vols. Paris: Cerf, 1967–76.
———. *Contra Celsum.* Trans. Henry Chadwick. Cambridge: Cambridge University Press, 1953.
Schroeder, Henry J., ed. *The Disciplinary Decrees of the General Councils: Texts, Translation, and Commentary.* Saint Louis, MO: Bitterden, 1937.
Vincent of Lérins. *The Commonitories.* Trans. Rudolph E. Morris. Vol. 9. New York: Fathers of the Church, 1949.
———. *Commonitorium.* CC Lat. Vol. 69.

Modern Criticism
Baker, Derek, ed. *Schism, Heresy, and Religious Protest.* Papers Read at the Tenth Summer Meeting and Eleventh Winter Meeting of the Ecclesiastical History Society. Cambridge: Cambridge University Press, 1972.
Bauer, Walter. *Orthodoxy and Heresy in Earliest Christianity.* Ed. and trans. Robert A. Kraft et al. Philadelphia: Fortress Press, 1971.
Chadwick, Henry. *Heresy and Orthodoxy in the Early Church.* Aldershot, UK: Variorum Reprints, 1991.
Ferguson, Everett, ed. *Orthodoxy, Heresy, and Schism in Early Christianity.* New York: Garland Press, 1993.
Grant, Robert McQueen. *Heresy and Criticism: The Search for Authenticity in Early Christian Literature.* Louisville: Westminster Press, 1993.
Jeanjean, Benoît. *Saint Jérôme et l'hérésie.* Paris: Institut d'Etudes Augustiniennes, 1999.
Le Boulluec, Alain. *La Notion d'hérésie dans la littérature grecque, IIe–IIIe siècles.* 2 vols. Paris: Etudes Augustiniennes, 1985.
Robinson, Thomas A. *The Bauer Thesis Examined: The Geography of Heresy in the Early Christian Church.* Lewiston, NY: Edwin Mellen, 1988.
Strousma, Guy G. *Hidden Wisdom: Esoteric Traditions and the Roots of Christian Mysticism.* Leiden: E. J. Brill, 1996.
Turner, Henry E. *The Pattern of Christian Truth: A Study in the Relation between Orthodoxy and Heresy in the Early Church.* London: A. R. Mowbray, 1954.

"MANICHAEANS" AND OTHER EARLY HERETICS
Medieval Texts
Adémar of Chabannes. *Historiarum libri iii.* MGH, Scriptores. Vol. 4, pp. 138, 143, and 148. "'Manichaeans' in Aquitaine" and "Heresy at Orléans." In Wakefield and Evans, pp. 73–76.
André de Fleury et al. *Les Miracles de Saint Benoît, écrits par Adrevald, Aimon, André, Raoul Tortaire et Hughes de Sainte Marie, moines de Fleury.* Ed. Eugène de Certain. Paris: Renouard, 1858.

———. *Vie de Gauzlin, abbé de Fleury / Vita Gauzlini, abbatis Floriacensis monasterii.* Ed. and trans. Robert-Henri Bautier and Gilette Labory. Paris: CNRS, 1969.

Anselm of Liège. *Gesta episcoporum Leodiensium.* MGH, Scriptores. Vol. 7, pp. 226–28. "Heretics at Châlons-sur-Marne." In Wakefield and Evans, pp. 89–93.

Council of Reims. In Mansi. Vol. 19, col. 742.

Gesta Synodi Aurelianensis. In Bouquet. Vol. 10, pp. 536–39.

Guibert of Nogent. *Autobiographie.* Ed. E. R. Labande. Paris: Les Classiques de l'Histoire de France au Moyen Age, 1981.

———. *Self and Society in Medieval France: The Memoirs of Abbot Guibert of Nogent.* Trans. John F. Benton. New York: Harper & Row, 1970. Rpt. Toronto: University of Toronto Press, 1984.

Hamilton, Janet and Bernard Hamilton, eds. *Christian Dualist Heresies in the Byzantine World, c. 650–c. 1405.* Manchester: Manchester University Press, 1998.

Heribert. *Epistola de haereticis Petragoricis.* PL. Vol. 181, cols. 1721–22. "A Warning from Périgueux." In Wakefield and Evans, pp. 138–39.

Jean de Fleury. Bouquet. Vol. 10, p. 498.

Paul de Saint-Père de Chartres. *Cartulaire de l'abbaye de Saint-Père de Chartres.* Vol. 1. Paris: Crapelet, 1840, pp. 109–15. "Heresy at Orléans: The Narrative of Paul, a Monk of Chartres." In Wakefield and Evans, pp. 76–81.

Rodolfus Glaber. *The Five Books of the Histories / Historiarum Libri Quinque.* Ed. and trans. John France. Oxford: Clarendon Press, 1989.

William of Newburgh. *Chronicles of the Reigns of Stephen, Henry II, and Richard I.* Ed. Richard Howlett. 2 vols. London: Her Majesty's Stationary Office and Kraus Reprint Corporation, 1884–1889.

———. *The History of William of Newburgh.* Trans. Joseph Stevenson. London, 1856.

Modern Criticism

Bautier, Robert-Henri. "L'Hérésie d'Orléans et le mouvement intellectuel au début du XIe siècle: Documents et hypothèses." In *Enseignement et vie intellectuelle (IX–XVI siècle).* Actes du 95ième Congrès national des sociétés savantes (Reims, 1970), Section de philologie et histoire jusqu'à 1610. Vol. 1. Paris: Bibliothèque nationale, 1975, pp. 63–88.

Bonnassaie, Pierre, and Richard Landes. "Une nouvelle hérésie est née dans le monde." In *Les Sociétés méridionales autour de l'An Mil: Répertoire des sources et documents commentés.* Ed. Michael Zimmermann. Paris: CNRS, 1992, pp. 435–59.

Brenon, Anne. "Les hérésies de l'An Mil: Nouvelles perspectives sur les origines du Catharisme." *Heresis* 24 (1995): 21–36.

Cohn, Norman. *The Pursuit of the Millennium: Revolutionary Messianism in Medieval and Reformation Europe and Its Bearing on Modern Totalitarian Movements.* Oxford: Oxford University Press, 1957. Rev., 1970.

Congar, Yves M.-J. "*Arriana haeresis* comme désignation du néomanichéisme au

XIIe siècle: Contribution à l'histoire d'une typification de l'hérésie au moyen âge." *Revue des sciences philosophiques et théologiques* 43 (1959): 449–61.

Cracco, Giorgio. "Le eresie del Mille: Un fenomeno di rigetto delle strutture feudali?" In *Structures féodales et féodalisme dans l'Occident méditerranéen (Xe–XIIIe s.): Bilan et perspectives de recherche.* Colloque, Ecole Française de Rome (10–13 octobre 1978). Paris: CNRS, 1978, pp. 345–60.

————. "Gli eretici nella *societas christiana* dei secoli XI e XII." In *La Christianità dei secoli XI e XII in Occidente: Coscienza e strutture di una società.* Atti della ottava settimana internazionale di studio Mendola (30 giugno–5 luglio 1980). Milano: Vita e pensiero, 1983, pp. 339–73.

————. "Riforma ed eresia in momenti della cultura europea tra X e XI secolo." *Rivista di Storia e Letteratua religiosa* 6 (1971): 411–77.

L'Ermetismo in Occidente nei secoli XI e XII. Atti della seconda settimana internationale di studio Mendola (30 agosto–6 settembre 1962). Milan: Società Editrice Vita e Pensiero, 1961.

Ilarino da Milano. "Le eresie popolari nel secolo XI nell'Europa occidentale." *Studi Gregoriani per la storia di Gregorio VII e della riforma Gregoriana.* Vol. 2. Roma: Abbazia di san Paolo, 1947, pp. 46–49.

Iogna-Prat, Dominique. *Order and Exclusion: Cluny and Christendom Face Heresy, Judaism, and Islam (1000–1150).* Ithaca: Cornell University Press, 2001.

————. *Ordonner et exclure. Cluny et la société chrétienne face à l'hérésie, au judaïsme et à l'Islam (1100–1150).* Paris: Aubier, 1998.

Landes, Richard. "La Vie apostolique en Aquitaine en l'An Mil: Paix de Dieu, culte des reliques, et communauté hérétiques." *Annales* 3 (mai–juin 1991): 573–93.

Leyser, Henrietta. *Hermits and the New Monasticism: A Study of Religious Communities in Western Europe, 1000–1150.* London: MacMillan, 1984.

Lobrichon, Guy. "The Chiaroscuro of Heresy: Early Eleventh-Century Aquitaine as Seen from Auxerre." In *The Peace of God: Social Violence and Religious Response in France around the Year 1000.* Ed. Thomas Head and Richard Landes. Ithaca: Cornell University Press, 1992, pp. 80–103.

Manselli, Raoul. "Il monaco Enrico e la sua eresia." *Bullettino dell'Istituto storico italiano per il medio evo e Archivio Muratoriano* 65 (1953): 1–63.

Moore, R. I. "Heresy, Repression, and Social Change in the Age of Gregorian Reform." In *Christendom and Its Discontents: Exclusion, Persecution, and Rebellion, 1000–1500.* Ed. Scott L. Waugh and Peter D. Diehl. Cambridge: Cambridge University Press, 1996, pp. 19–46.

Musy, Jean. "Mouvements populaires et hérésies au XIe siècle en France." *Revue historique* 253 (1975): 33–76.

Paravicini Bagliani, Agostino, and André Vauchez, eds. *Poteri carismatici e informali: Chiesa e società medioevali.* Palermo: Sellerio Editore, 1992.

Vauchez, André. "Diables et hérétiques: les réactions de l'église et de la société en occident face aux mouvements religieux dissidents, de la fin du Xe au début du XIIe siècle." In *Santi e demoni nell'alto medioevo occidentale (secoli V–XI).* Settimane di Studio sull'alto medioevo (Spoleto, 1989), pp. 45–60.

Vicaire, Marie-Humbert. *L'Imitation des apôtres: Moines, chanoines et mendiants, IVe–XIIIe siècles*. Paris: Editions du Cerf, 1963.

Walter, Johannes Wilhelm von. *Die ersten Wanderprediger Frankreichs: Studien zur Geschichte des Mönchtums*. 2 vols. Leipzig: Deicherschen Verlagshandlung, 1903.

CATHARS

Bibliography

Berne-Lagarde, Pierre de. *Bibliographie du catharisme languedocien*. Toulouse: Institut des Etudes Cathares, 1957.

Medieval Texts

Alain de Lille. *De fide catholica contra haereticos sui temporis*. PL, vol. 210, cols. 305–430. "Alan of Lille: A Scholar's Attack on Heretics." In Wakefield and Evans, pp. 214–20.

Bernard Gui. *Manuel de l'inquisiteur*. Ed. and trans. Guillaume Mollat. 2 vols. Paris: Champion, 1926–27. "Bernard Gui's Description of Heresies." In Wakefield and Evans, pp. 373–445.

———. *Practica inquisitionis heretice pravitatis*. Ed. Célestin Douais. Paris: Picard, 1886.

Caesarius of Heisterbach. *The Dialogue on Miracles*. Trans. Henry von Essen Scott and C. C. Swinton Bland. London: George Routledge and Sons, 1929.

———. *Dialogus miraculorum*. Ed. Joseph Strange. 2 vols. Cologne: J. M. Heberle, 1851.

Devic, Claude, and Joseph Vaissète, eds. *Histoire générale de Languedoc avec des notes et les pièces justificatives*. 16 vols. Paris: J. Vincent, 1730–45. Rpt. Toulouse: Privat, 1872–92.

Dossat, Yves, ed. *Les Hérésies et l'Inquisition, XIIe–XIIIe siècle: Documents et études*. Aldershot, UK: Variorum, 1990.

Douais, Célestin, ed. *Documents pour servir à l'histoire de l'Inquisition dans le Languedoc*. 2 vols. Paris: Renouard, 1890.

———, ed. *Les Sources de l'histoire de l'Inquisition dans le Midi de la France au XIIIe et XIVe siècles*. Paris: Renouard, 1881.

Eckbert of Schönau. *Sermones tredecim contra haereticos*. PL. Vol. 195, cols. 11–102. "Eckbert of Schönau: Sermon against the Cathars." In Moore, pp. 88–94.

Etienne de Bourbon. "Stephane de Borbone tractatus de diversis materiis praedicabilis." In *Anecdotes historiques, légendes et apologues tirés du recueil inédit d'Etienne de Bourbon, dominicain du XIIIe siècle*. Ed. Albert Lecoy de la Marche. Paris: Renouard, 1887, pp. 290–99.

Giacomo Capelli. *La Eresia catara*. Ed. Dino Bazzocchi. Bologna: Licinio Capelli, 1919. "James Capelli on the Cathars." In Wakefield and Evans, pp. 301–6.

Guillaume Pelhisson. *Chronique (1229–1244), suivie du récit des troubles d'Albi (1234)*. Ed. and trans. Jean Duvernoy. Paris: CNRS, 1994.

———. "The Chronicle of William Pelhisson." In Walter L. Wakefield, *Heresy, Crusade, and Inquisition in Southern France*. Berkeley: University of California Press, 1974, pp. 207–35.

Guillaume de Puylaurens. *Chronique, 1145–1275 / Chronica magistri Guillelmi de Podio Laurentii*. Ed. and trans. Jean Duvernoy. Paris: CNRS, 1976; rpt. Toulouse: Le Pérégrinateur, 1996.

————. *The Chronicle of William of Puylaurens: The Albigensian Crusade and Its Aftermath*. Trans. W. A. Silby and M. D. Silby. Woodbridge, Suffolk, UK: Boydell Press, 2003.

Hugh of Poitiers. *Historia Vizeliacensis monasterii*. PL. Vol. 194, esp. cols. 1681–82.

"Publicans at Vézelay." In Wakefield and Evans, pp. 247–49.

Maitland. S. R., ed. *Facts and Documents Illustrative of the History, Doctrine, and Rites of the Ancient Albigenses and Waldenses*. London: C. J. C. and F. Rivington, 1832.

Meyer, Paul, ed. "Le Débat d'Izarn et de Sicart de Figueiras." *Annuaire-bulletin de la Société de l'histoire de France* 16 (1879): 233–92.

Nelli, René, ed. and trans. *Ecrivains anticonformistes du Moyen Age occitan*. Vol. 2. *Hérétiques et politiques*. Paris: Editions Phébus, 1997.

Nicolau Eimeric. *Directorium inquisitorum*. Roma: Apud Georgium Ferrarium, 1587.

Nicolau Eymerich and Francisco Peña. *Le Manuel des Inquisiteurs*. Trans. Louis Sala-Molin. La Haye: Mouton, 1973.

Ralph of Coggeshall. *Chronicon anglicanum*. Ed. Joseph Stevenson. London: Longman, 1875.

Selge, Kurt Victor, ed. *Texte zur Inquisition*. Gutersloh: Mohn, 1967.

Tugwell, Simon, ed. *Early Dominicans: Selected Writings*. Mahwah, NJ: Paulist Press, 1982.

Modern Criticism

Arnold, John H. *Inquisition and Power: Catharism and the Confessing Subject in Medieval Languedoc*. Philadelphia: University of Pennsylvania Press, 2001.

Barber, Malcolm. *The Cathars: Dualist Heretics in Languedoc in the High Middle Ages*. Harlow, UK: Longman, 2000.

Berlioz, Jacques. *"Tuez-les tous, Dieu reconnaîtra les siens." La Croisade contre les Albigeois vue par Césaire de Heisterbach*. Portet-sur-Garonne: Editions Loubatières, 1994.

Borst, Arno. *Die Katharer*. Stuttgart: Hiersemann, 1953.

Brenon, Anne. *Les Femmes cathares*. Paris: Perrin, 1992.

Delaruelle, Etienne. "Le Catharisme en Languedoc vers 1200: Une enquête." *Annales du Midi* 72 (1960).

Delpoux, Charles. "Les Cathares et l'Inquisition à Toulouse et dans sa région." *Cahiers d'Etudes Cathares* 7 (1956): 83–95.

Dossat, Yves. *Les Crises de l'Inquisition toulousaine au XIIIe siècle (1233–1273)*. Bordeaux: Imprimerie Bière, 1959.

Duvernoy, Jean. *Le Catharisme*. Vol. 1. *La Religion des Cathares*. Toulouse: Privat, 1976.

————. *Le Catharisme*. Vol. 2. *L'Histoire des Cathares*. Toulouse: Privat, 1979.

Given, James B. *Inquisition and Medieval Society: Power, Discipline, and Resistance in Languedoc*. Ithaca: Cornell University Press, 1997.

Griffe, Elie. *Le Languedoc cathare de l'Inquisition (1229–1329)*. Paris: Letouzey et Ané, 1971.

Lambert, Malcolm. *The Cathars*. Oxford: Blackwell, 1998.

Lansing, Carol. *Power and Purity: Cathar Heresy in Medieval Italy*. Oxford: Oxford University Press, 1998.

Manselli, Raoul. *L'Eresie del male*. Napoli: Morano, 1963.

Mundy, John Hine. *Men and Women at Toulouse in the Age of the Cathars*. Toronto: Pontifical Institute of Mediaeval Studies, 1990.

La Persécution du Catharisme, XIIe–XIVe siècles. Actes de la 6e session d'histoire médiévale organisée par le Centre d'Etudes Cathares / René Nelli (1–4 septembre 1993). Carcassonne: Centre d'Etudes Cathares, 1993.

Runciman, Steven. *The Medieval Manichee: A Study of the Christian Dualist Heresy*. Cambridge: Cambridge University Press, 1947.

Thouzellier, Christine. *Catharisme et valdéisme en Languedoc à la fin du XIIe et au début du XIIIe siècle: Politique pontificale, controverse*. Paris: Presses Universitaires de France, 1966.

———. *Hérésies et hérétiques: Vaudois, Cathares, Patarins, Albigeois*. Roma: Edizioni di storia e letteratura, 1965.

Vicaire, Marie-Humbert. "Les Cathares albigeois vus par les polémistes." *Cahiers de Fanjeaux*. Vol. 3. *Cathares en Languedoc*. Toulouse: Privat, 1968, pp. 105–28.

Wakefield, Walter, *Heresy, Crusade, and Inquisition in Southern France*. Berkeley: University of California Press, 1974.

BERNARD OF CLAIRVAUX

Medieval Texts

Bernard of Clairvaux. *Opera*. Ed. Jean Leclercq, C. H. Talbot, and Henri Rochais. 8 vols. Roma: Editiones Cistercienses, 1957–77.

———. *Sermons on the Song of Songs*. 4 vols. Trans. Kilian Walsh and Irene M. Edmonds. Kalamazoo, MI: Cistercian Publications, 1979.

———. *The Letters of St. Bernard of Clairvaux*. Trans. Bruno Scott James. London: Burnes & Oates, 1953. Rpt. Kalamazoo, MI: Cistercian Publications, 1998.

Bishops of France. Letter to Pope Innocent II. Ed. Jean Leclercq. "Autour de la correspondence de s. Bernard." In *Sapientiae doctrina: Mélanges de théologie et de littérature médiévales offerts à Dom Hildebrand Bascour, O. S. B.* Louvain: Abbaye du mont César, 1980, pp. 185–98.

Exordium magnum Cisterciense, sive narratio de initio Cisterciensis ordinis. Ed. Bruno Griesser. Roma: Editiones Cistercienses, 1961.

Eberwin of Steinfeld. *Epistola ad S. Bernardum (Ep. 472)*. PL. Vol. 182, cols. 676–80. "Eversin of Steinfeld." In Moore, pp. 74–78.

Geoffrey of Auxerre. *Vita Prima*. PL. Vol. 185, cols. 301–68, at cols. 312–14, 410–16, 312–14, and 427–28. "Henry: St. Bernard's Mission, 1145." In Moore, 41–46.

John of Salisbury. *Historia Pontificalis/Memoirs of the Papal Court*. Ed. Marjorie Chibnall. London: Thomas Nelson & Sons, 1956.

————. *Metalogicon.* CCCM. Vol. 98. *Metalogicon.* Trans. Daniel D. McGarry. Berkeley: University of California Press, 1955. Rpt. Gloucester: Peter Smith, 1971.

Otto of Freising and Rahewin. *The Deeds of Frederick Barbarossa.* Trans. Charles Christopher Mierow with Richard Emery. New York: Columbia University Press, 1953.

————. *Gesta Friderici I. imperatoris.* MGH Scriptores. Vol. 46.

Peter the Venerable. *The Letters of Peter the Venerable.* Ed. Giles Constable. 2 vols. Cambridge, MA: Harvard University Press, 1967.

S. Bernardi Vita prima. PL. Vol. 180, cols. 222–643.

Modern Criticism

Arabeyre, Patrick et al., eds. *Vie et légendes de Saint Bernard de Clairvaux: Création, diffusion, réception (XIIe–XXe siècles).* Actes des Rencontres de Dijon (7–8 juin, 1991). Saint-Nicolas-Les Citeaux: Abbaye de Citeau: 1993.

Bredero, Adriaan H. *Bernard de Clairvaux (1091–1153): Culte et histoire.* Trans. Joseph Longton. Turnhout: Brepols, 1998.

Bounoure, Gilles. "Saint Bernard et les hérétiques du Sarlandais." *Bulletin de la Société Historique et Archéologique du Périgord* 116 (1989): 277–92.

————. "Le dernier voyage de saint Bernard en Aquitaine: La Piété des Périgourdins, l'utilité des dimanches, et la vitesse du cheval du saint Bernard." *Bulletin de la Société Historique et Archéologique du Périgord* 115 (1988): 129–34.

Brenon, Anne. "La lettre d'Evervin de Steinfeld à Bernard de Clairvaux de 1143: un document essentiel et méconnu." *Heresis* 25: 7–28.

Evans, G. R. *The Mind of St. Bernard of Clairvaux.* Oxford: Clarendon Press, 1983.

Gilson, Etienne. *The Mystical Theology of Saint Bernard.* Trans. A. H. C. Downes. London: Sheed & Ward, 1940. Rpt. 1955.

————. *La Théologie mystique de saint Bernard.* Paris: J. Vrin, 1934.

Haring, Nikolaus M. "Saint Bernard and the *Litterati* of His Day." *Citeau, Commentari, Cistercienses* 3 (1974): 199–222.

Kienzle, Beverly M. *Cistercians, Heresy, and the Crusade in Occitania, 1145–1229: Preaching in the Lord's Vineyard.* Woodbridge, UK: York Medieval Press, 2001.

————. "Tending the Lord's Vineyard: Cistercians, Rhetoric, and Heresy. The 1143 Sermons and the 1145 Preaching Mission." *Heresis* 25: 29–61.

Leclercq, Jean. *Bernard of Clairvaux and the Cistercian Spirit.* Kalamazoo, MI: Cistercian Publications, 1976.

————. "L'Hérésie d'après les écrits de S. Bernard de Clairvaux." In W. Lourdaux and D. Verhelst, eds., *The Concept of Heresy in the Middle Ages, 11th–13th Centuries.* Proceedings of the International Conference, Louvain (May 13–16, 1973). The Hague: Martinus Nijhoff, 1976. Rpt. Leuven: University Press, 1976, pp. 12–26.

————. *Recueil d'études sur Saint Bernard et ses écrits.* 2 vols. Roma: Edizioni di Storia e Letteratura, 1961–65.

Manselli, Raoul. "Everino di Steinfeld e san Bernardo di Clairvaux." In *Studie sulle eresie del secolo XII.* 2nd ed. Roma: Istituto Palazzo Borremini, 1975, pp. 145–56.

———. "San Bernardo e la religiosità populare." *Studi su S. Bernardo di Chiaravalle nell'ottavo centenario della canonizzazione.* Roma: Editiones Cistercienses, 1975, pp. 245–60.

McGuire, Brian P. *The Difficult Saint: Bernard of Clairvaux and His Tradition.* Kalamazoo, MI: Cistercian Publications, 1991.

Murray. Alexander Victor. *Abelard and St. Bernard: A Study in Twelfth-Century "Modernism."* Manchester: Manchester University Press, 1967.

Sommerfeldt, John R. *Bernardus Magister.* Papers Presented at the Nonacentary Celebration of the Birth of Saint Bernard of Clairvaux. Sponsored by the Institute of Cistercian Studies, Western Michigan University (10–13 May, 1990). Kalamazoo, MI: Cistercian Publications, 1992.

THE ALBIGENSIAN CRUSADE

Medieval Texts

Guilhem de Tudela and Anonymous Continuator. *Chanson de la croisade albigeoise.* Ed. Eugène Martin-Chabot. Vol. 1. Paris: Honoré Champion, 1931. Vol. 2. Paris: Les Belles Lettres, 1957. Vol. 3. Paris: Les Belles Lettres, 1961.

———. *The Song of the Cathar Wars: A History of the Albigensian Crusade.* Trans. Janet Shirley. Aldershot, UK: Ashgate, 1996.

Peter of les Vaux-de-Cernay. *The History of the Albigensian Crusade.* Trans. W. A. Silby and M. A. Silby. Rochester, NY: Boydell Press, 1998.

Pierre des Vaux-de-Cernay. *Hystoria albigensis.* Ed. Pascal Guébin and Ernest Lyon. 3 vols. Paris: Honoré Champion,1926–39.

Modern Criticism

Bagley, C. P. "*Paratge* in the Anonymous *Chanson de la Croisade Albigeoise.*" *French Studies* 21 (1967): 195–204.

Camproux, Charles. *Histoire de la littérature occitane.* Paris: Payot, 1953.

Delaruelle, Etienne. "L'Idée de la croisade dans la *Chanson* de Guillaume de Tudèle." *Annales de l'Institut d'Etudes Occitanes* (1962–63): 49–63.

Dossat, Yves. "La Croisade vue par les chroniqueurs." *Cahiers de Fanjeaux.* Vol. 4. *Paix de Dieu et guerre sainte en Languedoc au XIIIe siècle.* Toulouse: Privat, 1969, pp. 221–59.

Griffe, Elie. *Le Languedoc cathare au temps de la Croisade (1209–1229).* Paris: Letouzy & Ané, 1973.

Hamilton, Bernard. *The Albigensian Crusade.* London: The Historical Association, 1974. Rpt. in *Monastic Reform, Catharism, and the Crusades (900–1300).* London: Variorum Reprints, 1979, pp. 1–40.

Heur, Jean-Marie d'. "Sur la date, la composition et la destination de la *Chanson de la Croisade albigeoise* de Guillaume de Tudèle." In *Mélanges d'histoire littéraire, de linguistique et de philologie romanes offerts à Charles Rostaing.* Liège: Association des romanistes de l'Université de Liège, 1974, pp. 235–66.

Lafont, Robert. "Composition et rythme épiques dans la seconde partie de la *Chanson de la Croisade Albigeoise.*" *Revue de langue et littérature provençales* 9 (1962): 42–56.

————. "Guilhem de Tudela: Ses origines, les origines de son art." *Les Troubadours et l'état toulousain avant la Croisade (1209)*. Ed. Arno Krispin. Actes du Colloque de Toulouse (9 et 10 décembre, 1988). Paris: CELO / William Blake & Co., 1994, pp. 219–28.

Lejeune, Rita. "L'Esprit de croisade dans l'épopée occitane." *Cahiers de Fanjeaux*. Vol. 4. *Paix de Dieu et guerre sainte en Languedoc au XIIIe siècle*. Toulouse: Privat, 1969, pp. 143–64.

Macé, Laurent. *Les Comtes de Toulouse et leur entourage, XIIe–XIIIe siècles. Rivalités, alliances et jeux de pouvoir*. Toulouse: Privat, 2000.

Nelli, Suzanne. "Esclarmonde de Foix." *Cahiers d'études cathares* 6, no. 24 (1955): 195–204.

Pach, Rémi. "Un Poème patriotique médiéval: La *Chanson de la Croisade albigeoise*." *French Studies in Southern Africa* 22 (1993): 1–19.

Paterson, Linda. "La *Chanson de la Croisade albigeoise*: Mythes chevaleresques et réalités militaires." In *La Croisade: Réalités et Fiction*. Ed. Danielle Buschinger. Actes du Colloque d'Amiens (18–22 mars 1987). Göppingen: Kümmerle Verlag, 1989, pp. 193–203.

————. *The World of the Troubadours: Medieval Occitan Society, c. 1100–1300*. Cambridge: Cambridge University Press, 1993.

Roquebert, Michel. *L'Epopée cathare*. 4 vols. Toulouse: Privat, 1970–89.

Sumption, Jonathan. *The Albigensian Crusade*. London: Faber & Faber, 1978.

Weil, Simone (alias Emile Novis). "L'Agonie d'une civilisation vue à travers un poème épique." In *Le Génie d'Oc et l'homme méditerranéen*. *Cahiers du Sud* 249 (1943): 99–107.

MONTAILLOU

Medieval Texts

L'Inquisiteur Geoffrey d'Ablis et les Cathares du comté de Foix (1308–1309). Ed. Annette Pales-Gobilliard. Paris: CNRS, 1984.

Le Registre d'Inquisition de Jacques Fournier, évêque de Pamiers (1318–1325). Manuscrit Vat. lat. n. 4030 de la Bibliothèque Vaticane. Ed. Jean Duvernoy. 3 vols. Toulouse: Edouard Privat, 1965.

Le Registre d'Inquisition de Jacques Fournier, évêque de Pamiers (1318–1325). Trans. Jean Duverony. 3 vols. La Haye: Mouton, 1978.

van Limborch, Philippus. *Historia inquisitionis cui subiungitur Liber Sententiarum inquisitionis Tholosanae ab anno Christi MCCCCVII ad annum MCCCXXIII*. Amsterdam: H. Wetstenium, 1692.

Modern Criticism

Benad, Matthias. *Domus und Religion in Montaillou: Katholische Kirche und Katharismus im Überlebenskampf der Familie des Pfarrers Petrus Clerici am Anfang des 14. Jahrhunderts*. Tübingen: Mohr, 1990.

Biget, Jean-Louis. "Les Cathares devant les inquisiteurs en Languedoc." *Revue du Tarn* 146 (1992): 227–41.

Bordenave, Jean, and Michel Vialelle. *La Mentalité religieuse des paysans de l'Albigeois médiéval.* Toulouse: Privat, 1973.

Boyle, Leonard E. "Montaillou Revisited: *Mentalité* and Methodology." In *Pathways to Medieval Peasants: Papers in Medieval Studies.* Ed. J. A. Raftis. Toronto: Pontifical Institute of Mediaeval Studies, 1981, vol. 2, pp. 119–40.

Brenon, Anne. "Le Catharisme des montagnes: A la recherche d'un Catharisme populaire." *Heresis* 9 (1988): 53–74.

Cazenave, Annie. "Déviations scriptuaires et mouvements sociaux: Le Languedoc médiéval." In *Crises et réformes dans l'église de la réforme grégorienne à la préréforme.* Actes du 115e Congrès National des Sociétés Savantes, Avignon (1990), Section d'Histoire Médiévale et de Philologie. Paris: Editions du CTHS, pp. 117–34.

———. "L'Entraide cathare et la chasse à l'hérétique en Languedoc au XIIIe siècle." In *Pays de Langue d'Oc: Histoire et Dialectologie.* Actes du 96e Congrès National des Sociétés Savantes, Toulouse (1971), Section de Philologie et d'Histoire jusqu'à 1610, vol. 2. Paris: Bibliothèque Nationale, 1978, pp. 97–125.

Dondaine, Antoine. "Le Registre de J. Fournier, à propos d'une édition récente." *Revue de l'Histoire des Religions* 178 (octobre 1970): 49–56.

Davis, Natalie Zemon. "Les Conteurs de Montaillou." *Annales* 34, no. 1. (janvier–février 1979): 61–73.

Dossat, Yves. "Les Cathares d'après les documents de l'inquisition." In *Cahiers de Fanjeaux.* Vol. 3. *Cathares en Languedoc.* Toulouse: Privat, 1968, pp. 71–104.

———. *Les Crises de l'inquisition toulousaine (1233–1273).* Bordeaux: Bière, 1959.

———. "La crise de l'inquisition toulousaine de 1235 à 1236." *Revue d'histoire de l'Eglise de France* 37 (1951): 188–191.

———. "La crise de l'inquisition toulousaine en 1235–1236 et l'expulsion des dominicains." *Bulletin philologique et historique du Comité des traveaux historiques et scientifiques* (1953–54): 391–98.

Duvernoy, Jean. "Le Catharisme en Languedoc au début du XIVe siècle." In *Cahiers de Fanjeaux.* Vol. 20. *Effacement du Catharisme? (XIIIe–XIVe siècles).* Toulouse: Privat, 1986, pp. 37–56.

———. "La noblesse du comté de Foix au début du XIVe siècle." In *Pays de l'Ariège: Archéologie, histoire, géographie.* Actes du XVIe Congrès d'Etudes de la Fédération des sociétés académiques et savantes de Languedoc, Pyrénées, Gascogne, Foix (28–30 mai 1960). Montpellier: Fédération des sociétés académiques et savantes de Languedoc-Pyrénées-Gascogne, 1961.

———. "Pierre Autier." *Cahiers d'Etudes Cathares* 21, no. 47 (automne 1970): 9–49.

Given, James. B. *Inquisition and Medieval Society: Power, Discipline, and Resistance in Languedoc.* Ithaca: Cornell University Press, 1997.

Le Roy Ladurie, Emmanuel. *Montaillou: The Promised Land of Error.* Trans. and abr. Barbara Bray. New York: George Braziller, 1978. Rpt. New York: Vintage Books, 1979.

————. *Montaillou, village occitan de 1294 à 1324*. Paris: Editions Gallimard, 1975. Rev. ed., 1982.

Pales-Gobillard, Annette. "Le Catharisme dans le comté de Foix des origines au début du XIVe siècle." *Revue de l'Histoire des Religions* 189 (1976): 181–200.

Paul, Jacques. "Jacques Fournier, inquisiteur." *Cahiers de Fanjeaux*. Vol. 26. *La Papauté d'Avignon et le Languedoc, 1316–1342*. Toulouse: Privat, 1991, pp. 39–67.

Rosaldo, Renato. "From the Door of His Tent: The Fieldworker and the Inquisitor." In James Clifford and George E. Marcus, eds., *Writing Culture: The Poetics and Politics of Ethnography*. Berkeley: University of California Press, 1986, pp. 77–97

Vidal, J. M. "Les derniers ministres de l'albigéisme en Languedoc: Leurs doctrines." *Revue des questions historiques* 79 (1906): 55–107.

————. *Le Tribunal d'Inquisition de Pamiers*. Toulouse: Privat, 1905.

WALDENSIANS

Bibliography

Armand-Hugon, A. and Giovanni Gonnet. "Bibliografia valdese." *Bollettino della Società di Studi Valdesi* 93 (1953).

Medieval Texts

Alain de Lille. *De fide catholica contra haereticos sui temporis*. PL. Vol. 210, cols. 305–430. "Alan of Lille: A Scholar's Attack on Heretics." In Wakefield and Evans, pp. 214–20.

Anonymous of Laon. *Chronicon universale anonymi Laudunensis*. Ed. Georg Waits. MGH. Vol. 26, pp. 447 and 449. "The Origins of the Waldensian Heresy." In Wakefield and Evans, pp. 200–202. "The Waldensians at the Third Lateran Council: A Report in the Chronicle of Laon." In ibid., p. 203.

Bernard de Fontecaude. *Adversus Waldensium sectam liber*. PL. Vol. 204, cols. 793–840. "A Debate between Catholics and Waldensians." In Wakefield and Evans, pp. 210–13.

Bernard Gui. *Manuel de l'inquisiteur*. Ed. and trans. Guillaume Mollat. 2 vols. Paris: Champion, 1926–27. "Bernard Gui's Description of Heresies." In Wakefield and Evans, pp. 373–445.

————. *Practica inquisitionis heretice pravitatis*. Ed. Célestin Douais. Paris: Picard, 1886.

Burchard von Ursberg. *Die Chronik des Propstes Burchard von Ursberg*. Ed. Oswald Holder-Egger and Bernard von Simpson. Hannover und Leipzig: Hahnsche Buchhandlung, 1916. "A Reconciliation of a Group of Waldenses to the Church: Waldenses, Humiliati, and Friars Minor." In Wakefield and Evans, pp. 228–30. "Burchard of Ursperg: On the New Orders." In Peters, pp. 178–80.

Caesarius of Heisterbach. *The Dialogue on Miracles*. Trans. Henry von Essen Scott and C. C. Swinton Bland. London: George Routledge & Sons, 1929.

————. *Dialogus miraculorum*. Ed. Joseph Strange. 2 vols. Cologne: J. M. Heberle, 1851.

Chronicon universale anonymi Laudunensis. MGH, *Scriptores.* Vol. 26, pp. 447, 449. "The Origins of the Waldensian Heresy." In Wakefield and Evans, pp. 200–202.

David von Augsberg. *De inquisitione hereticorum.* Ed. Wilhelm Preger. "Der Tractat des David von Augsberg über die Waldesier." *Abhandlungen der historischen Classe der königlich bayerischen Akademie der Wissenschaften* 13, no. 2 (1878): 204–35. A short section translated as "David of Augsberg: On the Waldensians of Bavaria, 1270." In Peters, pp. 149–50.

Enchiridion Fontium Valdensium: Recueil critique des sources concernant les Vaudois au Moyen Age. Du IIIe Concile de Latran au Synode de Chanforan (1179–1532). Ed. Giovanni Gonnet. Vol. 1. *1179–1218.* (Only vol. 1 has been published). Torre Pellice: Claudiana, 1958.

Etienne de Bourbon. "Stephane de Borbone tractatus de diversis materiis praedicabilis." In *Anecdotes historiques, légendes et apologues tirés du recueil inédit d'Etienne de Bourbon, dominicain du XIIIe siècle.* Ed. Albert Lecoy de la Marche. Paris: H. Laurens, 1887, pp. 290–99. "Stephen of Bourbon on the Early Waldenses." In Wakefield and Evans, pp. 208–10. "Waldenses in the Thirteenth Century." In ibid., pp. 346–51.

Legendre, Olivier, and Michel Rubellin. "Valdès: Un 'exemple' à Clairvaux? Le plus ancien texte sur les débuts du Pauvre de Lyon." *Revue Mabillon* n.s., t. 11 (=t. 72) (2000): 187–95.

Nicolau Eimeric. *Directorium inquisitorum.* Roma: Apud Georgium Ferrarium, 1587.

Nicolau Eymerich and Francisco Peña. *Le Manuel des Inquisiteurs.* Trans. Louis Sala-Molin. La Haye: Mouton, 1973.

Passau Anonymous. *Quellen zur Geschichte der Waldenser.* Ed. Alexander Patschovsky and Kurt-Victor Selge. Gütersloh: Gerd Mohn, 1973, pp. 70–103. "The Passau Anonymous: On the Origins of Heresy and the Sect of the Waldensians." In Peters, pp. 150–63.

Walter Map. *De nugis curialium / Courtiers' Trifles.* Ed. and trans. M. R. James. Rev. C. N. L. Brooke and R. A. B. Mynors. Oxford: Clarendon Press, 1983.

Modern Criticism

Audisio, Gabriel. *The Waldensian Dissent: Persecution and Survival, c. 1170–c. 1570.* Trans. Claire Davison. Cambridge: Cambridge University Press, 1999.

———. "Were the Waldensians More Literate Than Their Contemporaries?" In Peter Biller and Anne Hudson, eds., *Heresy and Literacy, 1000–1530.* Cambridge: Cambridge University Press, 1994, pp. 176–85.

Biller, Peter. "Fingerprinting an Anonymous Description of the Waldensians." In Caterina Bruschi and Peter Biller, eds. *Texts and the Repression of Medieval Heresy.* Woodbridge, Suffolk, UK: York Medieval Press, 2003, pp. 163–93.

———. *The Waldenses, 1170–1530: Between a Religious Order and a Church.* Aldershot, UK: Ashgate Publishing, 2001.

Brenon, Anne. "The Waldensian Books," In Peter Biller and Anne Hudson, eds. *Heresy and Literacy, 1000–1530*. Cambridge: Cambridge University Press, 1994, pp. 137–59.

Cameron, Euan. *Waldenses: Rejections of Holy Church in Medieval Europe*. Oxford: Blackwell, 2000.

Clanchy, M. T. *From Memory to Written Record: England, 1066–1307*. 2nd ed. Oxford: Oxford University Press, 1993.

Deanesly, Margaret. *The Lollard Bible and Other Medieval Biblical Versions*. Cambridge: Cambridge University Press, 1920; rpt. 1966.

Delaruelle, Etienne. "Le Problème de la pauvreté vu par les théologiens et les canonistes de la deuxième moitié du XIIe siècle." *Cahiers de Fanjeaux*. Vol. 2. *Vaudois languedociens et Pauvres Catholiques*. Toulouse: Privat, 1967, pp. 48–63.

Duvernoy, Jean. "Les origines du mouvement vaudois." *Heresis* 13–14 (1989): 173–98.

———. "La Prédication des vaudois en Languedoc aux XIIIe et XIVe siècles, d'après les registres d'Inquisition." *Heresis* 30 (n.d.): 123–35.

Gonnet, Jean. "La figure et l'oeuvre de Vaudès dans la tradition historique et selon les dernières recherches." *Cahiers de Fanjeaux*. Vol. 2. *Vaudois languedociens et Pauvres Catholiques*. Toulouse: Privat, 1967, pp. 87–109.

———. "I primi valdesi erano veramente eretici." *Bollettino della Società di Studi Valdesi* 123 (1968): 7–17.

———. "La Prédication vaudoise à ses origines." *Heresis* 30: *La Prédication sur un mode dissident: Laïcs, femmes, hérétiques... (XIe–XIVe)*. Ed. Beverly M. Kienzle. Actes du 9e colloque du Centre d'Etudes Cathares / René Nelli. Couzia (26–30 août 1996). Carcassonne: Centre d'Etudes Cathares, 1999, pp. 93–121.

Gonnet, Jean, and Amedeo Molnar. *Les Vaudois au Moyen Age*. Torino: Claudiana, 1974.

Legendre, Olivier. "L'Hérésie vue de Clairvaux: Témoinage inédit d'un recueil cistercien d'*exempla* sur les movements hérétiques de la fin du XIIe siècle." *Heresis* 33 (décembre 2000): 69–78.

Little, Lester. *Religious Poverty and the Profit Economy in Medieval Europe*. Ithaca: Cornell University Press, 1970.

Maitland. S. R., ed. *Facts and Documents Illustrative of the History, Doctrine, and Rites of the Ancient Albigenses and Waldenses*. London: C. J. C. and F. Rivington, 1832.

Manteuffel, Tadeusz. *Naissance d'une hérésie: Les adeptes de la pauvreté volontaire au Moyen Age*. La Haye: Mouton, 1963.

Marthaler, Berard. "Forerunners of the Franciscans: The Waldenses." *Franciscan Studies* n.s. 18 (1958): 133–42.

Merlo, Grado G. *Identità valdesi nella storia e nella storigrafica*. Torino: Claudiana, 1991.

———. *Valdesi e Valdismi medievali*. Torino: Claudiana, 1984.

Molnar, Amedeo. *Storia dei Valdesi*. Vol. 1. *Dalle origine all'adesione alla Riforma (1176–1532)*. Torino: Claudiana, 1974.

Patschovsky, Alexander. "The Literacy of Waldensians from Valdes to c. 1400." In Peter Biller and Anne Hudson, eds. *Heresy and Literacy, 1000–1530.* Cambridge: Cambridge University Press, 1994, pp. 112–36.

Rubellin, Michel. "Au temps où Valdès n'était pas hérétique: Hypothèses sur le rôle de Valdès à Lyon (1170–1183)." In Monique Zerner, ed. *Inventer l'hérésie? Discours polémiques et pouvoirs avant l'Inquisition.* Nice: Z'éditions, 1998, pp. 193–217.

Selge, Kurt-Victor. "Caractéristiques du premier mouvement vaudois et crises au cours de son expansion." *Cahiers de Fanjeaux.* Vol. 2. *Vaudois languedociens et Pauvres Catholiques.* Toulouse: Privat, 1967, pp. 110–42.

———. *Die ersten Waldenser, mit Edition des "Liber Antiheresis" des Durandus von Osca.* 2 vols. Berlin: De Gruyter, 1967.

———. "La figura e l'opera di Valdez." *Bollettino della Società di Studi Valdesi* 136 (1974): 3–25.

Thouzellier, Christine. *Catharisme et valdéisme en Languedoc à la fin du XIIe et au début du XIIIe siècle: Politique pontificale—Controverses.* Paris: Presses Universitaires de France, 1969.

———. *Hérésie et hérétiques: Vaudois, Cathares, Patarins, Albigeois.* Roma: Edizioni di storia e letteratura, 1969.

Verdat, M. "Nouvelles recherches sur l'origine et la vie lyonnaise de Valdo." *Bollettino della Società di Studi Valdesi* 125 (1969): 3–11.

THE LIFE OF SAINT ALEXIS

Medieval Texts

La Vie de Saint Alexis. Ed. Christopher Story. Genève: Droz, 1968.

The *"Vie de Saint Alexis" in the Twelfth and Thirteenth Centuries: An Edition and Commentary.* Ed. Alison Goddard Elliott. Chapel Hill: University of North Carolina Department of Romance Languages, 1983.

Modern Criticism

Cazalles, Brigitte. "Saints' Lives." In *A New History of French Literature.* Ed. Denis Hollier. Cambridge, MA: Harvard University Press, 1989, pp. 13–18.

Elliot, Alison Goddard. "The *Triumphus Sancti Remacli*: Latin Evidence for Oral Composition." *Romance Philology* 22, no. 3 (February 1979): 292–98.

Gievsztor, Alexander. "*Pauper sum et peregrinus*: La Légende de saint Alexis en occident. Un idéal de pauvreté." In *Etudes sur l'histoire de la pauvreté (Moyen Age–XVIe siècle).* Ed. Michel Mollat. Paris: Publications de la Sorbonne, 1974, vol. 1, pp. 126–39.

Leupin, Alexandre. "Naming God: *La Vie de Saint Alexis.*" In *Barbarolexis: Medieval Writing and Sexuality.* Trans. Kate M. Cooper. Cambridge, MA: Harvard University Press, 1989, pp. 39–58 and 242–44.

Mölk, Ulrich. "La *Chanson de Saint Alexis* et le culte du saint en France aux XIe et XIIe siècles." *Cahiers de civilisation médiévale* 21 (janvier–mars 1978): 339–55.

Vitz, Evelyn Birge. "*La Vie de Saint Alexis*: Narrative Analysis and the Quest for the Sacred Subject." In *Medieval Narrative and Modern Narratology: Subjects and Objects of Desire*. New York: New York University Press, 1989, pp. 126–48.

TROUBADOURS

Medieval Texts

Biographies des Troubadours: Textes provençaux des XIIIe et XIVe siècles. Ed. Jean Boutière, Alexander Herman Schutz, and Irénée Marcel Cluzel. Paris: A.-G. Nizet, 1964. Rpt. New York: Burt Franklin, 1972.

Giraut de Bornelh. *The "Cansos" and "Sirventes" of the Troubadour Giraut de Borneil: A Critical Edition*. Ed. and trans. Ruth Verity Sharman. Cambridge: Cambridge University Press, 1989.

Guilhem de Montanhagol. *Les Poésies de Guilhem de Montanhagol, troubadour provençal du XIIIe siècle*. Ed. and trans. Peter T. Ricketts. Toronto: Pontifical Institute of Mediaeval Studies, 1984.

Guilhem de Poitiers. *The Poetry of William VI, Count of Poitiers, IX Duke of Aquitaine*. Ed. and trans. Gerald A. Bond. New York: Garland Publishing Co., 1982.

Peire Cardinal. *Poésies complètes du troubadour Peire Cardenal (1180–1278)*. Ed. René Lavaud. Toulouse: Edouard Privat, 1957.

Peire d'Alvernha. *Liriche*. Ed. Alberto del Monte. Torino: Loescher-Chiantore, 1955.

Raimbaut d'Auregna. *The Life and Works of the Troubadour Raimbaut d'Orange*. Ed. Walter T. Pattison. Minneapolis: University of Minnesota Press, 1952. Rpt. New York: AMS, 1983.

The Vidas of the Troubadours. Trans. Margarita Egan. New York: Garland Publishing Co., 1980.

Modern Criticism

Aroux, Eugène. *Dante hérétique, socialiste et révolutionnaire: Révélation d'un catholique sur le Moyen Age*. Paris: Renouard, 1854.

———. *L'Hérésie de Dante, démontrée par Francesca de Rimini, devenue un moyen de propagande vaudoise, et coup-d'oeil sur les romans de St.-Graal*. Paris: Renouard, 1857.

Belperron, Pierre. *La Croisade contre les Albigeois et l'union du Languedoc à la France (1209–1249)*. Paris: Plon, 1942.

Bernardac, Christian. *Montségur et le Graal: Le Mystère Otto Rhan [sic]*. Paris: Editions France-Empire, 1994.

Blum, Jean. *Les Cathares: du Graal au secret de la mort joyeuse*. Monaco: Editions du Rocher, 1991.

Breillat, Pierre. "Le Graal et les Albigeois." *Revue du Tarn* n.s. 10 (1944): 458–70, and 11 (1945): 99–109.

Davenson, Henri (Henri I. Marrou). "Autour de *L'Amour et l'Occident*." *Esprit* 7, no. 84 (1 sept. 1939): 765–68.

————. "Denis de Rougemont: *L'Amour et l'Occident.*" *Esprit* 7, no. 79 (1 avril 1939): 70–77.

————. *Les Troubadours.* Paris: Editions du Seuil, 1961.

Del Monte, Alberto. *Studie sulla poesia ermetica medievale.* Napoli: Giannini, 1953.

Diez, Frédéric [Friedrich]. *La Poésie des troubadours.* Trans. Ferdinand de Roisin. Paris: J. Labitte, 1845.

Duggan, Joseph H. "Ambiguity in Twelfth-Century French and Provençal Literature: A Problem or a Value?" In *Jean Misrahi Memorial Volume.* Ed. Hans R. Runte et al. Columbia, SC: French Literature Publications Co., 1977, pp. 136–49.

Fauriel, C. C. *Histoire de la poésie provençale.* 3 vols. Paris: B. Duprat, 1846.

Ferrante, Joan M. "Ab joi mou lo vers e·l comens." In W. J. J. Jackson, ed., *The Interpretation of Medieval Lyric Poets.* New York: Columbia University Press, 1980, pp. 93–128.

Gandillac, Maurice, et al. "Débat autour du catharisme et de l'amour courtois." *Entretiens sur la Renaissance du 12e siècle.* Cerisy-la-Salle (21–30 juillet 1965). Ed. Maurice de Gandillac and Edouard Jeauneau. La Haye: Mouton, 1968, pp. 437–48.

Garreau, Joseph. "Hérésie et politique chez Guilhem Figueria et Peire Cardinal." *Kentucky Romance Quarterly* 31, no. 3 (1984): 243–49.

Gaunt, Simon. *Troubadours and Irony.* Cambridge: University of Cambridge Press, 1989.

Jeanroy, Alfred. *La Poésie lyrique des troubadours.* Toulouse: Edouard Privat, 1934.

Kendrick, Laura. *The Game of Love: Troubadour Word Play.* Berkeley: University of California Press, 1988.

Lazar, Moshé. *Amour courtois et "fin'amors."* Paris: C. Klincksieck, 1964.

Mölk, Ulrich. *Trobar clus, trobar leu: Studien zur Dichtungstheorie der Trobadors.* München: Wilhelm Fink Verlag, 1968.

Nelli, René. *L'Erotique des troubadours.* Toulouse: Privat, 1963.

————. "Du Catharisme à l'amour provençal (d'après M. Briffault)." *Revue de synthèse* 64 (1948): 31–38.

————. "Le Catharisme vu à travers les troubadours." *Cahiers de Fanjeaux.* Vol. 3, *Cathares en Languedoc.* Toulouse: Privat, 1968, pp. 177–97.

————. "Le folklore de Montségur vu par Otto Rahn." *Folklore* (Carcassonne) 26, no. 1 (1973): 14–17.

Paden, William D. "*Utrum Copularentur:* Of Cors." *L'Esprit Créateur* 19 (1979): 70–83.

Paterson, Linda M. *Troubadours and Eloquence.* Oxford: Clarendon Press, 1975.

Péladan, Joséphin. *Le Secret des troubadours: De Parsifal à Don Quichotte.* Caen: Ker-Ys, 1906.

Peyrat, Napoléon. *Histoire des Albigeois.* 5 vols. Paris: Librairie Internationale, 1870–72.

Rahn, Otto. *Kreuzzug gegen den Gral: Die Tragödie des Katharismus.* Freiburg-im-Breisgau: Urban Verlag, 1933.

Roncaglia, Aurelio. "Trobar clus—discussion aperta." *Cultura neolatina* 29 (1969): 5–53.

Roquebert, Michel. *Les Cathares et le Graal*. Toulouse: Privat, 1994.

Rougemont, Denis de. *L'Amour et l'occident*. Paris: Librairie Plon, 1939.

———. *Love in the Western World*. Trans. Montgomery Belgion. New York: Harcourt Brace and Co., 1940; rpt. New York: Schocken Books, 1983.

Salverda de Grave, J. J. "Giraut de Borneil et la poésie obscure." In *Mélanges de linguistique et de philologie offerts à Jacq. van Ginneken*. Paris: C. Klincksieck, 1937, pp. 297–306.

Thouzellier, Christine. "Le Phénomène cathare et l'amour courtois." *Annales* (1964): 128–41.

Varga, Lucia. "Peire Cardinal était-il hérétique?" *Revue d'Histoire des Religions* 117 (juin 1938): 205–31.

van Vleck, Amelia. *Memory and Re-Creation in Troubadour Lyric*. Berkeley: University of California, 1991.

TRISTAN AND ISEUT

Bibliography

Shirt, David J. *The Old French Tristan Poems: A Bibliographical Guide*. London: Grant & Cutler, 1980.

Medieval Texts

Andreas Capellanus on Love. Ed. and trans. P. G. Walsh. London: Duckworth, 1982.

Bernart de Ventadorn. *The Songs of Bernart de Ventadorn*. Ed. Stephen G. Nichols Jr. Chapel Hill: University of North Carolina Press, 1965.

Béroul. *Le Roman de Tristan, poème du XIIe siècle*. Ed. Ernest Muret. Rev. ed. L. M. Defourques. 4th ed. Paris: Librairie Honoré Champion, 1982.

———. *The Romance of Tristran*. Ed. and trans. Norris J. Lacy. New York: Garland Publishing Co., 1989.

———. *The Romance of Tristran: A Poem of the Twelfth Century*. Ed. Alfred Ewert. 2 vols. Oxford: Blackwell, 1939; rpt. 1970–72.

Modern Criticism

Blakey, B. "Truth and Falsehood in the *Tristran* of Béroul." In *History and Structure of French: Essays in Honor of Professor T. B. W. Reid*. Oxford: Blackwell, 1972, pp. 19–20.

Bloch, R. Howard. "Tristan, the Myth of the State, and the Language of the Self." *Yale French Studies* 51 (1974): 61–81.

Blomme, Robert. *La doctrine du péché dans les écoles théologiques de la première moitié du XIIe siècle*. Louvain: Publications universitaires de Louvain, 1958.

Boase, Roger. *The Origin and Meaning of Courtly Love: A Critical Study of European Scholarship*. Manchester: Manchester University Press, 1977.

Burns, E. Jane. "How Lovers Lie Together: Infidelity and Fictive Discourse in the *Roman de Tristan*." *Tristania* 8, no. 2 (Spring 1983): 15–30. Rpt. in Burns, *Bodytalk: When Women Speak Out in Old French Literature*. Philadelphia:

University of Pennsylvania Press, 1993, pp. 203–50. Also rpt. in *Tristan and Isolde: A Casebook,* ed. Joan Tasker Grimbert. New York: Garland Publishing, 1995, pp. 75–93.

Caulkins, Janet Hillier. "The Meaning of *Pechié* in the *Romance of Tristan* by Béroul." *Romance Notes* 8 (1971–72): 545–49.

Cazenave, Michel. *Le Philtre et l'amour: La Légende de Tristan et Iseut.* Paris: J. Corti, 1969.

Denomy, Alexander. *The Heresy of Courtly Love.* Gloucester, MA: Peter Smith, 1965.

Dubuis, Roger. "*Dru* et *druerie* dans le *Tristran* de Béroul." In *Mélanges de Langue et de littérature françaises du Moyen Age offerts à Pierre Jonin.* Aix-en-Provence: Publications de CUERMA, 1979, pp. 221–31.

Dussol, Etienne. "A Propos du *Tristan* de Béroul: Du Mensonge des hommes au silence de dieu." In *Et c'est la fin pour quoy sommes ensemble: Hommage à Jean Dufournet. Littérature, histoire, langue du Moyen Age.* Ed. Jean-Claude Aubailly et al. 3 vols. Paris: Honoré Champion, 1993, pp. 525–33.

Ferrante, Joan M. "The Conflict of Lyric Conventions and Romance Form." In *In Pursuit of Perfection: Courtly Love in Medieval Literature.* Ed. Joan M. Ferrante and George D. Economou. Port Washington, NY: Kennikat Press, 1975, pp. 135–77.

Frappier, Jean. *Amour courtois et table ronde.* Genève: Droz, 1973.

———. "Structure et sens du *Tristan*: Version commune, version courtoise." *Cahiers de civilisation médiévale* 6 (1963): 255–80, 441–54.

Grimbert, Joan Tasker, ed. *Tristan and Isolde: A Casebook.* New York: Garland Publications, 1995.

Huchet, Jean-Charles. *Tristan et le sang de l'écriture.* Paris: Presses Universitaires de France, 1990.

Jonin, Pierre. "L'Esprit celtique dans le roman de Béroul." In *Mélanges de langue et de littérature médiévales offerts à Pierre le Gentil.* Paris: Société d'Edition de l'Enseignement Supérieur et Centre de Documentation Universitaire Réunies, 1973, pp. 409–20.

———. *Les Personnages féminins dans les romans français de Tristan au XIIe siècle: Etudes des influences contemporains.* Gap: Editions Ophrys, 1958.

———. "La ruse d'Yseut dans le *Tristan* de Béroul." In *Hommage au doyen Etienne Gros.* Faculté des lettres et sciences humaines d'Aix. Gap: Ophrys, 1959, pp. 77–84.

Kelly, Douglas. "La Vérité tristanienne: Quelques points de repère dans les romans." In *Tristan et Iseut, Mythe européen et mondial.* Ed. Danielle Buschinger. Actes du Colloque (10, 11 et 12 janvier, 1986), Université de Picardie. Göppingen: Kümmerle Verlag, 1987, pp. 168–81.

Lacy, Norris J. "Deception and Distance in Béroul's *Tristan*: A Reconsideration." *Journal of the Rocky Mountain Medieval and Renaissance Association* 6 (January 1985): 33–39.

———. "Irony and Distance in Béroul's *Tristan*." *French Review* 45, no. 3 (1971): 21–29.

Lazar, Moshé. *Amour courtois et 'fin'amors' dans la littérature du XIIe siècle.* Paris: C. Klincksieck, 1964.

La Légende de Tristan au Moyen Age. Actes du Colloque (16 et 17 janvier 1982), Université de Picardie. Göppingen: Kummerle Verlag, 1982.

Larmat, Jean. "La Religion et les passions dans le *Tristan* de Béroul." In *Mélanges de philologie et de littératures romanes offerts à Jeanne Wathelet-Willem.* Ed. Jacques de Caluwe. Liège: Cahiers de l'ARU, 1978, p. 344.

Lejeune, Rita. "Les 'influences contemporaines' dans les romans français de Tristan au XIIe siècle." *Le Moyen Age* 66 (1960): 143–62.

Loomis, Gertrude Schoepperle. *Tristan and Isolt: A Study of the Sources of the Romance.* Frankfurt: J. Baer, 1913. Rev. ed., New York: Franklin, 1970.

Newman, F. X., ed. *The Meaning of Courtly Love.* Albany: SUNY Press, 1968.

Newstead, Helaine. "The Equivocal Oath in the Tristan Legend." In *Mélanges Offerts à Rita Lejeune.* Gembloux: J. Duculot, 1969, vol. 2, pp. 177–85.

———. "The Tryst beneath the Tree: An Episode in the Tristan Legend." *Romance Philology* 9 (1955): 269–84.

Nichols, Stephen G., Jr. "Ethical Criticism and Medieval Literature: The *Roman de Tristan.*" In William Matthews, ed. *Medieval Secular Literature: Four Essays.* Berkeley: University of California Press, 1965, p. 68–89.

Ollier, Marie-Louise. "Le Péché selon Yseut dans le *Tristan* de Béroul." In *Courtly Literature: Culture and Context.* Ed. Keith Busby and Erick Kooper. Selected Papers from the Fifth Triennial Congress of the International Courtly Literature Society, Dalfsen, Netherlands (9–16 August, 1986). Amsterdam: John Benjamins Publishing Co., 1990, pp. 485–82.

———. "Le Statut de la Vérité et du mensonge dans le *Tristan* de Béroul." In *Tristan et Iseut: Mythe européen et mondial.* Ed. Danielle Buschinger. Actes du Colloque (10, 11 et 12 janvier, 1986), Université de Picardie. Göppingen: Kümmerle Verlag, 1987, pp. 298–318.

Payen, Jean-Charles. *Le Motif du repentir dans la littérature française médiévale (des origines à 1230).* Genève: Droz, 1967.

———. "Irréalisme et credibilité dans le *Tristan* de Béroul." In *Mélanges de philologie et de littératures romans offerts à Jeanne Wathelet-Willem.* Ed. Jacques de Caluwe. Liège: Cahiers de l'ARU, 1978, pp. 465–75.

———. "Lancelot contre Tristan: La Conjuration d'un mythe subversif (réflexions sur l'idéologie romanesque au Moyen Age)." In *Mélanges de langue et de littérature médiévales offerts à Pierre le Gentil.* Paris: SEDES et CDU Réunis, 1973, pp. 617–32.

———. "Ordre moral et subversion politique dans le *Tristan* de Béroul." In *Mélanges de Littérature du Moyen Age au XXe siècle offerts à Mademoiselle Jeanne Lods.* 2 vols. Paris: Collection de l'Ecole Normale Supérieure de Jeunes Filles, 1978, pp. 473–84.

———. "La Pensée d'Abélard et les textes romans du XIIe siècle." In *Pierre Abélard, Pierre le Vénérable: Les Courants philosophiques, littéraires et artistiques en occident au milieu du XIIe siècle.* Abbaye de Cluny (2 au 9 juillet 1972). Paris: CNRS, 1975, pp. 513–21.

Poirion, Daniel. "Le *Tristan* de Béroul: Récit, légende et mythe." *L'Information littéraire* 26 (1974): 199–207.

Regalado, Nancy Freeman. "Tristan and Renart: Two 'Tricksters.'" *L'Esprit Créateur* 16 (1976): 30–58.

Ribard, Jacques. "Le *Tristan* de Béroul: Un monde d'illusion." *Bulletin bibliographique de la Société internationale arthurienne* 31 (1979): 229–44.

———. "Tristan/Renart revisité." In *Studies in Honor of Hans-Erick Keller: Medieval French and Occitan Literature and Romance Linguistics.* Kalamazoo, MI: Medieval Institute Publications, 1993.

Russell, Jeffrey B. "Courtly Love as Religious Dissent." *Catholic Historical Review* 60 (April 1965–January 1966): 31–44.

Sargent-Baur, Barbara Nelson. "Between Fabliau and Romance: Love and Rivalry in Béroul's *Tristran.*" *Romania* 105 (1984): 292–311.

———. "La Dimension morale dans le *Roman de Tristran* de Béroul." *Cahiers de civilisation médiévale* 31, no. 1 (1988): 44–56.

———. "Truth, Half Truth, Untruth: Beroul's Telling of the Tristan Story." In *Craft of Fiction: Essays in Medieval Poetics.* Ed. Leigh A. Arrathoon. Rochester, MI: Solaris, 1984, pp. 394–421.

Sticca, Sandro. "Christian Ethics and Courtly Doctrine in Béroul's *Tristan et Iseut.*" *Classica et Mediaevalia* 29 (1968): 223–48.

Stone, Donald. "Realism and the Real Béroul." *L'Esprit Créateur* 5, no. 4 (Winter, 1965): 227.

Subrenat, Jean. "Sur le Climat social, moral, religieux du *Tristan* de Béroul." *Le Moyen Age* 82 (1976): 219–61.

Thompson, James Westfall. "Catharist Social Ideas in Medieval French Romance." *Romanic Review* 27, no. 2 (April–June 1936): 99–104.

Vàrvaro, Alberto. *Béroul's "Romance of Tristran."* Trans. John C. Barnes. Manchester: Manchester University Press, 1972.

Vinaver, Eugène. "La forêt de Morois." *Cahiers de civilisation médiévale* 1 (1968): 6.

COMIC TALES

Medieval Texts

Le Nouveau Recueil complet des fabliaux. Ed. Nico van den Boogaard and Willem Noomem. 10 vols. Assen: Van Gorcum, 1983–84.

Guillaume de Lorris and Jean de Meun. *Le Roman de la Rose.* Ed. Daniel Poirion. Paris: Garnier Flammarion, 1974.

Recueil général et complet des fabliaux des XIIIe et XIVe siècles. Ed. Anatole de Montaiglon and Gaston Raynaud. 6 vols. Paris: Librairie des Bibliophiles, 1872–90. Rpt. New York: Burt Franklin, n.d.

Rutebeuf. *Oeuvres complètes de Rutebeuf.* Ed. Edmond Faral and Julia Bastion. 2 vols. Paris: A. et J. Picard, 1959.

Modern Criticism

Bancourt, Paul. "Vol puni, vol impuni dans les fabliaux: Contribution à l'étude des rapports de la littérature et de la société au XIIIe siècle." In *La Justice au Moyen Age: Sanction ou impunité?* Aix-en-Provence: CUERMA, 1986, pp. 25–41.

Bédier, Joseph. *Les Fabliaux: Etudes de littérature populaire et d'histoire littéraire du Moyen Age.* Paris: Champion, 1893. Rpt. 1964.

Bloch, R. Howard. *The Scandal of the Fabliaux.* Chicago: University of Chicago Press, 1986.

Brusegan, Rosanna. "Les Fonctions de la ruse dans les fabliaux." *Strumenti critici: Rivista Quadrimestrale di Cultura e Critica Letteraria* 16 (giugno 1982): 47–48, 148–60.

———. "La Naïveté comique dans les fabliaux à seduction." In *Comique, satire et parodie dans la tradition renardienne et les fabliaux.* Ed. Danielle Buschinger and André Crépin. Actes du Colloque, Université de Picardie (15 et 16 janvier 1983). Göppingen: Kummerle, 1983, pp. 19–30.

———. "Le Personnage comme paradigme de traits dans les fabliaux." In *Epopée animale, fable, fabliau.* Ed. Gabriel Biancotto and Michel Salvat. Actes du IVe Colloque de la Société Internationale Renardienne, Evreux (7–11 septembre 1981). Paris: Presses Universitaires de France, 1984, pp. 157–67.

Cooke, Thomas D., and Benjamin L. Honeycutt, eds. *The Humor of the Fabliaux: A Collection of Critical Essays.* Columbia: University of Missouri Press, 1974.

Eichmann, Raymond. "The 'Her(m)ites' of the 'Boucher d'Abeville.'" *South Central Review* 2, no. 4 (Winter 1985): 1–8.

Lacy, Norris J. "The Fabliaux and Comic Logic." *L'Esprit Créateur* 16, no. 1 (1976): 39–45.

———. "Types of Esthetic Distance in the Fabliaux." In *The Humor of the Fabliaux: A Collection of Critical Essays.* Ed. Thomas D. Cooke and Benjamin L. Honeycutt. Columbia: University of Missouri Press, 1974, pp. 107–17.

Levy, Brian J. "Le Fabliau et l'exemple: Etude sur les recueils moralisants anglo-normands." In *Epopée animale, fable, fabliau.* Ed. Gabriel Biancotto and Michel Salvat. Actes du IVe colloque de la Société Internationale Renardienne, Evreux (7–11 septembre 1981). Paris: Presses Universitaires de France, 1984, pp. 311–21.

Menard, Philippe. *Les Fabliaux: Contes à rire du Moyen Age.* Paris: Presses Universitaires de France, 1983.

Muscatine, Charles. *The Old French Fabliaux.* New Haven: Yale University Press, 1986.

Nykrog, Per. *Les Fabliaux: Etude d'histoire littéraire et de stylistique médiévale.* Copenhagen: Munksgaard, 1957. Rpt., Genève: Droz, 1973.

Pitts, Brent A. "Merveilleux, Mirage, and Comic Ambiguity in the Old French Fabliaux." *Assays* 4 (1987): 39–50.

———. "Truth-Seeking Discourse in the Old French Fabliaux." *Medievalia et Humanistica* 15 (1987): 95–117.

Roguet, Yves. "La Violence comique des fabliaux." In *La Violence dans le monde médiéval.* Aix-en-Provence: CUERMA, 1994, pp. 455–68.

Schultz-Busacker, Elisabeth. "La Moralité des fabliaux: Considerations stylistiques." In *Epopée animale, fable, fabliau*. Ed. Gabriel Biancotto and Michel Salvat. Actes du IVe Colloque de la Société Internationale Renardienne, Evreux (7–11 septembre 1981). Paris: Presses Universitaires de France, 1984, pp. 525–47.

Serper, Arie. "Le Monde culturel des fabliaux et la réalité sociale." In *Third International Beast Epic, Fable and Fabliau Colloquium, Münster, 1979, Proceedings*. Ed. Jan Goosens and Timothy Sodmann. Cologne: Bohlau, 1981, pp. 392–403.

Williams, Alison. *Tricksters and Pranksters: Roguery in French and German Literature of the Middle Ages*. Amsterdam: Rodopi, 2000.

RICHEUT

Medieval Texts

"The Twelfth-Century French Poem of Richeut: A Study in History, Form, and Content." Ed. Donald Eugene Ker. Ph.D. diss., Ohio State University, 1976.

"Richeut, Old French Poem of the Twelfth Century, with Introduction, Notes, and Glossary." Ed. Irville Charles Lecompte. *The Romanic Review* 4, no. 3 (July–September 1913): 261–305.

Richeut: Edition critique avec introduction, notes et glossaire. Ed. Philippe Vernay Berne: Editions Francke, 1988.

Modern Criticism

Bédier, Joseph. "Le Fabliau de *Richeut*." In *Etudes romanes dédiées à Gaston Paris le 29 décembre 1890 (25e anniversaire de son doctorat ès lettres)*. Paris: Emile Bouillon, 1891, pp. 23–31. Rpt. in Bédier, ed., *Les Fabliaux: Etudes de littérature populaire et d'histoire littéraire du Moyen Age*. Paris: Emile Bouillon, 1893, pp. 265–70.

Foulet, Lucien. "Le Poème de *Richeut* et *Le Roman de Renart*." *Romania* 42 (1913).

Faral, Edmond. "Le Conte de *Richeut*. Ses rapports avec la tradition latine et quelques traits de son influence." *Cinquantenaire de l'Ecole Practique des Hautes Etudes*. Paris: Champion, 1921, pp. 253–70.

Lorcin, Marie-Thérèse. "La Prostituée des fabliaux est-elle intégrée ou exclue?" *Exclus et systèmes d'exclusion dans la littérature et la civilisation médiévales*. Aix-en-Provence: CUERMA, 1978, pp. 105–17.

Pallister, Janis L. "Forms of Realism in *Richeut*." *L'Esprit Créateur* 5 (1965): 233–39.

Vernet, André. "Fragments d'un *Moniage Richeut*?" *Etudes de langue et de littérature du Moyen Age offertes à Félix Lecoy*. Paris: Champion, 1973, pp. 585–97.

TRUBERT

Medieval Texts

Douin de Lavesne. *Trubert: Fabliau du 13e siècle*. Ed. Guy Raynaud de Lage. Genève: Droz, 1974.

Nouveau Recueil complet des Fabliaux. Ed Willem Noomen. Vol. 10. Assen, Netherlands: Van Gorcum, 1998, pp. 145–262, 360–75.

Modern Criticism

Badel, Pierre. *Le Sauvage et le sot, le fabliau de "Trubert" et la tradition orale.* Paris: Champion, 1979.

Batany, Jean. "Trubert: progrès et bousculade des masques." In *Masques et déguisements dans la littérature médiévale.* Ed. Marie-Louise Ollier. Montréal: Presses de l'Université de Montréal, 1988, pp. 25–34.

Bonafin, Massimo. "La Parodia e il briccone divino: Modelli letterari e modelli antropologici del *Trubert* di Douin de Lavesne." In *L'Immagine riflessa: Rivista di sociologia dei testi* 5 (1982): 237–72.

Bourdier, Jean-Pierre. "Pathelin, Renart, Trubert, Badins, Décepteurs." *Le Moyen Age* 98, no. 1 (1992): 71–84.

Dona, Carlo. *Trubert, o La Carriera di un furfante: genesi e forme di un antiromanzo medievale.* Parma: Pratiche, 1994.

Gravdal, Kathryn. "Trubert: The *Courtois Trompé.*" In *Vilain and Courtois: Transgressive Parody in French Literature of the Twelfth and Thirteenth Centuries.* Lincoln: University of Nebraska Press, 1989, pp. 113–40 and pp. 166–72.

Payen, Jean-Charles. "Goliardisme et Fabliaux: Interférences ou similitudes? Recherches sur la fonction idéologique de la provocation en littérature." In *Third International Beast Epic, Fable and Fabliau Colloquium, Münster, 1979, Proceedings.* Ed. Jan Goosens and Timothy Sodmann. Cologne: Bohlau, 1981, pp. 267–89.

———. "*Trubert* ou le triomphe de la marginalité." In *Exclus et systèmes d'exclusion dans la littérature et la civilisation médiévales.* Aix-en-Provence: CUERMA, 1978, pp. 119–33.

Raynaud de Lage, Guy. "Trubert est-il un personnage de fabliau?" In *Mélanges d'histoire littéraire, de linguistique et de philologie romanes offerts à Charles Rostaing.* Liège: Association des romanistes de l'Université de Liège, 1974, pp. 845–53.

RENART

Medieval Texts

Le Roman de Renart. Ed. Ernest Martin. vol. 1: *L'Ancienne Collection des branches,* 1882; vol. 2, *Les Branches additionelles,* 1885; vol. 3: *Les Variantes,* 1887. Strasbourg: Trübner et Leroux. Vol. 3, rpt. Berlin: De Gruyter, 1973.

Le Roman de Renart édité d'après le manuscrit de Cangé. Ed. Mario Roques. 6 vols. Paris: Champion, 1948–63.

Le Roman de Renart, édité d'après les manuscrits C et M. Ed. Fukumoto Naoyuki, Harano Noboru, and Suzuki Satoru. 2 vols. Tokyo: France Tosho, 1983–85.

Le Roman de Renart. Ed. Jean Dufournet and Andrée Méline. 2 vols. Paris: Garnier-Flammarion, 1970; rpt. 1985.

Modern Criticism

Alibert, D. "Approches de l'iconographie médiévale du renard: Enquête sur un marginal." In *Histoire et animal: Etudes.* Ed. Alain Couret, Frédéric Ogé, and

Annick Audiot. Toulouse: Presses de l'Institut d'Etudes Politiques, 1989, pp. 435–45.

Aspects of the Medieval Animal Epic. Ed. Edward Rombauts and Andries Welkenhuysen. Proceedings of the International Conference, Louvain (May 15–17, 1972). The Hague: Martinus Nijhoff, 1975.

Batany, Jean. "Renart et les modèles historiques de la duplicité vers l'an mille." In *Third International Beast Epic, Fable and Fabliau Colloquium, Münster, 1979, Proceedings.* Ed. Jan Goosens and Timothy Sodmann. Cologne: Bohlau, 1981, pp. 1–24.

———. *Scène et Coulisses du Roman de Renart.* Paris: SEDES, 1989.

Bellon, Roger. "Trickery as an Element of the Character of Renart." *Forum for Modern Language Studies* 22, no. 1 (January 1986): 34–52.

Bossuat, Robert. *Le Roman de Renart.* Paris: Hatier-Bouvin, 1957.

Combarieu du Gres, Micheline de, and Jean Subrenat. *Le Roman de Renart: Index des thèmes et des personnages.* Aix-en-Provence, CUERMA, 1987.

Le Diable au Moyen Age (doctrine, problèmes moraux, représentations). Colloque à Aix-en-Provence (3–5 mars 1978). Aix-en-Provence: CUERMA, 1979.

Dragonetti, Roger. "'Renart est mort, Renart est vif, Renart règne.'" *Critique* 34 (1978): 783–98. Rpt. in *La Musique et les lettres: Etudes de littérature médiévale.* Genève: Droz, 1986, pp. 419–34.

Dubarle, A. M. "Les Renards de Samson." *Revue du Moyen Age Latin* 7 (1951): 174–76.

Dufournet, Jean. *Du "Roman de Renart" à Rutebeuf.* Caen: Paradigme, 1993.

———. "La Réécriture dans 'La Confession de Renart' (Branche VII du *Roman de Renart*). Jeux et enjeux." In *A la Recherche du Roman de Renart.* Ed. Kenneth Varty. Vol. 1. Oak Villa, New Alyth: Lochee Publications, 1988.

Exclus et systèmes d'exclusion dans la littérature et la civilisation médiévales. Aix-en-Provence: CUERMA, 1978.

Flinn, John. *"Le Roman de Renart" dans la littérature française et dans les littératures étrangères au Moyen Age.* Toronto: University of Toronto Press, 1963.

Foulet, Lucien. *Le Roman de Renart.* Paris: H. Champion, 1914.

Goodich, Michael. "Sodomy in Medieval Secular Law." *Journal of Homosexuality* 1, no. 3 (1976): 295–302.

Gravdal, Kathryn. "Le *Roman de Renart:* The *Courtois Bestourné.*" In *Vilain et Courtois: Transgressive Parody in French Literature of the Twelfth and Thirteenth Centuries.* Lincoln: University of Nebraska Press, 1989, pp. 81–112 and 161–65.

Harano, Noboru. "Filz au Putain." *Reinardus* 3 (1990): 37–43.

Henderson, Arnold Clayton. "Animal Fables as Vehicles of Social Protest and Satire: Twelfth Century to Henryson." In *Third International Beast Epic, Fable and Fabliau Colloquium, Münster, 1979, Proceedings.* Ed. Jan Goosens and Timothy Sodmann. Cologne: Bohlau, 1981, pp. 160–73.

Herman, Gerald. "Old French *herite.*" *Romance Notes* 17 (1976–77): 328–34.

Jauss, H. R. *Untersuchungen zur mittelalterlichen Tierdichtung.* Tübingen: Max Niemeyer, 1959.

Jonin, Pierre. "Les Animaux et leur vie psychologique dans *Le Roman de Renart* (Branche I)." *Annales de la Faculté des Lettres d'Aix-en-Provence* 25 (1951): 63–82.

Lodge, Anthony. "L'eroe come *trickster* nel *Roman de Renart*." *Cultura Neolatina* 40 (1980): 55–65.

Lodge, R. A. "On the 'Character' of Renart in Branch I." In *Studies in Medieval Literature and Languages in Memory of Frederick Whitehead*. Ed. W. Rothwell et al. Manchester: Manchester University Press, 1973, pp. 185–99.

Orr, J. "*Bougre* as Expletive." *Romance Philology* 1 (1947–48): 71–74.

Regalado, Nancy Freeman. "Tristan and Renart: Two Tricksters." *L'Esprit Créateur* 16 (1976): 30–38.

Reichler, Claude. *La Diabolie: La séduction, la renardie, l'écriture*. Paris: Editions de Minuit, 1979.

Ribard, Jacques. "Tristan/Renart 'revisité.'" In *Studies in Honor of Hans-Erich Keller: Medieval French and Occitan Literature and Romance Linguistics*. Ed. Rupert T. Pickens. Kalamazoo, MI: Medieval Institute Publications, 1993, pp 181–94.

Rychner, Jean. "Renart et ses conteurs, ou 'le style de la sympathie.'" *Travaux de Linguistique et de Littérature* 9, no. 2 (1971): 309–22.

Scheidegger, Jean. *Le Roman de Renart, ou le texte de la dérision*. Genève: Droz, 1989.

Simpson, J. R. *Animal Body, Literary Corpus: The Old French "Roman de Renart."* Amsterdam: Rodopi, 1996.

Subrenat, Jean. "Les Confessions de Renart." *Epopée animale, fable, fabliau*. Ed. Gabriel Biancotto and Michel Salvat. Actes du IVe Colloque de la Société Internationale Renardienne, Evreux (7–11 septembre 1981). Paris: Presses Universitaires de France, 1984, pp. 625–40.

———. "Portraits de prélats dans *Le Roman de Renart*." *Reinardus* 4 (1991): 193–203.

Suomela-Harma, Elina. "*Le Roman de Renart* et les fabliaux." In *Et c'est la fin pour quoy sommes ensemble: Hommage à Jean Dufournet professeur à la Sorbonne Nouvelle: Littérature, histoire et langue du Moyen Age*. Ed. Jean-Claude Aubailly et al. Paris: Champion, 1993, pp. 1319–31.

Tilander, Gunnar. *Lexique du Roman de Renart*. Paris: Champion, 1924. Rpt. 1984.

Tregenza, W. A. "The Relation of the Oldest Branch of the *Roman de Renart* to the Tristan Poems." *Modern Language Review* 19 (1924): 301–5.

Varty, Kenneth. "An *Etat présent* of *Roman de Renart* Studies." In *Mélanges de philologie et de littératures romanes offerts à Jeanne Wathelet-Willem*. Ed. Jacques de Caluwe. Liège: Cahiers de l'ARU, 1978, pp. 699–716.

———. "Renart through the Looking Glass: The Passage of the Fox from One Fictitious World to Another in the *Roman de Renart*." *Bestia: Yearbook of the Beast-Fable Society* 3 (May 1991): 68–73.

———. *The "Roman de Renart": A Guide to Scholarly Work*. Lanham, MD: Scarecrow Press, 1998.

Voisenet, Jacques. "Le *Renart* dans le bestiaire des clercs médiévaux." *Reinardus* 9 (1996): 179–88.

Wackers, Paul. "*Mutorum Animalium Conloquium*; or, Why Do Animals Speak?"
    Reinardus I (1988): 163–74.
Zink, Gaston. "Le Vocabulaire de la ruse et de la tromperie dans les branches X et
    XI du *Roman de Renart.*" *L'Information Grammaticale* 43 (octobre 1989):
    15–19.

INDEX

Abelard, Peter, 4
Adémar de Chabannes, 47–48, 89
Aimeric de Montréal, 136–39, 150, 185
Alain de Lille, 194, 202, 202n. 59, 203, 204
Albi, 75
Albigensian Crusade, 6, 17, 80, 105–6, 185; at Carcassonne, 85; at Minerve, 70; and Raimon VI, 115–32; and Raimon Rogier, 132–49
Albigensians. *See* Cathars
Alexander, abbot of Cîteaux, 115
Alexander III, 189n. 7, 201, 202n. 59
Alexis, 189–91, 199–201
Amalric, Arnaut, 134
Andreas Capellanus, 152, 171n. 60, 184
Anonymous of Laon, 189, 192, 200, 201
Anonymous of Passau, 186, 194, 198–99, 203, 210, 211
apostates, 9
Apostles, 27–28, 54, 68, 203–4, 206
Aristotle, 213
Arnaut, Guilhem, 78, 113
Arnaut Daniel, 99; *vida*, 103
Aroux, Eugène, 84, 86
Aubri de Trois-Fontaines, 139
Augustine of Hippo, 5, 76, 195, 198; on heresy, 51–52, 53–56, 58n. 40
authority, 203–6
Avignonet, 78, 113, 142n. 88

Bagley, C. P., 148
Béatris de Béziers, 128, 130–31, 130n. 52
Béguines and Beghards, 5n. 12, 241

Belperron, Pierre, 86
Bernard of Clairvaux, 63–75, 214, 241
Bernart IV, count of Comminges, 115, 127, 128, 143
Bernart de Fontecaude, 202n. 59
Bernart de Ventadorn, 87, 152, 171–72
Béroul, 15. *See also* Tristan and Iseut
Béziers, 115, 125
Blanca de Laurac, 139, 146
Bloch, R. Howard, 159n. 18, 162n. 25
Boccaccio, Giovanni, 10, 243
Boulbonne, 140

Camproux, Charles, 148
Capelli, Giacomo, 70
Carcassonne, 19, 80, 87, 115, 125
Cardinal, Peire, 85n. 2, 106; "Ab votz d'angel, lengue' esperta, non bléza," 109–10; "Clergia non valc an mais tan," 110; "Clergue si fan pastor," 113; "Qui volra sirventes auzir," 110–11; "Un estribot farai que er mot maïstratz," 107–8, 112; "Un sirventes novel vueill comensar," 111
Casseneuil, 135
Catalonia, 19, 33, 43, 106, 149
catechumenate, 51, 58
Catharism, 6, 7, 29, 36, 105, 129; asceticism, 27, 29; *consolamentum*, 13, 24, 29, 112, 131, 145; dualism, 28, 239; *endura*, 29, 30; *melioramentum*, 29; views on cross, 32; views on Eucharist, 36; views on free will, 44, 111–12, 234, 154n. 7, 157

277

2